For my dear children
(children no more!):

I hope and pray that you'll enjoy reading this book
and share it with your friends and those whom you mentor.
May God stir in you and them a greater love for Jesus
and a deeper desire to follow him.

*"I have no greater joy than this:
to hear that my children are walking in truth."
(3 John 4 CSB)*

And for all seekers of truth:

May you find Jesus,
the only way to the Father.

*"I am the way, the truth, and the life.
No one comes to the Father except through me."
(John 14:6 CSB)*

"I have always longed for a work that helps us read the Gospels well, not merely to understand what happened but also to grasp their theological import. Success at that task is no small endeavor; it requires facility in historical context, literary structure, exegesis, and theology. In *The Jesus of the Gospels*, Köstenberger has brought all these qualities together in clear exposition so that we have a companion that walks us through the Gospel accounts, explaining the significance of each event the way the Gospel writer desired us to see them. This volume is an invaluable resource and a must-have for all those who yearn to know our Lord's life the way the biblical authors fully intended."

—Abner Chou, John F. MacArthur Endowed Fellow, The Master's University and Seminary

"In *The Jesus of the Gospels*, Andreas Köstenberger supplies a much-needed resource for an often neglected audience: college students. You get first-rate, up-to-date scholarship without getting bogged down in overly technical detours suitable only for doctoral students. In a clear, engaging, and inspiring way, Köstenberger centers on the most important questions and issues confronting students when they study the life of Jesus. As a well-respected and established evangelical scholar, Köstenberger offers a thorough treatment of Matthew, Mark, Luke, and John without losing sight of the one, fourfold gospel. Brilliantly done! I highly recommend *The Jesus of the Gospels*."

—J. Scott Duvall, J. C. and Mae Fuller Professor of New Testament, Ouachita Baptist University

"Whether you're new to the Bible or have been reading it your whole life, *The Jesus of the Gospels* will serve as a reliable companion to your reading. Providing a helpful mixture of explanations of terms and events, insights on Old Testament background, and overviews on how each Gospel is arranged, this book will serve to broaden and deepen your understanding of who Jesus is and what his ministry and message is all about."

—Nancy Guthrie, Bible teacher and author of *Saints & Scoundrels in the Story of Jesus*

"This text completes Köstenberger's three-volume venture in studying the life of Jesus. The other two books cover Jesus's earlier and latter days, respectively. The author's aim is to offer college-aged readers a reliable guide to pursue along with the Gospels in a personal or group setting. Commendations to both Andreas and Kregel Publications for publishing yet another solid work of research, wisdom, and application in this readable text."

—Gary R. Habermas, Distinguished Research Professor, Liberty University

"While we have many books about Jesus and the Gospels, we have very few that do what Andreas Köstenberger's does. Here, finally, is a volume that is introductory and accessible, but without sacrificing scholarly depth and up-to-date research. Such a combination will be a great benefit to college-aged students and to any Christian looking for a jargon-free overview of the Gospels."

—Michael J. Kruger, President and Professor of New Testament and Early Christianity, Reformed Theological Seminary

"This work is a succinct overview of the four evangelists' individual accounts of the life of Christ. Köstenberger is the guide you want for this pilgrimage through the four Gospels. Landmarks and contours are pointed out, light is shone on some of the more difficult texts, and there is even a plan to tour the four books in thirty days. Those who are journeying this terrain anew will be aided to know Jesus and to acknowledge the Gospels as the good news—the best news ever!"

—Abraham Kuruvilla, Senior Research Professor of Preaching and Pastoral Ministries, Dallas Theological Seminary

"Köstenberger's *The Jesus of the Gospels* is intended to be an introduction to the four Gospels for college students and, very intentionally, as an introduction to Jesus. The consistent focus on the biblical text ensures that the life and message of Jesus is indeed the center of the book. The fruit of many years of careful scholarship, this fine, easily accessible introduction is highly recommended for Christians and non-Christians alike."

—Eckhard J. Schnabel, Mary F. Rockefeller Distinguished Professor of New Testament, Gordon-Conwell Theological Seminary

"Andreas Köstenberger, one of the experts on the Gospels in our day, provides an accessible and heartwarming introduction to the Jesus of the Gospels. A wonderful resource for students and for all who wish to encounter Jesus Christ."

—Thomas R. Schreiner, James Buchanan Harrison Professor of New Testament Interpretation and Associate Dean, The Southern Baptist Theological Seminary

"In this helpful introduction to the Jesus of the canonical Gospels, Andreas Köstenberger helps us all to appreciate that Jesus was far too complex a historical and religious figure for one portrait to do him justice. We should be thankful that we have four, each of which contribute something to our overall understanding of our Savior. Portraits are not like bare photographs; they are inherently interpretative in their very nature, and so what we actually have in the New Testament are four distinct—but yet compatible—portraits of the real Jesus of both history and faith, which help us 'see him more clearly, love him more dearly, and follow him more nearly, day by day.' Highly recommended."

—Ben Witherington III, Amos Professor of New Testament for Doctoral Studies, Asbury Theological Seminary, and emeritus doctoral faculty, St. Andrews University

"Books on this subject may be so technical that only scholars can make sense of them. Not so here. The author makes wonderfully plain what the Gospel writers were convinced of—that Jesus is Lord, and that his life, teachings, self-sacrifice, and resurrection are not dead tales of the past. Rather, they are truths that remain life-changing right now. Read each Gospel with this book as a guide. It will give you fresh eyes for Jesus's meaning on the vast stage of first-century Jewish expectation and Roman history. And it will open up avenues for the informed personal commitment to Jesus *now* that all four Gospels commend."

—Robert W. Yarbrough, Professor of New Testament, Covenant Theological Seminary

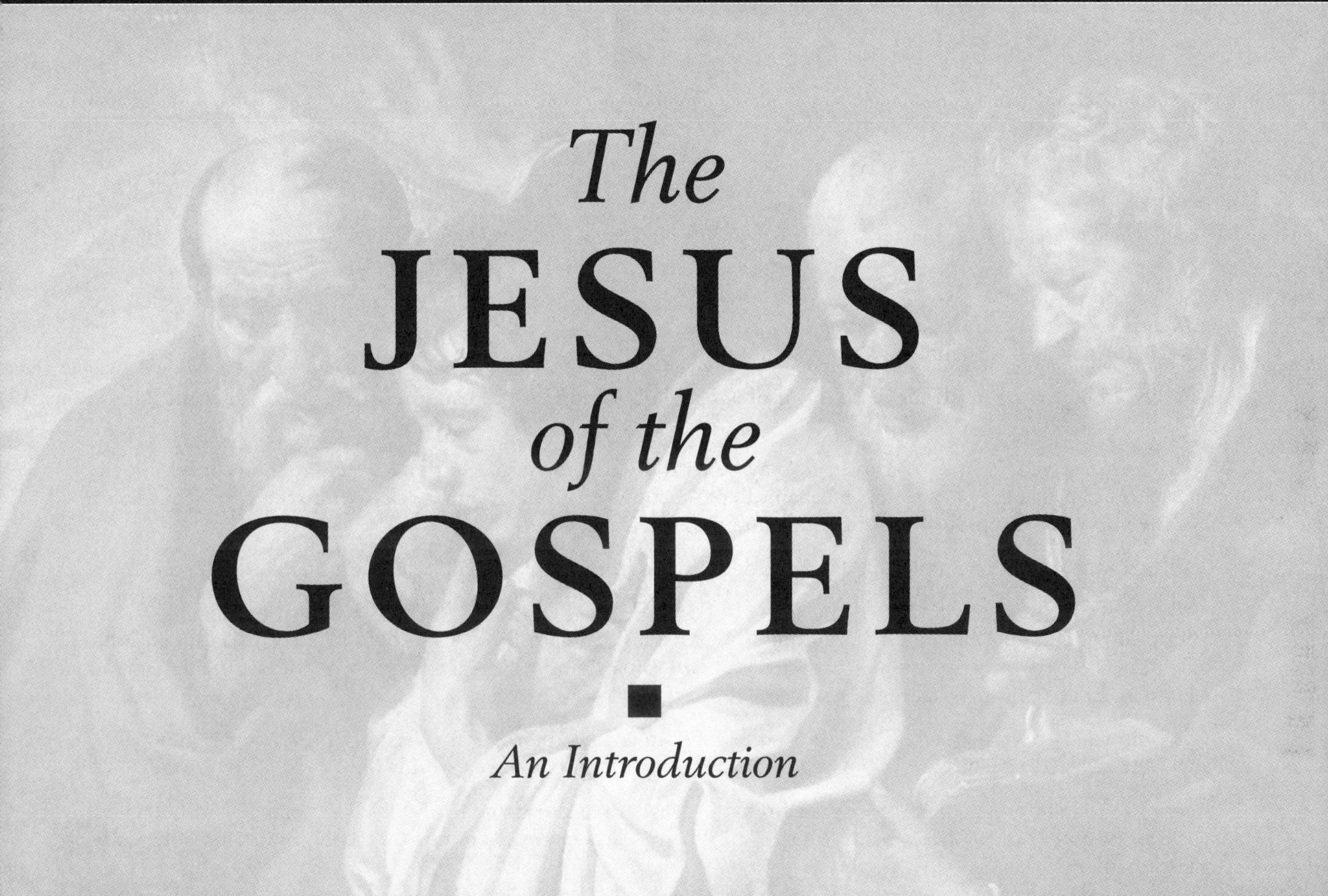

The JESUS of the GOSPELS

An Introduction

ANDREAS J. KÖSTENBERGER

KREGEL ACADEMIC

The Jesus of the Gospels: An Introduction

Published by Kregel Academic, an imprint of Kregel Publications, 2450 Oak Industrial Dr. NE, Grand Rapids, MI 49505-6020.

The Greek font, GraecaU, is available from www.linguistsoftware.com/lgku.htm, +1-425-775-1130.

ISBN 978-0-8254-4536-1

Printed in the United States of America

20 21 22 23 24 / 5 4 3 2 1

PREFACE

"Why another book on Jesus?" you may be asking. That's a fair question. There's certainly no lack of books on Jesus from a wide variety of perspectives, liberal to conservative. It seems like almost every biblical scholar has written a book on Jesus at some point in his or her career, both because Jesus is such an important figure and because books that have "Jesus" in the title attract a certain amount of attention and often sell well.

In my case, the idea for writing this book was triggered by a search for a suitable book that I could recommend to my college-age children. I wanted them to have a reliable guide by their side as they read the Gospels, informed by sound scholarship but accessible and jargon-free. Surveying the market, I found that most books on Jesus were either written for other scholars or penned in a popular, if not sensational, vein.

Also, I've already written two other books on Jesus, *The First Days of Jesus* and *The Final Days of Jesus*. It seemed therefore appropriate to "close the gap" by writing a book on the *life* of Jesus. In conceiving this project, I became convinced that the best way to do so was to write a succinct guide on each of the four Gospels, as this is how we know about Jesus. If we want to know Jesus, we need to read about the Jesus of the Gospels.

In writing this book, I was able to build on various previous publications on the subject, not only the above-mentioned works on Jesus but also *The Cradle, the Cross, and the Crown* and other material. I acknowledge Andrew Koetsier for doing some initial legwork (especially on sidebars) for the chapter on Matthew and Jimmy Roh for doing the same for Mark and Luke. Many thanks also to Kregel for accepting and publishing this work.

When working on this book, I realized like never before that God chose to transmit information about Jesus in the form of multiple narratives, stories meant to be read both progressively and in their entirety, as they lead us gradually to the realization of who Jesus is. There's simply no substitute for this kind of process and the resulting discovery! It's my desire that you share the same excitement I felt.

My vision for this book is that you'll use it in conjunction with reading one or several of the Gospels in a good English translation, whether by yourself or as part of a group. At the end of this book, you'll find a reading plan that divides each Gospel into units. You may find it helpful to read a section in a Gospel and then the portion on that section in the present volume. If you can only do one of these, by all means read the Gospel!

My aim with this volume is not to break new ground but to provide you with a practical tool for reading the Gospels in keeping with their intended purpose—that is, as relaying good news—and to get to know Jesus better, or even for the first time. Thank you very much for picking up this book and for your desire to learn more about Jesus. I pray that everything I've written will bring glory to him and help make him known.

INTRODUCTION

Who is Jesus? No question is more important or consequential than this. At a critical juncture during his time on earth, Jesus asked his followers, "Who do you say that I am?"[1] Centuries later, classics professor and Christian apologist C. S. Lewis argued that there are only three legitimate ways to answer this vital question: Jesus is a lunatic, a liar, or Lord.[2] So who do *you* say Jesus is? You may say, "Jesus is Lord. I'm one of his followers." Great! You may say, "He's a lunatic or liar." Or you may say, "I'm not sure. How can I know who Jesus is?" To find out, you'll want to take a closer look at the best ancient sources we have at our disposal regarding Jesus—the Gospels.[3]

In the first century, several of Jesus's followers and some of their associates composed accounts of Jesus's life and the things he said and did. Among these were Matthew (also known as Levi), a former tax collector called by Jesus to be one of his twelve apostles (messengers); Mark, a mentee and associate of Simon Peter, a fisherman and Jesus's most outspoken follower; Luke, a physician and close associate of Saul (also known as Paul), the undisputed leader of the early church; and John, a leading member of the Twelve and the last surviving apostle. The church put its stamp of approval on these four Gospels and affirmed that they provided one Gospel according to four witnesses, the fourfold Gospel according to Matthew, Mark, Luke, and John.[4]

---

1. Matthew 16:15; Mark 8:29.
2. See C. S. Lewis, *Mere Christianity* (New York: Macmillan, 1943), 56. For helpful background and discussion, see Justin Taylor, "Is C. S. Lewis's Liar-Lord-or-Lunatic Argument Unsound?" February 1, 2016, https://blogs.thegospelcoalition.org/justintaylor/2016/02/01/is-c-s-lewiss-liar-lord-or-lunatic-argument-unsound. True to his skeptical ways, Bart Ehrman has proposed a fourth alternative: Jesus as legend. But see the convincing refutation by Charles L. Quarles, "Lord or Legend: Jesus as the Messianic Son of Man," *Journal of the Evangelical Theological Society* 62 (2019): 103–24.
3. Gospel (*euangelion* in the original Greek) means "good news"; more on that shortly.
4. On the compilation of the various New Testament books into a collection of writings that eventually came to be known as the Christian "canon," see Andreas J. Köstenberger, L. Scott Kellum, and Charles L. Quarles, *The Cradle, the Cross, and the Crow*, 2nd ed. (Nashville: B&H, 2016), chapter 1.

This brings our initial question—Who is Jesus?—into even sharper focus. We can now ask, Who is the *Jesus of the Gospels*? Since we have in our Bibles one Gospel according to four witnesses, the Jesus of the Gospels will turn out to be a composite sketch by the four evangelists. As we'll see, Matthew presents Jesus as the Jewish Messiah, descendant of Abraham and David; Mark depicts him as the authoritative, miracle-working Son of God; Luke portrays him as the compassionate healer and Savior for all people; and John, last but not least, shows him to be the God-man and revealer of God the Father. If this were a multiple-choice question, we wouldn't have to choose: Jesus is all of these things! The correct answer would be "All of the above."

THE GOSPELS AS EYEWITNESS TESTIMONY

At the very outset, it's important to understand that the Gospels in our Bibles claim to be based on eyewitness testimony.[5] If you open your Bible and read any of the Gospels, therefore, you can read a firsthand account of Jesus's story written by those who saw him with their own eyes, heard him with their own ears, or conferred with those who did.[6]

That's what you'll want. You'll want your faith to be based on reliable testimony rather than on mere hearsay or some secondhand report that may not be historically accurate.

The bottom line, therefore, is this: if you're interested in knowing who Jesus really was, you should read one or several of the four Gospels. Better still, read all of them! In this way, you'll get a well-rounded picture of the most important person who ever lived—Jesus of Nazareth, the Messiah and Son of God—painted by those who knew him best or talked to those who did.

A COMPANION TO THE GOSPELS

Over the years, scholars have debated questions such as these: Are there any other Gospels that rival the four included in our Bibles? How can the four Gospels be viewed as objective, given that they were written by followers of Jesus? Were the Gospel writers biased? Do the Gospels ever contradict one another?

---

5. See Richard Bauckham, *Jesus and the Eyewitnesses: The Gospels as Eyewitness Testimony*, 2nd ed. (Grand Rapids: Eerdmans, 2017). Note, however, that Bauckham doesn't believe Matthew or John wrote their respective Gospels.
6. See 1 John 1:1 (NIV): "That which was from the beginning, which we have heard, which we have seen with our eyes, which we have looked at and our hands have touched—this we proclaim concerning the Word of life."

Important as these questions are, here we won't be unduly detained by such concerns.[7] Rather, I want to encourage you to read through each of the Gospels—or any one of them—for yourself first and form your own opinion, unclouded by the views of others. I want you to come face-to-face with Jesus and read the accounts of the four preeminent witnesses to the life of Jesus.

In this way, you can examine the evidence for yourself to come to an informed opinion regarding the one who asks you, "Who do *you* say that I am?" Or, if you're one of his followers already, reading the Gospels—or reading them again—will help you get to know him even better.

This book, as mentioned, is not intended as a substitute for reading the Gospels but rather as a companion to them.[8] In the following pages, we'll follow the story of Jesus as told by the four Gospel writers. What you'll find is that these four accounts paint beautiful portraits of Jesus the Jewish Messiah, the miracle-working Son of God, the compassionate healer and Savior of the world, and the divine-human revealer.

THE GOSPELS AS GOOD NEWS

It's now fashionable to read the Gospels as stories. This practice is certainly commendable, as the Gospels are narratives—literary compositions that are carefully crafted to provide a coherent account of a historical character, Jesus of Nazareth. What's more, as historical narratives, the Gospels, as mentioned, contain reliable information corroborated by eyewitnesses.

In fact, ancient Jewish laws called for a minimum of two or three witnesses to support any given claim.[9] In our Bibles, we don't have merely two or three witnesses; we have four! While each evangelist tells the story of Jesus in his own distinctive way, all four Gospels are grounded in the historical fabric of events making up the life of Jesus.

---

7. If you're interested in those kinds of questions, you may want to consult Andreas Köstenberger, Darrell Bock, and Josh Chatraw, *Truth Matters: Confident Faith in a Confusing World*, or in greater depth, *Truth in a Culture of Doubt: Engaging Skeptical Challenges to the Bible* (both Nashville: B&H, 2014). See also the resources provided on my website, www.biblicalfoundations.org. Cf. Peter J. Williams, *Can We Trust the Gospels?* (Wheaton, IL: Crossway, 2018), who discusses matters such as non-Christian sources for Jesus, the Gospel writers' factual accuracy, undersigned coincidences among the Gospels, the reliability of the New Testament text, and alleged contradictions.
8. I recommend the *ESV Reader's Gospels* (Wheaton, IL: Crossway, 2015), featuring the English Standard Version, but there are many other fine English versions and study Bibles on the market. For a helpful compendium of geographical essays on the Gospels, see Barry J. Beitzel, ed., *Lexham Geographic Commentary on the Gospels* (Bellingham, WA: Lexham, 2017).
9. See Deuteronomy 19:15.

And yet the Gospels are more than stories. They're even more than true, historically accurate accounts. What makes the Gospels so precious and worth reading and sharing is that they're good news. In fact, that's what "gospel" literally means in the original Greek: "good news"!

That said, calling the gospel *good* news is the greatest understatement of all time. Yes, the Gospels convey good news, but they do much more: they contain amazing, terrific, life-giving news worthy to be celebrated and broadcast far and wide. As you read the Gospels, please remember that they're a lot more than mere stories: they're news that have the potential to radically change people's lives.

You may ask, exactly how are the Gospels good news? Well, let's look and find out! You can read the Gospels in any order; they all give an accurate portrait of who Jesus is. For our purposes, we'll follow the order in which the Gospels are found in our Bibles and start with the Gospel of Matthew.

As we read Matthew's account of Jesus, let's ask ourselves the question: How is what Matthew tells us about Jesus good news? Sound good? All right, then, we're almost ready to get started. But first let's locate our study in the history of Jesus research. After all, we're not the first who set out on a journey to get to know the Jesus of the Gospels.[10]

10. Then again, if you can't wait to jump right into your own reading and study of the Gospels, by all means feel free to skip the next chapter and go straight to chapter 2!

CHAPTER 1

Situating This Book in the History of JESUS RESEARCH

"The very best 'Life of Christ' is the four gospels. We read them with delight."

—Charles Haddon Spurgeon

Chapter 1

WHO DO PEOPLE SAY THAT I AM?

The life of Jesus is not primarily a life to be contemplated or even admired; it's a call to response and action.[1] As mentioned, Oxford don C. S. Lewis memorably argued that Jesus is either a liar, a lunatic, or Lord.[2] If he's a liar or lunatic—or, as a skeptic by the name of Bart Ehrman recently suggested, a legend—then of course we can readily dismiss him as a fraud or hold him at arm's length as a fable. Yet I ask you: Is this really the most credible conclusion to draw from reading the primary sources we have about Jesus, the four New Testament Gospels? In order to find out, we need to read the Gospels and do so with an open mind and with a sound strategy. But as we'll see, in the history of Gospels and Jesus scholarship, that's something many unfortunately haven't done.

What's more, if Jesus is in fact Lord and has supreme authority over the universe and all of humanity, this means that you and I shouldn't approach him merely with interested curiosity but with a readiness to obey and an eagerness to follow him. As Jesus told his followers, "If anyone would come after me, let him deny himself and take up his cross daily and follow me."[3] At a critical juncture in his messianic mission here on earth, Jesus took his closest followers aside and asked them, "Who do people say that I am?" When his disciples reported to him a variety of responses, he followed up with an even more pointed, deeply personal question: "But who do *you* say that I am?"

So, who do *you* say Jesus is? Before I became a Christian, I spent much of my time trying to solve the world's (i.e., everybody else's!) problems, quick to diagnose what was wrong with those around me while being slow to take the log out of my own eye. But when I encountered Jesus, I came to realize that he called me to decide: Who did *I* think he was? How would *I* respond to the one who died for me on the cross to offer me forgiveness and salvation out of sheer love and grace? By his mercy, I realized that I desperately needed what he had to offer and chose to follow him. But, of course, I was not the first to encounter Jesus (and many of you have had similar journeys of faith). For now, I hope you'll join me on a brief tour of the history of Jesus research. Who did scholars over the past few centuries say Jesus was? And what can we learn from their quest for the historical Jesus as we read the Gospels today?

---

1. Charles Spurgeon quote on page 17: Charles Haddon Spurgeon, *The Metropolitan Tabernacle Pulpit*, vol. 24 (Pasadena, TX: Pilgrim, 1878), 459. I owe this reference to my student Ed Romine.
2. C. S. Lewis, *Mere Christianity* (New York: Macmillan, 1943), 56; cf. Lewis, *God in the Dock* (Grand Rapids: Eerdmans, 2014), 100–101.
3. Luke 9:23. See the classic work by Dietrich Bonhoeffer, *The Cost of Discipleship* (London: SCM, 1948; orig. ed. Munich: Kaiser, 1937).

LIVES OF JESUS AND GOSPEL HARMONIES

The centuries following the Enlightenment period, which witnessed the rise of human confidence in autonomous critical reason, saw an increasing proliferation of so-called "lives of Jesus." These were accounts of the life of Jesus that often owed considerably more to the imagination and philosophical outlook of the person writing the account than to the actual life of Jesus, the first-century Palestinian Jew portrayed in the canonical Gospels. Albert Schweitzer, the German biblical scholar and later medical doctor, humanitarian, and Nobel Peace Prize–winner, masterfully chronicled this phenomenon in his work *The Quest of the Historical Jesus*.[4] In fact, Schweitzer believed that "the greatest achievement of German theology is the critical investigation of the life of Jesus."[5]

As Schweitzer noted, "We are dealing here with the most vital thing in the world's history. There came a Man to rule over the world; He ruled it for good and for ill, as history testifies. . . . He continues, notwithstanding, to reign as the alone Great and alone True."[6] Schweitzer shows how the practitioners of the quest for the historical Jesus sought to rediscover the "Jesus of history" by peeling off layers of theological tradition, enlisting the historical Jesus "as an ally in the struggle against the tyranny of dogma." In that noble pursuit, however, Schweitzer discovered, "each individual created Him in accordance with his own character." In fact, "there is no historical task," Schweitzer continued, that "so reveals a man's true self as the writing of a Life of Jesus."[7] This pronouncement should give anyone who endeavors to write a life of Jesus pause.

In conceiving of a game plan for the present volume, I had to ask myself the honest question: How am I going to do any better than those scholars whom Schweitzer had surveyed? What makes me think that I can improve on these earlier scholars who recreated Jesus in their own image? Is it not likely that I will do the same? The answer, I concluded, lies largely in being faithful to the available sources for the life of Jesus. If I was going to adhere closely to the contours of revelation provided in the canonical sources—the Gospels of Matthew, Mark, Luke, and John in their final canonical form—this was my best, if not only, hope, because adhering closely to these sources alone would keep me from imposing onto the data my own reconstruction that then, in effect, would replace the actual first-century accounts.

Remarkably for a critical scholar, Schweitzer observed that our sources for the life of Jesus are remarkably rich: "There are few characters of antiquity about whom we possess

4. Albert Schweitzer, *The Quest of the Historical Jesus: A Critical Study of Its Progress from Reimarus to Wrede* (London: Adam & Charles Black, 1911).
5. Schweitzer, *Quest*, 231.
6. Schweitzer, *Quest*, 2.
7. Schweitzer, *Quest*, 4.

so much indubitably historical information, of whom we have so many authentic discourses." What's more, unlike other historical figures, Jesus "stands much more immediately before us, because He was depicted by simple Christians without literary gift."[8] At the same time, Schweitzer contended, the first three Gospels provide only a sampling of anecdotes, while John includes a mere selection of events and discourses; "yawning gaps" remain.[9] Schweitzer may have exaggerated the incomplete nature of the Gospel witness to the life of Jesus, but it's true that the gaps in the various biblical accounts do invite a certain amount of speculation that has the potential of distorting our study of Jesus.

In the remainder of his book, Schweitzer proceeded to probe the nature of Jesus's messianic consciousness and to bemoan the difficulty, even impossibility, of reconstructing a full-fledged life of Jesus—understood as a blow-by-blow account—given the incomplete information provided by the four canonical Gospels. Like Adolf Schlatter, he expresses commendable reserve against allowing "historical imagination" to fill in what is left unaddressed in the sources, resulting in scholarly "fables."[10] Surveying the (then-recent) history of scholarship on the historical Jesus, Schweitzer diagnosed that no real progress had been made in the preceding century from David Friedrich Strauss (writing in 1835) until the 1890s.[11] So much for the illusion of progress in biblical scholarship! If anything, scholars had been looking themselves in the mirror and described what they saw.

Strauss, in fact, had popularized the idea that the category of history must be replaced with the notion of myth; miracles have no place in modern scientific investigation. Later, the Tübingen school bequeathed on subsequent scholarship the Markan-priority hypothesis and the conviction that the Synoptic Gospels—Matthew, Mark, and Luke—are far superior to John as historical documents.[12] Not only was Mark the first to write his Gospel, scholars concluded, but his Gospel alone provided a historically intelligible (though not necessarily infallible) portrait of the life of Jesus. In his own attempt "to bring order into the chaos of the Lives of Jesus,"[13] Schweitzer proceeded to discuss Jesus as a first-century Jewish apocalyptic prophet who believed that the end was near and preached a message of the impending kingdom of God, only to be ambushed by one of his closest followers (Judas) and end up on a Roman cross. In the ultimate analysis, therefore, Schweitzer found the "historical Jesus" to be strangely elusive.

---

8. Schweitzer, *Quest*, 6. We will return to this question later in this introduction.
9. Schweitzer, *Quest*, 7.
10. Schweitzer, *Quest*, 8. Cf. Adolf Schlatter, *The History of the Christ: The Foundation of New Testament Theology*, trans. Andreas J. Köstenberger (Grand Rapids: Baker, 1997), 20.
11. Schweitzer, *Quest*, 9. Cf. David Friedrich Strauss, *The Life of Jesus* (originally published in 1835).
12. Schweitzer, *Quest*, 10.
13. Schweitzer, *Quest*, 12.

Ironically, Schweitzer clearly perceived the shortcomings of the historical-critical method. "We modern theologians are too proud of our historical method, too proud of our historical Jesus, too confident in our belief in the spiritual gains which our historical theology can bring to the world," he writes. A Jesus pressed to conform to the constraints of the historical method is "too small," he observed, lamenting how then-recent portraits of Jesus had recast his denial of the world into people's acceptance of it. This in turn robbed Jesus's message of its power: "Many of the greatest sayings are found lying in a corner like explosive shells from which the charges have been removed." Jesus was not a nineteenth- or twentieth-century German theologian; he was a first-century Jew. In effect, scholars had retrojected their own thoughts back into history and had made them speak to them out of the past.[14]

Schweitzer's closing remarks regarding the historical Jesus are worth quoting in full: "He comes to us as One unknown, without a name, as of old, by the lake-side, He came to those men who knew Him not. He speaks to us the same word: 'Follow thou me!' and sets us to the tasks which He has to fulfil for our time. He commands. And to those who obey Him, whether they be wise or simple, He will reveal Himself in the toils, the conflicts, the sufferings which they shall pass through in His fellowship, and, as an ineffable mystery, they shall learn in their own experience Who He is."[15]

With admirable consistency, Schweitzer subsequently abandoned any further scholarly pursuits and spent the rest of his life in the African jungle as a medical doctor.[16] While he couldn't penetrate the inscrutable mystery of the true identity of Jesus, he sought to obey his call to self-sacrificial, self-denying service.

It would be too convenient to dismiss Schweitzer's musings as the confused ramblings of a scholar caught up in his own time and culture. While I for one am not prepared to embrace Schweitzer's dire verdict, or his Christ-mysticism, I do believe that those who fail to learn from history are doomed to repeat it.[17] When it comes to the study of Jesus, Schweitzer has rightly drawn our attention to some of the challenges we face.

---

14. Schweitzer, *Quest*, 398. We see a similar phenomenon in our day: see Andreas J. Köstenberger and Michael J. Kruger, *The Heresy of Orthodoxy: How Contemporary Culture's Fascination with Diversity Has Reshaped Our Understanding of Early Christianity* (Wheaton, IL: Crossway, 2010). If the subtitle hadn't already been long enough, we would have added "Jesus" to it, like this: "How Contemporary Culture's Fascination with Diversity Has Reshaped Our Understanding *of Jesus* and Early Christianity." Thus, we find that the more things change, the more they stay the same. Or, as the ancient sage put it, "there is nothing new under the sun" (Ecclesiastes 1:9).
15. Schweitzer, *Quest*, 403.
16. For a brief biographical sketch, see "Albert Schweitzer," Biblical Foundations, accessed September 21, 2015, http://www.biblicalfoundations.org/albert-schweitzer.
17. The original quote is commonly attributed to the Spanish-American philosopher George Santayana (1863–1952). Winston Churchill changed the quote slightly in a 1948 speech to the British House of Commons.

To begin with, we're confronted with limitations in our historical sources (including the four Gospels in our Bibles). John, for his part, frankly acknowledges that he must be highly selective.[18] Historical-critical scholars—including the infamous Jesus Seminar—have by and large sought to solve this dilemma by engaging in historical reconstruction, undergirded by a strong dose of anti-supernaturalism. This has typically resulted in a truncated picture of Jesus, excising his miracles and even the resurrection. It has also opened a gaping rift between history and theology.[19] Schweitzer himself sought to overcome this rift by appealing, as was common in his day, to the "spirit" of Jesus that still speaks to us through the Gospels and calls us to follow.[20] Others, like Martin Kähler, dichotomized between the "historical Jesus" and the "Christ of faith."[21] Yet others, such as the famous German scholar Rudolf Bultmann, following in the tradition of David Friedrich Strauss, opted to engage in a dubious program of demythologization, stripping off the supernatural from the life of Jesus in order to recontextualize it for an "enlightened" modern readership.[22]

However, I submit that we don't need to succumb to skepticism toward the Gospel records. If the Gospels are reliable, albeit not exhaustive, we needn't separate the Jesus whose story they tell, each in their own distinctive way, from the existential impact he has had on those who have followed him during the days of his earthly mission and beyond.

For this reason, rather than embarking on a quest for the Jesus of history, we should engage in a study of *the Jesus of the Gospels*. It is not that the Jesus of the Gospels is an unhistorical Jesus simply because he is the literary (or, perhaps better, the canonical or textual) Jesus. Rather, as we'll discuss further below, if the Gospels represent accounts penned by reliable eyewitnesses, then the textual Jesus and the historical Jesus will closely cohere (though you might say that the Gospel portraits of Jesus are refracted through the perception of the four evangelists, like multiple artists may each paint their own distinctive portrait of a given individual).

---

18. John 20:30–31; 21:24–25.
19. Made famous by the German philosopher Gotthold Ephraim Lessing (1729–1781), who spoke of the "ugly ditch" of history that, he argued, cannot be used to prove the contingent truths of reason. "On the Proof of the Spirit and of Power," in *Lessing: Philosophical and Theological Writings*, ed. and trans. H. B. Nisbet (Cambridge: Cambridge University Press, 2005), 87.
20. By "spirit" Schweitzer didn't mean the Holy Spirit but the abstract notion of a person's influence as postulated by individuals such as the German idealist philosopher Georg Wilhelm Friedrich Hegel (1770–1831) in his work *The Phenomenology of Spirit*, in development of another German intellectual giant, the philosopher Immanuel Kant (1724–1804).
21. Martin Kähler, *The So-called Historical Jesus and the Historic, Biblical Christ*, trans. Carl E. Braaten (Minneapolis: Augsburg Fortress, 1964; original German edition 1892).
22. See Rudolf Bultmann, *New Testament and Mythology and Other Basic Writings*, ed. and trans. Schubert M. Ogden (Philadelphia: Fortress, 1984), 1–14 and throughout (original German edition 1941).

What's more, the manuscript evidence we possess indicates that the text of the Gospels has been faithfully preserved and transmitted since their composition by the original authors, so that we can have a high degree of confidence that the Gospels in our Bibles—faithful translations of the Greek original—are accurate representations of what the Gospel writers wrote.[23] History and literature thus work in tandem as vehicles of divine revelation regarding Jesus.[24]

What this means, then, is that, in our quest to get to know the real Jesus, we must place our trust in the Gospels as reliable witnesses to the life of Jesus. For some of us, this will be a big step. It can be unsettling to think that our knowledge of Jesus boils down to trust, but the Scriptures reassure us that the information provided about Jesus in the four Gospels is rock-solid and backed up by firsthand personal experience.

The unrivaled authority of the four biblical Gospels also means, I believe, that the whole enterprise of historical Jesus research is fundamentally misguided. Whenever a scholar attempts to provide a reconstruction of the life of Jesus in distinction from, or even opposition to, the canonical Gospels, the danger looms large that this reconstruction takes the place of the biblical Gospels themselves. This, I would argue, is the case even when such a reconstruction is not undergirded by a historical-critical agenda but is conceived in more constructive terms, as in the case of a harmony approach to the life of Jesus.[25]

THE APPROACH TAKEN IN THIS BOOK: FIVE THESES

It follows that those who would like to examine the witness of the Gospels regarding knowing Jesus as he truly revealed himself should read the Gospels that we have as they have come down to us. I say this for the following five reasons:

1. God chose to provide us with four canonical, inspired Gospels, and the church recognized this by including these four Gospels in its canon. As a matter of fact, the church fathers strongly contended that there could only be four Gospels, just like there is north and south, east and west. The New Testament boasts no harmony of the life of Jesus.[26]

23. If you're interested in this question, you may want to read chapter 8, "Tampering with the Text: Was the New Testament Text Changed along the Way?" in Köstenberger and Kruger, *Heresy of Orthodoxy*.
24. On the "hermeneutical triad" of history, literature, and theology, see Andreas J. Köstenberger and Richard D. Patterson, *Invitation to Biblical Interpretation: Exploring the Hermeneutical Triad of History, Literature, and Theology* (Grand Rapids: Kregel, 2011). Second edition forthcoming in 2021.
25. See further below.
26. Thus, the approach taken in this volume differs from that of Darrell Bock, who uses a harmony approach for the Synoptic Gospels; see Darrell L. Bock with Benjamin I. Simpson, *Jesus according to Scripture: Restoring*

2. We should recognize that the Gospels each provide accurate and distinctive yet personal and complementary accounts of Jesus's life. We should appreciate the historical, literary, and theological insights they provide without pitting them against each other as if diversity necessarily meant contradiction or disparity.[27]

3. We should read all four Gospels rather than preferring one or several of them to the others. Among other things, this means that we should affirm the historical value of John's Gospel alongside that of the other Gospels and read all four accounts to derive the maximum benefit when learning about the canonical witness to the life of Jesus.[28]

4. Out of respect for the New Testament canon, it's best to discuss the Gospels in their canonical order: first Matthew, then Mark, Luke, and John.[29] I believe this is true regardless of the order in which the Gospels were written. Mark may well have been the first to do so. But in the end, the Bibles we have put Matthew first, and this is how we should proceed as well.

---

the Portrait from the Gospels, 2nd ed. (Grand Rapids: Baker, 2017). Craig L. Blomberg opts for both a survey of individual gospels and a harmony presentation; see *Jesus and the Gospels: An Introduction and Survey*, 2nd ed. (Nashville: B&H, 2009).

27. This is the problematic assumption underlying the work by Bart D. Ehrman, *Jesus, Interrupted: Revealing the Hidden Contradictions in the Bible (And Why We Don't Know about Them)* (New York: HarperCollins, 2010); see the critique in Köstenberger, Bock, and Chatraw, *Truth Matters*.

28. While Friedrich Schleiermacher still affirmed the historical value of John's Gospel, subsequent scholarship routinely disparaged John's historicity, preferring the Synoptic Gospels and here particularly Mark. Increasingly, even Matthew and Luke were relegated to secondary status. More recently, some scholars have sought to remedy this negative view of John's historical value by positing a two-strand tradition, Mark and John, each of which may be of historical value—but not both at the same time! This is a doubtful remedy, as it still forces us to choose between one or the other, Mark or John, who cannot both be reliable. Hence, such scholars continue to uphold the view that the New Testament Gospel accounts are contradictory. See, e.g., D. Moody Smith, *The Fourth Gospel in Four Dimensions: Judaism and Jesus, the Gospel and Scripture* (Columbia: University of South Carolina Press, 2008). Paul N. Anderson, in *The Fourth Gospel and the Quest for Jesus: Modern Foundations Reconsidered*, Library of New Testament Studies 321 (London: T&T Clark, 2006) and other works, calls for a "fourth quest" of the historical Jesus and a rehabilitation of the historicity of John's Gospel, which is very commendable, but his reconstruction of the emergence of the Gospel tradition is highly conjectural and still does not escape some of the problems encountered by modern critical scholarship.

29. This differs from Blomberg, *Jesus and the Gospels*; Mark L. Strauss, *Four Portraits, One Jesus: A Survey of Jesus and the Gospels* (Grand Rapids: Zondervan, 2007); and Richard B. Hays, *Reading Backwards: Figural Christology and the Fourfold Gospel Witness* (Waco, TX: Baylor University Press, 2014), all of whom discuss Mark first on the basis of Markan priority.

5. We should affirm, as the early church did, that the four canonical Gospels are in fact "the fourfold Gospel"—that is, *one* gospel according to *four* witnesses, Matthew, Mark, Luke, and John.[30] This attests to the essential unity among the Gospels regarding the key events in Jesus's life, particularly his crucifixion, burial, and resurrection.

What we should *not* do is reduce the fourfold gospel witness to a skeleton (minus the supernatural), such as in the famous "Jefferson Bible," or a harmony of key events in the life of the historical Jesus. Nor should we substitute a historical timeline of events in Jesus's earthly ministry for reading the actual Gospel narratives.[31]

For these reasons, what I've chosen to do in this book is to provide a resource for reading the four canonical Gospels by closely tracking with their respective story lines and theological emphases. In addition, I've suggested some proper points of application along the way, since, as I mentioned, the life of Jesus is not merely a proper object of study but first and foremost a call to action, a call to follow Jesus and to become more like him, both in our own character and in the way we relate to others.

This approach also promises to help us develop a better grasp of how the gospel of salvation in Jesus Christ is central to the fourfold Gospel witness. Rather than dichotomizing between the elusive "Jesus of history" and the existential "Christ of faith," we'll be able to come to know *the Jesus of the Gospels*—and thus of the gospel!—and be equipped to follow the one who calls us. This will help us not only to recognize him as Savior and Lord but also to join him on mission: to take up our cross on a daily basis and to identify with him in a world that desperately needs to see and hear that "God so loved the world that he gave his only Son, that whoever believes in him should not perish but have eternal life."[32]

---

30. Cf. Martin Hengel, *The Four Gospels and the One Gospel of Jesus Christ* (Harrisburg, PA: Trinity Press International, 2000). See also Hays, *Reading Backwards*, who places a special emphasis on reading the Gospels in view of Israel's Scriptures; and Jonathan Pennington, *Reading the Gospels Wisely: A Narrative and Theological Introduction* (Grand Rapids: Baker, 2012), chapters 4 and 5.

31. Some may argue that we should do both: read the four Gospels individually and in conjunction with one another *and* provide a survey of the overall Gospel timeline. However, it's hard to see how this completely avoids the problems mentioned above regarding reconstructing a harmony from the existing Gospels. While it's certainly the case that as we read the four Gospels we form a mental composite of the various events and teachings in the life of Jesus, it's best to hold this conglomerate construct as tentatively as possible and to subordinate it to the cumulative impact of the fourfold Gospel witness.

32. John 3:16.

READING THE GOSPELS TODAY

How, then, should we read the Gospels? Let me share with you four ways of reading the Gospels that will help us get to know the real Jesus of the Gospels.

Reading the Gospels as a Unified Witness

In keeping with the early church's understanding, as mentioned, we should understand the individual Gospels as unified documents within the larger rubric of the fourfold Gospel. When you look at your English Bible—or, if your language proficiency permits, your Greek New Testament—you'll notice that the actual title of the individual Gospels is *not* "The Gospel of Matthew," "The Gospel of Mark," and so forth, but "The Gospel *according to* Matthew," "The Gospel *according to* Mark," and so forth.

Thus, in a sense, we don't have *four* Gospels but *one* Gospel according to four witnesses—Matthew, Mark, Luke, and John. This is not merely a pedantic point; in fact, it's exceedingly important for us to let the implications of this insight sink in. The church doesn't have four gospels; it proclaims one, and only one, unified gospel. Therefore, let's not divide or separate what God has brought together (to recontextualize Jesus's saying regarding divorce) in the church's canon of Scripture.[33] We may not always be able to read through a given Gospel in our Bibles in one sitting, or even in multiple subsequent ones. But we should never lose sight of the fact that the one gospel, given to us in the canon in form of a fourfold witness, is unified.

What's more, the Gospels constitute not merely a canonical, or literary, unity; they represent a unity in every sense of the term, including a historical and theological one. In other words, the Gospels are not merely a unified literary and canonical document; they also attest to the same historical set of events and teachings in the life of Jesus and reflect unified theological convictions expressed by Jesus and embraced by the biblical authors and the early church.[34] And while the titles of the four Gospels are not themselves part of these Gospels (they are what scholars call "para-text"), they were affixed to the Gospels at a very early stage and clearly reflect the church's common understanding of their role and function in the life of the early church.[35]

Thus, we should embrace a both-and rather than either-or mentality in reading the Gospels. We should sit at the feet of each of the four Gospel witnesses to arrive at a full-orbed understanding of who Jesus is. And we should resist the notion that reading the Gospels confronts us with the challenge of choosing between mutually contradic-

---

33. Cf. Matthew 19:6.
34. I've tried to elaborate on this point together with Michael Kruger in *The Heresy of Orthodoxy*.
35. Martin Hengel, "The Titles of the Gospels and the Gospel of Mark," in *Studies in the Gospel of Mark* (London: SCM, 1985), 64–84.

tory accounts: either we embrace, say, Mark's account while discarding John's, or vice versa (or holding that both are wrong). This may have the appearance of enlightened critical scholarship but is clearly not the way in which the original writers intended their Gospels to be read, nor in which the early Christians themselves conceived of the relationship between the Gospels.

Reading the Gospels as Eyewitness Testimony

From the vantage point of history, we should read the Gospels as eyewitness testimony. Of the four Gospels, it is particularly John who stakes a strong claim to being an eyewitness. Ironically, as mentioned, many Enlightenment thinkers disputed this claim, in part because John's account is rather different from the other three canonical Gospels and in part because they conceived of history and theology in disjunctive rather than complementary terms.[36] This is not the place to provide a thorough vindication of John's historical reliability, though several reputable scholars have attempted to do so in recent years.[37] Suffice it to say that anyone who approaches John's Gospel with an open mind will likely conclude that John is interested in both history and theology and that these two dimensions should not be pitted against each other. In fact, the truth of John's theology rests in large part on his historical reliability.[38]

Luke, for his part, claims in his opening preface that his account is based on eyewitness testimony.[39] He frankly acknowledges that he himself was not an eyewitness but notes that he, as a good historian, carefully researched his subject matter by accessing accounts of those who were eyewitnesses in compiling his own narrative. In this way, Luke is honest and transparent and, while not himself an eyewitness, makes a virtue out

---

36. The first such frontal challenge to John's historicity came from the German scholar Karl Gottlieb Bretschneider in a work called *Probabilia de evangelii et epistolarum Ioannis Apostoli indole et origine cruditorum judiciis modeste subjecit* in 1820. Bretschneider wrote in Latin; the work has never been translated. Translated into English, his title reads: *Probability Concerning the Character and Origin of the Gospel and Epistles of John, the Apostle, Modestly Submitted to the Judgment of the Erudite* (see William J. Baird, *History of New Testament Research*, vol. 1: *From Deism to Tübingen* [Minneapolis: Fortress, 1992], 312). Bretschneider backed away from his criticism only two years later (1822), but the seeds of doubt and criticism had been sown, and many others followed in his footsteps in the decades that followed. See my critique, "Frühe Zweifel an der johanneischen Verfasserschaft des vierten Evangeliums in der modernen Interpretationsgeschichte," *European Journal of Theology* 5 (1996): 37–46; English translation: "Early Doubts of the Apostolic Authorship of the Fourth Gospel in the History of Modern Biblical Criticism," in *Studies in John and Gender: A Decade of Scholarship*, Studies in Biblical Literature 38 (New York: Peter Lang, 2001), chapter 2.
37. See, e.g., Craig L. Blomberg, *The Historical Reliability of John's Gospel: Issues and Commentary* (Downers Grove, IL: InterVarsity Press, 2001).
38. As argued in the still-valuable work by Leon Morris, *Studies in the Fourth Gospel* (Grand Rapids: Eerdmans, 1969), esp. his essay "History and Theology in the Fourth Gospel," 65–138.
39. Luke 1:1–4.

of necessity; rather than compiling, or drawing on, one eyewitness account, he bases his Gospel on multiple eyewitness accounts to which he had access. As Richard Bauckham observes in his landmark work *Jesus and the Eyewitnesses*, Luke's procedure here is fully in keeping with first-century standards for historiography (history writing), which must be based on eyewitness testimony to be credible.[40] Matthew and Mark, likewise, can be shown to have followed accepted conventions for history writing in the first century.

Reading the Gospels as Narratives

From a literary vantage point, we should read the Gospels as narratives. This means that we should come to appreciate them as self-contained literary works, consisting of literary units and subunits, complete with plots, subplots, a set of major and minor characters, and so forth. As mentioned, this is vital, particularly since this is the form in which information regarding the life of Jesus has come down to us. Respecting Scripture, therefore, also means respecting the literary boundaries and characteristics attached to the respective Gospel accounts. Conflating these into a hypothetical reconstruction of the life of Jesus, no matter how well intentioned, is therefore counterproductive if not misguided and most likely misleading. In fact, in the hands of critical scholars, such a project will likely result in a truncated portrait of Jesus, whether stripped of the miraculous, demythologized into existential categories, or subjected to various other modifications. Establishing the likely historicity of key events in the life of Jesus may be of limited apologetic value in dealing with modern-day skeptics[41] but is an inadequate substitute for reading the four canonical Gospels as coherent and complementary accounts reflecting eyewitness testimony.

Recent literary scholarship has given us vital and valuable tools for reading the Gospels as narratives. In the past few decades, scholars have increasingly come to appreciate the fact that the Gospel accounts display a large variety of literary features that can be studied with great profit by students of Scripture.[42] This includes their overarching plotline, characterization, setting, and various literary structuring or other devices.[43]

40. Richard Bauckham, *Jesus and the Eyewitnesses: The Gospels as Eyewitness Testimony*, 2nd ed. (Grand Rapids: Eerdmans, 2017); See also Craig S. Keener, Christobiography: Memory, History, and the Reliability of the Gospels (Grand Rapids: Eerdmans, 2019).
41. For a largely positive example, see Darrell L. Bock and Robert L. Webb, *Key Events in the Life of the Historical Jesus: A Collaborative Exploration of Context and Coherence* (Grand Rapids: Eerdmans, 2010).
42. Classic works include David Rhoads and Donald Michie, *Mark as Story: An Introduction to the Narrative of a Gospel* (Philadelphia: Fortress, 1982; 3rd ed. David Rhoads, Joanna Dewey, and Donald Michie [Philadelphia: Fortress, 2012]); Robert C. Tannehill, *The Narrative Unity of Luke-Acts*, 2 vols. (Philadelphia: Fortress, 1987); and R. Alan Culpepper, *Anatomy of the Fourth Gospel: A Study in Literary Design* (Philadelphia: Fortress, 1983).
43. See, e.g., chapters 5 and 9 (on Old and New Testament narrative, respectively), in Köstenberger and Patterson, *Invitation to Biblical Interpretation*.

Without imposing modern-day categories onto the biblical text, we can benefit from reading the biblical Gospels as literary wholes rather than compartmentalizing them into smaller, possibly even disparate, units. This holistic reading of narratives will enable us to appreciate their character as coherent stories (without implying lack of historicity) both on their own terms and in relation to other accounts.

This balanced, empathetic reading will also enable us to keep the literary and theological diversity of the four evangelists in tension with their underlying unity and will keep us from jumping to the conclusion that they stand in necessary contradiction. In fact, reading all four accounts in relation to one another will provide us with a theological richness that is simply unattainable by reading only one or two Gospel accounts. What many have called the "Synoptic problem," therefore, at a closer look turns out to be a "Synoptic opportunity," if not a "Synoptic blessing." The same goes on a broader scale for reading the Synoptics in conjunction with John's Gospel.

Reading the Gospels One at a Time

How, then, should we read the Gospels? Like eating an elephant, as the saying goes (one bite at a time), it's best to read the Gospels one at a time (vertically), tracking with their plotlines and with the ways in which they characterize their one major character, Jesus, with regard to what he did (his actions) and what he said (his teachings).[44] All of this is part of the biblical portrait of Jesus's messianic mission, which in turn is rooted in a long stream of prophetic predictions that, in Jesus, have come to fulfillment.[45] The life of Jesus can't be understood apart from the first days of Jesus (e.g., the virgin birth) or the final days of Jesus (his crucifixion and resurrection).[46]

And yet the middle of this story—the story of Jesus's three-and-a-half-year earthly ministry centering on his training of the Twelve and his eventual crucifixion and resurrection—is pregnant with meaning and significance and promises to repay rich dividends for those who engage in this study with open minds and hearts. Who knows, the Spirit of Jesus may perform open-heart surgery on you as you read the pages of this

44. That said, it is of course also appropriate to read the Gospels horizontally—that is, enjoy the Gospels in all their richness and gather what we can glean from *all* the Gospels about a given event or topic. While our primary focus in this book is on reading the Gospels vertically (one at a time), on a secondary level we will occasionally comment on how a given event in one Gospel is supplemented by information in another, or even how to reconcile apparently contradictory information in multiple Gospels.

45. See Andreas J. Köstenberger and Alexander E. Stewart, *The First Days of Jesus: The Story of the Incarnation* (Wheaton, IL: Crossway, 2015). This is also the primary thesis underlying the treatment of Hays, *Reading Backwards*.

46. See Köstenberger and Stewart, *First Days of Jesus*; Andreas J. Köstenberger and Justin Taylor with Alexander Stewart, *The Final Days of Jesus: The Most Important Week of the Most Important Person Who Ever Lived* (Wheaton, IL: Crossway, 2014).

book and as you read the Gospels themselves as they, with one voice, testify to Jesus the Messiah, who has staked a claim also on your life as your only rightful Savior, Master, and King.[47]

The early church assigned symbols to each of the Gospels taken from Ezekiel's vision reflected in the book of Revelation: a man, a lion, a bull, and an eagle.[48] The church father Jerome writes that Matthew starts out his Gospel with a man: "Jesus, the son of David, the son of Abraham." Mark begins with a voice roaring like a lion: "A voice of one shouting in the desert, 'Prepare the way of the Lord.'" Luke features Zechariah the priest, making the bull a fitting sacrificial symbol. John rose up on eagle's wings, "hastening toward higher matters," presenting Jesus as the preexistent Word of God.[49]

While not directly grounded in Scripture, these symbols stir the imagination as we set out to explore each of the Gospels individually.[50] They help us realize that each of the Gospels was written by a different evangelist, and that each Gospel has a different personality, as it were, just as we today recognize different personality types. Few would argue that there should only be one personality type—that would be boring! It is similar with the Gospels. Let's therefore enjoy the richness, variety, and diversity reflected in the Gospels as the personality of each Gospel writer shines through in the way they paint a unique portrait of Jesus.

---

47. While space doesn't allow me to reproduce the Gospel texts themselves in this volume, I'd strongly urge you to read each of the Gospels in their entirety. Toward that end, I'd highly recommend the *ESV Reader's Gospels* (Wheaton, IL: Crossway, 2015).
48. Ezekiel 1:5, 10; cf. Revelation 4:6–9.
49. See Matthew 1:1; Mark 1:3; Luke 1:5; John 1:1. Cf. St. Jerome, *Commentary on Matthew*, trans. Thomas P. Scheck, The Fathers of the Church 117 (Washington, DC: Catholic University of America Press, 2008), 55. Note that Irenaeus assigns the four symbols differently (Mark as eagle, John as lion; *Against Heresies* 3.11.8 [*Ante-Nicene Fathers* 1.428]), while Augustine proposes a yet different arrangement (Matthew as lion, Mark as man; *Harmony of the Four Gospels* 1.9; see Jerome, *Commentary on Matthew*, 55n37).
50. Cf. Richard A. Burridge, *Four Gospels, One Jesus? A Symbolic Reading*, 3rd ed. (Grand Rapids: Eerdmans, 2014). Burridge discusses the Gospels in the order Mark—Matthew—Luke—John, following the narrative contours in broad strokes. His "symbolic reading" is grounded in the ancient symbols for the Gospels.

CHAPTER 2

The Good News according to MATTHEW

Jesus the Jewish Messiah, Descendant of Abraham and David

JUST THE FACTS
Good news of salvation delivered by Matthew (Levi)
Former tax collector for the Roman occupying force
Follower of Jesus and member of the Twelve

WHO WAS MATTHEW?

Matthew, called Levi in the other Gospels, was one of the twelve apostles of Jesus.[1] Matthew himself includes his calling narrative in the Gospel: "As Jesus went on from there, he saw a man named Matthew sitting at the tax collector's booth. 'Follow me,' he told him, and Matthew got up and followed him." After this, Matthew reports that Jesus and his disciples had dinner at his house along with many other tax collectors and so-called sinners. When the Pharisees objected, Jesus retorted that he had come to call sinners, not the righteous.[2]

Shortly thereafter, "Matthew the tax collector" is mentioned as one of the twelve apostles Jesus appointed.[3] Matthew's background and special interest in tax-related issues come occasionally to the fore, such as when he alone includes the account of Jesus and Peter paying the temple tax or discusses paying taxes to Caesar.[4] Like John, Matthew wrote as a member of the twelve apostles and an eyewitness of the earthly mission of Jesus.

HOW DOES MATTHEW TELL THE STORY OF JESUS?

For the most part (there is some topical arrangement), Matthew tells the story of Jesus in chronological order, moving from Jesus's birth (the virgin birth) and infancy to his public ministry, culminating in Jesus's crucifixion, burial, and resurrection. Jesus's

1. See Matthew 9:9 NIV; cf. Mark 2:14; Luke 5:27. On Matthew as an author, see Charles L. Quarles, *Matthew*, Exegetical Guide to the Greek New Testament (Nashville: B&H, 2017), 5–6.
2. Matthew 9:9–13.
3. Matthew 10:3.
4. Matthew 17:24–27; 22:15–22.

ministry proceeds geographically from Galilee—where Jesus is shown to engage in multiple cycles of ministry in ever-increasing circles—to Judea and from there to Judea's capital, the city of Jerusalem.

Matthew organizes Jesus's teaching in the form of five major discourses or "books of Jesus," like the five Old Testament books of Moses (the Pentateuch) and the five books of Psalms.[5] In these discourses, Matthew portrays Jesus as the new Moses who gives a new law (the Sermon on the Mount, chaps. 5–7), as the messianic shepherd who gathers and commissions a Jewish remnant—the twelve apostles—to preach the good news of the kingdom of God (chap. 10), and as the rabbinic teacher of parables of the kingdom (chaps. 13, 18) and of end-time events climaxing in his return (chaps. 24–25).

Matthew clearly delineates each of these teaching portions by concluding transitional phrases that (with slight variations) conform to the formula "When Jesus had finished saying these things. . . ."[6] In addition to these discourses, Matthew, throughout his Gospel, alternates between discourse (teaching) and narrative (story) sections, portraying Jesus as the Jewish Messiah in both word and deed.

WHAT ARE SOME OF MATTHEW'S DISTINCTIVE EMPHASES?

The first evangelist presents Jesus as the long-awaited Messiah predicted or typologically prefigured across a broad spectrum of passages in the Hebrew Scriptures (Law, Prophets, and Writings). Matthew styles his Gospel as a continuation of God's dealings with Israel and cites numerous Old Testament passages to highlight the identity of Jesus as the Jewish Messiah.

The first evangelist cites the Old Testament more than fifty times (compared to a combined total of sixty-five for the other three Gospels) and alludes to it an additional two hundred-plus times. Matthew's close connection with the Old Testament is further reinforced by the placement of his Gospel as the first book of the New Testament. The fact that Matthew, alone among the Gospels, starts out with a genealogy of Jesus makes it the perfect starting point for the New Testament and a fitting "first Gospel" in the fourfold Gospel canon.

In many ways, therefore, Matthew introduces both the fourfold Gospel canon and the entire New Testament; and as we read his narrative, we'll do well to keep one finger in the pages of the Old Testament—Israel's Scriptures. In the introduction alone, Matthew presents Jesus as fulfilling as many as six Old Testament prophecies.

5. See Quarles, *Matthew*, 8.
6. Matthew 7:28; 11:1; 13:53; 19:1; 26:1.

For those of us who are Gentiles (i.e., non-Jews)—probably the majority of those reading this—we may legitimately ask: What's the relevance of a Gospel that presents Jesus distinctly as the Jewish Messiah for us who are Gentiles? The answer is at least twofold.

First, even for us Gentiles, it's important to realize that our Christian faith is firmly rooted in Jewish soil, in the story and history of God's dealings with Israel, culminating in Jesus's coming in keeping with Old Testament promises.

Second, while Matthew depicts Jesus as the Jewish Messiah in the line of Abraham and David, in the course of the Gospel the scope of salvation gradually widens from Jews to Gentiles. At first, it is wise men who come from afar to worship the infant Messiah; later, Jesus heals a Canaanite woman; at last, the risen Jesus commissions his followers—a Jewish believing remnant—"Go therefore and make disciples of all nations" until "the end of the age."[7] This shows that, while presenting Jesus as the Jewish Messiah, Matthew's Gospel is highly relevant to all people, Jews as well as Gentiles.

WHAT ARE THE MAJOR CONTOURS OF MATTHEW'S ACCOUNT?

Introduction: Jesus the Messiah, Descendant of Abraham and David (1:1–4:16)

Jesus's Work in Galilee (4:17–18:35)

- Work in Galilee, Part 1 (4:17–25)
- *Discourse #1: Jesus's Inaugural Address: The Sermon on the Mount (5:1–7:29)*
- Work in Galilee, Part 2 (8:1–9:38)
- *Discourse #2: Commissioning of the Twelve (10:1–42)*
- Work in Galilee, Part 3 (11:1–12:50)
- *Discourse #3: Stories about God's Kingdom (13:1–53)*
- Work Farther North (13:54–17:27)
- *Discourse #4: Stories about God's Kingdom (18:1–35)*

Jesus's Work in Judea and His Death, Burial, and Resurrection (19:1–28:20)

- Jesus's Work in Judea and Jerusalem (19:1–23:39)
- *Discourse #5: Teaching about the End Times and God's Kingdom (24:1–25:46)*
- Jesus's Death, Burial, Resurrection, and the Great Commission (26:1–28:20)

7. The "Great Commission": Matthew 28:19–20.

INTRODUCTION: JESUS THE MESSIAH, DESCENDANT OF ABRAHAM AND DAVID (1:1–4:16)

The Genealogy of Jesus (1:1–17)

The opening phrase of Matthew's Gospel, "The book of the genealogy" (Greek *Biblos geneseōs*), mirrors the language used to introduce both the creation account and the genealogy of Adam in the book of Genesis.[8] The first evangelist isn't telling a new, unconnected story; he's telling a story with deep roots in God's creation of humanity and the covenants God established with his people Israel as recorded in the Hebrew Scriptures—the Messiah's "genesis"!

Matthew is one of two evangelists (the other being Luke) who includes a genealogy in his Gospel, yet there are several conspicuous differences.

1. Matthew puts his genealogy at the very beginning, as an introduction to Jesus's messianic birth in Bethlehem in keeping with prophetic prediction, while Luke includes his genealogy right before the inception of Jesus's public ministry.[9]

2. Matthew presents his genealogy in ascending order (starting with Abraham and moving forward to end with Jesus), while Luke presents his in descending order (starting with Jesus and moving backward to end with Adam).

---

8. See Genesis 2:4 and 5:1. Beyond this, the phrase echoes the title of the first book of the Bible, the book of Genesis (Quarles, *Matthew*, 14).
9. Luke 3:23–38.

3. Matthew traces Jesus's ancestry back to Abraham, the father of the Jewish nation, accentuating Jesus's Jewishness; Luke traces it back all the way to Adam, stressing more broadly Jesus's humanity.

4. Counting Mary, the mother of Jesus, Matthew includes five women in Jesus's genealogy—which, as far as genealogies are concerned, is highly unusual, especially considering which women are included:

   - Tamar, Judah's daughter-in-law who posed as a harlot (Genesis 38)
   - Rahab, a former Jericho prostitute (Joshua 2)
   - Ruth, a Moabite woman and great-grandmother of David (Book of Ruth)
   - "Uriah's wife"—that is, Bathsheba—later David's wife and mother of Solomon (2 Samuel 11)
   - Mary, the mother of Jesus

Most likely, Matthew includes these women as part of his argument for the plausibility of the virgin birth. In that regard, the presence of these women in Jesus's genealogy serves to demonstrate that the appearance or reality of scandal was not unprecedented in messianic history; and since Jews widely believed God acted consistently in history, this demonstration would likely have added persuasiveness to Matthew's account of the virgin birth.

Tamar posed as a harlot; Rahab once was one. Ruth might have been perceived as scandalous in that she and Boaz spent the night under the same roof (though without actual scandal). Bathsheba—here called "Uriah's wife"—was embroiled in a scandal with David. And Mary conceived a child out of wedlock!

Without removing the marvel, miracle, and mystery from the virgin birth, Matthew argues therefore that the virgin birth, considered scandalous by some (including initially by Joseph; see below), should not necessarily pose a stumbling block to those who questioned Jesus's true paternity; counterintuitive and highly unusual it may be, but God had worked in unusual ways before, including even the possibility or reality of scandal.[10]

5. Matthew's genealogy differs from Luke's in several respects, which raises the question as to why they're so different. Unfortunately, the issue is too complex to address fully here.[11] Suffice it to say that the conventional wisdom that Matthew

10. Plus, Matthew will shortly invoke biblical prophecy of a virgin being with child—Isaiah 7:14—that he claims was fulfilled in Jesus.

11. For more detail, see Nancy S. Dawson, *Genealogies of the Bible*, eds. Eugene H. Merrill and Andreas J. Köstenberger (Grand Rapids: Zondervan, forthcoming). See also David R. Bauer, "Genealogy," in *Dictio-*

> traces Jesus's lineage through Joseph while Luke does so through Mary is likely inadequate to account for the differences. Compounding the complexity is the fact that "became the father of" leaves open whether a given ancestor was the biological or legal father of another person (e.g., through adoption). As a result of this and other factors, lineage shifts occasionally occurred. Also, both genealogies are selective or use different methods that are complementary and not necessarily contradictory. For example, the genealogies in Matthew and Luke begin to diverge when arriving at king David, at which point Matthew continues to trace Jesus's ancestry through Solomon (Matthew 1:6–7) while Luke continues with Nathan, Solomon's brother (Luke 3:31). This double ancestral helix inexorably results in a dual lineage for Jesus.

But why would Matthew start his Gospel with a genealogy in the first place? From our modern Western perspective, introducing the story of Jesus with a detailed list of his ancestors hardly excites (though some of us may enjoy dabbling in genealogical research). But for Jewish first-century readers, the genealogy served an absolutely vital function: to validate Jesus's messianic ancestry. If Jesus was in fact the long-awaited Messiah, he must come from the line of David, through whose royal lineage God promised to establish an eternal dynasty.[12] At the very outset of his genealogy, therefore, Matthew introduces "Jesus Christ"—that is, Jesus the Messiah—as both the "son of David" and the "son of Abraham."[13] As the son of David, Jesus was the messianic king of Israel, the one who would reign over God's people for all eternity. As the son of Abraham, Jesus was the fulfillment of God's promise to Abraham that in him "all the families of the earth" would be blessed.[14]

In addition, Matthew shows his careful arrangement by framing his presentation of Jesus's genealogy in the form of a chiastic (A-B-C-C′-B′-A′) structure:

A Jesus Christ
  B Son of David
    C Son of Abraham (1:1)
    C′ Abraham (1:2)
  B′ David (1:6)
C′ Christ (1:16).

---

nary of Jesus and the Gospels, 2nd ed., eds. Joel B. Green, Jeannine K. Brown, and Nicholas Perrin (Downers Grove, IL: InterVarsity Press, 2013), 299–303.

12. 2 Samuel 7:13.
13. Matthew 1:1.
14. Genesis 12:1–3.

As mentioned above, Matthew's genealogy of Jesus, similar to Luke's, is not exhaustive but rather selective (i.e., Matthew skipped certain generations he considered less significant, at least for his purposes). In addition, Matthew employed a Jewish literary device called *gematria* (numerical symbolism). Accordingly, he structured his genealogy in three blocks of fourteen generations each (whereby fourteen is a multiple of seven, symbolically conveying the notion of perfection):

- Fourteen generations from Abraham to David (his patriarchal lineage)
- Fourteen generations from David to the Babylonian exile (his royal lineage)
- Fourteen generations from the Babylonian exile to Jesus[15]

Not only this, but the name "David" in Hebrew has a numerical value of fourteen when letters are converted into numbers, like this:[16]

- *Dalet* (Hebrew *d*) = 4
- *Waw* (Hebrew *v*) = 6
- *Dalet* (Hebrew *d*) = 4
- Total = 14

For Jewish readers, this numerical symbolism applied to Jesus would have added further persuasiveness to Matthew's argument that Jesus was the Davidic Messiah. In his genealogy, the first evangelist had furnished incontrovertible proof that the number of generations for each of the three salvation-historical periods presented in his listing of Jesus's ancestry added up to fourteen, the exact numerical value of the name "David"! Now you may be unimpressed, but Matthew didn't write his Gospel originally for twenty-first-century Westerners but for first-century Jews.[17] In all these ways, Matthew has provided an orderly account of Jesus's messianic pedigree—as mentioned, genealogies were not necessarily expected to be comprehensive in the ancient Near East—which reflected God's purposeful design and providential ordering of history.

Finally, there's an interesting twist toward the end of the genealogy. While the repeated refrain throughout the genealogy is "X was the father of Y," when the reader arrives at the

---

15. Matthew 1:17.
16. Note that there are no letters for vowels in Hebrew, only consonants; vowels are pointed below a given letter but not counted as letters themselves, which is why the *a* and *i* in "David" are not represented or counted in the conversion of letters into numbers below.
17. Note, by the way, that this in no way condones everything that's done with *gematria* in ancient times or even today. I've seen people do crazy things with numerical symbolism (such as calculating the number of the "beast"—the Antichrist—in Revelation)!

end of the genealogy, upon reading "Matthan the father of Jacob, and Jacob the father of Joseph," the familiar pattern suddenly breaks off. Rather than writing, "and Joseph *the father of Jesus*," Matthew writes, "Joseph *the husband of Mary*," adding, "of whom Jesus was born, who is called Christ."[18] That is, Jesus was born "of Mary," his actual *mother*, but Joseph, while being Mary's husband, was not Jesus's actual *father*! Rather, Joseph was merely Jesus's adoptive, or legal, father; Jesus's actual Father was God. In this way, the end of Matthew's genealogy anticipates the account of the virgin conception and birth of Jesus that is about to follow and that it is designed to introduce.[19]

SON OF DAVID

From the very beginning of his Gospel, Matthew presents Jesus as the "son of David."[20] Jesus's Davidic descent is a major emphasis in the opening genealogy. Jesus is the Messiah who inherits God's dynastic promises to David and who will establish and exercise God's rule over Israel in an eternal kingdom. In Matthew 1:6, David is identified as "David *the* king." He was not merely *a* king; he was *the* king, and Jesus is his promised descendant who has come to fulfill God's covenant with him and with his people.[21]

In the body of Matthew's Gospel, the title "Son of David" attaches to actions that signify Jesus's messianic identity in the line of David. On two occasions blind men cry out to Jesus, "Have mercy on us, Son of David!"[22] In each case Jesus heals them, fulfilling Old Testament promises that the Messiah will give sight to the blind.[23] Echoing another Isaianic prophecy Jesus had already applied to himself,[24] Jesus heals a demon-oppressed man who is both deaf and mute. In response, the crowds marvel and ask, "Can this be the Son of David?"[25] In 15:21–28, a Canaanite woman pleads with Jesus to heal her daughter: "Have mercy on me, O Lord, Son of David." Jesus promptly obliges, and their interchange reveals that while Jesus, as

18. Matthew 1:16.
19. Matthew 1:18–25.
20. Matthew 1:1.
21. 2 Samuel 7:12–16.
22. Matthew 9:27; 20:30–31.
23. Isaiah 32:1–3; 33:17.
24. See Matthew 11:4–5 and Isaiah 35:5–6; 61:1.
25. Matthew 12:23.

the Son of David, came as Israel's Messiah, his coming would ultimately bring salvation to the Gentiles as well.

When Jesus enters Jerusalem at the onset of his passion, crowds hail him with cries of "Hosanna to the Son of David!"[26] While all the evangelists feature accounts of the crowd's acclamation at Jesus's triumphal entry,[27] Matthew alone includes the address "Son of David." What's more, only Matthew draws attention to the fact that after Jesus heals the blind and lame in the temple, the children sing songs of praise to him: "Hosanna to the Son of David!" In both his introduction of Jesus and the description of his earthly ministry, therefore, Matthew presents Jesus as the long-awaited King, the rightful heir to David's throne and the ruler of God's people.[28]

The Virgin Birth (1:18–25)

Matthew's depiction of Jesus's virgin conception, Bethlehem birth, and early boyhood underscores Jesus's uniqueness and connects his coming with God's promises to his people Israel. A young virgin named Mary—a very common name in first-century Palestine—finds herself pregnant, not by Joseph her fiancé, but by the Holy Spirit.[29] While greatly distressed by Mary's pregnancy, Joseph, "being a just man," resolves to divorce her quietly.[30] Yet before he can do so, an angel appears to him in a dream, poignantly addressing him as "son of David"[31] and directing him to take Mary as his wife: "Marry Mary!"[32] What's more, the angel reveals the gender and name of the child growing in Mary's womb: it is a male child, a son, and his name will be Jesus—which in Hebrew means "Yahweh (God) saves"—"for he will save his people from their sins."[33] In keeping with Isaiah's prophecy,

---

26. Matthew 21:9.
27. Mark 11:9; Luke 19:38; John 12:13.
28. See Andreas J. Köstenberger and Alexander E. Stewart, *The First Days of Jesus: The Story of the Incarnation* (Wheaton, IL: Crossway, 2015), 29–91.
29. Matthew 1:18, 20. On Jewish betrothal and marriage customs, see Michael J. Wilkins, *Matthew*, in *Zondervan Illustrated Bible Backgrounds Commentary*, vol. 1, *Matthew, Mark, Luke*, ed. Clinton E. Arnold (Grand Rapids: Zondervan, 2002), 11.
30. In that day, dissolving an engagement required a certificate of divorce. This shows that first-century Jews considered betrothal binding, akin to marriage.
31. See the discussion of Jesus's genealogy above.
32. Matthew 1:19–20. OK, that's not a direct quote but my paraphrase. It works better in English than in Hebrew!
33. Matthew 1:21. See the discussion in Quarles, *Matthew*, 21.

the Messiah will be born of a young woman, a virgin.[34] In addition to "Jesus," he will also be called "Immanuel"—which, as Matthew notes, in Hebrew means "God with us," conveying God's continual presence with his people in fulfillment of the new covenant Jesus would establish with the believing remnant of Israel at the Last Supper.[35]

The Wise Men's Worship (2:1–12)

Matthew states matter-of-factly that "Jesus was born in Bethlehem of Judea in the days of Herod the king."[36] He will develop the messianic implications of Jesus's Bethlehem birth shortly. For now, he continues by narrating the journey of wise men from the East following the path of a star in search of one "born king of the Jews."[37] Over time, numerous legends have grown around this story, such as that these wise men were "kings from Orient" and that their number was three, presumably because they brought three gifts. There may have been three wise men, but if so, they were almost certainly not kings. In any case, more important than their exact occupation is the function of these characters within Matthew's Gospel as a whole. In this regard, the story of the wise men illustrates a recurring set of themes in the Matthean narrative: varying responses to Jesus, and his reach beyond the Jewish people to the Gentile world.[38] What's more, ironically, King Herod, the vassal ruler of Judea, is a type of "Pharaoh" ruling in Jerusalem, which has become a type of "spiritual Egypt."[39]

Coming first to Jerusalem, the wise men find an anxious King Herod (the Great; see below), who outwardly professes a desire to worship the baby but inwardly sees him as a threat to his own power.[40] Herod enlists the help of the Jewish high priests and scribes in determining where the Messiah was to be born. Without a moment's hesitation, they

34. Matthew 1:23a; cf. Isaiah 7:14. Controversy has surrounded Matthew's use of this passage to prove the virgin birth of Jesus, because the original woman in Isaiah was only a "young woman," not a virgin. But that doesn't necessarily invalidate Matthew's point. *Of course* Jesus's virgin birth was unique! Matthew simply tried to point out that the Messiah being born of a young woman—in his case, an actual virgin—was prophetically anticipated in Old Testament Scripture. See Wilkins, *Matthew*, 13.

35. Matthew 1:23b; cf. 26:26–29. As the fourth evangelist puts it, "The Word [i.e., the preexistent Jesus] became flesh" (John 1:14).

36. Matthew 2:1. Regarding geographical matters, see Paul H. Wright, "The Birthplace of Jesus and the Journeys of His First Visitors (Matt 2:1–12; Luke 2:1–20)," in *Lexham Geographic Commentary on the Gospels*, ed. Barry J. Beitzel (Bellingham, WA: Lexham, 2017), 1–9.

37. Matthew 2:2.

38. For a thorough discussion of Matthew's birth narrative, see Köstenberger and Stewart, *First Days of Jesus*, chapters 1–4. See also Benjamin A. Foreman, "Matthew's Birth Narrative (Matt 2:1–18)," in Beitzel, *Lexham Geographic Commentary*, 19–29.

39. This connection is made explicit in Revelation 11:8, where Jerusalem, the place where "the Lord was crucified," is figuratively called "Egypt."

40. Matthew 2:3; cf. 2:8, 16.

tell him, "In Bethlehem of Judea," just as the prophet Micah had predicted. According to Micah, a "ruler who will shepherd my people Israel" was to be born in the village of "Bethlehem, in the land of Judah."[41] At this, King Herod, again ironically, "commissions" the wise men to go to Bethlehem to "search diligently for the child," feigning, as mentioned, a desire to worship him.[42] In his cynical, flippant, and insincere attitude, Herod represents the people and (in particular) rulers of the world who are more interested in preserving their lifestyle and protecting their turf than in submitting to Christ's authority and worshiping him.

The wise men follow the star to Bethlehem in search for the infant king.[43] Upon going "into the house," they see "the child" with Mary.[44] At once, they prostrate themselves in worship and present precious gifts to the child: gold (a gift for royalty), frankincense (a priestly item), and myrrh (perhaps prophetically conveying the grief associated with Jesus's eventual crucifixion).[45] In this, the wise men provide a stark contrast to Herod as Gentiles who approach Jesus in a reverent and worshipful attitude. After this, having been warned in a dream by an angel, they don't return to King Herod but travel back to their country by another route. Strikingly, the same chief priests and scribes who correctly identified the birthplace of the Messiah never seem to have gone to Bethlehem themselves to see if the Messiah was in fact born there. Their inaction betrays indifference toward the Messiah that would later turn into animosity and even outright hatred. Thus ironically, the wise men—Gentiles—rather than the Jewish scribes, emerge as true worshipers, foreshadowing the Great Commission to "make disciples of all nations" at the end of the book.

THE HERODS IN THE NEW TESTAMENT

Sorting out the different Herods in the New Testament can be quite confusing. The Herodian dynasty played an important role in the political setting of Jesus's ministry. There are as many as six Herods to be kept apart:

41. Matthew 2:6; see Micah 5:2.
42. Matthew 2:7–8.
43. Matthew 2:1–12. See Wilkins, "The Christmas Star," in *Matthew*, 16.
44. The two terms, "the house" and "the child," are put in quotation marks to indicate that most likely the wise men arrived in Bethlehem some time after Jesus's birth in that Jesus seems to be no longer in a manger and is no longer an infant but a child. This runs counter to most popular depictions, which have the wise men arrive at the scene of Jesus's birth on the night Jesus was born (e.g., *The Nativity Story*, directed by Catherine Hardwicke [New Line Cinema, 2006]).
45. Matthew 2:10–11.

1. *Herod the Great*: This Herod (Herod I) was the Roman client king of Judea who is mentioned in Matthew 2:1–12. He was responsible for the rebuilding of the temple in Jerusalem and known for his many ambitious, grandiose building projects. He was also responsible for slaughtering the infants at Bethlehem following Christ's birth. The emperor Augustus famously quipped that it was better to be Herod's pig (*hus*) than his son (*huios*). Herod the Great died in 1 (or 4) BC.[46]

2. *Herod Archelaus*: This Herod was the son of Herod the Great and was appointed as the ruler (ethnarch) of Judea, Idumea, and Samaria. Mary and Joseph were afraid to return to Galilee under Archelaus's rule (Matthew 2:22), possibly because of his reputation for excessive brutality. He was eventually deposed and banished to Gaul by Augustus in AD 6.

3. *Herod Philip*: This Herod was the half-brother of Archelaus and Antipas and the son born to Herod by his fifth wife, a woman from Jerusalem named Cleopatra. He was appointed as tetrarch over several northern Galilean provinces in 4 BC. He rebuilt the city of Panias and renamed it Caesarea Philippi, in distinction from Caesarea Maritima, which was close to where Jesus discussed his messianic identity with his disciples (Matthew 16:13–20; Mark 8:27–30).[47] He died in AD 33/34.

4. *Herod Antipas*: This Herod was the younger brother of Archelaus and was appointed as tetrarch over Galilee. Jesus's ministry took place in Galilee during Antipas's reign. He divorced his wife in favor of Herodias, the wife of his half-brother Philip. He was criticized for this unlawful act by John the Baptist, which led to the latter's arrest and beheading at his order (Matthew 14:1–12; Mark 6:14–29). When Antipas later hears of Jesus, he thinks that John the Baptist has been raised from the dead (Luke 9:7–9). Jesus calls him "that fox" (Luke 13:32) and is sent by Pilate to him for a hearing during his trial (Luke 23:6–12). Similar to Archelaus, Antipas was banished to Gaul and died after AD 39.[48]

46. For more detailed sketches, see Wilkins, *Matthew*, 18; Mark Strauss, *Luke*, in Arnold, *Zondervan Illustrated Bible Backgrounds Commentary*, vol. 1, *Matthew, Mark, Luke*, 330.
47. See Wilkins, *Matthew*, 102.
48. See David E. Garland, *Mark*, in Arnold, *Zondervan Illustrated Bible Backgrounds Commentary*, vol. 1, *Matthew, Mark, Luke*, 241.

5. *Herod Agrippa I*: This Herod was the grandson of Herod the Great and assumed control of his uncle Philip's territory along with Galilee and Judea. He is depicted as a persecutor of the early Christian church and was responsible for having James executed and Peter imprisoned (Acts 12:1–19). Luke tells his readers that this Herod died suddenly for accepting divine praise in Acts 12:21–23. Herod Agrippa I died in AD 44.

6. *Herod Agrippa*: This Herod (also known as Herod Agrippa II or Agrippa) was the son of Herod Agrippa I and the great-grandson of Herod the Great. He was only seventeen years old when his father died and too young to rule over his father's extensive territories. In due course, he assumed control over the territories of Philip as well as territory near the Sea of Galilee. Agrippa assumed authority over temple affairs in Jerusalem while Festus served as the governor of Judea. Paul appeared before Agrippa prior to his appeal to Caesar (Acts 25:13–27). Herod Agrippa II died around AD 93.

Escape to Egypt, Herod's Rage, and Return to Nazareth (2:13–23)

The ensuing events reveal God's sovereign hand in protecting Jesus from the murderous designs of King Herod. Having been warned by the angel of the Lord in a dream (notice that the angel tells Joseph to take "the child and his mother" away, again hinting at the fact that while Mary was Jesus's mother, Joseph was not Jesus's biological father), Joseph takes his young family to Egypt to remain there until Herod's death, which, history tells us, took place shortly thereafter in 1 (or 4) BC (this means that Jesus's birth must have taken place prior to this time, most likely in 5 and 1 BC).[49] The narrative of the escape of Joseph, Mary, and Jesus to Egypt and the execution of Jewish male children by Herod echoes the escape of Moses and the execution of Jewish male children at the time of the exodus.[50] It also fulfills the statement by the Old Testament prophet Hosea, "Out of Egypt I called my son."[51] Just as God called Israel "his son" out of Egypt into the Promised Land, Matthew contends (citing Hosea), so God called Jesus "his Son" out of Egypt back into the Holy Land.

49. Note that there was a computation error when, much later, our current calendar was set, resulting in the strange fact that Jesus was born sometime between 5 and 1 BC ("before Christ").
50. See Exodus 1–2.
51. Matthew 2:15, citing Hosea 11:1.

When discovering that the infant Messiah had eluded his grasp, Herod is enraged and orders all male children two years old and under in Bethlehem and vicinity to be killed, unwittingly fulfilling Jeremiah's prophecy that "a voice was heard in Ramah . . . Rachel weeping for her children."[52] In light of what we know of Herod's personality and character from other sources, this senseless act of violence sadly comports with the historical record. Mercifully, since Bethlehem was a small village, the mad king's edict may have applied to no more than one or two dozen children. While the contexts in Hosea and Jeremiah on the one hand and in Matthew on the other differed in that the former wrote prior to the Messiah's coming while Matthew interpreted these prophetic writings in hindsight in view of actual events in Jesus's life,[53] the proofs the first evangelist adduces for Jesus's messianic identity would likely have been highly persuasive to his original Jewish readers. Matthew's portrayal of Jesus begins to paint the picture of him as the new Moses who delivers and instructs God's people and who will shortly take center stage when delivering his inaugural address, the famous Sermon on the Mount.[54]

Finally, in response to another angelic vision, Joseph brings his family to Nazareth, a city in Galilee, where Jesus would live for the remainder of his childhood.[55] This, too, happened "so that what was spoken by the prophets might be fulfilled": "He would be called a Nazarene"—that is, Jesus of Nazareth.[56] Unlike the references in Hosea and Jeremiah discussed above, however, the source of the present quote is hard to pinpoint. Perhaps Matthew doesn't have one specific passage in mind but alludes more broadly to the connection between Nazareth and messianic prophecies in Isaiah involving the Hebrew word *nezer*, "root."[57] As mentioned, there were no vowels in the Hebrew alphabet, and so there would have been a close connection between the consonants in "NaZaReth" and "NeZeR" (the messianic "Root" of Jesse, King David's father, predicted by the prophet Isaiah). In all these ways, then—the Messiah's birthplace, the escape to Egypt, the slaughter of the infant boys in Bethlehem, and Jesus's boyhood in Nazareth—Matthew observes that Jesus fulfilled Old Testament expectations regarding the Messiah. No matter how you look at him, he perfectly fits the (messianic) bill!

52. Matthew 2:18, citing Jeremiah 31:15.
53. And, it might be added, that while modern-day critical scholars balk at Matthew's use of the Old Testament here . . .
54. Matthew 5–7; see discussion below.
55. Matthew 2:19–20. Regarding the reference in Matthew 2:22 to Archelaus's rule in Judea that caused Joseph to settle in Galilee instead, see the sidebar "The Herods in the New Testament" above. Note the preponderance of dreams and angelic visions in Jesus's birth narrative, underscoring the degree of divine intervention and the uniqueness and momentous nature of Jesus's arrival.
56. Matthew 2:23. On matters of geography, see Paul H. Wright, "The Size and Makeup of Nazareth at the Time of Jesus (Matt 2:23)," in Beitzel, *Lexham Geographic Commentary*, 30–41.
57. E.g., Isaiah 11:1, 10.

MATTHEW'S AND THE OTHER GOSPELS' USE OF THE OLD TESTAMENT

A big part of Matthew's purpose, as mentioned, is the demonstration that Jesus, as the Jewish Messiah, fulfilled Old Testament Scripture. The introduction to Matthew's Gospel is particularly pronounced in its consistent emphasis on scriptural fulfillment. As Matthew shows, Jesus strikingly fulfilled an entire matrix of Old Testament messianic predictions, including the following:

- Isaiah 7:14: The Messiah will be born of a virgin.[58]
- Micah 5:2: The Messiah will be born in Bethlehem.[59]
- Hosea 11:1: The Messiah will be called out of Egypt.[60]
- Jeremiah 31:15: The Messiah's birthplace will witness the slaughter of infants.[61]
- Isaiah 40:3: The Messiah's arrival will be heralded by a voice in the wilderness.[62]
- Isaiah 9:1–2: The Messiah will begin his ministry in Galilee.[63]

The underlying premise is that all the pieces of the messianic puzzle point to Jesus. The Old Testament predicted that the Messiah would be born in Bethlehem: Jesus was born in Bethlehem. The Old Testament predicted that the Messiah would be born of a virgin: Jesus was born of a virgin. And so forth. What's more, Matthew is not alone in his emphasis on scriptural fulfillment; the other Gospels are very similar in this regard.

So, as you read the Gospels, you'll want to pay close attention to instances where an evangelist cites an Old Testament passage. Many of those will indicate prophetic *prediction and fulfillment* in Jesus. Sometimes this will take on the form of *typology*, in which a typical pattern, person, or

58. Matthew 1:22–23.
59. Matthew 2:6.
60. Matthew 2:15.
61. Matthew 2:18.
62. Matthew 3:3.
63. Matthew 4:14–16. For a list of Jesus's fulfillment of Old Testament prophecies, see Charles L. Quarles, *A Theology of Matthew*, Explorations in Biblical Theology 11 (Phillipsburg, NJ: P&R, 2013), 28–29.

event in Israel's history is said to correspond to Jesus as the matching antitype. An example of this is Moses's lifting up of the bronze serpent in the wilderness so that the people of Israel could look at the serpent and not die of snakebites, which Jesus said corresponds to Jesus himself being lifted up on a cross so that people can look at him and not die eternally.[64]

You'll usually be able to tell an Old Testament quotation by an introductory formula such as "All this took place to fulfill what the Lord had spoken by the prophet."[65] Often the New Testament author will presuppose the Old Testament context, so you'll do well to look up the source passage in the Old Testament in order to be able to understand the quotation of that passage in a given Gospel context better.

In addition, there are many other ways in which the Old Testament significantly affects the evangelists' portrait of Jesus. This includes the use of Old Testament symbols, such as that of a messianic shepherd, or the exodus motif, including the signs and wonders performed by Moses. As the church father Augustine (AD 354–430) once wrote, "The New Testament lies hidden in the Old and the Old Testament is unveiled in the New."[66] I believe that as you'll read through the Gospels, you'll find Augustine's statement abundantly confirmed.

64. John 3:14–15.
65. Matthew 1:22.
66. *Quaest. in Hept.* 2, 73.

INTRODUCTION: JESUS THE MESSIAH, DESCENDANT OF ABRAHAM AND DAVID (1:1–4:16, CONT.)

The Mission of John the Baptist, Forerunner of the Messiah (3:1–12)

The narrative now shifts to the ministry of John the Baptist, who appeared in the Judean wilderness urging the Jewish people to "repent, for the kingdom of heaven is at hand."[67] That a prophet would call God's people to repentance was nothing new; the announcement that "the kingdom of heaven" was on the verge of arriving, on the other hand, was nothing short of momentous.[68] As in all the Gospels, John the Baptist identifies himself as a "voice of one crying in the wilderness, 'Prepare the way of the Lord,'" envisaged by the prophet Isaiah.[69] The reference to an unspecified "voice" draws attention away from the one making the announcement to the one who is to come—the Messiah. The wilderness locale is reminiscent of Israel's wanderings there during the exodus from Egypt. What John the Baptist is essentially announcing (and Matthew is echoing) is that the Messiah would lead a new exodus by which God would deliver his people. God's people should prepare for the advent of this new messianic age by way of repentance. John's attire resembles that of the flamboyant Old Testament prophet Elijah, who likewise donned "a garment of (camel) hair and a leather belt around his waist."[70]

John's preaching of repentance and confession of sins meets with a huge response among the ordinary people, but when the Jewish leaders come to John, he

---

67. Matthew 3:1–2.
68. Note that "heaven" is a euphemism for "God" here and throughout Matthew's Gospel.
69. Matthew 3:3; cf. Isaiah 40:3. On the wilderness setting, see Aubrey L. Taylor, "Ministry in the Wilderness (Matt 3:1–12; Luke 3:1–20)," in Beitzel, *Lexham Geographic Commentary*, 42–52.
70. Matthew 3:4; cf. 2 Kings 1:8.

denounces them in harsh terms; their appeal to Abraham won't save them.[71] For them, there'll be only judgment, for "God is able from these stones to raise up children for Abraham."[72] In other words, God didn't need them to populate his messianic community; he can start over from scratch![73] This caution would also ring in Matthew's readers' ears, many of whom would have been Jews. Unless they repented and put their trust in the Messiah, their Jewish heritage wasn't going to save them![74] That said, John's baptizing activity was only the beginning; one mightier than he would follow after him who would baptize not with mere water but with "the Holy Spirit and fire."[75]

Jesus's Baptism by John (3:13–17)

That figure who is infinitely mightier than John the Baptist now appears on the scene: Jesus the Messiah. He comes to the Jordan River to be baptized by John.[76] John voices the question that will be on the mind of every reader of the narrative: "I need to be baptized by you, so why do you come to me?" Typically, the lesser would be baptized by the greater. What's more, wasn't John's a baptism of repentance? If Jesus were to be baptized by John, wouldn't that indicate that he was a sinner in need of repentance? This may be a plausible way of reasoning in human terms, but Jesus himself brushes all such concerns aside, reassuring John that he should go ahead with the baptism so as "to fulfill all righteousness."[77] Apparently, this was part of Jesus's identification with sinners without implicating Jesus himself in any sin himself.[78]

When Jesus is subsequently baptized, as soon as he emerges from the water, the heavens open and the Spirit of God descends and rests on him like a dove (conveying the notion of a new creation, as the Spirit of God is shown to be hovering above the waters at the original creation in Genesis 1:2), and a voice from heaven—God the

71. See the discussion of Jesus's genealogy above.
72. Matthew 3:5–10.
73. Jesus makes this same point in several of his parables, including that of the wicked tenants.
74. Incidentally, the same continues to be true today: just because you grew up in a Christian home, or have Christian parents, or were born and raised in what some might consider a Christian country, doesn't mean you're going to be allowed to enter God's heaven unless you repent and believe in Christ.
75. Matthew 3:11–12. "Fire" most likely serves as an emblem of divine judgment.
76. Matthew 3:13. On the setting, see Aubrey L. Taylor, "Wilderness Events: The Baptism and Temptation of Jesus (Matt 3:13–4:11; Luke 3:21–4:15)," in Beitzel, *Lexham Geographic Commentary*, 53–64.
77. Matthew 3:15.
78. Cf., e.g., Paul's words in Romans 8:3–4: "For God has done what the law, weakened by the flesh, could not do. By sending his own Son in the likeness of sinful flesh and for sin, he condemned sin in the flesh, in order that the righteous requirement of the law might be fulfilled in us, who walk not according to the flesh but according to the Spirit."

Father—declares, "This is my beloved Son, with whom I am well pleased."[79] This declaration, too, is reminiscent of Old Testament messianic passages by which Jesus is identified as the Messiah and suffering servant who will provide forgiveness for sinners by sacrificing his life for them.[80] The Father's commendation of his Son makes clear that Jesus isn't a self-proclaimed Messiah (see the temptation narrative below); he is the Son of God who does the will of the Father and, as a result, God is pleased.

The Temptation of Jesus (4:1–11)

The scene of the narrative shifts once again as Jesus is "led by the Spirit into the wilderness to be tempted by the devil."[81] Again, the wilderness reference connects Jesus's experience with Israel's during the exodus.[82] Jesus's forty days of temptation show that he truly came to "fulfill all righteousness."[83] Where the Israelites failed to be faithful to God during their forty years of wandering in the wilderness, Jesus remains faithful and demonstrates his identity as the true Son of God. The connection with Moses, wilderness Israel, and the exodus is significantly reinforced by the fact that all three Old Testament passages Jesus quotes in response to Satan's temptations come from Deuteronomy 6–8, Moses's address to the Israelites before entering the Promised Land. All these were lessons that the Israelites should have learned:

- "Man shall not live by bread alone, but by every word that comes from the mouth of God."
- "You shall not put the Lord your God to the test."
- "You shall worship the Lord your God and him only shall you serve."[84]

At Jesus's baptism, we saw that Jesus came to "play by the rules," being committed to fulfilling "all righteousness." In fact, he went even beyond what could reasonably have been expected when he, the sinless Son of God, submitted to baptism. Here at Jesus's temptation, we see that once again Jesus refuses to succumb to Satan's lie that Jesus, as the Messiah, can write his own ticket.

79. Matthew 3:17.
80. Psalm 2:7; Isaiah 42:1.
81. Matthew 4:1 NIV.
82. Cf. Matthew 3:1–3.
83. Matthew 4:1–11; see 3:15. Righteousness is an important theme in Matthew's Gospel, especially in the early portions; see the reference to those who hunger and thirst for righteousness (5:6), Jesus's requirement that his followers' righteousness exceed that of the Pharisees (5:20), and his command that his disciples seek first the kingdom of God and his righteousness (6:33).
84. Deuteronomy 8:3; 6:16; 6:13 (in that order) cited in Matthew 4:4, 7, 10.

First, when hungry, Jesus, if he had wanted to, could have turned stones into bread (just like he turned water into wine at the Cana wedding in John 2), but he refused to take matters into his own hands. He was committed to trust in God's provision rather than acting independently as Adam and Eve had done in the garden. How often are we tempted to take matters into our own hands rather than trusting God, say, when looking for a job or even for a marriage partner?

Second, when the devil dared him to jump off the pinnacle of the temple, with Satan even quoting Scripture (!) to appear "biblical," Jesus again didn't take the bait but refused to put God to the test. True, Jesus had angels at his command who would have softened his fall (in fact, notice how, as soon as the temptations are over, "angels came and were ministering" to Jesus); but this would have been to claim special status when Jesus had chosen to empty himself of his divine prerogatives.[85]

Finally, when Satan offered to give Jesus all the kingdoms of the world "and their glory," Jesus climactically rebuked him, saying, "Be gone, Satan!" As the true Israelite, he'd worship none other than God alone (even though he himself, as the Son of God, could have commanded worship). We, too, should never make a pact with the devil, even if he promises us fame or fortune; as Jesus would later tell his followers, "For what will it profit a man if he gains the whole world and forfeits his soul?"[86]

At these temptations, Jesus showed his humility and obedience to God's will as revealed in Scripture. As Jesus said of himself later in Matthew's Gospel, "I am gentle and lowly in heart."[87] At the very inception of his public ministry, therefore, Jesus is revealed as the true Israel. Here we see both his identification with Israel, and with humanity in general, and a marked contrast with Israel's wilderness experience. Where Israel was disobedient, Jesus was obedient. Where Israel, in particular the wilderness generation, failed to enter the Promised Land because of unbelief, and Moses's successor Joshua was unable to conquer the land completely, this "Son of God" will succeed and bring about a new exodus effecting permanent deliverance from sin—ultimately through his death on a cross—and bring believers into their eternal rest. As Jesus will exclaim later in the Gospel, "Come to me, all who labor and are heavy laden, and I will give you rest."[88] At the end of the temptation, the devil withdraws, and angels come and attend to Jesus.[89]

85. Cf. Philippians 2:6–7.
86. Matthew 16:26; Mark 8:36; Luke 9:25.
87. Matthew 11:29.
88. Matthew 11:28; see also 11:29–30.
89. Matthew 4:11–12.

The Beginning of Jesus's Public Work (4:12–16)

Upon hearing that John the Baptist had been arrested (we learn elsewhere in the Gospels that this is related to Herod Antipas, the ruler of Galilee, whose marriage to Herodias, the former wife of Herod's half-brother Philip, John had dared to denounce),[90] Jesus withdraws to Galilee. The reader was told earlier that Jesus had come from Galilee to the Jordan River to be baptized by John, and that at the temptation the Spirit first led him into the wilderness, and subsequently the devil took Jesus to the temple in the "holy city" (i.e., Jerusalem) and to a "very high mountain."[91] Now Jesus goes back to Galilee, moving from Nazareth where he had grown up[92] to Capernaum "by the sea" (i.e., on the shores of the Sea of Galilee; "sea" in this case means a rather large lake).

At this, Matthew introduces the setting in which Jesus the Messiah will begin his public ministry in both word and deed.[93] Again in keeping with Old Testament prophecy, Jesus commences his work in Galilee, declaring the arrival of God's kingdom in terms identical to John the Baptist's earlier message: "Repent, for the kingdom of heaven is at hand."[94] This shows that John's message was accurate, and that John's and Jesus's messages were essentially one and the same—the big difference, of course, being that John was heralding Jesus's arrival on the scene whereas, now that Jesus had appeared, the kingdom was being inaugurated. As Jesus would later tell the Jewish leaders when asked when the kingdom would come, "The kingdom of God is in your midst"; that is, in Jesus the King, the kingdom had already arrived.[95]

RECAP

In his introduction, Matthew has sketched a comprehensive portrait of Jesus even before Jesus formally launches his public ministry. As to his ancestry, Jesus is the descendant of Abraham (his patriarchal lineage) and David (his royal lineage). As to his human birth, he is the son of Mary whom the Holy Spirit conceived in her womb.

90. The story is told in the form of a flashback in Matthew 14:1–12 and Mark 6:14–29; cf. Luke 9:7–9.
91. See Matthew 3:13; 4:1, 5, 8.
92. Cf. Matthew 2:23.
93. Matthew 4:12.
94. Matthew 4:17; cf. Matthew 3:2; see Isaiah 9:1–2. Together with 3:2, 4:17 constitutes a literary *inclusio*, whereby the identical messages of John the Baptist and Jesus provide the opening and closing bookends of the literary unit of 3:1–4:17 (introduced by "In those days" and concluded by "From that time"), which transitions the Matthean narrative from Jesus's growing-up years in Nazareth through John the Baptist's ministry to the beginning of Jesus's ministry.
95. See Luke 17:20–21. In another sense, of course, the advent of the kingdom of God still awaits the consummation of Jesus's reign at his return at the end of time (cf. Revelation 19:11–16).

As to the global scope of his coming, he is worshiped by Gentile wise men who have come from afar. As to the world's receptivity toward his coming, he is opposed at once by King Herod, while Israel's leaders, though acknowledging that the Messiah would be born in Bethlehem, all but ignore the news of his birth (though increasingly they'd fiercely oppose him). This rejection leads to Jesus being brought out of Egypt, signifying that he will lead a new exodus, and to him settling in Nazareth, signifying that his ministry will ultimately reach the Gentiles and that he is the messianic root that had sprung up in keeping with Isaiah's prophecy.

Also in keeping with Isaiah's prophecy, Jesus is heralded by his messianic forerunner, John the Baptist, who administers a baptism of repentance and even baptizes Jesus—who is in no need of repentance—so that "all righteousness be fulfilled." Jesus's temptation is placed strategically between his baptism and the inception of his public ministry. At the very outset, Jesus resists the temptation to be a self-seeking, self-promoting Messiah; instead, he presents himself as a humble and obedient Servant who is willing to do things God's way. What's more, the fact that Jesus's ministry begins in Galilee, again in keeping with Old Testament prophecy, signals that Jesus is an outsider who will be rejected by the religious establishment in Jerusalem.

In all these ways, Matthew's readers have received a thorough introduction to the narrative of Jesus's ministry spanning the next three and half years, during which Jesus will engage in an extensive teaching and healing ministry and train the twelve apostles for their mission. In due course, Jesus's ministry will culminate in his crucifixion, burial, and resurrection. At the very outset, then, Matthew has provided a compelling apologetic for Jesus as Israel's Messiah, leaving no stone unturned in unearthing numerous Old Testament prophecies that would find their fulfillment in Jesus. Indeed, it's hard to imagine anyone other than this assiduous tax collector with a penchant for detail and numbers proving more conclusively that Jesus is Israel's Messiah, the Son of God, in keeping with an intricately woven web of Old Testament promises.

JESUS'S WORK IN GALILEE (4:17–18:35)

Work in Galilee, Part 1 (4:17–25)

JESUS'S WORK IN GALILEE (4:17–18:35)

In keeping with Old Testament prediction, Jesus began his ministry in Galilee, a province north of Jerusalem, the capital of Judea.[96] While he was born in Bethlehem in Judea, he started his public work in the Galilean north, indicating, as mentioned, his status as an outsider in opposition to the Jewish religious establishment based in Jerusalem. While he would occasionally travel to Jerusalem for major religious festivals such as the Passover, Jesus would be based in Galilee. In fact, all the apostles (with the possible exception of Judas, the traitor) were from Galilee; many of them were fishermen.

When Jesus was a young boy, his parents established residence in Nazareth, southwest of the Sea of Galilee. This is where Jesus likely grew up as the son of Mary and the adoptive son of Joseph, a carpenter, from whom he would have learned the same trade. Apparently, Joseph died prior to Jesus's public ministry, as he is never mentioned in the Gospels as still living. This meant that Jesus, as Mary's oldest son, would have been responsible for her and the family. Later, the adult Jesus established a residence at Capernaum on the north shore of the Sea of Galilee; thus Matthew calls Capernaum Jesus's "own city."[97]

As you read through the first two thirds of Matthew, Mark, and Luke, you'll want to familiarize yourself with the geography of Galilee and with some of the major towns that frequently serve as the sites of Jesus's major teachings and miracles. Often Jesus and his disciples are shown to cross over the Sea of Galilee (which, as mentioned, is really a very large lake) from one side of the lake to the other, or Jesus is teaching people who are assembled on the shore while sitting in a boat. Anyone who has been to the Holy Land can attest to the natural beauty of Galilee and will not soon forget seeing a sunset over the Sea of Galilee.

Work in Galilee, Part 1 (4:17–25)

After all these preliminaries, Jesus now begins his public ministry by calling his first followers: Simon Peter and Andrew, as well as James and John, the sons of Zebedee, two

96. Matthew 4:12–16.
97. Matthew 9:1. See Aubrey L. Taylor, "Capernaum: A Strategic Home for the Messiah (Matt 4:12–17; Luke 4:14–41; John 4:43–45)," in Beitzel, *Lexham Geographic Commentary*, 84–91. See also Elaine A. Phillips, "The Domestic Architecture of Capernaum and Beyond: A Window into 1st-Century Life (Matt 9:1–8; etc.)," in Beitzel, *Lexham Geographic Commentary*, 108–16.

pairs of Galilean brothers.[98] He promises these disciples—all of whom were fishermen—that if they followed him, he would make them "fishers of people."[99] Matthew records that, at Jesus's call, these four men "immediately" left their nets and boats (and, in James and John's case, also their father Zebedee) and followed Jesus.[100] The willingness of these men to leave their occupation—and temporarily even their families—in order to attach themselves to Jesus shows that entering into a committed relationship with Jesus is more important even than family ties. Jesus would often highlight this truth in the course of his teaching, especially when would-be disciples approached him, many of whom ultimately turned out to be unwilling to pay the price of following him, finding it impossible to prioritize following Jesus over their natural relations and material possessions.[101]

While Matthew's Gospel has been, and will continue to be, primarily focused on *Jesus*, from this point on the *disciples* emerge as significant characters in the narrative as well. While they've been called by Jesus to follow him, they've only begun their journey of discovering who this Jesus really is and of exploring the calling he has extended to them to follow in his steps. At this point in the narrative, right at the end of his lengthy introduction to the Messiah's background and origins, Matthew presents a concluding statement that aptly sums up Jesus's ministry in Galilee.[102] His message had consisted in "teaching . . . and proclaiming the gospel of the kingdom," while his deeds had consisted in "healing every disease and every affliction among the people."[103] As Jesus the Messiah declared the arrival of God's kingdom and provided living proof that in him the kingdom had already arrived, his reputation continued to grow, and large crowds followed him wherever he went.

THE GREATER MOSES

Throughout his Gospel, Matthew presents Jesus as the greater Moses, exceeding the salvation-historical contribution of the great lawgiver and deliverer of Israel at the exodus. Parallels between Jesus and Moses surface initially in the circumstances surrounding their respective births.

98. Matthew 4:18–20.
99. Matthew 4:19. See the discussion of this phrase and its possible Old Testament background at Mark 1 in chapter 3 of this volume.
100. Matthew 4:20, 22.
101. E.g., the "rich young ruler": Matthew 19:16–22.
102. Matthew 4:23–25. Jesus's work in Galilee continues until chapter 16. See Alexander H. Vernon, "The Words and Teachings of Jesus in the Context of Galilee (Matt 5:13–16; etc.)," in Beitzel, *Lexham Geographic Commentary*, 134–48.
103. Matthew 4:23.

Matthew's narrative of the journey of Joseph, Mary, and Jesus to Egypt to escape the execution of Jewish male children by King Herod echoes the narrative of Moses's birth and the execution of Jewish male children in the early chapters of the book of Exodus.[104]

Parallels between Jesus and Moses are also palpable in Jesus's ascent of a mountain at the onset of Jesus's ethical discourse, the Sermon on the Mount, which is reminiscent of Moses's ascent of Mount Sinai to receive the law from God.[105] Jesus's walking on the water brings to mind Moses's leading the people of Israel in the miraculous crossing of the Red Sea.[106] Jesus's feeding of the multitude is reminiscent of God's miraculous provision of manna for the people of Israel in the wilderness under Moses's leadership.[107]

These and other parallels between Jesus and Moses identify Jesus as the fulfillment of Moses's prophecy in Deuteronomy 18:15–19 regarding a future prophet like Moses whom God would raise up to deliver his people. As Charles Quarles notes, "Matthew's presentation of Jesus as the prophet like Moses fulfilled an important theological purpose: it identified Jesus as the Savior of his people in a powerful way. Although modern Christians think of Moses primarily as a lawgiver, to the ancient Jews he was far more. Moses was recognized as a redeemer, deliverer, and savior."[108]

Like Moses, Jesus came to redeem and deliver God's people. While Moses was used by God to deliver Israel from slavery, Jesus, the greater Moses, came to rescue God's people permanently from their sins.[109] As Craig Blomberg observes, "Jesus is 'greater than' all three major Old Testament categories of national leaders—prophet, priest, and king. He is thus no new Moses but one far greater than Moses."[110] Thus Matthew portrays Jesus as Messiah, the son of David and of Abraham, and the greater Moses—terrific news indeed!

104. Matthew 2:13–18. See Exodus 1–2.
105. Matthew 5:1–2. The phrase "he went up on the mountain" recurs in 14:23 and 15:29.
106. Matthew 14:22–33; cf. Exodus 14:15–31.
107. Matthew 14:13–18; 15:29–39.
108. Andreas J. Köstenberger, L. Scott Kellum, and Charles L. Quarles, *The Cradle, the Cross, and the Crown: An Introduction to the New Testament* (Nashville: B&H, 2009), 37.
109. Matthew 1:21; 20:28.
110. Craig L. Blomberg, *Matthew*, New American Commentary (Nashville: Broadman, 1992), 31.

DISCOURSE #1: JESUS'S INAUGURAL ADDRESS: THE SERMON ON THE MOUNT (5:1–7:29)
Introduction (5:1–16)
The Setting (5:1–2)
The Beatitudes (5:3–12)
The Disciples' Identity as Salt and Light (5:13–16)

DISCOURSE #1: JESUS'S INAUGURAL ADDRESS: THE SERMON ON THE MOUNT (5:1–7:29)

The famous Sermon on the Mount, arguably the greatest body of ethical teaching of all time, one that has truly shaped Western civilization, constitutes the first of five discourses in Matthew's Gospel containing Jesus's teaching on the kingdom. You can think of it as the first of five "books of Jesus." As already mentioned, these discourses provide the framework for the remainder of the narrative as Matthew alternates between Jesus's teachings (discourses) and actions (healings, demon exorcisms, nature miracles, and so forth). What's more, these discourses "can be understood as providing progressive illumination of the nature and values of God's kingdom as the story proceeds to its culmination."[111]

R. T. France has fittingly called the Sermon on the Mount "The Discourse on Discipleship," centering on the radically new lifestyle demanded of Jesus's followers who will form a "Christian counterculture."[112] Charles Quarles adds, "For those who affirm the deity and authority of the Lord Jesus, no portion of Scripture could possibly be more important for defining the nature of Christian discipleship and the lofty ethic that should characterize God's people."[113] The Sermon on the Mount provides Jesus's most direct teaching for how his followers are to live and relate to one another and to the

111. Jeannine K. Brown, "Gospel of Matthew," in Green, Brown, and Perrin, *Dictionary of Jesus and the Gospels*, 574.

112. To borrow John R. W. Stott's term. See R. T. France, *The Gospel of Matthew*, New International Commentary on the New Testament (Grand Rapids: Eerdmans, 2007), 153.

113. Charles L. Quarles, *The Sermon on the Mount*, NAC Studies in Bible & Theology (Nashville: B&H, 2011), 1.

world in light of their submission to the Messiah in God's kingdom. What a powerful vision undergirding Jesus's messianic mission!

Quarles provides the following outline based on the literary structure of the sermon:[114]

- I. Introduction (5:1–16)
  - A. The Setting (5:1–2)
  - B. The Beatitudes (5:3–12)
  - C. The Disciples' Identity as Salt and Light (5:13–16)
- II. Body: Greater Righteousness (5:17–7:12)
  - A. Demand for Greater Righteousness (5:17–20)
  - B. The Disciples' Obedience to the Law (5:21–48)
  - C. The Disciples' Avoidance of Hypocrisy (6:1–18)
  - D. The Disciples' Priorities (6:19–34)
  - E. The Disciples' Relationships (7:1–12)
- III. Conclusion (7:13–29)
  - A. Two Roads and Gates (7:13–14)
  - B. Two Trees and Fruits (7:15–20)
  - C. Two Confessions (7:21–23)
  - D. Two Hearers and Builders (7:24–27)
  - E. The Response (7:28–29)

Introduction (5:1–16)

The Setting (5:1–2)

Matthew's description of the setting of the sermon invites parallels to the setting of comparable events in the Old Testament. Throughout the Old Testament, as well as in Matthew, mountains are sites of divine revelation.[115] Specifically, as mentioned, Jesus's ascent of the mountain to speak to his disciples harks back to Moses's ascent of Mount Sinai to receive the law to give to Israel.[116] The setting of the sermon thus depicts Jesus as the greater Moses, a characterization that Matthew, as noted, sustains throughout the sermon, particularly in the remainder of the present chapter, and in his entire Gospel.[117]

114. Quarles, *Sermon on the Mount*, 17–18, given here in adapted form. Quarles's outline provides further subpoints for each of the main points of the body of the sermon.

115. See Terence L. Donaldson, *Jesus on the Mountain: A Study in Matthean Theology*, Journal for the Study of the New Testament Supplement Series 8 (Sheffield: Sheffield Academic Press, 1990).

116. Exodus 19:3.

117. See especially the refrain "You've heard that it was said . . . But I say to you" or an equivalent (Matthew 5:21, 27, 31, 33, 38, 43). Cf. Köstenberger, Kellum, and Quarles, *The Cradle, the Cross, and the Crown*, 21.

The Beatitudes (5:3–12)

At the very outset, Jesus extols virtuous characteristics of the inhabitants of God's kingdom (the so-called Beatitudes, from Latin *beatus*, "happy" or "blessed"). In turn, Jesus pronounces blessings on

- the poor in spirit,
- those who mourn,
- the meek,
- those who hunger and thirst for righteousness,
- the merciful,
- the pure in heart,
- the peacemakers, and
- those who are persecuted for the sake of righteousness.[118]

Jesus doesn't elaborate on the need for grace or on the empowerment of the Holy Spirit. These topics will be broached later by New Testament writers such as the apostle Paul. For now, in his inaugural address, Jesus's purpose is simply to lay out his program, so to speak, his platform on which he will run, somewhat comparable to the inaugural address of a US president who has just been elected to office (though, of course, the analogy breaks down fairly quickly if pressed too far). One may think of these eight characteristics of the kingdom as consisting of two sets of four attributes each, in which both sets end on the note of "righteousness."[119] Rather than focus on outward characteristics, Jesus here zeroes in on people's hearts. It is those who are humble, meek, merciful, pure in heart, and peacemakers who will inherit and inhabit God's kingdom. Clearly, we can't be those kinds of people apart from the enablement of God's Spirit. And yet the Beatitudes give us the ideal for which to aim by way of aspiration, and the impossibility of achieving or even approximating these kinds of characteristics will drive us only closer to God and help us realize our desperate dependence on him.

---

118. Note that, in the original Greek, the first four of these kingdom virtues are alliterated, beginning with the letter *pi*. This would have aided memorization and presents Jesus's words in a poignant, memorable way. See Peter J. Williams, *Can We Trust the Gospels?* (Wheaton, IL: Crossway, 2018), 108, who also notes other memorable features. In addition, Williams argues that Jesus originally delivered the Sermon on the Mount in Greek, which is a view few (if any) other scholars would hold. More likely, Matthew presented Jesus's teaching in alliterated form when composing his Gospel.

119. Note that Luke, in the comparable passage, features only four beatitudes balanced with four woes: see Luke 6:20–26.

The Disciples' Identity as Salt and Light (5:13–16)

Next, Jesus turns to his followers' relationship with the world around them. He likens the desired nature of their relationship to salt and light. "Salt" means that Christ's followers should give flavor to the world in which they live. They should be distinct and spiritually set apart themselves, and thus give the world a distinctive taste of what it's like to be Christ's followers rather than blending in with the culture and being indistinguishable from it, as the church so often is today.[120]

"Light" means that Christians should set a high moral standard—not through self-effort but in the power of the Spirit. Rather than adding to the world's moral darkness, they should stand out and be a source of light to those around them who live in darkness. The twin images of salt and light thus underscore the countercultural identity of Jesus's followers, whose lives are to be marked by the kind of purity and integrity (righteousness) that will lead others to see their good works and give glory to their heavenly Father.[121]

120. See Wilkins, *Matthew*, 36.
121. Matthew 5:16.

DISCOURSE #1: JESUS'S INAUGURAL ADDRESS: THE SERMON ON THE MOUNT (5:1–7:29, CONT.)
Body: Greater Righteousness (5:17–7:12)
Demand for Greater Righteousness (5:17–20)
The Disciples' Obedience to the Law (5:21–48)
The Disciples' Avoidance of Hypocrisy (6:1–18)
The Disciples' Priorities (6:19–34)
The Disciples' Relationships (7:1–12)

DISCOURSE #1: JESUS'S INAUGURAL ADDRESS: THE SERMON ON THE MOUNT (5:1–7:29, CONT.)

Body: Greater Righteousness (5:17–7:12)

Demand for Greater Righteousness (5:17–20)

Jesus will shortly contrast his teaching with that found in the Old Testament. Anticipating his listeners' question as to the relationship between his teaching and "the Law and the Prophets" (i.e., the Old Testament Scriptures), Jesus states emphatically that he hasn't come to abolish the Law or the Prophets but rather to fulfill them.[122] Notice, however, that the contrast is not between "abolish" and "uphold" but rather between "abolish" and "fulfill." One might say that by fulfilling the Old Testament Scriptures, Jesus in a sense *did* abolish the law, though not in such a way that the law was set aside without finding its deeper fulfillment in him. For example, Jesus's followers no longer need to keep Old Testament food laws, or to fast, or to keep the Sabbath, nor do they need to tithe. But this doesn't mean they're free to do anything they want! Rather, in Jesus, and in the Spirit, they've been introduced to an even deeper understanding of God and his righteous requirements.[123] What's more, in Jesus they've received redemp-

122. Matthew 5:17–48. Notice that the references to "the Law and the Prophets" in 5:17 and 7:12 form an *inclusio*, demarcating the body of the Sermon of the Mount.

123. Notice that the apostle Paul picks up this same issue as well in several of his letters, such as Romans and 1 Corinthians.

tion and forgiveness of sins, and in the Spirit they've now been given the ability to live righteous lives that are pleasing to God.

Imagine that: Jesus was accused of having a low view of Scripture! In truth, of course, he held to a very high view of Scripture. Elsewhere he says, almost as an aside, that "Scripture cannot be broken,"[124] and in the course of his teaching Jesus cites Scripture numerous times. Even his opponents admitted that his mastery of the Scriptures was unequalled, despite his lack of formal rabbinic training.[125] At one point he tells his opponents, "If you believed Moses, you would believe me; for he wrote of me. But if you do not believe his writings, how will you believe my words?"[126] In the present case, he argues strenuously that he fulfilled Scripture rather than setting it aside. That's because he was the Messiah predicted in the Scriptures and because he had authority over the Scriptures and understood their deeper meaning. He taught not only with rabbinic but with messianic authority.

Predictably, Jesus's teaching and practice (e.g., healing on the Sabbath) were going to prove offensive to those who rigidly adhered to the law.[127] Yet what Jesus's detractors failed to realize was that the law was not an end in itself but rather a means to an end; it pointed to the coming of Christ (the prophetic dimension of the law) and had been given to hold people accountable to the righteous standards of a holy God. As far as New Testament teaching on the matter is concerned, Jesus here only provides the opening salvo; it would be left to the apostle Paul to comment much more extensively on the way in which Christ had become the "end of the law" and his followers had been called to live by a new law: the law of the Spirit.[128] What's more, when Jesus described himself as the fulfillment of the Law and the Prophets, this was perfectly in keeping with Matthew's claim throughout his opening chapters that Jesus was the Messiah who fulfilled a whole slew of Old Testament messianic promises and predictions.[129]

The Disciples' Obedience to the Law (5:21–48)

Jesus's fulfillment of the Law and the Prophets doesn't absolve his disciples from their responsibility to live righteous lives; in fact, it increases it: "Unless your righteousness exceeds that of the scribes and Pharisees, you will never enter the kingdom of

124. John 10:35.
125. See, e.g., John 7:15.
126. John 5:46–47.
127. E.g., the Pharisees later on in the Gospel who alleged that Jesus's teaching and practice conflicted with the law's teaching on the Sabbath (Matthew 12:1–8) and ritual purity (Matthew 15:1–20).
128. See Romans 10:4 and Paul's teaching in Romans 6–8.
129. See discussion of Matthew 1:1–4:17 above. Cf. D. A. Carson, *Expositor's Bible Commentary*, vol. 8, *Matthew and Mark*, rev. ed. (Grand Rapids: Zondervan, 2010), 174: "Therefore, we see in 'fulfill' exactly the same meaning as in the formula quotations, which in the prologue (Mt 1–2) have already laid great stress on the prophetic nature of the OT and the way it points to Jesus."

heaven."[130] Jesus's call to righteous living is vastly different from the external compliance with the law with which the scribes and Pharisees were concerned; rather, his call was to heartfelt obedience lived out in daily actions. Just as the Old Testament law commanded, disciples of Jesus are to do the following:

- Control their anger: hatred is spiritual murder; before you worship, be reconciled to your brother.[131]
- Pursue sexual purity: lust is spiritual adultery; be radical in dealing with what causes you to sin.[132]
- Honor the covenant of marriage: don't divorce your spouse, except for sexual immorality.[133]
- Speak with honesty and integrity: don't swear any oaths; simply be a person of your word.[134]
- Resist the temptation to take their own revenge: don't resist evil; rather, go the extra mile.[135]
- Love their enemies and pray for those who persecute them: otherwise, they're no better than pagans who love those who love them.[136]

While general wisdom can be found in many times and places, the teaching of the Sermon of the Mount is truly unique. While even unbelievers could subscribe to the ideals enunciated in Jesus's teaching, only believers will be able to live consistently and in a heartfelt way in keeping with these principles. What is needed is nothing less than a radical inner transformation and divine spiritual enablement. Only regenerate believers can truly love, consistently refrain from lust, control their desire for revenge when wronged, and, above all, love their enemies. Loving one's enemy doesn't come naturally! Yet this is what Jesus requires of his followers. He doesn't merely demand what's hard; he demands the impossible! And yet he doesn't lower his standards just to render his expectations more easily attainable. To the contrary, he insists, "You therefore must be perfect, as your heavenly Father is perfect."[137] And just because, on this side of eternity, perfection is impossible, this doesn't mean we should stop trying—with God's help.

130. Matthew 5:20.
131. Matthew 5:21–26.
132. Matthew 5:27–30.
133. Matthew 5:31–32.
134. Matthew 5:33–37.
135. Matthew 5:38–42.
136. Matthew 5:43–47.
137. Matthew 5:48.

The Disciples' Avoidance of Hypocrisy (6:1–18)

Continuing on the topic of righteousness, which he has sounded in the Beatitudes—twice—and reiterated at the outset of his instructions regarding the deeper meaning of the law, Jesus now addresses the question of how his followers should "practice their righteousness" before others.[138] He had previously told his disciples that unless their righteousness exceeded that of the Pharisees—who were known to be scrupulous with regard to keeping even the most minute matters in the law—they would never enter God's kingdom. Those with a reputation for righteousness in Jesus's day thought they were OK if they didn't break the Ten Commandments ("You shall not kill," "You shall not commit adultery," "You shall not bear false witness," and so forth), but Jesus held his followers to a much higher standard: "Don't hate," "Don't lust," "Keep your word." What's more, rather than merely loving their fellow Jews, they should love even their enemies.[139] Talk about raising the bar!

At this, Jesus turns to the so-called three pillars of Judaism—prayer, fasting, and almsgiving—pious acts that identified someone as a righteous person before others.[140] Jesus's underlying concern, once again, is a person's motivation: Why did people pray, fast, or give alms in public in the first place? Was it because they truly loved God? Or was it merely to impress others with their piety? If their motive truly was to honor God, Jesus argued, they would be content to perform their good works in secret; after all, God sees everything, so he knows what we're doing, and will reward us on the last day.[141] But if people did their pious acts primarily so that people could see how spiritual they were, they stood condemned as hypocrites, actors who put on a good show without having the hearts to back it up. But God, who sees the heart, was not fooled. Neither was Jesus!

When giving, then, people shouldn't "let their left hand know what their right hand is doing."[142] In other words, giving should be discreet and non-ostentatious. If our trust is in God, and our giving is ultimately to God, we won't give merely so others can see how generous we are. When we pray, no flowery language is required. Nor do God's people need to utter lengthy prayers. We can just talk to God, our heavenly Father who already knows what we need even before we ask. At this, Jesus gives an example prayer, the so-called Lord's Prayer (or, perhaps better, the "Disciple's Prayer").[143] This prayer is conspicuous for putting God first: the honor of his name, the arrival of his kingdom, the accomplishment of his will. Christ's followers want nothing more than the advance of God's kingdom. In that context, they'll humbly ask God to give them the necessary

138. Matthew 6:1; cf. Matthew 5:6, 10, 20.
139. Cf. Matthew 5:21–48.
140. Matthew 6:1–18.
141. See the steady refrain, "And your Father who sees in secret will reward you" (Matthew 6:4, 6, 18).
142. Matthew 6:3.
143. Matthew 6:9–12.

food to eat,[144] to forgive their sins, and to guard them from temptation. Finally, fasting, too, should be done in secret, not so others can see how spiritual we are.

The Disciples' Priorities (6:19–34)

Next, Jesus moves beyond "practicing one's righteousness" to the underlying values he seeks to promote and inculcate in his followers. This teaching portion culminates in his command that his disciples "seek first the kingdom of God and his righteousness."[145] In many ways, this command sums up the ethos of the entire Sermon on the Mount. Rather than putting their own interests and concerns first, as natural as that might be for frail and finite human beings, Jesus wants his followers to trust God to provide for their needs in the larger context of his universal reign. Rather than fit God into our own little world, we should find our place in God's big world. Rather than doing what we feel like doing and then ask God to bless our activities, we should find out what God is doing in this world and then join him on his mission. This is the essence of Jesus's call to discipleship as well. We're called to follow *him*, rather than expect him to follow *us*!

In this vein, Jesus urges his disciples to value what is eternal and spiritual rather than what is merely temporary and material. It's foolish to store up earthly possessions that won't last while neglecting to invest in eternal realities that will pay rich dividends in the heavenly realm. Rather than seeking treasure on earth, Jesus's followers are to store up treasure in heaven: "For where your treasure is, there your heart will be also."[146] With razor-sharp logic, Jesus argues "No one can serve two masters." Therefore, his followers "cannot serve God and money."[147] Again, Jesus cuts to the chase with his challenge. How often do we try to have our cake and eat it too—to be "good Christians" and yet pursue successful careers and the American dream? To be good parents and yet spend the lion's share of our time at work or in other pursuits? Rather than living ambivalent or even schizophrenic lives, Jesus wants us to put God first—wholeheartedly and without reservations.

At this, Jesus anticipates an objection that many will predictably raise: But what about my need for daily necessities—food, clothing, and shelter? Aren't those legitimate concerns? Jesus answers, "Yes, I know; you're right to be concerned about these things. But look around you: Doesn't God take care of lesser parts of his creation such as birds or flowers? If he does—and he does—can he not also be trusted to take care of the crown of his creation—us?" Just as Jesus had earlier challenged his followers to rise above the level of nonbelievers who love only those who love them, he now asks again the probing

144. See Gordon Franz, "Grain, Wine, and Oil: The Essentials of Life (Matt 6:11, 25–33)," in Beitzel, *Lexham Geographic Commentary*, 327–37.
145. Matthew 6:33.
146. Matthew 6:21.
147. Matthew 6:24.

question: If believers are anxious about material provisions, how are they different from unbelievers? Therefore, Jesus's followers should trust in *God's* ability to provide for their daily needs and let *God's* priorities define their values, goals, and pursuits. They should seek *God's* kingdom and *his* righteousness, "and all these things will be added" to them![148] While this Godward focus does require faith, it will remove anxiety from our hearts. And more importantly, such an attitude of dependent trust will honor God in that it shows that he can be trusted to be faithful to provide for the creatures he has made.

The Disciples' Relationships (7:1–12)

Jesus also speaks out against hypocritical judgment of others: "Don't judge, so that you won't be judged."[149] This verse is rapidly replacing John 3:16 as the most popular and widely known verse in the Bible in our culture. Unfortunately, however, it is often taken out of context. Jesus is *not* saying that we should practice spineless tolerance, condoning the sins of others.[150] Rather, he is confronting the insincere, biased condemnation of others by those who fail to apply the same standard of judgment to themselves. Jesus likens this inconsistency and double standard to the hyperbolic and hilarious example of a man who tries to remove a tiny piece of wood from another person's eye while failing to take care of a huge log in his own. How ironic and even bizarre it would be if anyone were to do this in real life! And yet, spiritually speaking, this is what we do all the time.

This again shows that Jesus possesses a keen knowledge of sinful human nature: we criticize others for any number of shortcomings, whether arrogance, selfishness, or lack of compassion, but are completely oblivious to the fact that we're guilty of the same shortcomings ourselves. So, then, Jesus is not cautioning us against holding others accountable, just against applying a hypocritical double standard that faults others while being unwilling to be held to that same standard ourselves. In his words, "You hypocrite, *first* take the log out of your own eye, and *then* you will see clearly to take the speck out of your brother's eye." The key is the proper order, *first* and *then*. In judging, we need to start with ourselves and confront sin in our own lives. If we do this, we'll see clearly. We won't be motivated by bias, envy, anger, or any other number of improper motives. Then, we can—and should—help others with their own shortcomings, and we'll do so in a manner that is helpful and healing rather than vindictive and judgmental.

Finally, notice the contrast between the log in our own eye and the speck in the other person's eye. We tend to magnify others' faults and minimize our own, when in fact the opposite may be true: our faults are much greater, and those of others are far

148. See Franz, "Essentials of Life."
149. Matthew 7:1–6.
150. A good book on this is D. A. Carson, *The Intolerance of Tolerance* (Grand Rapids: Eerdmans, 2012).

less egregious by comparison. Starting with confronting our own faults will thus also restore much-needed perspective and keep relationships in proper balance. This is great advice for a wide variety of situations, whether in marriage or relationships at work or in the church. So, then, Jesus is *not* saying, "Don't ever judge." Rather, what he *means* is, "Don't judge others unless you've first confronted your own faults. *Then* approach the other person, not with an attitude of smug self-righteousness and moral superiority (as the Pharisees were wont to do), but with an attitude of humility and compassion."

In what follows, Jesus builds on his previous comments regarding God's provision for the earthly needs of his followers.[151] Having already given his disciples a model prayer asking for God to provide their "daily bread," he now continues to instill confidence in answered prayer in his followers on the basis of his intimate knowledge of his heavenly Father, in particular the Father's goodness and generosity. We should never doubt the goodness of God and, like trusting children, should never hesitate to approach him in prayer with our needs and requests. In an argument from the lesser to the greater, Jesus says, "If you then, who are evil (!), know how to give good gifts to your children, how much more will your Father who is in heaven give good things to those who ask him!"[152] Of course, Jesus's instructions for answered prayer are given here in the context of the values and priorities of God's kingdom, which presupposes that we don't ask with selfish motives but seek to determine God's will in our lives.

Not only should Jesus's followers ask so they can receive; they should also do good to others. This Jesus sums up with the maxim "So whatever you wish that others would do for you, do also to them"—the famous Golden Rule.[153] Those who live by this rule will never regret it. Jesus contends that "this is the Law and the Prophets," by which he means that the Golden Rule sums up the tenor of the entire Scriptures! This is quite a statement to make and a truth to ponder. Paul would later write, "Do nothing from selfishness or empty conceit, but with humility of mind regard one another as more important than yourselves; do not *merely* look out for your own personal interests, but also for the interests of others."[154] Later in Matthew's Gospel, Jesus is asked what the "greatest commandment in the law" is, and he replies that it is the command to love God wholeheartedly, adding the corollary command to love one's neighbor as oneself. "On these two commandments," Jesus affirms, "depend all the Law and the Prophets."[155] Thus we could say that the Golden Rule is equivalent to loving God supremely and to loving others as we love ourselves.

151. Cf. Matthew 6:32: "Your heavenly Father knows that you need them all."
152. Matthew 7:11. Luke specifies that the "good gift" par excellence is the gift of the Holy Spirit (Luke 11:13).
153. Matthew 7:12. See Wilkins, "The Golden Rule," in *Matthew*, 52.
154. Philippians 2:3–4.
155. Matthew 22:36–40.

DISCOURSE #1: JESUS'S INAUGURAL ADDRESS: THE SERMON ON THE MOUNT (5:1–7:29, CONT.)
Conclusion (7:13–29)
Two Roads and Gates (7:13–14)
Two Trees and Fruits (7:15–20)
Two Confessions (7:21–23)
Two Hearers and Builders (7:24–27)
The Response (7:28–29)

DISCOURSE #1: JESUS'S INAUGURAL ADDRESS: THE SERMON ON THE MOUNT (5:1–7:29, CONT.)

Conclusion (7:13–29)

Two Roads and Gates (7:13–14)

As he moves toward the end of his teaching on God's kingdom, Jesus registers a series of cautions. First, he points out that there are two roads and two gates; in fact, the gate to salvation is narrow and hard to find, while the gate to destruction is wide and well traveled. Realistically, only few will choose the path of discipleship; most will be too attached to this world to be willing to put God first. Jesus makes the same point in the parable of the sower and the soils.[156] While this may be unsettling to some, it helps manage expectations. As Jesus points out elsewhere, even in one's own family there will often be those who choose not to embrace Jesus's teaching. Yet Jesus's disciples must follow "the road less traveled."[157]

Two Trees and Fruits (7:15–20)

Second, Jesus speaks to his followers about two trees and two kinds of fruit, warning them against "wolves in sheep's clothing," false prophets who are out to wreak havoc in

156. Matthew 13:1–23; Mark 4:1–20; Luke 8:4–15.

157. I'm alluding here to the title of a book by M. Scott Peck, *The Road Less Traveled* (New York: Simon & Schuster, 1978), without endorsing all the content of his self-help book!

his disciples' lives. Jesus's advice is simple: look at the (rotten) fruit in the lives of these deceivers and pretenders! By a simple yet inexorable natural law, good trees bear good fruit, while bad trees bear bad fruit. Similarly, if anyone leaves destruction and misery in his wake, he can't be a good teacher or true prophet.

Two Confessions (7:21–23)

Third, Jesus tells his followers to be discerning about two confessions: While many claim to be his disciples, not all who lodge this claim are genuine followers of Jesus. In fact, many who call Jesus "Lord"—that is, profess to acknowledge his authority over their lives and even do many things in his name—have no true knowledge of Jesus, and, as a result, Jesus will disavow knowing them on judgment day![158] The lesson is obvious: Don't be fooled by false professions of faith! Also, make sure you're not self-deceived about being a follower of Jesus without being regenerated and a genuine citizen of his kingdom!

Two Hearers and Builders (7:24–27)

After instructing his disciples about two roads and gates, two trees and fruits, and two confessions, Jesus closes the Sermon on the Mount with an illustration about two hearers and builders. He has imparted a series of powerful, penetrating instructions; now he issues a challenge of application to those who heard his teaching. In so doing, Jesus memorably and poignantly casts a vision of two builders. The first built his house on rock, and when storms and floods came, the house stood firm. The other built his house on sand, and when the elements raged against that house, it promptly collapsed.

This truly is a timeless illustration; we often read in the news about people whose entire belongings were swept away by major floods, fires, or storms, often very unexpectedly. The lesson, therefore, is this: mere hearing is not enough; the real test is whether we put Jesus's teaching into practice. Obedience to Christ puts one's life on solid footing, and when challenges come—as they certainly will, whether loss of a job or loved one, terminal illness such as cancer, and ultimately death—our lives will be weatherproof and rock-solid because they're built on the unshakeable truth of God's Word.

The Response (7:28–29)

Jesus's teaching left the crowds amazed, for he was instructing them "as one who had authority, and not as their scribes."[159] There's no question—the Sermon on the Mount is truly unique among all other moral instruction. In fact, a plausible case could be

158. Matthew 7:21–23.
159. Matthew 7:29.

made that it is the greatest ethical discourse of all time. Just think of the many truths from this sermon that have made it into our common cultural heritage and discourse:

- Anyone who looks at a woman lustfully has already committed adultery in his heart[160]
- Go the extra mile[161]
- Love your enemies[162]
- Don't let your right hand know what your left hand is doing[163]
- The Lord's Prayer[164]
- No one can serve two masters[165]
- Seek first his kingdom and his righteousness[166]
- Don't judge, so you won't be judged[167]
- Take the log out of your own eye[168]
- The Golden Rule[169]
- Wolves in sheep's clothing[170]
- Building one's house on sand rather than rock[171]

All these phrases have become part of our cultural vocabulary in the West (and other parts of the world as well). And yet many don't know the larger context in which Jesus gave these instructions: his spiritual, supernatural, transcendent vision of God's kingdom that he sought to impart to those who were willing to leave behind the attachments and affections of this world in order to follow the one who was sent to earth by his heavenly Father and who was conceived in Mary's womb by the Holy Spirit—the Messiah and Son of God.

160. Matthew 5:28.
161. Matthew 5:41.
162. Matthew 5:44.
163. Matthew 6:33.
164. Matthew 6:9–13.
165. Matthew 6:24.
166. Matthew 6:33.
167. Matthew 7:1.
168. Matthew 7:3–5.
169. Matthew 7:12.
170. Matthew 7:15.
171. Matthew 7:24–27.

RECAP

What a powerful inaugural address Jesus has given, dwarfing any such address by a newly elected president or national leader by comparison! Two thousand years later, we're still captivated by the Sermon on the Mount and the high and noble vision of humanity it conveys. And yet only those who follow the Messiah unconditionally and wholeheartedly have it within their grasp to live out the noble ethical ideals he projects. It's one thing to catch the vision; it's quite another to be able to attain to its ideals by the indwelling Holy Spirit.

For, in the end, Jesus's words do more than merely cast a humanistic vision of humanity at its best. Rather, the Messiah here specifies the characteristics of God's heavenly kingdom, which in the lives of his followers can begin already here on earth. Jesus will elaborate on this later on in the Gospel in his numerous "kingdom parables," illustrations of various aspects of God's spiritual kingdom that has come to invade human existence in the person of the coming King, Jesus the Messiah.[172]

172. See Discourses 3, 4, and 5 in Matthew 13, 18, and 24–25 below.

JESUS'S WORK IN GALILEE (4:17–18:35, CONT.)

Work in Galilee, Part 2 (8:1–9:38)

Jesus's Display of His Messianic Authority, Part 1 (chap. 8)

On the heels of the Sermon on the Mount, Matthew provides "the crispest of summaries of the promises and demands of the coming kingdom."[173] The following narrative portion, then, presents a representative sample of Jesus's ministry—in fact, half of Jesus's miracles recorded in the Gospel are found in this section—impressively and comprehensively underscoring his messianic authority. I say "impressively" and "comprehensively" because the various miracles narrated in this unit show Jesus's authority over an impressive array of realms: the demonic world, sickness, the natural realm, and even death. Nothing, Matthew seems to be saying, is off limits for Jesus's messianic authority, which not only spans all of human earthly existence but extends even to the supernatural realm. Specifically, we see Jesus

- cleansing a leper (8:1–4);
- healing the paralyzed servant of a Roman centurion (8:5–13);[174]
- healing the sickness of Simon Peter's mother-in-law (8:14–15);[175]

173. Reggie M. Kidd, "Matthew," in *A Biblical-Theological Introduction to the New Testament*, ed. Michael J. Kruger (Wheaton, IL: Crossway, 2016), 50.
174. Note the reference to feasting with Abraham, Isaac, and Jacob in the kingdom of heaven in 8:11–12, which is unique to Matthew and not found in the Markan and Lukan parallels, underscoring Matthew's Jewish orientation and special interest in Abraham (cf. 1:1, 2, 17).
175. Reading only Matthew's account, one might get the impression Jesus simply saw Peter's mother-in-law ill and lying in bed and took the initiative to heal her. However, the other Synoptic evangelists make clear that others were interceding for her (Mark 1:30; Luke 4:38). Also, while both Matthew and Mark refer to Peter's mother-in-law having a fever, Luke (the doctor) says she had a "high fever," which would explain why Jesus's intervention was needed and urgent. Finally, while Matthew says Jesus touched her hand (8:15), Luke adds the further detail that Jesus "stood over her and rebuked the fever" (Luke 4:39). All three evangelists uniformly note that as soon as Jesus had healed her, Peter's mother-in-law got up and served them.

- calming a powerful storm on the Sea of Galilee by his mere word (8:23–27); and
- delivering two Gadarene men from demon possession (8:28–34).

Then, in the following chapter (see below), Jesus is

- healing a paralytic (9:1–8);
- raising a synagogue ruler's daughter from the dead (9:18–19, 23–26) and stopping a woman's twelve-year-long discharge of blood (9:20–22);
- giving sight to two blind men (9:27–31); and
- opening the mouth of a demon-possessed mute man (9:32–34).[176]

Following the healings of a leper, a paralyzed man, and Peter's mother-in-law, Matthew cites the Old Testament once again, telling us that Jesus's miracles serve to identify him as the servant of the Lord of Isaiah's prophecy who would take up our infirmities and bear the diseases of God's people.[177] So we see here that Jesus's healing ministry is a kind of foreshadowing of the deeper reality that Jesus, in his very own person, came to take our diseases and infirmities upon himself, ultimately by dying for us on the cross! In this way, all of Jesus's healing miracles point to the deeper reality of his true identity: that he is the servant of the Lord who came to take all our sicknesses and evil afflictions upon himself to set us free from our bondage to sin and its entailments, whether physical or spiritual.

So we see a deeper underlying unity linking Jesus's teaching and his actions and miracles. It's not merely that Jesus practices what he preaches, and that he walks his talk, but that what he says and what he does is grounded in who he is. The same should be true for us: Who are we? What is our identity? If you're a Christian, then your identity is that you're "in Christ." You're a son or daughter of the King; you're made in God's image; you're indwelt by the Holy Spirit. Both our words and our actions should be grounded in that reality of being in Christ.

Jesus is also identified as the Messiah who alone has the power to open the eyes of the blind, to unstop the ears of the deaf, to make the lame leap like a deer, and to loosen the tongue of the mute to sing for joy.[178] What's more, Jesus's compassion is not limited to Jews but extends even to Gentiles, such as the centurion's servant or

176. Interspersed with these accounts of Jesus's powerful messianic interventions in the natural and supernatural world are Jesus's instructions about discipleship to a would-be follower, a Jewish scribe (8:18–22); Jesus's call of Matthew, a former tax collector (9:9–13); and Jesus's response to a question about fasting brought to him by disciples of John the Baptist (9:14–17; see below).

177. Matthew 8:17; see Isaiah 53:4.

178. See Isaiah 35:5–6.

the Gadarene demoniac. Significantly, it is the Gentile centurion who is commended for his faith, which stands in stark contrast even to the disciples who are characterized as those of "little faith," and infinitely more so the hardened Pharisees who attribute Jesus's power to Satan.[179] Thus, Jesus is not only the Messiah for the Jewish people; his messianic authority extends even to Gentiles and thus to all of humanity.

179. Matthew 8:10, 26; 9:34.

JESUS'S WORK IN GALILEE (4:17–18:35, CONT.)

Work in Galilee, Part 2 (8:1–9:38, cont.)

Jesus's Display of His Messianic Authority, Part 2 (chap. 9)

The focus of this narrative section is to demonstrate Jesus's messianic identity through the healing of a paralytic, the raising of a girl from the dead, the giving of sight to two blind men, and the opening of the mouth of a demon-possessed mute man. Jesus's mighty works, in turn, are cast within the framework of his training of a select group of followers for mission. The call of Matthew sees the first evangelist join those whom Jesus had called previously, such as Peter and Andrew, James and John, just in time before Jesus appoints his twelve apostles.[180] The unit closes with a transitional paragraph that both summarizes Jesus's work thus far ("teaching," "proclaiming the good news of the kingdom," "healing") and foreshadows the commissioning of the Twelve to join in their Master's mission.[181] Jesus's description of the crowds as "harassed and helpless, like sheep without a shepherd" echoes Moses's words at the transition of leadership from him to Joshua and serves as an indictment of the Jewish leaders who, in keeping with Ezekiel's prophecy, were useless shepherds.[182]

RECAP

The account of Jesus's work in Galilee in the present unit powerfully underscores the authority of Jesus noted at the end of the Sermon of the Mount. Jesus is not merely Messiah in word, providing powerful spiritual lessons and pieces of instruction; he is Messiah in deed as well, proving his messianic authority in a series of striking manifestations. The message to Matthew's readers couldn't be more pointed and powerful: Jesus can heal. Jesus can expel demons. Jesus can command the forces of nature. Jesus can

180. Matthew 9:9–13. See 10:1–4 below.
181. Matthew 9:35–38.
182. Matthew 9:36; cf. Numbers 27:17; Ezekiel 34:5.

even raise people from the dead! This, too, is in fulfillment of Old Testament prophecy regarding the Messiah, in particular Isaiah's depiction of the servant of the Lord who would take people's infirmity upon himself and set them free, both physically and spiritually. In this way, the Sermon of the Mount and the composite of healing narratives in chapters 8 and 9 serve as a powerful one-two punch that leaves the reader thoroughly impressed with Jesus's messianic credentials.

DISCOURSE #2: COMMISSIONING OF THE TWELVE (10:1–42)
The Mission of the Twelve (10:1–4)
Instructions for the Mission (10:5–15)
The Expectation of Persecution and How to Respond (10:16–33)
The Radical Effects of Jesus's Mission and Supporters (10:34–42)

DISCOURSE #2: COMMISSIONING OF THE TWELVE (10:1–42)

The narrative portion of the previous two chapters now gives way to the second discourse featured in Matthew's Gospel, the commissioning of the Twelve. There is a certain historical uniqueness to this discourse at this particular juncture in Jesus's ministry. Not everything that is said here applies directly to the church today (e.g., the limitation of the mission of the Twelve to Israel), though on a principial level there is much we can learn about what it means to follow Jesus. R. T. France provides the following outline of what is also called Jesus's "Missionary Discourse":[183]

1. The Context of the Mission (9:35–38)
2. The Mission of the Twelve (10:1–4)
3. Instructions for the Mission (10:5–15)
4. The Expectation of Persecution (10:16–21)
5. How to Respond to Persecution (10:22–33)
6. The Radical Effects of Jesus's Mission (10:34–39)
7. The Rewards of Mission (10:40–42)
8. Jesus Resumes His Mission (11:1)

The Mission of the Twelve (10:1–4)

The context of the Missionary Discourse is Jesus's denunciation of Israel's faithless shepherds—the Pharisees and Sadducees—and his exhortation to his disciples to "pray

183. Adapted from France, *Gospel of Matthew*, 371–415. France includes 9:35–38 and 11:1 as the bookends of the discourse.

earnestly to the Lord of the harvest to send out laborers into the harvest."[184] The disciples who pray and follow Jesus's call will become the first answer to their own prayers for additional workers to reap the rich spiritual harvest that lies ahead. Consequently, Jesus proceeds to appoint twelve "apostles"—messengers or emissaries—who will "serve as the nucleus of a newly reconstituted spiritual Israel."[185]

Instructions for the Mission (10:5–15)

As he sends the Twelve on their mission, Jesus provides the following instructions. First, they're to focus exclusively on the "lost sheep of the house of Israel" rather than on Gentiles or even Samaritans.[186] Jesus's mission was foremost to the Jewish people, as it was God's purpose to bless all the families of the earth through Abraham, and Jesus his descendant.[187] Only after the Jewish leaders, representing the nation as a whole, had rejected Jesus and, sanctioned by the Roman governor, put him on the cross did Jesus open the door to the Gentiles, giving them access to his new messianic community, the church made up of all those who believe in Jesus as Messiah.

The message the Twelve are given to proclaim is the same as that preached by John the Baptist and Jesus himself: "The kingdom of heaven is at hand."[188] Their work is an extension of that of Jesus. Like their Master, they are to "Heal the sick, raise the dead (!), cleanse lepers, [and] cast out demons."[189] They're to do their work free of charge and take only minimal supplies on their journey. When entering a city, they're to seek out the hospitality of worthy individuals and lodge there for the duration of their stay. If rejected, they should shake the dust off their feet and move on to another place. They can be sure that God's judgment on those who reject them will be severe.

The Expectation of Persecution and How to Respond (10:16–33)

While mission is the primary subject of the discourse, "a prominent subtext is the hostile response which that mission is to meet."[190] This calls for realistic expectations. Not everyone will receive Jesus's emissaries with open arms. Thus, they must be "wise as serpents and innocent as doves."[191] Just as hostility has already begun to mount against

184. Matthew 9:36–38.
185. Matthew 10:2–3; see Köstenberger, Kellum, and Quarles, *The Cradle, the Cross, and the Crown*, 22–23.
186. Matthew 10:6.
187. Cf. Genesis 12:1–3.
188. Matthew 10:7.
189. Matthew 10:8.
190. France, *Gospel of Matthew*, 370.
191. Matthew 10:16.

Jesus, so his followers will suffer persecution for his sake.[192] They will be dragged into court and be flogged in synagogues, but they needn't be anxious because "the Spirit of [their] Father" will speak through them.[193]

In fact, opposition will arise even within their own families, and they will be "hated by all" (!) for his name's sake.[194] Nevertheless, this chilling prospect shouldn't discourage them because it is a sure sign that they're following in the footsteps of their Master.[195] What's more, they should view such opposition as a sobering call to fear God rather than people, resting in his provision and looking to him for vindication.[196] The most precious assurance Jesus can give them is that on judgment day he will acknowledge before his heavenly Father everyone who acknowledges him.[197] This is why we shouldn't be afraid to identify with him in this world.

The Radical Effects of Jesus's Mission and Supporters (10:34–42)

The closing portion of Jesus's instructions to the Twelve brings into even sharper focus the cost of discipleship for those who choose to follow Jesus. Jesus has "not come to bring peace, but a sword."[198] Rather than a person's life improving, their decision to follow Christ may in fact make matters worse, at least initially, in keeping with the Old Testament prophet Micah's prediction that a person's enemies will be the very members of his own household.[199] This will prove to be a supreme test of loyalty. As Jesus puts it, in a statement that epitomizes his call to discipleship,

> Whoever loves father or mother more than me is not worthy of me,
> and whoever loves son or daughter more than me is not worthy of me.
> And whoever does not take his cross and follow me is not worthy of me.
> Whoever finds his life will lose it,
> and whoever loses his life for my sake will find it.[200]

One has to admire Jesus for not sugarcoating what it means to enlist in his spiritual army. No one could ever say they didn't know what they were getting themselves

192. Matthew 10:18; cf. 9:3, 11, 14, 34.
193. Matthew 10:20.
194. Matthew 10:21–22.
195. Matthew 10:24–25.
196. Matthew 10:26–33.
197. Matthew 10:32.
198. Matthew 10:34.
199. Matthew 10:35–36, citing Micah 7:6.
200. Matthew 10:37–39.

into when following Jesus! Too often today, we hedge about the challenges potential converts to Christianity will face. Jesus didn't do that—not even close. He was blunt in predicting that his followers would face intense hatred and persecution, even from those closest to them. Nevertheless, Jesus is eminently worthy to be followed. He would give his life for his followers so they could be forgiven and saved and spend eternity with him in God's presence. And following Jesus would have many rewards both in this life and in the life to come.

RECAP

Jesus's calling and commissioning of twelve apostles is a vital part of his messianic mission. While the central part of his mission was his death on the cross, followed by his burial and resurrection, Jesus spent much of his three-and-a-half-year earthly ministry training the Twelve for their future mission following his departure. Thus, while the first Matthean discourse, the Sermon on the Mount, provides the ethic of God's kingdom, the second "book of Jesus," the Missionary Discourse, is equally vital in that it presents the nucleus of Jesus's messianic community, a remnant of believing Israel, which would carry on his mission following the saving events that were to transpire toward the end of Jesus's earthly existence as recounted in the so-called passion narrative.

In this way, the Missionary Discourse will culminate in the concluding commission, the "Great Commission," at the end of Matthew's Gospel, a fitting climax to the entire Gospel with Jesus's call for his followers to "go and make disciples of *all the nations*." While in the Missionary Discourse, as mentioned above, the Twelve are to go only to the "lost sheep of the house of Israel," the risen Jesus, following the resurrection, will dramatically extend the scope of his vision, and mission, to "all the nations." But more about that later when we'll discuss the Great Commission at the end of Matthew's Gospel. For now, let's look what happens next as discourse again gives way to narrative in the oscillating rhythm between word and deed in this Gospel.

JESUS'S WORK IN GALILEE (4:17–18:35, CONT.)
Work in Galilee, Part 3 (11:1–12:50)
The Query from John the Baptist (11:1–19)
Denunciation of Unbelief and Invitation to Learn from Jesus (11:20–30)
Jesus's Authority over the Sabbath (12:1–14)
Jesus's Messianic Healing Ministry and the Blasphemy against the Holy Spirit (12:15–37)
The Sign of Jonah and Jesus's True Mother and Brothers (12:38–50)

JESUS'S WORK IN GALILEE (4:17–18:35, CONT.)

Work in Galilee, Part 3 (11:1–12:50)

With the transition statement "When Jesus had finished instructing his twelve disciples," Matthew now moves on to the third cycle of Jesus's work in Galilee. While this section of Matthew's narrative is less clearly defined and includes a mixture of Jesus's words *and* actions, a main theme that emerges is the varying responses to Jesus the Messiah. As R. T. France observes,

> In chs. 11–12 we shall be introduced to a variety of people who are responding in different ways to what they are seeing and hearing, different ways of reacting to the coming of the Messiah. There are the wholly positive portraits of the "children" who have been given the ability to discern the truth (11:25–27) and of Jesus's true family who do the will of God (12:46–50). There is the puzzled John the Baptist, wanting to believe but still unsure (11:2–6). . . . But there are also the local towns which have rejected Jesus's appeal (11:20–24), and in ch. 12 we read a succession of stories which illustrate the growing opposition to Jesus from the religious authorities, including not only the cynical demand for an authenticating sign (12:38–42) and the very threatening accusation that Jesus is in league with the devil (12:22–32) but also the beginning of an explicit threat to Jesus's life (12:14).[201]

201. France, *Gospel of Matthew*, 417.

Sometimes it can be bewildering to read through such a long Gospel as Matthew's. The evangelist has strung together a long series of shorter literary units (which scholars call "pericopes"), and it is often hard to discern the underlying logic. Often, we see the Gospels oscillate between Jesus's training of the Twelve on the one hand and his interaction with the crowds or even his opponents on the other. In this way, the Gospel writer chronicles the various responses to Jesus—whether positive or negative—and thus builds drama and suspense along an escalating plotline that inexorably leads to the climax: the crucifixion, burial, and resurrection of Jesus. Try to read the following narrative unit (chaps. 11–12), and the one after that as well (13:53–17:27), and see if having a better understanding of the evangelist's underlying rationale and narrative purpose makes it easier to see what binds the various individual pericopes together.

The Query from John the Baptist (11:1–19)

The opening reference to John in prison harks back to Matthew's earlier comment, "Now when he heard that John had been arrested," at the inception of Jesus's ministry just prior to the Sermon on the Mount.[202] Now the scene shifts to John in prison. Apparently, John, who at first had boldly proclaimed that Jesus was the Messiah, is now plagued by doubt and so sends his followers to Jesus to inquire whether he truly is "the one who is to come"—shorthand for the Messiah.[203] Words are cheap, and actions speak louder than words, so Jesus, rather than giving a direct answer in the affirmative, points John and his disciples to his *deeds*. Painting a composite picture made up of various messianic passages in the book of Isaiah, Jesus provides an impressive list of messianic credentials:

> Go and tell John what you hear and see:
> the blind receive their sight and
> the lame walk,
> lepers are cleansed and
> the deaf hear, and
> the dead are raised up, and
> the poor have good news preached to them.[204]

Earlier, Matthew had quoted Isaiah's portrait of the Messiah's work: "He took our illnesses and bore our diseases."[205] Here we see that Jesus knows himself to be the Mes-

202. Matthew 4:12.
203. Matthew 11:3.
204. Matthew 11:4–5; cf., e.g., Isaiah 26:19; 29:18–19; 35:5; 42:7, 18; 61:1.
205. Matthew 8:17, citing Isaiah 53:4.

siah fulfilling Old Testament prophecy. At this, Jesus goes and tells the crowds that John was not only a prophet but "more than a prophet." He was the "messenger" whose coming the prophet Malachi had announced, the one who would come to prepare the way of the Messiah.[206] In fact, Jesus asserts, "among those born of women there has arisen no one greater than John the Baptist."[207] This emphatically underscores the vital salvation-historical function John possessed as the Messiah's forerunner. Indeed, as Jesus points out, John was the capstone of "all the Prophets and the Law."[208]

Rightly understood, therefore, John was "Elijah"—not literally, of course, which he had rightly denied, but the latter-day Elijah who would powerfully testify to the coming Messiah.[209] Yet "this generation," Jesus lamented, was like children who couldn't agree on which game to play. John was too austere, while Jesus was too permissive, a glutton and drunkard, a friend of tax collectors and "sinners"![210] Too bad neither John nor Jesus conformed to people's expectations of what kinds of individuals the Messiah and his forerunner were to be! Again, Jesus shows himself to be an astute observer of human nature and points out with masterful irony that people's unbelief wasn't due to lacking messianic manifestations on his part but rather due to inaccurate expectations on theirs.

Denunciation of Unbelief and Invitation to Learn from Jesus (11:20–30)

Jesus proceeds to denounce the cities where he had performed most of his miracles yet which didn't repent, noting that their judgment would be exceedingly severe.[211] By contrast, he goes on to praise his Father in heaven that he had hidden "these things" (presumably Jesus's messianic identity) from the worldly wise but revealed them to little children.

In what scholars have called the "thunderbolt from the Johannine blue" (also found in Luke), Jesus here speaks in what can only be described as Johannine language, which proves that John didn't necessarily make up the statements of Jesus he records in his Gospel as is often alleged: "All things have been handed over to me by my Father, and no one knows the Son except the Father, and no one knows the Father except the Son and anyone to whom the Son chooses to reveal him."[212] Sounds like something straight out of John's Gospel!

---

206. Matthew 11:10, citing Malachi 3:1.
207. Matthew 11:11.
208. Matthew 11:13. Note that Jesus here states that not only the Prophets but also the Law "prophesied." See the discussion of Matthew 5:17 above.
209. Note that later on, at the transfiguration of Jesus, Moses and Elijah appear to converse with Jesus, whereby Moses possibly represents the Law and Elijah the Prophets.
210. Matthew 11:16–19.
211. Matthew 11:20–24.
212. Matthew 11:27.

Jesus identifies himself as a gentle and humble Messiah, inviting those who are weary and heavy-laden—most likely because of the unreasonable religious burdens (their "yoke") put on them by the religious leaders—to come to him so that he can give them rest for their souls.[213] The topic of rest sets the stage for what comes next.

Jesus's Authority over the Sabbath (12:1–14)

Some of the opposition Jesus was talking about rears its ugly head when the Pharisees object to Jesus's disciples plucking and eating heads of grain in the fields.[214] To us, this may seem like a small issue, but the problem was that this happened on the Sabbath and violated some of the Pharisees' numerous regulations as to what a person could or couldn't do on this Jewish day of rest. By way of background, the Old Testament tells us that God rested on the seventh day of creation (the Hebrew word for "rest" is *shabbat,* hence "Sabbath").[215] Later on, keeping the Sabbath day holy is included as one of the Ten Commandments.[216]

Over time, zealous Jews developed Sabbath observance into an art form by amassing a plethora of stipulations, some bordering on the obtuse, ridiculous, or even bizarre. Thus, while Jesus's disciples may have violated some of the Pharisees' added regulations, they didn't actually violate the Old Testament Sabbath commandment at all. Remember: exactly how people were to "keep the Sabbath day holy" was a matter of interpretation and application; and the Pharisees' overly scrupulous, legalistic rules and regulations got so bogged down in minutiae that the underlying purpose of the Sabbath command—to give people a day of rest—got lost in the shuffle.

Compared to the religious establishment, Jesus, their Teacher and Master, took a more compassionate and reasonable approach. After all, his disciples were hungry, and no harm was done if they helped themselves to some heads of grain. In fact, Jesus adduced an incident in Old Testament times when David and his men had done much the same![217] In addition, Jesus cited another Old Testament passage which the Pharisees had overlooked: "I desire mercy, and not sacrifice."[218] All their scrupulous religious law-keeping was in vain, as it lacked mercy and perspective. "Something greater than the temple" was here,[219] and they had entirely missed it. Jesus was greater than the Sabbath!

---

213. Matthew 11:28–29.
214. Matthew 12:1–8.
215. Genesis 2:2–3.
216. Exodus 20:8–11; Deuteronomy 5:12–15.
217. Read the story recounted in 1 Samuel 21:1–6.
218. Matthew 12:7, citing Hosea 6:6. Note this is now the second time Jesus cites this verse from Hosea; he had done so earlier at Matthew 9:13, in a passage also included in Mark and Luke, though only Matthew includes the quote from Hosea. This, along with the fact that Matthew here includes a second instance where Jesus cited this passage, suggests a special Matthean emphasis on this topic.
219. Matthew 12:6.

The demonstration of Jesus's authority over the Sabbath lies close at hand, as in the following narrative Jesus enters a synagogue and promptly heals a paralyzed man there.[220] Jesus draws the inexorable conclusion: "So it is lawful to do good on the Sabbath."[221] Further hardened, the Pharisees begin to plot to take Jesus's life; Jesus withdraws, yet heals all who follow him. The incident teaches a powerful lesson on grace and Christian freedom as opposed to myopia and legalism. Talk about missing the forest for the trees! Here the Messiah has appeared, and the Pharisees reject him because of their traditions, which have in effect replaced the Word of God itself.

That's easy to do, so we need to be careful to distinguish between what God's Word is actually (inerrantly) saying and our (fallible) interpretation of it. We certainly shouldn't try to impose our own doubtful interpretation of scriptural commands onto others as the Pharisees had done, especially if we're not even prepared to keep those ourselves or find clever ways to rationalize our noncompliance. In this rather oppressive religious climate, Jesus's teaching comes as a breath of fresh air, and the common people can breathe a sigh of relief and let their lungs fill with the air of God's grace, love, and forgiveness. As Jesus said elsewhere, new wine must be put into new wineskins. Or as we would say, it's a whole new ball game!

Jesus's Messianic Healing Ministry and the Blasphemy against the Holy Spirit (12:15–37)

At this point in his narrative, Matthew interjects a lengthy quotation from the prophet Isaiah that sums up the Messiah's healing ministry perfectly.[222] The Messiah is God's chosen Servant on whom God's Spirit rests. Gentle and humble, he champions righteousness and is the hope of Gentiles as well.

The tension between Jesus and the Pharisees continues to escalate when he heals a blind and mute man.[223] The common people are inclined to think Jesus is the son of David, triggering the Pharisees' rather outlandish argument that Jesus is able to cast out demons only by the power of Satan himself. Jesus promptly exposes their flawed logic by retorting, in a now classic argument, that "a house divided against itself will not stand."[224] Many people mistakenly think the statement was coined by Abraham Lincoln, who used it with reference to the issue of slavery shortly before the Civil War in the United States. Why would Satan cast out his own demons? Jesus asked. That didn't make any sense at all.

220. Matthew 12:9–14.
221. Matthew 12:12.
222. Matthew 12:18–21, citing Isaiah 42:1–4. See the quotation of Isaiah 53:4 in Matthew 8:17 above.
223. Matthew 12:22–32.
224. Matthew 12:25.

Going on the counteroffensive, Jesus pressed, "But if it is by the *Spirit of God* that I cast out demons, then the kingdom of God has come upon you."[225] And in a shot across the bow, he warns the Pharisees against committing the unpardonable sin of blasphemy against the Holy Spirit. If you accuse me of casting out demons by Satan when in fact I'm doing so by the Spirit, Jesus asserted, be careful, because in so doing you're not only attacking me; you're also offending the Holy Spirit, which, he said in vintage humility, is an even greater offense. In addition, of course, by speaking of "blasphemy against the Spirit," Jesus asserts the Spirit's deity.[226]

He adds the now famous affirmation that a tree is known by its fruit; in like manner, people's hearts are revealed by the words they speak. On judgment day, we'll have to give an account to God for every careless word we've spoken. Ouch! That's a sobering thought.

The Sign of Jonah and Jesus's True Mother and Brothers (12:38–50)

Yet the scribes and Pharisees are not easily silenced. Instead, they demand a sign from Jesus to validate his messianic claims. Calling them "an evil and adulterous generation," Jesus offers only the "sign of Jonah." Just as Jonah was in the large fish for three days and nights, so Jesus would rise from the dead after three days.[227] Yet both Nineveh and the queen of Sheba would rise up in the final judgment to testify against the Jewish leaders (note that both the Ninevites and the queen of Sheba were Gentiles). Yet now someone even greater than Solomon was here![228] Jesus's opposition, however, is going from bad to worse.

The unit closes with the arrival of Jesus's mother and brothers (interestingly, no sisters are mentioned here), who ask to speak to him. In another lesson on faith and discipleship, Jesus responds that whoever does the will of his Father is part of his spiritual family. To be a disciple of Jesus is to be a member of a new spiritual family, the family of God.[229] In this way, Matthew's narrative transitions from the escalating conflict with the Pharisees to yet another significant discourse gathering portions of Jesus's teaching on the nature of God's kingdom.

---

225. Matthew 12:28.
226. Matthew 12:31.
227. Matthew 12:39–40. Note that some are perturbed by the fact that Jesus was crucified on Friday afternoon and rose Sunday morning, so, technically, he rose after three days and *two* nights (not three), counting partial days (like Friday and Sunday). However, Jewish people routinely called a day "a day and a night," so while there is the appearance of a discrepancy, such exists only in the mind of the modern reader, but not in that of the ancient reader.
228. Matthew 12:41–42.
229. Matthew 12:46–50.

RECAP

In the most recent two chapters (11–12), Matthew has narrated the third part of Jesus's work in Galilee. Following the Missionary Discourse in chapter 10, this narrative portion commenced with the query from John the Baptist whether Jesus in fact is the Messiah. In response, Jesus simply pointed to his actions, which were in keeping with messianic prophecy. Jesus proceeded to denounce the Galilean cities in which he had performed many of his miracles, affirming that Gentiles who believed in Old Testament times would pronounce judgment on these cities. He also praised his Father in heaven who had chosen to reveal himself to those who lacked status in this world. Over against his Jewish opponents, Jesus asserted his authority over the Sabbath and warned them against blaspheming the Holy Spirit. They would be given no sign of his authority other than the "sign of Jonah," which prefigured his future burial and resurrection after three days. Again, we see how the entire narrative portion revolves around Jesus's messianic claims and credentials, which he amply demonstrates but which tragically continue to be rejected by the Jewish religious leaders.

THE KINGDOM OF HEAVEN

The central topic in Jesus's teaching according to the Gospel of Matthew is the kingdom of heaven.[230] Both John the Baptist, Jesus's forerunner, and Jesus begin their ministries by calling on the people of Israel to "repent, for the kingdom of heaven is at hand."[231] Jesus, for his part, travels "throughout all Galilee, teaching in their synagogues and proclaiming the gospel of the kingdom."[232]

What is this kingdom whose coming Jesus announces? David Turner's summary is apt: "Generally, the kingdom of heaven refers to the nearness or even presence of the rule of God in the person, works, and teaching of Jesus but there are times when it implies or clearly describes the future

230. Matthew uses the expression "kingdom of heaven" thirty-two times in his Gospel (the expression is found nowhere else in the Gospels) and the expression "kingdom of God" five times. What's more, in fifteen of the nineteen times Matthew employs the word "kingdom" with no qualification, the context indicates that he is speaking of the kingdom of God. See the discussion of "kingdom of heaven" in David L. Turner, *Matthew*, Baker Exegetical Commentary on the New Testament (Grand Rapids: Baker, 2008), 37–44.

231. Matthew 3:2; 4:17.

232. Matthew 4:23.

reign of Jesus upon the earth."[233] There's a sense in Matthew's Gospel that Jesus is teaching about a kingdom that in him has already arrived. At the same time, it's equally apparent that the kingdom won't be completely realized until his return. Thus, Jesus teaches about a kingdom that is already inaugurated but not yet consummated.

As Jeannine Brown noted, Jesus's five major discourses in Matthew's Gospel "can be understood as providing progressive illumination of the nature and values of God's kingdom as the story proceeds to its culmination."[234]

- The first discourse, the Sermon on the Mount (chaps. 5–7), lays the framework for the values and ethic of the kingdom.
- In the second discourse (chap. 10), Jesus gives instructions to his disciples as they take the message of the kingdom "to the lost sheep of the house of Israel."[235]
- The third discourse (13:1–53) includes several parables, most notably the parable of the sower, on the coming of the kingdom and the various responses to it.
- The fourth discourse (chap. 18) includes another series of parables, which Jesus employs to teach on what relationships in the kingdom of God are to look like.
- Finally, the fifth major discourse (chaps. 24–25) conveys Jesus's teaching on his return, at which time the kingdom will be consummated.

While Jesus's coming signified the coming of the kingdom of heaven first to Israel, it is eventually presented to all who acknowledge Jesus as Messiah. As Grant Osborne observes, "All three Synoptic Gospels present the kingdom as coming in the incarnation, life, death, and resurrection of Jesus; but Matthew especially centers on the ethical implications of this. The church is the kingdom community, and the Sermon on the Mount is the final Torah of the kingdom reality."[236]

---

233. Turner, *Matthew*, 43 (Scripture references omitted).
234. Brown, "Gospel of Matthew," 574.
235. Matthew 10:6.
236. Grant R. Osborne, *Matthew*, Zondervan Exegetical Commentary on the New Testament (Grand Rapids: Zondervan, 2010), 33.

For Matthew, "righteousness" is a life lived in accordance with these kingdom demands, and all people will be judged in keeping with how they've lived their lives.[237] In the coming of Jesus, the kingdom of heaven has already come near. The arrival of the kingdom demands that all who encounter Jesus either repent of their sin and follow him (e.g., the Twelve) or reject him (the Jewish leaders), resulting in eternal reward or judgment when the kingdom is consummated.

As we've seen, much learned ink has been spilled by scholars trying to figure out what Jesus meant when he talked about the kingdom of God. In the ultimate analysis, I believe grasping Jesus's teaching on God's kingdom isn't so much an intellectual challenge as something requiring spiritual insight. Essentially, Jesus came down from heaven to show us, in his three and a half years of public ministry, what heaven is like. As Revelation tells us, heaven will be a place where "'there will be no more death' or mourning or crying or pain."[238] So when Jesus heals the sick and even raises the dead, he shows us what living forever in God's presence will be like. No one will die; no one will get sick. There'll be no more suffering or sorrow. In short, Jesus gives us a sneak preview of heaven. He is God's messenger, his agent—his one and only Son—who doesn't merely *tell* us what God's kingdom will be like; he *shows* us! And it is a *kingdom* because God's rule and reign will be supreme. All the forces of evil will have been subdued forever. As John tells us in the book of Revelation, the devil and his minions will be banished from God's—and our—presence forever.[239]

So, do you want to know what God's kingdom is like? Look at Jesus! Listen to what he says about the kingdom of God, and look at what he does. It's really quite amazing: on the cross, Jesus has already done everything for us. All we need to do is believe! That's such a small thing, and yet, like Jesus's first followers, we often find it hard to do. Also, Jesus repeatedly speaks about being "worthy" of him as his

237. Matthew 16:27.
238. Revelation 21:4 NIV.
239. Revelation 20:7–10.

disciple.[240] Do we grasp what a privilege it is to have been redeemed by Jesus—reclaimed as his special possession—and to have been called to his service? Truth is, many of us are still busy building our own "kingdoms" while asking Jesus to bless our efforts! We use pious, spiritual language, rationalizing it's all about *him*—when, more often than not, our "kingdom" work may be mostly about *us*. It shouldn't be so. Following Jesus entails submitting to *his* authority. We need to let *him* call the shots and be content to be soldiers in his spiritual army. In this way, already now we're preparing for living in God's kingdom—the supreme, unchallenged reign of God for all eternity.

240. See, e.g., Matthew 10:37–39.

DISCOURSE #3: STORIES ABOUT GOD'S KINGDOM (13:1–53)

Chapter 13 contains the third major discourse in Matthew's Gospel, in which Jesus explains the spiritual dynamics of the kingdom of heaven. Jesus's chosen teaching tools here are parables—stories or similes conveying spiritual truths.[241] It's possible, if not likely, that, rather than delivering all these parables in one sitting, Jesus may have told them over a period of time and that Matthew, the first evangelist, conveniently gathered them in one place for his readers in order to give them a composite picture of what God's kingdom was going to look like according to Jesus. It's also possible, however, that Jesus *did* in fact tell all these parables in one sitting. Either way, they're collected here in Matthew's Gospel.

The Parable of the Sower (13:1–23)

In a series of parables, then, Jesus explains the variety of responses to himself and his message up to that point in his ministry. By now his followers would have wondered why, if Jesus was in fact the Messiah, the Jewish leaders didn't recognize him as such. In the first, most extensive parable of the discourse, the parable of the sower, Jesus provides an answer to this pressing question. In the parable, a sower goes out into a field to sow seeds; some fall along the path and are eaten by birds; some fall on rocky ground and wither away; some fall among thorns and are choked; and some fall on good soil and flourish. The four types of soil are emblematic of a spectrum of spiritual heart conditions. According to Jesus, there were a variety of reasons why many rejected his message—Satan's work, external opposition, or a preoccupation with the things of this world. He goes on to cite a passage from Isaiah, indicating that Israel's rejection of Jesus the Messiah fulfilled Old Testament prophecy.[242] Even in Isaiah's day, Jesus avers, most Jews weren't willing to receive God's message; it is no different in his day.

---

241. Essentially, parables are fictional but realistic stories Jesus made up to convey a spiritual truth (or truths), usually about an aspect of God's kingdom. On interpreting parables, see chapter 9 in Köstenberger and Patterson, *Invitation to Biblical Interpretation*.

242. Matthew 13:1–23; see Isaiah 6:9–10.

This makes it much easier to understand why Jesus met with such significant resistance and explains that the magnitude of opposition toward Jesus in no way proved that his messianic claim was spurious. Rather, the problem lay squarely with the hearts of those who opposed him and was anticipated already by Old Testament prophets such as Isaiah. Nevertheless, there remained a minority who heard Jesus's message and received it (e.g., the Twelve); such people with receptive hearts would bear rich spiritual fruit. It's significant that the parable of the sower comes first, both here and in Mark's Gospel, as it is foundational to understanding the Jewish rejection of Jesus and his reception by a Jewish remnant. In many ways, therefore, this is the quintessential parable that opens up our understanding of all of Jesus's parables.

Jesus's parable of the sower is instructive not only for his original disciples but for us today as well. We often wonder why it is that those around us aren't catching on and seem indifferent to the gospel. The lesson is this: Don't let the apathy, resistance, or even hostility to spiritual things of those around you keep you from following Jesus and from serving him faithfully. You can't control how others respond; they'll have to make their own decision about Christ and will have to give an account for rejecting him one day. In the meantime, don't let the lack of response to Jesus and the gospel from others make you insecure or cause you to wane in your enthusiasm for serving him. As Paul would write later, "Let us not lose heart in doing good, for in due time we will reap if we do not grow weary."[243]

Seven Additional Kingdom Parables (13:24–53)

Similar to the parable of the sower, the remaining parables gathered in this chapter each answer an important question Jesus's followers likely had at this juncture of Jesus's ministry. Personally, as I try to discern the core teaching in a given parable, I've found it helpful to ask myself: "What question in the minds of his disciples (or, in some cases, his opponents) at that particular point in time was Jesus trying to answer by telling a given parable?" This is what scholars call the "life-setting of Jesus." In addition, they also talk about the "life-setting of the church," essentially meaning the reason why a given evangelist included a particular parable in his Gospel because of its relevance to his primary target audience. In light of this, let's take a quick look at each of the remaining parables in this chapter.

In the parable of the weeds, Jesus accounts for the continuing presence of evil in the world and reassures his disciples that at the proper time—at the final judgment—he will punish the wicked and reward the righteous.[244] All that's required, therefore, is

243. Galatians 6:9 NASB.

244. Matthew 13:24–30, explained at 13:36–43.

patience. There's no need to take matters into one's own hands, nor do God's people need to worry that evil will permanently go unpunished.

Through the parables of the mustard seed and the leaven, Jesus portrays the unexpected and remarkable growth of the kingdom.[245] If for the moment Jesus's followers constitute only a "little flock," not to worry—it's God's good pleasure to give them the kingdom.[246] And they won't always be as small; Jesus's vision is that his messianic community will grow gradually yet steadily until it is large enough to benefit many others.

Through the parables of the hidden treasure and the precious pearl, Jesus shows that God's kingdom is exceedingly precious and worthy of any sacrifice his followers may be called on to make.[247] This answers the question why so many aren't following Jesus at this point in time: they're simply unwilling to pay the price. It also reassures those who did choose to follow Jesus that their sacrifice will ultimately be worth it.

The parable of the dragnet, similar to the parable of the weeds, portrays the final judgment, at which God will separate the righteous from the wicked and those who reject the King and his kingdom will be judged.[248] While this separation has yet to take place, Jesus's followers need not worry that those who seem to prosper but are not followers of Jesus will end up ahead. It ain't over till the Son of Man comes on judgment day!

Finally, the parable of the scribe depicts Jesus's disciples as better qualified to teach God's law than the scribes and Pharisees. In their storeroom of instruction, they hold "both old and new treasures" (the Old Testament and the teachings of Jesus, respectively).[249] Thus this simple simile provides a fitting conclusion to the series of parables included in this chapter.

In fact, one might reasonably argue that one such scribe who brings out from his storeroom of instruction both old and new treasures is none other than the first evangelist himself, who has treated his readers to a veritable smorgasbord of spiritual lessons regarding the nature of God's kingdom. He has explained that God's kingdom is primarily a matter of the heart: those whose hearts are good soil will eagerly receive it and flourish spiritually, while those with wicked, distracted, or anxious hearts won't find it within themselves to accommodate Jesus's teaching on the kingdom permanently in their lives. In the latter's case, the problem lies not with Jesus or his followers but with their own spiritually unsettled hearts (though note that there's still hope: let's pray that God will fertilize many rocky or thorny hearts and turn them into good, receptive soil).

---

245. Matthew 13:31–35.
246. Luke 12:32.
247. Matthew 13:44–46.
248. Matthew 13:47–50.
249. Matthew 13:51–52; see Köstenberger, Kellum, and Quarles, *The Cradle, the Cross, and the Crown*, 26.

RECAP

In this chapter, Matthew has gathered a series of parables Jesus told to instruct his followers about the nature of God's kingdom. While at present Christ's followers find themselves confronted with the messy reality that it is often not easy to determine who is a citizen of the kingdom and who isn't, no worries—simply leave separating the wheat from the weeds up to God, and he'll take care of this task on judgment day. No worries also if at the moment God's kingdom seems rather small; just keep being faithful, and over time it'll grow. And remember: God's kingdom is like hidden treasure or a precious pearl. No sacrifice is too great for purchasing that most desirable item of all. In all these ways, Jesus calmed the nerves and soothed the hearts of his followers who may have started to wonder by that time, in light of the limited response Jesus received, whether leaving their livelihoods and families had been the right choice. Hang with me, Jesus says; trust me, it'll be all right.

Which reminds me of a little anecdote in my own life. When traveling through Europe, my family ran into a series of minor difficulties. Having taken the speed train through the British Chunnel from London to Paris, we had rented a car in the French capital but had lost our way, and my limited French made it difficult to ask for directions (no GPS yet). While some of us were getting worried, my daughter Tahlia (who sat in the back of our car) piped to the front, "Guys! Don't worry! Everything is going almost perfectly!" Praise God for my daughter's positive disposition! The tension was immediately defused, and before too long things started looking up. Ever since, Tahlia's comment has become a standard saying in our family when things aren't going so well at the time. It's as if Jesus were telling his disciples at this juncture of his ministry, "Don't worry! Everything is going almost perfectly! Trust me, and everything is going to be all right."

JESUS'S WORK IN GALILEE (4:17–18:35, CONT.)
Work Farther North (13:54–17:27)
The Rejection of Jesus in Nazareth (13:54–58)
The Tragic End of John the Baptist (14:1–12)
Jesus Feeds the Multitudes, Walks on Water, and Heals the Sick (14:13–36)

JESUS'S WORK IN GALILEE (4:17–18:35, CONT.)

Work Farther North (13:54–17:27)

The Rejection of Jesus in Nazareth (13:54–58)

With the phrase "And when Jesus had finished these parables," Matthew's Gospel moves from instruction back to narrative. Not only is Jesus rejected by the Jewish leaders, who have grown increasingly antagonistic and adversarial; he is rejected even by the people in his own hometown, the city of Nazareth. While Jesus's contemporaries recognized his unusual wisdom and mighty works, they weren't truly receptive to his message. As Jesus trenchantly remarked, "A prophet is not without honor except in his hometown and in his own household."[250] Familiarity breeds contempt. Those closest to us often take us for granted. Again, Jesus proves to be an incisive student of people's hearts; in fact, as a sign of his deity, he knows exactly what's motivating them. Because of their persistent unbelief, Jesus didn't perform many miracles in his hometown.[251]

Jesus's rejection by the people of Nazareth is in keeping with his instruction of his followers in the Missionary Discourse in chapter 10, discussed above.[252] It also foreshadows the execution of John the Baptist that lies close at hand as well as Jesus's own demise later on, as narrated in the passion narrative. Similarly, you and I may often experience that it is hardest to witness to our Christian faith in the context of our own families. We should take heart, because Jesus's experience was no different. Neverthe-

250. Matthew 13:57.
251. Matthew 13:58.
252. Cf. Matthew 10:11–15.

less, we shouldn't give up, because as we can see in Jesus's case, his brothers (and hopefully his sisters as well) did become believers after his resurrection.[253] And whether or not we see spiritual fruit as a result of our gospel living and speaking, our focus should be on bearing witness—and leaving the results to God.

The Tragic End of John the Baptist (14:1–12)

The narrative continues with the heart-wrenching story of the execution of John the Baptist.[254] Interestingly, this is the only narrative portion in Matthew's Gospel that is not explicitly about Jesus, which shows the respect and significance awarded to John the Baptist and his salvation-historical role as forerunner to Jesus. Oddly, as a segue to the story, Herod Antipas, the ruler of Galilee, upon hearing about Jesus's growing reputation, surmises that he is John the Baptist raised from the dead (indicating that, at this point in time, the Baptist is no longer alive). This occasions the narrative of John's beheading in the form of a historical flashback (a literary technique not uncommon in literature and movies even today).

You can read the sad, gruesome story on your own. What started out with John's powerful witness to Jesus at the Jordan River had given way to doubt and now ended in tragic death, triggered by John's prophetic confrontation of Galilee's ruler for his illicit relationship.[255] Nevertheless, John's major salvation-historical purpose of "preparing the way for the Lord" has been fulfilled. The one John heralded—Jesus the Messiah—and his mission continue, while John the Baptist's life and ministry have come to a close. What's more, though not in every gory detail, John's execution foreshadows what will happen to Jesus at the hands of the unholy alliance between the Jewish leaders and the Roman authorities in due course.

Jesus Feeds the Multitudes, Walks on Water, and Heals the Sick (14:13–36)

In what follows, Matthew presents several miracles of Jesus that further serve to demonstrate his messianic authority.[256] Jesus doesn't merely talk about the coming of God's kingdom; he provides tangible proof that he is the King, and that in encountering his person and work people can get a foretaste of what the kingdom of God will be like.[257] After John's death, Jesus seeks a place of solitude, but the crowds

253. See, e.g., Acts 1:14.

254. Thus, both narrative units, chapters 11–12 and chapters 14–17, start with a narrative about John the Baptist: in the former case, his nagging doubts as to whether Jesus really was the Messiah; in the present case, his gruesome death at the hands of Herod Antipas.

255. Cf. Matthew 11:2–3.

256. Matthew 14:13–16:12.

257. See the sidebar "The Kingdom of Heaven" above.

follow him wherever he goes.[258] This shows his considerable appeal to ordinary people, who respond in great numbers and are increasingly attracted to Jesus and what he has to offer.

Consistent with his normal practice, Jesus doesn't turn people away but instead again proves to be the compassionate messianic healer.[259] In contrast with the decadent feast of Herod that led to the beheading of John the Baptist,[260] the feeding of five thousand men—plus women and children—features Jesus's miraculous provision of an abundant meal from a mere five loaves of bread and two small fish.[261] The way Matthew tells the story evokes reminiscences of God's provision of manna for the Israelites in the wilderness.[262] Just like God fed the people of Israel during the exodus, so now Jesus takes up the mantle and miraculously feeds God's people, showing himself to be the greater Moses and messianic Shepherd-King.

Immediately following this public miracle, Jesus also amazes his disciples with the private miracle of walking on water on the Sea of Galilee.[263] The disciples show their superstition and unbelief by surmising the figure they see is actually a ghost, and these grown, rugged men "cried out in fear"![264] But Jesus immediately reassures them that it is he. By walking on the water, Jesus invokes the image of God striding on the surface of the water in Old Testament times.[265] This powerfully associates him with God and even identifies him as God, and provides a stark contrast to his superstitious followers who are terrified of (supposed) ghosts.

At this, Peter is emboldened to ask Jesus to tell him to walk on water as well! Jesus simply tells him to come. Peter steps out of the boat and into the water and starts walking toward Jesus. Yet when he takes his eyes off Jesus and looks at the wind, he begins to sink and pleads with Jesus to rescue him. Jesus immediately takes his hand, chiding him for his lack of faith. The whole incident leads the shaken disciples to worship Jesus and declare, "Truly you are the Son of God."[266]

---

258. Matthew 14:13. On the setting of the two feedings of the multitudes, see Gordon Franz, "The Feedings of the Multitudes: When, Where, and Why? (Matt 14:13–21; 15:29–39; etc.)," in Beitzel, *Lexham Geographic Commentary*, 237–46. See also John A. Beck, "The Geography of Forgiveness (Matt 14:13–21; 15:29–39; 16:5–12)," in Beitzel, *Lexham Geographic Commentary*, 258–64; and Perry G. Phillips, "Natural Amphitheaters along the Sea of Galilee (Matt 14:13–21; 15:29–39; Mark 6:30–44; 8:1–10; Luke 9:10–17; John 6:1–14)," in Beitzel, *Lexham Geographic Commentary*, 265–69.
259. Matthew 14:14.
260. Matthew 14:2–12.
261. Matthew 14:13–21. This is one of the few stories found in all four Gospels.
262. See Exodus 16.
263. Matthew 14:22–36.
264. Matthew 14:26.
265. See Job 9:8: "He alone stretches out the heavens and treads on the waves of the sea" (NIV).
266. Matthew 14:33.

It seems that, at this point of the narrative, the truth finally begins to sink in (pun intended) for the disciples that Jesus really is the Messiah, the Son of God. On a deeper level, the story also instructs us about the life of faith. As the author of Hebrews tells his readers, we need to "fix our eyes on Jesus" and run the race of faith with endurance.[267] The moment we get distracted and look at our circumstances, we'll get shaky. Give Peter a lot of credit, though, for asking Jesus to tell him to walk on water in the first place, and for immediately crying out for Jesus to save him when he began to sink!

Incidentally, this interplay between the disciples and the crowds is characteristic of the way in which all four Gospels—including Matthew—paint a contrast between Jesus's revelation of his true messianic nature to the inner circle he has chosen (the Twelve, the nucleus of his new messianic community) and to those who follow him from a distance, benefiting from his miracles but without truly understanding who Jesus is. John, the fourth evangelist, will later relabel Jesus's miracles "signs" in order to draw attention to the fact that they were more than mere demonstrations of his power; properly understood, they were signposts to who he was—the Messiah and Son of God.[268] Thus, the crowds have their stomachs filled for a few hours, but soon they'll be hungry again. Those who understand that this is but a sign of Jesus's messianic mission and believe, however, will receive eternal life, and their spiritual hunger and thirst will be forever quenched.

The action continues unabated. No sooner do Jesus and the disciples come ashore on the other side of the lake than the people there recognize Jesus. The chapter has started out with a reference to "the fame of Jesus," which had reached even Herod Antipas, Galilee's ruler. The chapter ends with another reference to Jesus's reputation for his miracle-working power, which has spread throughout the entire region. As a result, many come to him, believing that if they simply "touch the fringe of his garment," they will be healed. And they are![269]

---

267. Hebrews 12:1–2.

268. See esp. John 20:30–31 and the discussion of Jesus's messianic signs in John's Gospel in chapter 5 below.

269. Matthew 14:36.

JESUS'S WORK IN GALILEE (4:17–18:35, CONT.)

Work Farther North (13:54–17:27, cont.)

Tradition, Tradition (15:1–20)

In chapter 12 we saw that the Pharisees gave Jesus grief about his disciples' eating ears of grain on the Sabbath.[270] Now they come to Jesus—all the way from Jerusalem—with a similar grievance: "Why do your disciples break the tradition of the elders? For they do not wash their hands when they eat." Jesus immediately goes on the offensive: "And why do *you* break the commandment of God for the sake of your tradition?"[271] In other words, God's actual commandments have priority over man-made traditions. By putting their own traditions in the place of God's commandments, the Pharisees have in fact set aside the word and will of God.

Jesus immediately provides an example of such travesty pertaining to the commandment to honor one's father and mother.[272] By dedicating certain things to God, the Pharisees had cleverly sidestepped this command. Then, when their parents needed material assistance, they would say, "So sorry! I'd love to help, but I really can't, because what I would have otherwise given to you, I've already committed to God!" Quoting Isaiah, Jesus denounces them for paying mere lip service to God while having hearts full of corruption, selfishness, and greed. All their "worship" was empty and devoid of meaning. God wasn't fooled!

270. Matthew 12:1–8.
271. Matthew 15:1–3, emphasis added.
272. Cf. Exodus 20:12; Deuteronomy 5:16. See also Exodus 21:17; Leviticus 20:9.

Jesus isn't done yet. Calling people to himself, he further explains the matter to them. The problem, he insists, is not unwashed hands or what goes *into* a person (potentially "defiled" food). Rather, the problem is what comes *out of* a person, rooted in their heart condition. The Pharisees—denounced by Jesus as "blind guides"—predictably are offended, but Peter asks Jesus to explain "this parable" (here probably in the sense of "illustration").

After chiding Peter and the others (plural "you" in the original Greek) for their lack of understanding, Jesus states the obvious: what people eat is shortly discarded through the digestive process, but what comes out of their hearts is the source of all kinds of wickedness—"evil thoughts, murder, adultery, sexual immorality, theft, false witness, slander."[273] A corrupt, sinful, perverted heart is what defiles a person; unwashed hands defile no one. Wow, what a powerful refutation of the petty, pusillanimous Pharisees! They probably left with their heads still spinning. Perhaps they'll be more careful next time before challenging Jesus. Clearly, if you're keeping score, this round goes overwhelmingly to the Messiah.

Jesus Heals Many (including Gentiles) and Feeds the Multitudes (Again!) (15:21–39)

Following his exchange with the Pharisees, Jesus withdraws northward from Galilee to the Gentile district of Tyre and Sidon.[274] There, he encounters a Canaanite woman calling out to him, "Have mercy on me, O Lord, Son of David," and imploring him to heal her demon-possessed daughter.[275] In stark contrast to the unbelieving Jewish leaders, this woman approaches Jesus with what he himself recognizes as "great faith." In response to her faith and pleas for mercy, Jesus heals her daughter. At this news, great crowds come to him with their lame, blind, crippled, and mute, "and many others." Jesus heals them all, and people glorify "the God of Israel."[276]

Jesus's encounter with the Canaanite woman and his healing ministry among the crowds of Gentiles signal that the scope of his mission will ultimately encompass both Jews and Gentiles.[277] This is further underscored by the feeding of the four thousand men (again, plus women and children), which resembles his earlier feeding of the five thousand, except that this time the feeding takes place in Gentile territory.[278] While

273. Matthew 15:19.

274. Matthew 15:21. See Emily J. Thomassen, "Jesus's Journey into Gentile Territories (Mark 7:24–31; Matt 15:21–29," in Beitzel, *Lexham Geographic Commentary*, 247–57.

275. Matthew 15:22–29.

276. Matthew 15:30–31.

277. Matthew 28:19: "Make disciples of all nations."

278. Not to mention small details such as that this time there are seven loaves and a few small fish, and seven basketsful of leftovers. See Franz, "Feedings of the Multitudes."

Matthew makes clear that Jesus's messianic mission is directed preeminently to Israel, he also affirms Jesus's love and compassion for Gentiles, who didn't previously belong to the people of God.[279] Following the feeding, Jesus dismisses the crowds, gets into a boat, and departs for the region of Magadan.[280]

279. See the conversation between Jesus and the Canaanite woman, esp. Matthew 15:24–26.
280. Matthew 15:39. See Gordon Franz, "Ancient Harbors of the Sea of Galilee (Matt 4:18–22; 8:28–34; 14:15–22; 15:32–39; etc.)," in Beitzel, *Lexham Geographic Commentary*, 219–36.

JESUS'S WORK IN GALILEE (4:17–18:35, CONT.)

Work Farther North (13:54–17:27, cont.)

Give Me a Sign (16:1–12)

Upon his return to Jewish territory, Jesus is once again confronted by a group of Pharisees and Sadducees who are seeking to test him. What else is new? Despite Jesus's numerous and frequent public miracles, they disingenuously ask him for "a sign from heaven" to legitimate his messianic authority and to demonstrate his messianic identity.[281] In response, Jesus chides this "evil and adulterous generation" for being able to interpret the signs of the weather but being unable to interpret the signs of the times.[282] They're skilled in navigating the waters of this world while being intransigent to matters of the spiritual realm.

Jesus's answer is exactly the same as last time.[283] Again, the only sign those people will receive is "the sign of Jonah"—that is, Jesus's resurrection after three days. In other words, no signs for them! Fact is, Jesus has given a large amount of proofs for his messianic identity. The only thing that's puzzling is how the Pharisees could have missed them all. What will it take to satisfy them? They're unmasked as utterly disingenuous and unreasonable.

281. Matthew 16:1–4.

282. See Elaine A. Phillips, "Jesus's Interpretation of Weather Patterns (Matt 16:1–4; Luke 12:44–55)," in Beitzel, *Lexham Geographic Commentary*, 278–85.

283. Cf. Matthew 12:38–42.

Never one to pass over a teachable moment, Jesus takes the opportunity to warn his followers against the "leaven" (i.e., corrosive teaching) of the Pharisees and Sadducees.[284]

Breakthrough: "You Are the Christ" (16:13–28)

The narrative proceeds to the climax of Jesus's Galilean ministry, Peter's confession at Caesarea Philippi far north in Herod Philip's territory straight east of Tyre.[285] Just recently, the Pharisees and Sadducees had asked Jesus for a sign (which he had refused to give). Now Jesus poses a series of pointed question of his own to his disciples. Jesus's first question is this: "Who do people say that the Son of Man [Jesus] is?" His disciples' answer makes clear there is currently no consensus: "Some say John the Baptist, others say Elijah, and others Jeremiah or one of the prophets." Strikingly, Jesus doesn't even engage their answer but immediately proceeds to ask his follow-up question: "But who do *you* say that I am?" In this way, Jesus challenges his disciples to make up their own minds regarding him rather than merely following others' opinions based on stereotype, prejudice, or other unwarranted preconceived notions of who the Messiah is going to be.

Peter, speaking for the disciples, replies, "You are the Christ [the Messiah], the Son of the living God."[286] Finally! Someone in the narrative understands who Jesus really is! Yet Jesus immediately deflects credit from Peter for correctly identifying Jesus's true identity, saying this realization didn't come from human insight but rather had its origin in divine revelation (though Jesus does call Peter "blessed").[287] Playing off Peter's name, *Petros* (which means "rock"), Jesus adds that it is on this "rock" (presumably, Peter's confession of Jesus as Messiah) that he will build his church—his new messianic community—and the "gates of hell" will begin to crumble and give up those who were headed for eternal destruction.[288] Jesus's promise that he himself will build his church has rightly given great encouragement and reassurance to those who struggled with limited fruit or hard soil in their church-planting efforts.

Also, Jesus will give Peter the "keys of the kingdom of heaven," which historically meant that Peter would be involved in opening access to the church to Jews, Samaritans, and Gentiles as recorded in the book of Acts.[289] At this, Jesus sternly warns his disciples not to tell

---

284. Matthew 16:5–12.

285. Matthew 16:13–20, emphasis added; cf. 15:21. See Elaine A. Phillips, "Peter's Declaration at Caesarea Philippi (Matt 16:13–23; Mark 8:27–30; Luke 9:18–20)," in Beitzel, *Lexham Geographic Commentary*, 286–97.

286. Matthew 16:16.

287. Matthew 16:17.

288. Note that this is one of only two references to the "church" (*ekklēsia*) in all the Gospels combined (the other reference is in Matthew 18:18). Cf. Quarles, *Matthew*, 188, who glosses the Greek word *ekklēsia* as "community, congregation." He adds, "The term was used frequently in the OT to describe 'the congregation of Israel/God.' . . . Jesus will form a new, or renewed, congregation. . . . Jesus will gather this new people for God."

289. See Acts 2, 8, and 10.

anyone that he was the Messiah—the so-called messianic secret, found especially in Mark but present also in Matthew and Luke. Most likely, Jesus knew that people would typically misunderstand what it meant for him to be the Messiah, as they commonly looked for a national deliverer rather than someone who would set people free spiritually. Most certainly, they didn't look for a crucified Messiah, as the ensuing narrative will shortly make clear.

Now that Peter has acknowledged Jesus as the Messiah—the major turning point in the narrative—Jesus begins to talk to his followers candidly about what his future destiny will be.[290] This attests powerfully to Jesus's amazing divine foreknowledge and also makes the important apologetic point that none of the adverse events that Jesus would encounter caught him by surprise. Rather, the entire script of Jesus's life—including his crucifixion, burial, and resurrection—was written by the sovereign God for the sake of our salvation! Peter, however, in a bizarre twist in the story, takes Jesus aside and begins to "rebuke" him (though one can hardly fault Peter for lack of confidence!), objecting, "No way! This is never going to happen to you!" In effect, he denies the necessity of the cross (not to mention that he claims to know the future better than Jesus).

Jesus, in turn, at once sharply rebukes Peter: "Get behind me, Satan!" Wow! Did Jesus just call Peter "Satan" (i.e., adversary)? How quickly fortunes can change! Just a few moments ago, Jesus had called Peter "blessed" upon his acknowledgment of Jesus as the Christ, the Son of the living God. Now he calls him "Satan," saying, "You are a hindrance to me." By this Jesus means that his crucifixion, no matter how painful, is absolutely necessary for our salvation, and he is therefore determined to carry out God's plan. Peter, on the other hand, has just revealed that, when acknowledging Jesus as Messiah, he didn't fully understand what he was saying.

A Messiah—but not a crucified one! This is the prototypical misunderstanding of which the first evangelist wants to disabuse his readers—that the Messiah will be a conquering King, not a suffering Savior. Jesus will have none of it. This shows that even those closest to Jesus were completely taken aback by his suggestion that he must be killed. Not only did they love him and didn't want to lose him; they didn't understand how Jesus could be killed and still be the Messiah. The two seemed to be mutually contradictory. Either Jesus was the Messiah or he would be killed; it couldn't be both. This makes the Jewish myth that the disciples stole Jesus's body and invented his resurrection so unbelievable. His disciples were utterly incapable of concocting such a myth. If Jesus were to rise from the dead, he would do so completely against all expectations—never mind that he told his followers repeatedly that he must be killed and on the third day rise again!

The implication for Jesus's followers is that anyone who would "come after" Jesus (i.e., follow him) must likewise "deny himself and take up his cross." That is, Jesus's

290. Matthew 16:21–23.

followers must be prepared to identify publicly with Jesus and to suffer rejection by unbelievers just like he did. If we want to follow Jesus but disavow suffering with him, we'll be like Peter, who objected to a crucified Messiah. We'll be like the preachers of the "health and wealth gospel" who tell others that they can have "their best life now."[291] Tell me: Does that sounds like the gospel Jesus preached? No; it makes a mockery of the cross and of Jesus's insistence that taking up one's cross is essential for Christian discipleship. A noncrucified disciple is a contradiction in terms. As the German theologian Dietrich Bonhoeffer put it, commenting on this very passage, "When Christ calls a man, he bids him come and die."[292] Not only will he, the Messiah, suffer, but every disciple who follows him must be prepared likewise to "take up his cross" and even possibly "lose his life" for Jesus's sake. Even so, Jesus promises his disciples that they will see "the Son of Man coming in his kingdom" before they die.

Mountaintop Experience: Jesus's Glorious Transfiguration (17:1–13)

Only six days later, Jesus's statement comes literally true when his three closest disciples—Peter, James, and John—ascend a high mountain with him and in a vision see Jesus supernaturally transformed before their very eyes.[293] Jesus's "face shone like the sun, and his clothes became white as light"—apocalyptic language later replicated in John's vision of Jesus in the book of Revelation.[294] As he had just predicted, Jesus will be killed, but after this will be glorified and exalted; the Transfiguration provides Jesus's inner circle with a "sneak preview" of his resurrected glory. As R. T. France notes, "Jesus's identity as the Son of God, first declared in 3:17 (at his baptism), is now reiterated with the same heavenly authority just at the time when his declaration about his coming suffering and death might have led some to question it."[295]

What's more, Moses and Elijah appear, representing the Law and the Prophets, and converse with Jesus in a sort of salvation-historical powwow. Peter, never a man of inaction,

---

291. See Costi W. Hinn, *God, Greed, and the (Prosperity) Gospel* (Grand Rapids: Zondervan, 2019). See also the movie *American Gospel*, directed by Brandon Kimber 9Transition Studios, 2018), which chronicles the many lies underlying this so-called gospel, which is really no saving message at all but leaves people in error and bondage.
292. Dietrich Bonhoeffer, *The Cost of Discipleship* (New York: Simon & Schuster, 1995), 89. The entire chapter 4, "Discipleship and the Cross," is well worth reading.
293. On the mountain motif in Matthew's Gospel, see Terence L. Donaldson, *Jesus on the Mountain: A Study in Matthean Theology* (Sheffield: Sheffield Academic Press, 1990). On the setting, see Benjamin A. Foreman, "The Geographical Significance of the Transfiguration (Matt 17:1–13; Mark 9:2–13; Luke 9:28–36)," in Beitzel, *Lexham Geographic Commentary*, 298–307. On the "high mountain" of Jesus's transfiguration, see Wilkins, *Matthew*, 106, who leans toward Mount Hermon rather than the traditional site of Mount Tabor.
294. Matthew 17:2; cf. Revelation 1:16: "his face was like the sun."
295. France, *Gospel of Matthew*, 642.

proposes to make tents for each of them, but his proposal is at once overshadowed by God's voice from heaven declaring, as earlier at Jesus's baptism, "This is my beloved Son, with whom I am well pleased."[296] The disciples are terrified, but Jesus tells them not to fear, and when they look up, Moses and Elijah are gone! The sight of Elijah later triggers in the minds of the disciples the question as to when Elijah would come. Jesus instructs them that he had already come in the form of John the Baptist.[297]

Jesus's transfiguration is another high point (literally!) in the narrative, in some ways even topping the climax of Peter's confession of Jesus as the Christ, the Son of the living God, at Caesarea Philippi. The event left an indelible mark in the mind of Peter, who refers to it in his second letter over thirty years later.[298] In language and imagery similar to the account of Moses coming down from Mount Sinai after meeting with God in the book of Exodus, the transfiguration shows Jesus as the greater Moses, the Savior and Deliverer of God's people.[299] Moses couldn't see the glory of God on the mountain and live; Jesus, on the other hand, reflects the very glory of God. He is the promised Messiah, the Son of God, who has come to save and redeem his people so they can enter God's kingdom.

Back Down in the Valley: Mountain-Moving Faith, Paying the Temple Tax (17:14–27)

On their way down the mountain, Jesus instructs the three disciples not to tell anyone of the vision they've just seen until after his resurrection from the dead. He also reiterates that his path to glory will include rejection and suffering.[300] When they reach the foot of the mountain, they find a crowd waiting for them, and a man approaches Jesus, pleading with him to have mercy on his son who is demon-possessed and suffers from epilepsy. Apparently, while Jesus was on the mountain, the disciples had tried to cast out the demon but were unsuccessful because of their lack of faith.[301] At once, Jesus expels the demon and tells his disciples that all they need is faith as small as a mustard seed, which reminds the reader of Jesus's earlier parable of the mustard seed.[302]

At this, Jesus predicts for the second time that he'll be killed and raised on the third day, which again greatly distresses the disciples. The narrative portion concludes with the interesting, even intriguing, account of Jesus having a private conversation with

296. Matthew 17:5; cf. 3:17.
297. Matthew 11:13–14.
298. 2 Peter 1:16–18.
299. See Exodus 34:29–35 and the discussion of Matthew's portrait of Jesus at the end of this chapter.
300. Matthew 17:9.
301. Matthew 17:14–21.
302. Matthew 17:20; cf. 13:31–32.

Peter about paying the temple tax (a topic that would have been of special interest to Matthew, a tax collector). Even though, Jesus points out, they should have been exempt from paying it, he tells Peter in a sort of off-handed, aw-shucks way to cast his fishing line into the lake and he would find a shekel in the mouth of the first fish he'd catch. "Take that," Jesus says, "and give it to them for me and for yourself."[303] Amazing!

RECAP

A lot has happened since Jesus last instructed his followers with a series of kingdom parables in chapter 13. Jesus has been rejected in his hometown of Nazareth; John the Baptist has been beheaded (a flashback). Jesus has publicly fed a multitude of five thousand and privately walked on water in front of his disciples, who worshiped him and confessed him to be the Son of God. Despite his many miraculous healings, his opponents relentlessly press charges against him, claiming that he violated the tradition of the elders. Jesus, however, retorts that it was in fact they who broke the Word of God such as when they devised clever schemes to circumvent the commandment to honor their parents. By contrast, a Canaanite in the northern region exhibits remarkable faith, and Jesus heals her daughter, not to mention many others. A second time, Jesus feeds a multitude; this time he feeds four thousand in Gentile territory.

Again, his opponents press him for a sign, which he refuses. Even his disciples fail to cue in when he warns them against the "leaven" of the Pharisees and Sadducees. Yet the breakthrough comes when Peter acknowledges Jesus as "the Messiah, the Son of the living God" (even though Peter doesn't understand that Jesus must be crucified). The floodgates are now opened, and Jesus speaks freely of his impending suffering and instructs his followers that they, too, must take up their cross and follow him. Shortly thereafter, Jesus's inner circle of three sees Jesus in all his transfigured glory as he will be in his kingdom. Upon his return, Jesus heals a demon-possessed man, challenging his spiritually impotent disciples to have "faith the size of a mustard seed." Jesus's second passion prediction is followed by an astonishing miracle when Jesus tells Peter to catch a fish with a coin in its mouth so he and Peter can pay the temple tax.

303. Matthew 17:24–27. The tax was a half-shekel per person, so one shekel would have paid the tax for two people.

DISCOURSE #4: STORIES ABOUT GOD'S KINGDOM (18:1–35)

Relationships in the Community (18:1–14)

Discipline and Forgiveness (18:15–35)

DISCOURSE #4: STORIES ABOUT GOD'S KINGDOM (18:1–35)

Thus far, Matthew has showcased three major discourses of Jesus: the Sermon on the Mount (chaps. 5–7), the commissioning of the Twelve (chap. 10), and parables of the kingdom (chap. 13). Now he intersperses into the narrative portion of his Gospel yet another discourse of Jesus (Discourse #4), containing additional parables through which Jesus once again instructs his followers about the values and priorities in God's kingdom. In these realistic, true-to-life stories, Jesus paints a composite picture of what life and relationships in the messianic community, the kingdom of God, will look like. Grant Osborne outlines the fourth major discourse in Matthew's Gospel as follows:[304]

- I. Relationships in the Community (18:1–14)
  - A. The Greatest in the Kingdom (18:1–4)
  - B. Warning against Causing Others to Sin (18:5–9)
  - C. The Problem of Wandering Sheep (18:10–14)
- II. Discipline and Forgiveness (18:15–35)
  - A. Discipline and Reconciliation (18:15–20)
  - B. The Absolute Need for Forgiveness (18:21–35)

Relationships in the Community (18:1–14)

The discourse begins with a question posed by Jesus's disciples, "Who is the greatest in the kingdom of heaven?"[305] One wonders why they asked that question. Were they aspiring to spiritual greatness? Or were they after status, power, and position, trying to elbow their way to the top? The answer is probably the latter; yet Jesus at once discerns their underlying motivation. In response, teaching them an object lesson, he calls a child to himself, places him in their midst, and tells his followers that if they want to enter God's kingdom, they

304. Osborne, *Matthew*, 666–98.
305. Matthew 18:1.

must become like this little child.[306] Most likely, the disciples were at a loss as to what Jesus meant. Become like a little child? This hardly was what they had in mind; it certainly wasn't the answer they expected. Of course, this was not lost on Jesus. He deliberately tried to jolt them into the realization that success in his kingdom was achieved by means that were vastly different from climbing the ladder of success in the world. According to Jesus, his followers must forsake all worldly status and take the stance of a powerless, unpretentious child.

So, are you a young seminarian who wants to pastor a church one day? Perhaps you're like the young man with whom I talked several years ago. I asked him, "So what position are you looking for when you get out of seminary?" Without a moment's hesitation he said, "Senior pastor." When I gently probed, "What about associate? Would you consider taking an associate position?" he said, "No. I want to be a senior pastor." What struck me as odd in his case was not only that he was set on being a senior rather than associate pastor but that the young man was only twenty-five years old! In another instance, I saw the curriculum vitae of an older pastor who listed in great detail how many baptisms he had performed in churches he had pastored previously, and even the numerical and percentage growth he oversaw in pastoring previous congregations. I also talked to a deacon recently who told me he wanted to teach an equipping class because this was expected of a person aspiring to be an elder. In all these cases, it occurred to me that there may have been a career mindset present in these individuals that was at odds with Jesus's teaching on greatness in the kingdom (though it is, of course, hard to judge motives).

Not only should Jesus's followers be willing to humble themselves and become like little children themselves; they should also be willing to receive other "little ones"—those of little or no worldly status—in his name and avoid leading any of them astray.[307] They should treat the grave danger of sin with utmost fervency, whatever it takes, as "it is better for you to enter life crippled or lame than with two hands or two feet to be thrown into eternal fire."[308] This reiterates Jesus's earlier warning, "If your right eye causes you to sin, tear it out and throw it away. For it is better that you lose one of your members than that your whole body be thrown into hell. And if your right hand causes you to sin, cut it off and throw it away. For it is better that you lose one of your members than that your whole body go into hell."[309] Sin kills! Sin keeps us in bondage, breaks our relationship with God and others, and makes us miserable in the end. Don't believe Satan's lies that sin is pleasurable and alluring—even fun. It *always* leads to misery. Truly, we are our own worst enemy.

306. Jesus builds on the theme of "little ones" in the remainder of the first half of the discourse "in a way which clearly goes beyond literal children to include fellow-members of the disciple community in their insignificance and vulnerability" (see Matthew 18:2–5, 6, 10, 14; France, *Gospel of Matthew*, 674).
307. Matthew 18:4–6.
308. Matthew 18:7–9.
309. Matthew 5:29–30.

Jesus continues to impress the precious value of even a single person—no matter how lowly—on his followers by telling them the parable of the lost sheep. First, he asserts that "their angels always see the face of my Father who is in heaven." Also, just like a man who has a hundred sheep goes after his one lost sheep because every sheep is precious to him, so God doesn't want even one precious sheep of his to perish.[310] This is a moving illustration of the value God places on every human life, not only in terms of physical life, but even more in terms of people's spiritual destiny. Elsewhere in the New Testament, Jude compares evangelism to snatching a person out of a burning house![311] O that I would sense the same degree of urgency when encountering a person who doesn't know, love, and follow Christ! In addition, Jesus's parable may also serve to illustrate God's sovereign will to preserve his disciples, even those who may temporarily wander away from him.[312]

Discipline and Forgiveness (18:15–35)

In the same vein, Jesus proceeds to outline a process of confronting a straying brother with the purpose of restoring that brother to the fellowship of believers. This shows that sin must be taken seriously not only by individuals but also by the believing community as a whole. This process looks as follows:

- *Step 1: Private Confrontation.* Go and confront the sinning person by yourself.
    - If he listens, he is restored to fellowship.
- *Step 2: More Formal Confrontation.* If he doesn't listen, take one or two others along so as to establish a given charge before two or three witnesses.
    - If he listens, he is restored to fellowship (implied).
- *Step 3: Public Announcement.* If he still doesn't listen, bring the matter to the church as a whole.
    - If he listens, he is restored to fellowship (implied).
- *Step 4: Church Discipline.* If he still doesn't listen, put him out of the fellowship.[313]

In this way, the community of believers holds fellow believers accountable, helping true fellow believers face up to their sin and encouraging them to repent, while exposing those who really aren't believers at all and removing them from the church. Thus, only those who are genuine believers will be members of the community, and those who aren't will be purged—upholding the biblical principle of regenerate membership. In this process, Jesus

310. Matthew 18:10–14.
311. Jude 23.
312. See Köstenberger, Kellum, and Quarles, *The Cradle, the Cross, and the Crown*, 252–53.
313. Matthew 18:15–17.

awards genuine authority to the leadership of the church—what they bind on earth will be bound in heaven, and what they loose on earth will be loosed in heaven—reiterating what he told Peter earlier when informing him that he would give him the keys to the kingdom of heaven.[314] Not only does Jesus affirm church leaders in their authority; he also promises them his spiritual presence throughout the process: "For where two or three are gathered in my name, there am I among them."[315] After his resurrection, Jesus will promise his followers his continuing spiritual presence as they go and make disciples of all nations.[316]

At the outset of the fourth major discourse of Jesus in Matthew's Gospel, the disciples asked Jesus the question, "Who is the greatest in the kingdom of heaven?" Jesus responded by affirming their need for humility and stipulated a process of accountability for those in the community of believers who needed to be confronted and repent of their sin. Now, Peter asks a second question: "How often do I need to forgive a person who sins against me?" Answering his own question, Peter asks, "Seven times?" Presumably, Peter thought forgiving a person seven times was exceedingly generous. Yet, in response, Jesus affirms that the correct answer to Peter's question is "Seventy-seven times" or even "Seventy times seven"—that is, an infinite number of times! There is no limit to forgiveness!

To illustrate this point, Jesus tells the parable of the unforgiving servant.[317] The main point is that Jesus's followers should extend forgiveness to the same extent to which they themselves have received forgiveness from God. Since God's grace, by definition, has no limits, neither should our forgiveness. By contrast, those who don't forgive others as God has forgiven them will be objects of God's wrath for the double standard they've applied—receiving God's unlimited forgiveness yet putting limits on their own.

Forgiving others who have deeply hurt us is hard. It hurts when other people slander us, deceive us, or wrong us in a variety of ways. But no one ever said forgiveness was easy. It cost God the life of his one and only Son! Nevertheless, we're called to forgive other people because we ourselves are forgiven people. Let's never forget that. We're the recipients of God's precious grace; as a result, we have the privilege to extend grace to others—those who don't deserve it! But neither do we.[318] As C. S. Lewis put it, "To be a Christian means to forgive the inexcusable because God has forgiven the inexcusable in you."[319]

---

314. Matthew 18:18; cf. 16:19.
315. Matthew 18:18–20.
316. Matthew 28:20.
317. Matthew 18:21–35.
318. Some may ask, "Should I forgive someone who sinned against me but who has not repented of his or her sin?" I believe the answer is yes, even though forgiveness will not be efficacious on the part of the person who has wronged another but has yet to repent of his or her sin.
319. C. S. Lewis, "On Forgiveness," in *The Weight of Glory: And Other Addresses* (New York: HarperCollins, 2001), 182. See his reflection on pp. 181–83.

JESUS'S WORK IN JUDEA AND HIS DEATH, BURIAL, AND RESURRECTION (19:1–28:20)

Jesus's Work in Judea and Jerusalem (19:1–23:39)

When Is Divorce Legitimate? (19:1–12)

The Kingdom of Heaven and Little Children (19:13–15)

A Wealthy Young Man and the Requirements for Discipleship (19:16–30)

JESUS'S WORK IN JUDEA AND HIS DEATH, BURIAL, AND RESURRECTION (19:1–28:20)

At the beginning of Jesus's ministry, I briefly discussed the geography of Galilee. There, we saw that Jesus started out his ministry in the Galilean north as an outsider, opposite the Jewish religious establishment based in Judea's capital, Jerusalem. Now, we see Jesus travel toward Jerusalem, in an ominous sign that his earthly ministry is about to end. In keeping with scriptural prediction, he must be rejected by the Jewish authorities and be killed—not for his own sins but for those of the people.

As you read through the following chapters, you'll want to familiarize yourself with the geography of Judea. This was the province in the south that in Old Testament times was distinct from the ten provinces in the north (called Israel) that were taken into Assyrian exile in approximately 722 BC. Judea, for its part, succumbed to the Babylonians and was taken into exile in three stages starting in 605 BC. Jesus's outsider status is underscored by the fact that when he visited Jerusalem, he typically spent the night outside the city in nearby Bethany.

In addition, you'll want to familiarize yourself with the layout of the city of Jerusalem. This includes the location of the temple and the area surrounding it; Golgotha, the place where Jesus died; the garden of Gethsemane, where Jesus prayed the night before his arrest, trials, and crucifixion; the pools of Siloam and Bethesda; and the locations of the Hinnom and Kidron Valleys and of the Mount of Olives, where Jesus taught his disciples about the immediate and more distant future, including the temple's destruction and his return.

Jesus's Work in Judea and Jerusalem (19:1–23:39)

When Is Divorce Legitimate? (19:1–12)

Again, Matthew transitions from a discourse to a narrative portion by way of the phrase "Now when Jesus had finished these sayings." Significantly, after four cycles of ministry in Galilee from the inception of his ministry until now, Jesus now leaves Galilee and enters "the region of Judea beyond the Jordan" to commence his journey to Jerusalem, the capital of Judea, to fulfill his mission to Israel there. Large crowds continue to follow him, and he continues to heal those who come to him.[320] Jesus's popularity with the crowds again stands in marked contrast to the opposition of Jesus's nemeses, the Pharisees, who test him with another trick question: "Is it lawful to divorce one's wife for any cause?"[321] Notice that Matthew, as his Gospel is written to Jews, regularly includes Jesus's interchanges with the Jewish religious establishment on a variety of disputed matters. In this he differs from Mark, whose Gospel is primarily addressed to (Roman) Gentiles, who would have had less interest in technical matters pertaining to the Jewish interpretation of the Hebrew Scriptures.[322]

The present issue is a case in point. As we learn from a Jewish compilation of rabbinic teachings called the Mishnah, dating from around AD 200, first-century Jews held a range of views on the matter of divorce. On the one side was the conservative rabbinic school of Shammai, who interpreted the relevant stipulation in the law of Moses that a man may divorce a woman only for matters of "some indecency in her" in terms of sexual immorality—that is, adultery.[323] On the other side was the liberal school of Hillel, who interpreted the same stipulation more broadly in terms of a woman doing "anything that was displeasing to her husband." When asking "Is it lawful to divorce one's wife *for any cause*," therefore, the Pharisees were asking Jesus to align himself with one of the current rabbinic schools. Was he siding with the conservative school of Shammai or the liberal school of Hillel (whom they had quoted)? Either way, he was going to antagonize the other side.

In his response, Jesus evades the trap in an unexpected manner. Rather than merely providing his own interpretation of the disputed phrase in the book of Deuteronomy, Jesus takes his listeners back to the very beginning, to God's original plan for marriage:

---

320. Matthew 19:1–2.

321. Matthew 19:3–12. See the discussion of this passage in Andreas J. Köstenberger with David W. Jones, *God, Marriage, and Family: Rebuilding the Biblical Foundation*, 2nd ed. (Wheaton, IL: Crossway, 2010), 223–32, 275–85.

322. Note, however, that Mark does include several of Jesus's rabbinic disputes with the Pharisees and scribes, including the present one (albeit in much less detail).

323. See Deuteronomy 24:1.

"Have you not read that he who created them from the beginning made them male and female?" He continues that it was also God who said in the Scriptures, "Therefore a man shall leave his father and his mother and hold fast to his wife, and the two shall become one flesh." The obvious conclusion was this: "So they are no longer two but one flesh. What therefore God has joined together, let not man separate."[324] In other words, God's original plan was for marriage to be for life. In this way, Jesus took a position that was even stricter than the conservative position of Shammai.

Not taking no for an answer, however, the Pharisees ask the obvious follow-up question, "Then why did Moses command one to give a certificate of divorce?" to which Jesus masterfully retorted: this was merely a concession to human hard-heartedness and never meant to replace God's original design for marriage.[325] Jesus was here not to accommodate a lower standard but to reiterate God's original purpose. Along the way, he did, however, uphold the interpretation of the phrase in Deuteronomy as referring to sexual immorality (Greek *porneia*): "And I say to you: whoever divorces his wife, *except for sexual immorality*, and marries another, commits adultery."[326] Not that husbands were commanded to divorce their wives in case of adultery, but they were permitted to do so as a concession (note that in Old Testament times adultery was considered to sever the marriage covenant and was punishable by stoning of the guilty party).[327]

Now Jesus's own disciples—no longer the Pharisees—follow up by saying, "If such is the case of a man with his wife, it is better not to marry."[328] In other words, "Jesus, your standard is too high! Remaining with one's wife for life is an unattainable ideal!" This shows how common divorce was in Jesus's day and how even devout Jews (apparently including even Jesus's own disciples) had accommodated themselves to human sinfulness in this regard. But Jesus doesn't back down. All he is willing to say is that there are some who have the gift of celibacy (i.e., of remaining unmarried); if anyone has that gift, he should refrain from marrying in the first place! Again, Jesus leaves both the Pharisees and even his own disciples gasping for air at the loftiness of his ethical teaching and spiritual vision.

You may ask, why did Matthew even include this interchange in a Gospel that is designed to show that Jesus is the Messiah in keeping with Jewish prophetic expectations? Great question! A Gospel that narrowly focuses on the demonstration of Jesus's messianic identity may be expected to accentuate primarily Jesus's healing ministry and working of other miracles. Matthew does that, and in overwhelming number, but

---

324. Matthew 19:4–6; cf. Genesis 1:27, 2:24.
325. Matthew 19:7–8.
326. Matthew 19:9.
327. Cf. Leviticus 20:10.
328. Matthew 19:10.

he also shows Jesus's authority as a Teacher in the way he interprets the Scriptures in a manner far superior to the leading exegetes and scholars of the day.

In this vein, the continued confrontations between Jesus and the Pharisees on matters of interpretation of the Scriptures serve to illustrate that Jesus is the final and authoritative interpreter of God's law.[329] Thus, Jesus's teaching authority is part of his messianic authority. Consequently, the risen Jesus commands his followers to go and make disciples of all nations, baptizing them and "teaching them to observe all that I have commanded you."[330] Similarly, there may be those today who tell the church to focus primarily on works of the kingdom while deemphasizing instruction in the Scriptures. Matthew's Gospel shows that such a unilateral focus is misguided; Jesus's followers must be thoroughly conversant with the Scriptures and teach others to be the same. The Great Commission entails teaching people to observe all that Jesus commanded! More on that later.

The Kingdom of Heaven and Little Children (19:13–15)

Following this latest interchange, people bring children to Jesus so that he can lay hands on them and pray for them. The disciples, who already have forgotten what Jesus just recently told them about citizens of God's kingdom becoming like children, rebuke those who brought them.[331] In turn, Jesus pointedly rebukes them, reaffirming that the kingdom of heaven belongs to children such as these.

A Wealthy Young Man and the Requirements for Discipleship (19:16–30)

Next, a man approaches Jesus, asking, "Teacher, what good deed must I do to have eternal life?"[332] In response, Jesus urges him to keep the commandments. The man replies that he has kept them all; what does he still lack? Jesus replies that he should sell his possessions and give to the poor.[333] At this, the young man goes away regretfully, as he cannot part with his wealth.[334] To those who would follow Jesus, he graciously exposes their hearts' attachments to family or material possessions. While it is natural for us to get attached to those things, it's still true that nothing must be more important in our lives than Jesus. We need to trust him in the way we handle all other attachments and submit all our affections to him. If we do, he'll often give those things back to us, but he'll purge our hearts from possessiveness and a desire to control our life's circumstances rather than yielding control to him.

---

329. Cf. Matthew 5:17–20.
330. Matthew 28:20.
331. Cf. Matthew 18:1–4.
332. Matthew 19:16.
333. Matthew 19:17–21; cf. Jesus's earlier teaching that his followers accumulate treasures in heaven, not on earth, in Matthew 6:19–34.
334. Matthew 19:22.

Correspondingly, we need to learn to hold our plans and relationships with an open hand and to allow God access to our entire lives, rather than withholding certain cherished parts of our lives from him.[335] God will respect our choices and won't compel us to relinquish control; this is a decision we must make voluntarily. It is the right choice, even though it may hurt because we have to give up something we love dearly. Jesus asks us to give up things we cherish because he loves us and because he wants nothing to stand between us and God. This is what it means to deny ourselves, take up our cross, and follow him. Jesus knows that it's hard for us to part with material possessions, conceding that "it is easier for a camel to go through the eye of a needle than for a rich person to enter the kingdom of God."[336] Again, as in the case of Jesus's "hard" teaching on divorce, the disciples are aghast: "Then who can be saved?"[337] Jesus responds that what is impossible for people is possible with God. In other words, it takes divine enablement for humans to part with what they treasure most in this world.

Ever the opportunist, Peter pops up: "Look, we've left everything and followed you. What's in it for us, then?" Jesus's answer takes your breath away: "Truly, I say to you, in the new world, when the Son of Man will sit on his glorious throne, you who have followed me will sit on twelve thrones, judging the twelve tribes of Israel. And everyone who has left houses or brothers or sisters or father or mother or children or lands, for my name's sake, will receive a hundredfold and will inherit eternal life." He adds the cautionary note, "But many who are first will be last, and the last first."[338] In other words, the kingdom of God will bring about a dramatic reversal: those with great power and wealth on earth will be shut out, while the powerless and poor will be put in charge.[339]

Taken together, the two accounts of the children and of the wealthy young man provide a poignant picture of the kingdom of God. As Craig Blomberg observes, "The children turn out to be nearer to the kingdom than most have suspected; the rich man demonstrates that he is further away than most would have guessed."[340]

---

335. This is the underlying thesis of the classic booklet by Robert Boyd Munger, *My Heart, Christ's Home* (first published in 1954).
336. Matthew 19:24. John Piper says regarding this passage, "One thing is crystal clear: a camel cannot go through the eye of a needle. It is impossible. And if you have ever heard anyone say that this is a reference to a gate in the wall around Jerusalem which was so small that a camel had to get down low and take the load off its back, there is no such gate and the context will not allow such an interpretation." "How to Get a Camel through a Needle's Eye," Desiring God, April 30, 2000, https://www.desiringgod.org/messages/how-to-get-a-camel-through-a-needles-eye.
337. Matthew 19:25.
338. Matthew 19:27–30.
339. See the Beatitudes at the beginning of Jesus's Sermon on the Mount (Matthew 5:3–12).
340. Blomberg, *Matthew*, 296.

JESUS'S WORK IN JUDEA AND HIS DEATH, BURIAL, AND RESURRECTION (19:1–28:20, CONT.)

Jesus's Work in Judea and Jerusalem (19:1–23:39, cont.)

The Parable of the Workers in the Vineyard (20:1–16)

To illustrate another aspect of God's kingdom, Jesus tells the parable of the workers in the vineyard. In it, a vineyard owner hires various workers at different hours of the day. At the end of the day, he pays everyone the same daily wage regardless of when they were hired. The first ones hired complain that it isn't fair that those who were hired toward the end of the day are paid the same amount as they, but the vineyard owner insists that it is fair: he has paid them the contractual amount. If he chooses to be gracious toward those hired later, that is his prerogative. This is yet another brilliant parable by which Jesus makes the important point that God is sovereign in extending grace to undeserving sinners, and that none of us is in a position to complain that God was "too gracious" to another person.

Of course, in salvation-historical terms, this parable applied uniquely to the Jewish religious leaders who complained about Jesus fraternizing with tax collectors and Gentile "sinners." They couldn't legitimately complain that God gave the same grace he had given to them to these Johnny-come-latelies in the history of salvation. Jesus makes a similar point in the parable of the prodigal son, which is included only in Luke's

Gospel.[341] In the present case, Jesus ends the parable with the statement "So the last will be first, and the first last," which makes clear that Jesus told the parable to illustrate the point he had made about the reversal of fortunes in the kingdom in response to Peter's question at the end of the previous chapter.[342] Again, the sublime wisdom and inherent truth in Jesus's teaching leaves the reader in awe.

Jesus Predicts His Suffering for the Third Time (20:17–19)

As they're headed toward Jerusalem, Jesus takes his disciples aside and for a third time predicts his impending betrayal, crucifixion, and resurrection, specifying that the chief priests and scribes would condemn him (his Jewish trial) and subsequently hand him over to the Gentiles (i.e., Pilate and the Roman soldiers, the Roman trial) to be mocked, flogged, and crucified.[343] This adds drama and suspense, as it heightens the reader's expectation of the events Jesus is predicting with increasing intensity and specificity. It also serves to focus Matthew's account on Jesus's passion, which is at the very heart of the gospel.

An Impudent Request (20:20–28)

Soon thereafter, the mother of James and John (Mrs. Zebedee) approaches Jesus, together with her sons (!), and asks him to grant her sons positions of honor in his kingdom, one on his right and one on his left. When Jesus asks them if they can "drink the cup" he must drink, they confidently yet foolishly assert that they can. The other disciples, for their part, are indignant with James and John, most likely because they didn't think to ask first!

One may conceivably excuse Mrs. Zebedee for her presumption, and perhaps even admire her for her motherly advocacy of her sons, as she may not have been present when Jesus instructed his disciples only recently about true greatness in the kingdom. But how could the *disciples themselves* have forgotten so quickly what Jesus had said in response to their question as to who would be greatest in the kingdom of heaven?[344] What about the object lesson he had taught them by placing a little child in their midst? Similar to the earlier misunderstanding about the "leaven of the Pharisees and Sadducees," Jesus's earlier teaching had failed to make an impression.[345]

Patient teacher that he is, Jesus reiterates that greatness in God's kingdom differs radically from greatness in the world. It is measured not by power or prestige but by service

341. Luke 15:11–32.
342. Cf. Matthew 19:30.
343. Matthew 20:17–19; cf. 16:21; 17:22–23.
344. Matthew 18:1.
345. Matthew 16:5–12.

and humility. In fact, even Jesus himself "came not to be served but to serve, and to give his life as a ransom for many."[346] This shows that Jesus didn't merely take on a stance of servanthood when dying on the cross for our sins; he did so throughout his entire sojourn on earth. In this way, he modeled one of the key characteristics of God's kingdom—humble service of others and treating others as more important than oneself.

Two Blind Men (20:29–34)

Still on their way to Jerusalem, passing through Jericho, Jesus is followed by a great throng of people. When two blind men sitting on the side of the road hear that Jesus is passing by, they yell on top of their lungs, "Lord, have mercy on us, Son of David!" When the people in the crowd tell them to stop bothering Jesus (who, they surmise, has more important things to do than being held up by blind beggars, like going to Jerusalem), they cry all the louder, instinctively sensing that this is their once-in-a-lifetime opportunity to be healed. At this, Jesus stops, engages them in conversation, and, full of compassion, touches their eyes. They recover their sight at once and follow him. This is another example of Jesus's mercy toward sinners. He is not the ruthless, powerful ruler many expected; he is the gentle, humble, and merciful servant of the Lord who is touched by human suffering and headed for Jerusalem to take our suffering upon himself in complete identification with our human predicament and sin.

346. Matthew 20:25–28.

JESUS'S WORK IN JUDEA AND HIS DEATH, BURIAL, AND RESURRECTION (19:1–28:20, CONT.)

Jesus's Work in Judea and Jerusalem (19:1–23:39, cont.)

Jesus's Triumphal Entry into Jerusalem (21:1–11)

The long journey to Jerusalem that the readers of Matthew's Gospel have anticipated virtually from the very beginning has almost come to a climax. Jesus arrives at the village of Bethphage by the Mount of Olives, close to the Holy City. He instructs two of his disciples to go into the village, where, it seems, divine providence has already orchestrated all circumstances, so that they can secure a colt and donkey that are needed for Jesus's triumphal entry into Jerusalem.[347] As Matthew notes, this, too, took place in order to fulfill the prophetic word announcing to Zion (i.e., Jerusalem) that her king would be coming to her, humbly mounted on a donkey.[348]

Everything transpires just as Jesus had predicted, foreshadowing the way in which the entire proceedings surrounding his arrest and crucifixion will unfold in keeping with God's sovereign plan. Jesus enters Jerusalem seated on a donkey in humble royal demeanor in keeping with scriptural prophecy, and the inhabitants of the city hail him

347. Matthew 20:1–3.

348. Matthew 21:4–5, citing Zechariah 9:9.

as the long-awaited Son of David, the Jewish Messiah and King. If it weren't for Jesus's threefold prediction that he would be betrayed and killed, the reader would have to assume that the story has a happy ending: the Messiah comes to the Holy City of Jerusalem, and its inhabitants welcome him with open arms! Unfortunately, appearances are deceiving, and events will soon take a sudden turn for the worse.

Jesus's Cleansing of the Temple (21:12–17)

Having entered Jerusalem, Jesus first heads to the temple.[349] Arriving at the temple grounds—that is, the area surrounding the actual temple building—Jesus finds the place a bustling center of commerce where merchants are making a fast shekel selling sacrificial animals and money changers charge steep exchange rates for converting people's money into the proper (Tyrian) temple currency. This background explains why Jesus engages in the rather unusual and startling action of driving out all sellers and buyers in the temple area and overturns the money changers' tables and pigeon sellers' chairs. Quoting the Old Testament prophets Isaiah and Jeremiah, Jesus objects that the temple was supposed to be a "house of prayer" but those profiteers had made it into a "den of robbers."[350]

Following this rather unpleasant incident at which Jesus acts like a prophet cleansing the house of God, the blind and lame come to him, still in the temple area, to be healed. At this, children cry out, "Hosanna to the Son of David!" The chief priests and scribes are indignant, hinting that Jesus should tell the children to be quiet, which again indicates the Jewish leadership's rising antagonism toward Jesus. As one might expect, Jesus doesn't grant their request but instead quotes an Old Testament psalm with the reproachful introduction, "Have you never read: 'Out of the mouth of infants and nursing babies you have prepared praise'"?[351] This shows that Jesus interprets everything that happens in his earthly messianic mission in light of a matrix of Old Testament predictions. Also, he views not only the prophetic books but also the Law and even the Psalms as prophetic and as pointing forward to his coming.[352] One senses that Jesus's relationship with the Jewish leaders is going from bad to worse, and they must be seething at yet another rebuffed request from Jesus.

Jesus's Withering Indictment of the Fig Tree (21:18–22)

Jesus spends that night in Bethany near the city; remarkably, he never stays overnight in Jerusalem. On his return to the city, Jesus engages in another puzzling activity.

349. See Chris McKinny, "Southern Temple Mount Excavations (Matt 21:1–11; 23:13–39; etc.)," in Beitzel, *Lexham Geographic Commentary*, 442–61.

350. Matthew 21:12–13; cf. Isaiah 56:7; 60:7; Jeremiah 7:11.

351. Matthew 21:16, citing Psalm 8:2.

352. See discussion of Matthew 5:17 above.

Hungry, he wants to grab a fig from a nearby tree but finds the tree has no fruit, only leaves. At once, he curses the barren tree, and it withers instantly. Again, Jesus's action seems strange, even bizarre. It's hard to believe Jesus simply lost his temper! Perhaps it's best to understand the cursing of the fig tree as a form of acted-out parable. In the present case, the tree gave the appearance of fruit—in fact, it is the very purpose of existence for fig trees to bear figs—yet there was none. "The cursing of the fig tree," therefore, "foreshadowed the destruction of Jerusalem, which had failed to produce the fruit of righteousness God expected of it."[353]

The disciples, for their part, marvel at Jesus's power to curse a tree by mere fiat, and the tree immediately complies. Like telling Peter to catch a fish and he'll find a coin in it with which to pay the temple tax for both of them, or predicting the precise circumstances that the disciples will encounter when securing a donkey for Jesus to ride on at his entry into the city, there's an almost eerie feeling about Jesus: Who is this guy? Where does he get his powers? There clearly was something supernatural about him that defied mere human rational explanations. It must have been quite something to be with Jesus! You'd never know what might happen next. In the present case, Jesus uses the fig tree incident to reinforce with his disciples the importance of faith. If they have faith, they'll be able to move spiritual mountains and will receive whatever they ask for in prayer.[354]

Who Do You Think You Are? Jesus's Authority Challenged (21:23–27)

Back in the temple area after having thrown out the merchants and money changers the previous day, Jesus immediately finds himself the center of attention once again. With crowds surrounding them, the chief priests and elders confront Jesus pointedly and ask him what makes him think he has the authority to do these things. Does he think he has authority over what happens in the temple area? That was *their* turf! Jesus discerns that their question is insincere, and nothing but a masked challenge (in other words, they're not really asking who gave him authority to do these things). So, rather than answering their question straightforwardly and telling them that it was *God* who authorized him, Jesus responds with a counter-question (as I said a moment ago, you never know what to expect with Jesus!): Who was the one who authorized John's baptism?

In this, Jesus was cleverly exploiting the fact that most considered John to be a prophet (like Elijah). So, if the chief priests and elders denied that God sent John,

353. Köstenberger, Kellum, and Quarles, *The Cradle, the Cross, and the Crown*, 29.
354. See John A. Beck, "A Lesson on Prayer from the Landscape (Matt 21:18–22)," in Beitzel, *Lexham Geographic Commentary*, 408–13.

they would find themselves contradicting common opinion regarding him. But if they agreed, then on what basis could they deny that Jesus was similarly sent by God, as John was his forerunner? Notice that Jesus here, for argument's sake, lowers the bar and is content to be regarded as a divinely commissioned prophet like John. In the present instance, Jesus blunts the force of their challenge, and the face-off ends in a stalemate. His interrogators reply, "We don't know." Jesus retorts, "Neither will I tell you where I get my authority from." At this, they retreat, humiliated once again. Needless to say, the interchange does nothing to alleviate tensions between Jesus and the religious leaders.

JESUS'S WORK IN JUDEA AND HIS DEATH, BURIAL, AND RESURRECTION (19:1–28:20, CONT.)

Jesus's Work in Judea and Jerusalem (19:1–23:39, cont.)

A Trilogy of Parables: The Two Sons, the Wicked Tenants, and the Wedding Feast (21:28–22:14)

After this latest confrontation with the Jewish authorities, Jesus tells three parables that deal with the leaders' rejection of him. The first, the parable of the two sons, draws a contrast between his own disciples and the Jewish leaders.[355] The first son, like those who submitted to John's baptism, rebelled at first but later chose to submit to his father's authority and did what he asked. The second son, like the Jewish leaders, pledged obedience but in the end failed to obey. Which son carried out his father's instructions? The lesson of the parable was that the tax collectors and prostitutes who showed genuine contrition would enter the kingdom of God ahead of the Jewish leaders who failed to truly repent.[356]

355. Matthew 21:28–32.
356. Matthew 21:32.

In a second parable, the parable of the wicked tenants, Jesus tells of tenant farmers of a vineyard who, having been left in charge, mistreat, abuse, and even kill every servant the master sends to collect fruit at harvest time.[357] The parable culminates with the tenants killing the vineyard owner's very own son. When Jesus asks his listeners what punishment the tenants should receive, they reply that they should be killed, and the vineyard be entrusted to others. At this, Jesus declares that in fact it is *they* who are the wicked tenants! Jesus told the parable as a stern warning to the Jewish leaders that God would punish them by taking the kingdom of God away from them and giving it to "a people producing its fruits."[358] The lesson is similar to that of the cursed fig tree. The parable depicts Israel's abuse of previous prophets and her murderous rejection of God's Son. In keeping with Old Testament prediction, Jesus identifies himself as "the stone that the builders rejected [which] has become the cornerstone."[359] Again, the chief priests and Pharisees are enraged and renew their resolve to kill Jesus.

In a third parable, the parable of the wedding feast, Jesus tells the story of a king giving a joyous wedding celebration for his son.[360] When he sends out his servants to invite people to the wedding, they refuse to attend because they have more important things to do; some even kill the servants. The king destroys them and burns their city and sends his servants out again to summon as many as would come, and there was a large wedding. At the end, the king comes upon a wedding guest without proper attire; he has him bound and cast out. This suggests that those who are invited must come prepared to play by God's rules, unlike the wedding guest who came without proper attire. Often people think they can write their own rules and in the end God will accept them; this parable rejects such presumption. The story closes with Jesus's pithy pronouncement, "For many are called, but few are chosen." This is a telling commentary on the salvation-historical moment at which Jesus and the people find themselves. God has called many, but few have responded; in fact, many have rejected his gracious offer of salvation in his Son. As a result, God will invite others who will be more receptive to God's kind invitation.

Testing Jesus: On Taxes, Marriage in the Resurrection, and the Great Commandment (22:15–40)

Following Jesus's three denunciation parables, the Jewish leaders begin to lay a series of traps for him in search of a justification for killing him. These traps pertain to paying

357. Matthew 21:33–46.
358. Matthew 21:43.
359. Matthew 21:42; cf. Psalm 118:22–23.
360. Matthew 22:1–14.

taxes (always a controversial issue),[361] the nature of marriage in the resurrection,[362] and the greatest commandment in the law.[363] In each case, Jesus masterfully deflects their attacks and demonstrates both his wisdom and the authoritative nature of his teaching.

The first trap consists in the question "Is it lawful to pay taxes to Caesar?" If Jesus were to respond in the affirmative, he would antagonize Jewish zealots who agitated for overthrowing the Roman overlords and engaged in various kinds of civil disobedience. If he were to respond in the negative, the Jewish leaders could rightfully report Jesus to the Romans as a rebel and zealot himself, a traitor who needed to be censored by Rome. Jesus, however, masterfully sidesteps this trap by asking for a common Roman coin, a denarius, and querying whose picture is on that coin. "Caesar's" is the answer. Jesus's reply cuts to the chase: "Therefore render to Caesar the things that are Caesar's, and to God the things that are God's." Once again, Jesus's opponents are silenced.

The second trap involves Sadducees, who denied the future resurrection because they only affirmed the authority of the five books of Moses, which, they claimed, did not explicitly mention the resurrection. In order to make their case, and to ridicule the whole idea, they concoct the hypothetical scenario of a woman having been married seven times. "In the resurrection, therefore," they ask, "of the seven, whose wife will she be?" You can just see their smug facial expressions as they think they have shrewdly posed a dilemma that Jesus cannot resolve. Yet once again Jesus eludes the trap with ease. Pointedly calling God "the God of Abraham, and the God of Isaac, and the God of Jacob"—all featured in the book of Genesis, the first book in the Pentateuch, whose authority the Sadducees recognized—Jesus affirms that God is a God of the living, not the dead. What's more, Jesus intriguingly reveals that in the resurrection people will no longer marry but be like angels. Wow! The Sadducees are nowhere to be seen. They have been "silenced," while the crowds are "astonished."[364]

At this, the Pharisees take their turn. One of them asks Jesus about the greatest commandment in the law. Jesus parries the challenge with no problem. It is to love God with all our heart, soul, and mind, and to love one's neighbor as oneself: "On these two commandments depend all the Law and the Prophets." Test passed again with flying colors!

Now Let Me Ask You a Question: Whose Son Is the Messiah? (22:41–46)

Interestingly, the chapter ends not with a question by Jesus's opponents but with a query of his own. Jesus asks the Pharisees, "What do you think about the Christ?

361. Matthew 22:15–22.
362. Matthew 22:23–33.
363. Matthew 22:34–40.
364. Matthew 22:33–34.

Whose son is he?" They reply, "The son of David." He follows up: "How is it then that David, in the Spirit, calls him Lord . . . ?" At this, he quotes Psalm 110:

> The Lord said to my Lord,
> "Sit at my right hand,
> until I put your enemies under your feet."

"If then David calls him Lord," Jesus asks, "how is he his son?" That's a pretty good question! No one was able to give an answer. The answer, it appears, is that there is a plurality in the Godhead, encompassing both God the Father and God the Son, and that it is God the Father who told God the Son to sit at his right hand. But admitting this would have required the Pharisees to depart from their rigid monotheism, according to which there was only one God. That was, of course, true, but it was also true that this God existed in three persons, what in subsequent theology has been called the Trinity.[365]

We've seen that Jesus was able to answer all his opponents' questions with incredible acuity and wisdom, while they, on the other hand, were completely dumbfounded by both his answers and his counter-questions. In all these ways, Jesus emerges not only as the rightful Messiah but also as the authoritative Teacher who can speak of his "Father in heaven" and of "the kingdom of God" because he knows both God the Father and his kingdom from firsthand experience. This unique identity as Son of God gives Jesus the authority to teach what God's kingdom is like and what God requires from those who would follow him. It also gives him authority to interpret the Hebrew Scriptures in a way that is far superior to the interpretation of the Jewish experts in the law. As a result, Jesus's responses leave the Jewish leaders at a complete loss, so that "from that day [no one dared] to ask him any more questions."[366]

It's truly tragic that many of Jesus's contemporaries never learned that it was hugely arrogant for them to suppose they were smarter than Jesus. But what about us today? How often do we think we're smarter than Jesus? We may not come right out and say it, but if we act in unbelief, or substitute God's solution for an alternate course of action of our own, don't we in effect say we know better than God? Also, those who don't accept God's "foolish" plan of salvation—sending his one and only Son to die for us on a Roman cross—imply, in effect, that they're smarter than God. The brilliant scientist Stephen Hawking wrote in his final book prior to his death, "There is no God. No one

365. For further discussion, see Andreas J. Köstenberger and Scott R. Swain, *Father, Son and Spirit: The Trinity and John's Gospel*, New Studies in Biblical Theology 24 (Downers Grove, IL: InterVarsity Press, 2008), chapter 1.
366. Matthew 22:46.

created the universe and no one directs our fate."[367] Suffering from Lou Gehrig's disease for most of his adult life, Hawking faced some grave trials and adverse circumstances. Sadly, he rejected God and died an atheist.

Woe to You: Scribes and Pharisees, Hypocrites! (23:1–36)

Following the series of challenges from the religious establishment, Pharisees and Sadducees alike, Jesus warns the crowds and the disciples against the Jewish leaders. They sit in Moses's seat, Jesus says, so they're in rightful positions of authority.[368] So, do what they tell you; but realize that they themselves aren't practicing what they're preaching.[369] They lay heavy spiritual burdens on others but themselves don't lift a finger. They "do all their deeds to be seen by others" and "love the place of honor at feasts and the best seats in the synagogues."[370] They enjoy the perks that come with their jobs and are infatuated with their own power—but they've forgotten that they were given their position to serve others' interests, not merely their own! By contrast, Jesus's followers shouldn't elevate anyone to the exalted position of "Teacher" or "Father"—the only Father believers have is God in heaven—but should exhibit a lifestyle of humility: "the greatest among you shall be your servant."[371] This again bears a chilling resemblance to the mentality of leaders today, even some Christian leaders, who are often detached from rank-and-file church members and live a comfortable life themselves while doing little to alleviate the suffering of those they're charged to shepherd.

Next, in a withering series of seven "woes" reminiscent of prophetic parlance in the Old Testament, Jesus scathingly condemns the hypocrisy of the Jewish scribes and Pharisees:[372]

- They shut heaven's door in people's faces, so that not only will they not enter God's kingdom but others won't be able to do so either.
- They spare no efforts to convert people to their sect, so they can make them "twice as much a child of hell" (!) as they are.
- They're blind guides who pervert the biblical teaching on the taking of oaths, using it to their own advantage.

---

367. Stephen Hawking, *Brief Answers to the Big Questions* (New York: Bantam Books, 2018), 38.
368. On "Moses's seat" and other aspects of the setting of the present passage, see Paul H. Wright, "Indicting Hypocrisy with Imagery from the Temple Mount (Matt 23:1–36; Luke 11:37–42)," in Beitzel, *Lexham Geographic Commentary*, 414–30. See also Wilkins, *Matthew*, 140.
369. Matthew 23:1–12.
370. Matthew 23:3–6.
371. Matthew 23:11.
372. Matthew 23:13–39; cf. Isaiah 5:8–24; Amos 5:18–20; Micah 2:1–4; Habakkuk 2:6–20.

- They tithe scrupulously, even minor spices, while neglecting the "weightier matters of the law": justice, mercy, and faithfulness.
- They thinly veil their greed and self-indulgence; they're in dire need of repentance but won't repent.
- They're masters at projecting a certain public image: everything looks great on the outside but terrible on the inside.
- They're guilty of righteous blood and are destined straight for hell; but they'll be held accountable.

Lament over Jerusalem (23:37–39)

Finally, Jesus laments the coming desolation of Jerusalem: "O Jerusalem, Jerusalem, the city that kills the prophets and stones those who are sent to it!" For now, it's goodbye, as the city won't see Jesus again until he comes as the triumphant messianic king, and people will welcome him, saying, "Blessed is he who comes in the name of the Lord."[373] While eerily reminiscent of his triumphal entry into the city at his first coming, the accolades will soon turn into accusations, and the city will turn its back on Jesus. Only at his return will Jesus be welcomed by the city and its inhabitants that previously rejected him. In this way, Jesus casts an end-time vision that transcends his immediate circumstances and encompasses future salvation-historical events at the end of time.

RECAP

We've seen how Jesus moved into Judea and engaged in increasingly heated confrontations with the Jewish religious leaders. Some Pharisees kicked things off by questioning Jesus regarding his views on divorce. The disciples rebuked those who brought children to Jesus, while a young man—the rich young ruler—comes to Jesus but shrinks back from following him because he is too attached to his earthly possessions. Humanly speaking, these were disheartening encounters. Even the parable of the vineyard workers is told by Jesus in response to some apparent criticism. For the third time, Jesus predicts his imminent passion. The mother of James and John asks him for special privileges for her boys; they're overconfident, while the others are indignant. Seems like now there is infighting among Jesus's inner ranks too. Leaving Jericho, Jesus is approached by two blind beggars; moved by compassion, he heals them.

At this, Jesus enters Jerusalem, humbly mounted on a donkey. He proceeds to cleanse the temple, which people had converted from a house of prayer to a den of robbers. He curses the fig tree as an indictment of the Jewish nation that failed to bear spir-

373. Matthew 23:37–39.

itual fruit for the kingdom. After yet another challenge of his authority by the Jewish leaders, Jesus tells a series of three denunciation parables (the parables of the two sons, the vineyard owner, and the wedding feast). This is followed by three "tests" of Jesus: on paying taxes to Caesar, on marriage in the resurrection, and on the greatest commandment. The interchange concludes with Jesus's test of his own: Whose son is the Messiah? Tellingly, they have no answer. The unit concludes with Jesus's pronouncement of seven woes on the Pharisees and his lament over Jerusalem. The stage is set for his end-time discourse and for the narrative of his passion—his crucifixion, burial, and resurrection.

DISCOURSE #5: TEACHING ABOUT THE END TIMES AND GOD'S KINGDOM (24:1–25:46)
The Olivet Discourse (24:1–51)
Jesus's Prophecy and the Disciples' Question (24:1–3)
Possible Signs of the End (24:4–14)
The Abomination of Desolation and Destruction of the City (24:15–22)
Imposters, Cosmic Upheaval, and the Coming of the Son of Man (24:23–31)
The Timing of the Destruction of the Temple and of Jesus's Return (24:32–36)
Conclusion (24:37–51)

DISCOURSE #5: TEACHING ABOUT THE END TIMES AND GOD'S KINGDOM (24:1–25:46)

At this, Matthew presents the fifth and final extended teaching portion of his Gospel, which consists of the Olivet Discourse and a final series of kingdom parables.[374]

374. For a similar outline, see Andreas J. Köstenberger, Alexander E. Stewart, and Apollo Makara, *Jesus and the Future: Understanding What He Taught about the End Times* (Bellingham, WA: Lexham, 2017), 33–84. Notice that I conflate some of the headings in the discussion below.

The Olivet Discourse (24:1–51)

Jesus's Prophecy and the Disciples' Questions (24:1–3)

The discourse is occasioned by a stroll Jesus and his followers are taking on the temple grounds and the disciples' excited remarks about the splendor of the sanctuary.[375] Putting a damper on their enthusiasm, Jesus wastes no time predicting the destruction of the temple, affirming that "there will not be left here one stone upon another that will not be thrown down."[376] As they later sit down on the Mount of Olives halfway back to where they would stay for the night, it is apparent that Jesus's followers are still processing his earlier remark about the temple's destruction. They ask Jesus a two-pronged question: "Tell us, *when* will these things be, and *what* will be the sign of your coming and of the close of the age?"[377] It is in response to this question that Jesus provides his teaching on the end times, the so-called Olivet Discourse found with some variation in all three Synoptic Gospels.[378]

Possible Signs of the End (24:4–14)

Tackling his disciples' two-part question in reverse order, Jesus first addresses the part dealing with signs preceding "these things"—that is, the destruction of the temple (remember, their remarks about the temple triggered the discourse). He starts with a warning against messianic pretenders who will appear and deceive many.[379] There'll be man-made conflicts—both wars and rumors of wars—as well as natural disasters such as famines or earthquakes.

Also, God's people will experience great tribulation and even martyrdom, with the result that many will fall away and betray and hate one another. They'll also witness a proliferation of false prophets and an increase of lawlessness, violence, and crime, and the Christian commitment of many will wane and falter. Yet none of this is the actual sign; all is part of the proclamation of the good news of God's kingdom to all the nations of the world.

Jesus cautions his disciples against being too quick to assume they know when the temple's destruction is at hand. Even when speaking of various portents of its demise,

375. See Todd Bolen, "Magnificent Stones and Wonderful Buildings of the Temple Complex (Matt 24:1–2; Mark 13:1–2; Luke 21:5–6)," in Beitzel, *Lexham Geographic Commentary*, 462–75.

376. Matthew 24:2.

377. Matthew 24:3.

378. On the entire Olivet Discourse, see the detailed discussion in Köstenberger, Stewart, and Makara, *Jesus and the Future*, 31–86.

379. For a list of messianic pretenders in the years AD 30–70, see Köstenberger, Stewart, and Makara, *Jesus and the Future*, 42–44.

such as great wars or natural disasters or major waves of persecution, he makes clear these are not yet the actual signs. Jesus's words to his followers call for Christian faithfulness to persevere in the face of intensifying persecution and wisdom in discerning the signs preceding the temple's demise.

The Abomination of Desolation and Destruction of the City (24:15–22)

The previous section has indicated what would happen prior to the signs of the temple's destruction. Now Jesus reveals the actual sign: the "abomination of desolation spoken of by the prophet Daniel, standing in the holy place," that is, the temple.[380] At this point, the evangelists Matthew and Mark add the parenthetical comment, "let the reader understand."[381] As the book of 1 Maccabees makes clear, the initial fulfillment of Daniel's prophecy was the erection of a "desolating sacrilege on the altar of burnt offering" by the Seleucid (Greek) ruler Antiochus Epiphanes IV in 167 BC. Apparently, Antiochus sacrificed a pig on the altar of the temple in blatant disregard of Jewish sensibilities regarding eating pork in order to provoke and humiliate them. The Maccabean revolt ensued, and miraculously the small band of Judean rebels defeated the Seleucids and ushered in a century of Jewish self-rule (164–163 BC).[382]

The temple was rededicated in 164 BC, which marked the beginning of the Jewish festival of Hanukkah, celebrated also by Jesus and his disciples.[383] Yet Jesus's renewed reference to the "abomination of desolation" indicates that Antiochus's offense didn't exhaust Daniel's prophecy but awaited further fulfillment. Luke makes clear that this fulfillment would take place, at least in part, at the temple's destruction by the Romans in AD 70: "When you see Jerusalem surrounded by armies, then know that its desolation has come near."[384] At that time, Jesus advises his followers to flee Judea and head for the mountains.[385] This would be a time of great tribulation, too much to humanly endure, but for the sake of the elect God would put a limit on the time of the Roman siege of Jerusalem. Later reports indicate the incredible amount of suffering inflicted on its inhabitants by the Romans.[386]

---

380. Matthew 24:15; cf. Daniel 8:13; 9:27; 11:31; 12:11.
381. Matthew 24:15; Mark 13:14.
382. Cf. 1 Maccabees 1:54, 59; Josephus, *Jewish Antiquities* 12.253. For additional ancient references, see Köstenberger, Stewart, and Makara, *Jesus and the Future*, 53–54.
383. Cf. John 10:22.
384. Luke 21:20. At the same time, the events of the year 70 would serve as a foretaste of the even more momentous cluster of events surrounding the return of Christ (the second coming); see the discussion under the next heading (24:23–31) below.
385. Matthew 24:16.
386. See Köstenberger, Stewart, and Makara, *Jesus and the Future*, 58.

Imposters, Cosmic Upheaval, and the Coming of the Son of Man (24:23–31)

The word "then" marks a transition in the discourse. Most likely, Jesus is here moving from the time leading up to the destruction of the temple to the more distant coming of Jesus, the "Son of Man."[387] There will be various imposters, both false messiahs and false prophets. Performing "great signs and wonders," their intention will be "to lead astray, if possible, even the elect."[388] But God's people must not be deceived: "For as the lightning comes from the east and shines as far as the west, so will be the coming of the Son of Man."[389] No one will be able to miss the second coming, because it'll be a highly visible, public event.

The coming of the Son of Man himself will be accompanied by cosmic upheaval, causing the tumbling of sun, moon, and stars. Then the "sign of the Son of Man" will appear in heaven, and "all the tribes of the earth will mourn," as they will "see the Son of Man coming on the clouds of heaven with power and great glory."[390] And the angels will come with great fanfare and gather the elect.

The Timing of the Destruction of the Temple and of Jesus's Return (24:32–36)

Concluding the discourse, Jesus compares the sign of his return to a fig tree when summer approaches and its branches become tender and it puts out its leaves. At this, at least in part, Jesus answers the disciples' question as to "*when* these things will happen": "Truly, I say to you, this generation will not pass away until all these things take place."[391] That is, Jesus's words will come true within one generation! Some of those disciples who heard Jesus say these things would be alive when the temple would be destroyed.

While several of the apostles were martyred prior to the year 70, we know that at least one apostle, John the son of Zebedee, lived to a ripe old age until toward the end of the first century, so he would certainly have been alive during the temple's destruction in the year 70.[392] Jesus adds that while heaven and earth—the world as we know it—will come to an end, his words will certainly come to pass;[393] and no

387. Matthew 24:27.
388. Matthew 24:24.
389. Matthew 24:27.
390. Matthew 24:30.
391. Matthew 24:34. On the phrase "this generation," see Köstenberger, Stewart, and Makara, *Jesus and the Future*, 75–77.
392. In fact, I've argued in several publications that the destruction of the temple constituted an important occasion for John's writing of his Gospel. See, e.g., "The Destruction of the Second Temple and the Composition of the Fourth Gospel," in *Challenging Perspectives on the Gospel of John*, ed. John Lierman, Wissenschaftliche Untersuchungen zum Neuen Testament 2/219 (Tübingen: Mohr Siebeck, 2006), 69–108.
393. Matthew 24:35; cf. 5:18.

one—not the angels, and not even Jesus himself—knows the exact time of his return, only God the Father.[394]

Conclusion (24:37–51)

In conclusion, Jesus explains that the time of his coming will be like the universal flood in Noah's day. When it arrives, it'll be too late to prepare. Therefore, Jesus counsels, "Stay awake, for you do not know on what day your Lord is coming."[395] Also, his return will be like the coming of a thief. No thief in his right mind will announce when he'll break into your house! (Though I've read some news stories where thieves did some pretty dumb things, such as forgetting their cell phones at the scene of the crime.[396]) "Therefore, you also must be ready, for the Son of Man is coming at an hour you do not expect."[397]

Jesus gives yet another illustration of his future return in the parable of the faithful and wicked slaves. The faithful slave is ready for his master's return no matter when it happens. The wicked slave, on the other hand, in view of his master's delay mistreats others and indulges in various kinds of pleasures. Again, Jesus's point remains the same: believers need to be in a constant state of readiness for Jesus's return no matter when it happens.[398] In essence, we should live each day as if Jesus were coming back today.

Jesus's coming will be good news for believers, especially those suffering persecution who eagerly await his return. It'll be terrible news for the unbelieving world, because it means that God's patience will have run out and there will no longer be any opportunity to repent and be saved. What we see in Jesus's instruction on the end times, therefore, is that he uses the near-destruction of the temple to point to the more distant time of his return. In both cases, tribulation would precede the arrival of these events, but God would protect all faithful believers.

394. Matthew 24:36.
395. Matthew 24:42.
396. If you're interested in "dumb thieves" stories, go to the *World* magazine website, https://world.wng.org, and type "Quick Takes" in the search bar. Then, search for "thief," and you will find several examples. Enjoy!
397. Matthew 24:44.
398. Matthew 24:37–51.

DISCOURSE #5: TEACHING ABOUT THE END TIMES AND GOD'S KINGDOM (24:1–25:46, CONT.)

Parables of the Ten Virgins and Talents, and the Final Judgment (25:1–46)

The Parable of the Ten Virgins (25:1–13)

The Parable of the Talents (25:14–30)

The Final Judgment: Separating Sheep from Goats (25:31–46)

DISCOURSE #5: TEACHING ABOUT THE END TIMES AND GOD'S KINGDOM (24:1–25:46, CONT.)

Parables of the Ten Virgins and Talents, and the Final Judgment (25:1–46)

The Parable of the Ten Virgins (25:1–13)

Seamlessly, the Gospel continues with additional parables related to the topic of Jesus's return at the end of time. Jesus has just spoken of the faithful and wise servant who is ready for his master's return even if it should be delayed. He now tells the parable of the ten virgins, five of whom were foolish and five were wise. Again, the scenario involves a delay, this time on the part of the bridegroom. The wise virgins were prepared and ready, while the foolish ones were not and ended up being caught off guard by the bridegroom's eventual return. The foolish virgins asked the wise ones to share their oil with them, but the wise ones refused, saying there wouldn't be enough for all of them. Then the wise virgins joined in the wedding celebrations, while the foolish virgins were shut out. Again, this is a picture of Christ's return and the final judgment. Jesus's followers should make every effort to stay in a constant state of readiness even if there is an apparent delay in Christ's return. In Jesus's words, "Watch therefore, for you know neither the day nor the hour," a statement that ties in directly with Jesus's closing statement of the Olivet Discourse.[399]

399. Matthew 25:13; cf. 24:36.

The Parable of the Talents (25:14–30)

Jesus continues by telling the parable of the talents, which features a man leaving for a trip and entrusting his servants with various amounts of talents (a unit of currency, not a "talent" as we would use the word today). One servant received five talents, another two, and yet another one talent. Then the man left on his journey. Upon his return ("after a long time"), the man settled accounts with his servants. What had they done with the stewardship they received? The first had made five more talents, the second an additional two. Both were thus commended by their master for their faithfulness: "Well done, good and faithful servant." But when the master came to the third and final servant, the servant said he was afraid of his master and consequently had buried the talent in the ground. Then he simply gave the money back to the master. At this, the master chastised the servant and told him he should have invested the money. And he ordered the talent to be given to the first servant, who already had ten talents. The lesson is this: "For to everyone who has will more be given, and he will have an abundance. But from the one who has not, even what he has will be taken away."[400] Jesus told this parable to impress on his followers the importance of faithful and wise stewardship of all that the Lord has given them, a stewardship that is not limited to money but includes all our earthly possessions.

The Final Judgment: Separating Sheep from Goats (25:31–46)

At this, Jesus projects the breathtaking vision of his return and the final judgment that will ensue at that time. Jesus will come back in all his glory and with myriads of angels, and he will sit on his throne and gather all nations as a shepherd separating the sheep from the goats. What is striking is Jesus's method of judgment. Rather than focus on words, Jesus focuses on actions. Not only this, he identifies with those in the world who are hungry and thirsty, lack clothing, or suffer in prison. On one side are those who fed the hungry, clothed the naked, and visited those in prison. On the other side are those who failed to do so. When the latter protest, "When did we see you hungry or thirsty or a stranger or naked or sick or in prison, and did not minister to you?" Jesus will say to them, "Truly, I say to you, as you did not do it to one of the least of these, you did not do it to me."[401]

One theme that several of Jesus's end-time parables have in common is that those who are being judged or who are caught unprepared make various kinds of excuses. The servant who had received the one talent blamed his inaction on the perceived harshness of his master, but to no avail. Likewise, the "goats" on Jesus's left in the present parable excuse their inaction by saying they never saw Jesus hungry, thirsty, naked, or in prison, so they did nothing to help the poor. Again, however, their excuse avails to nothing, and

400. Matthew 25:29.
401. Matthew 25:44–45.

they are judged. As in the conclusion to the Sermon on the Mount, Jesus is adamant that our Christian faith be translated into concrete action. In this way, proclaiming and believing the gospel and doing good works are inextricably wedded together. Jesus's half-brother James would later continue to make this point in his letter written most likely only about a decade after Jesus's earthly ministry.[402]

MESSIAH IN MATTHEW

Matthew's Gospel presents Jesus as Israel's Messiah promised in their own Scriptures. Virtually every significant event of Jesus's life is shown to fulfill Scripture.[403] By connecting the events of Jesus's life to Scripture, Matthew demonstrates that "God's present activity in Jesus fulfills Israel's story and Scriptures."[404] Matthew's use of fulfillment quotations ("This took place to fulfill . . .") also emphasizes "the sovereign control of history by God, who governs all of human history to fulfill his will."[405]

For Matthew, the life of Jesus fulfills or completes all the promises of God found in the Scriptures.[406] As R. T. France observes, "Among the gospels Matthew stands out for his sustained and creative presentation of this theme of fulfillment in Jesus."[407] The Scriptures in their entirety look forward to a coming Messiah. Matthew skillfully documents that Jesus is the now-revealed Messiah who has come in keeping with this long-held prophetic anticipation.

While Matthew, from the outset of his Gospel, presents Jesus as the promised Messiah, he also makes clear that Jesus's coming was not in line with the messianic expectations held by most Jewish people of his day. Many first-century Jews were looking for a powerful national deliverer who would free them from oppression by the Romans, while Jesus, at his

402. James 1:22–27.
403. See Köstenberger, Kellum, and Quarles, *The Cradle, the Cross, and the Crown*, 34, for a chart of these Old Testament citations.
404. Brown, "Gospel of Matthew," 578.
405. Osborne, *Matthew*, 38. See Matthew 5:17: "Do not think that I have come to abolish the Law or the Prophets; I have not come to abolish them but to fulfill them."
406. In the words of the apostle Paul, "all the promises of God find their Yes in him" (2 Corinthians 1:20).
407. France, *Gospel of Matthew*, 11.

first coming, came to suffer and die as the suffering servant depicted in the book of Isaiah.

Matthew also shows that Jesus repeatedly predicted his own suffering, death, and resurrection.[408] At the same time, he notes that even Jesus's closest followers failed to understand that the Messiah must suffer and die.[409] Against this backdrop, Matthew presents Jesus as the righteous sufferer featured in the Psalms.[410] He came "not to be served but to serve, and to give his life as a ransom for many."[411] In the words of the angel to Joseph, "You shall call his name Jesus, for he will save his people from their sins."[412]

RECAP

By way of brief review, it may be helpful to see what has happened since the end of the previous discourse.

- Jesus leaves Galilee and enters Judea (19:1), where he ministers to children and encounters the rich young ruler.
- On his way to Jerusalem, he again tells his followers that he will be killed and on the third day rise again (19:17–19).
- In Jericho, he heals two blind men (19:29–34).
- From Bethphage and the Mount of Olives, he enters Jerusalem humbly mounted on a donkey (21:1–11).
- He cleanses the Jerusalem temple, stays overnight in Bethany outside the city, and on his return to Jerusalem curses the fig tree (21:12–22).
- He teaches in the temple area and is challenged by the Jewish leaders, whom he denounces in a series of seven withering woes (21:23–23:39).
- Leaving the temple, the disciples draw Jesus's attention to its beauty, triggering the end-time Olivet Discourse, followed by several parables on end-time readiness (chaps. 24–25).

408. Matthew records four such specific predictions: 16:21; 17:22–23; 20:18–19; 26:2.
409. Most poignantly Peter, who, in response to Jesus's first prediction, proclaimed, "Far be it from you, Lord! This shall never happen to you" (Matthew 16:22).
410. See Matthew's quotations of Psalms 22:1, 7–8, 18; 69:21 in Matthew 27:34–35, 39, 43, 46, 48.
411. Matthew 20:28.
412. Matthew 1:21.

All these events have taken place in or near Jerusalem. The action has slowed down significantly. There is an oscillating pattern of Jesus spending the night outside the city and then in the morning returning to the city to teach in the temple area. There, he is challenged by the Jewish leaders and instructs his followers about their need to be ready for his return. What's remarkable is that Jesus hasn't even died and risen yet, and already he is talking to his followers about his return! This shows remarkable faith and vision. Jesus anticipates that the events of his passion will inexorably ensue, in keeping with God's predetermined, sovereign plan, and sets his sights already on what will happen after these events, both in the decades following the ascension (the destruction of the temple in AD 70) and in the more distant future, in his return and final judgment.

JESUS'S DEATH, BURIAL, RESURRECTION, AND THE GREAT COMMISSION (26:1–28:20)
The Plot against Jesus: The Last Supper, His Arrest, and Jewish Trial (26:1–75)
A Hideous Plot (26:1–5)
Anointed for Burial (26:6–13)
The Traitor Makes His Move (26:14–16)
The Last Supper (26:17–29)
Prediction of Peter's Denials (26:30–35)
Praying at Gethsemane (26:36–46)
Betrayed, Arrested, and Abandoned (26:47–56)
Jesus's Jewish Trial before the Sanhedrin (26:57–68)
Peter's Threefold Denial (26:69–75)

JESUS'S DEATH, BURIAL, RESURRECTION, AND THE GREAT COMMISSION (26:1–28:20)

The last of Jesus's five discourses featured in Matthew's Gospel transitions to the concluding passion narrative with the customary phrase "When Jesus had finished all these sayings."

The Plot against Jesus: The Last Supper, Arrest, and Jewish Trial (26:1–75)

A Hideous Plot (26:1–5)

In the Matthean narrative it's now only two days until Passover.[413] Again, Jesus reminds his disciples that he is about to be delivered into the hands of the Jewish authorities in order to be crucified.[414] No one can legitimately say that Jesus was caught unaware or failed to anticipate the events surrounding the crucifixion.[415] To the contrary, he is utterly determined to accomplish God's purpose for his life. Talk about a purpose-driven life![416] If ever there was one, this is it. Not only is Jesus determined to follow through with God's plan; the Jewish leaders, likewise, have their minds made up and are shown merely to wait for the right time to arrest Jesus. But they're afraid that Passover may not be the right time, as Jerusalem is at that time flooded with pilgrims from everywhere.[417]

Anointed for Burial (26:6–13)

After this preamble, the narrative shifts to the house of Simon the leper (not mentioned elsewhere) in the village of Bethany.[418] While Jesus and the others are eating, a woman approaches him with a bottle of very expensive perfume and pours it over Jesus's head. That's definitely an event those who saw it would remember for some time! While Jesus's disciples decry the expensive waste, Jesus tells them that the woman (no doubt without realizing it) has anointed him for burial. This strikes an ominous note at the outset of the proceedings against Jesus.

Almost on parallel tracks, we witness the unfolding of the plot of the Jewish leaders on one hand and the plan of God on the other. In fact, God's plan is sovereignly accomplished *through* the evil designs of Jesus's opponents. As in the case of Joseph the patriarch, what Jesus's enemies have meant for evil, God is working out for good—the salvation of humankind.[419] Jesus affirms that the woman's act of devotion will be proclaimed

413. "Passover" in the Gospels variously refers to Passover week, synonymous with the weeklong Feast of Unleavened Bread, or the actual day of Passover commencing Passover week, when people ate the Passover meal to commemorate Israel's deliverance from Egypt (see, e.g., Matthew 26:1, 17–18; Mark 14:1, 12–16; Luke 22:1, 7–13; cf. Exodus 12:18–20; Leviticus 23:4–14). See Erez Soref, "Passover, Unleavened Bread, Firstfruits," in *A Handbook on the Jewish Roots of the Christian Faith*, eds. Craig A. Evans and David J. Mishkin (Peabody, MA: Hendrickson, 2019), 74–80.

414. Matthew 26:1–2.

415. As was essentially argued by Albert Schweitzer, whose work we have considered extensively in chapter 1 above.

416. I'm alluding here to the bestselling book by Rick Warren, *The Purpose-Driven Life* (Grand Rapids: Zondervan, 2002).

417. Matthew 26:3–5.

418. Matthew 21:17 mentions that Jesus lodged in Bethany previously, perhaps at the same house?

419. Genesis 50:20; cf. Romans 8:28.

"in the whole world . . . in memory of her."[420] This prediction, too, has come true, as the event is included in three of the four Gospels, and whole books have been written on this event and the woman who performed it.[421]

The Traitor Makes His Move (26:14–16)

At this, Judas Iscariot, one of the Twelve, approaches the Jewish leaders and offers to betray Jesus for thirty pieces of silver.[422] The price harks back to a reference in Zechariah, where the prophet receives that same amount and throws it to the potter.[423] According to the book of Exodus, thirty pieces of silver was the price of a slave.[424] It may be an insult that the price for betraying Jesus is nothing more than that paid for a slave; it may also be ironic that Jesus died to set people free from slavery to sin and death. In any case, Judas's willingness to betray Jesus at last will give the authorities a foothold within Jesus's inner circle. This will help them arrest Jesus in an inconspicuous manner, opening the door for them to proceed with Jesus's arrest during Passover week.

The Last Supper (26:17–29)

With Passover approaching, Jesus again instructs his disciples to make the necessary preparations, similar to fetching the donkey at his triumphal entry. Just like at that previous occasion, everything works out exactly as Jesus has predicted.[425] That evening, Jesus celebrates Passover with his disciples. While they're eating, he announces, no doubt with a heavy heart, that one of them—Judas Iscariot—would betray him.[426] After this, he institutes the Lord's Supper by taking first a piece of bread and subsequently a cup, saying, "Take, eat; this is my body," and, "Drink of it, all of you, for this is my blood of the covenant, which is poured out for many for the forgiveness of sins."[427] Jesus would not drink wine again until the end-time celebration depicted in the book of Revelation, the Marriage Supper of the Lamb, in his Father's kingdom.[428]

---

420. Matthew 26:13.
421. Somewhat ironically, the woman has also become an icon of the feminist movement: see Elizabeth Schüssler Fiorenza, *In Memory of Her: A Feminist Theological Reconstruction of Christian Origins* (New York: Crossroad, 1983). See my wife Margaret's critique in *Jesus and the Feminists: Who Do They Say That He Is?* (Wheaton, IL: Crossway, 2008), chapter 8.
422. Matthew 26:14–16.
423. Zechariah 11:12–13.
424. Exodus 21:32; cf. Zechariah 11:13.
425. Matthew 26:17–19.
426. Matthew 26:20–25.
427. Matthew 26:26–29.
428. Revelation 19:6–9.

To this day, we celebrate the Lord's Supper regularly as part of our worship gatherings. We see here how the Jewish Passover served as the foundation on which the Lord's Supper was built. In fact, the last Passover—at least for Jesus and his apostles—was also the first Lord's Supper. The underlying symbolism is highly significant. In the first instance, Passover commemorates the blood of a sacrificial animal that became the means of salvation for believing Israelites on the eve of the exodus. In the second instance, the Lord's Supper is instituted to commemorate the blood of Jesus's sacrifice that became the means of salvation for all who believe, on the eve of the crucifixion. This shows the deep Jewish roots of Christianity.[429] It also shows the all-important advance from one era to the other in that Jesus, in keeping with Old Testament prophecy, established a new covenant with a believing Jewish remnant—the twelve apostles—that, as the New Testament book of Hebrews teaches, rendered the old covenant obsolete.[430]

This is why, now that Jesus has come, died, and risen, all people—including Jews—need to believe that Jesus is the Messiah who brought the final sacrifice for sins on the cross to procure salvation and eternal life. It's inadequate to persist in unbelief or agnosticism with regard to Jesus. In fact, taking an adversarial or even neutral stance toward Jesus is to reject God's gracious gift of his one and only Son and to dismiss the cruel death Jesus endured on behalf of sinners. For this reason, even Jewish people, whether in Matthew's day or ours, need to acknowledge that Jesus is the Messiah and trust him in order to be saved; no longer can they rely on their Jewish heritage and think that just because they are Jews—God's chosen people—they'll be saved regardless of whether they believe in Jesus.

Prediction of Peter's Denials (26:30–35)

At the end of the meal, Jesus and his disciples sing a hymn and head to the Mount of Olives east of the city. There, Jesus invokes Old Testament prophecy predicting that his disciples would all abandon him following his arrest.[431] Peter vehemently protests Jesus's prediction, declaring that "though they all fall away because of you, I will never fall away."[432] In response, Jesus predicts that not only will Peter fall away but he'll deny Jesus three times before the rooster crows at sunrise the next day.

---

429. See Craig A. Evans and David Mishkin, eds., *The Handbook of Jewish Roots of the Christian Faith* (Peabody, MA: Hendrickson, 2019).
430. See chapter 1 on Hebrews in Andreas J. Köstenberger, *Handbook on Hebrews through Revelation* (Grand Rapids: Baker, 2020).
431. Matthew 26:31. See Zechariah 13:7.
432. Matthew 26:33.

Praying at Gethsemane (26:36–46)

After this, Jesus takes his disciples to the garden of Gethsemane.[433] The tension is palpable, and the sense of drama and suspense almost unbearable. Fully aware of what is about to happen, Jesus gathers his inner circle who had been with him at the transfiguration—Peter, James, and John—and asks them to watch and pray with him. Just imagine what it would have been like to be with Jesus during his final hours prior to the crucifixion! Leaving them at a distance, Jesus cries out to the Father, asking if there could be any way for him to escape the cross, yet ultimately pledging submission to the Father's will. Three times he returns to his disciples only to find them sleeping. Sadly, they're unable to stand with him in his darkest hour. Jesus, on the other hand, is victorious in prayer. Just as so many times when Jesus prayed before important occasions, his victory at Gethsemane would pave the victory at Golgotha.

Betrayed, Arrested, and Abandoned (26:47–56)

At last, Judas arrives with an armed mob assembled by the Jewish leaders, at which Jesus declares, "See, the hour is at hand, and the Son of Man is betrayed into the hands of sinners."[434] Approaching Jesus, Judas gives him a kiss of friendship—the infamous "Judas kiss"—identifying him to the mob as the one they should take into custody. The mystery of one among Jesus's inner circle betraying him to the authorities truly makes one shudder. Like the other apostles, Judas has been with Jesus for over three years, having seen countless demonstrations of his messianic authority. And yet, in keeping with God's plan, his heart remained hard and cold and unaffected by the spiritual transformation God intended to take place. In this way, Judas stands forever as a chilling reminder that someone may conform externally to what is expected of a follower of Christ for a period of time yet ultimately reveal that he never truly put his trust in Jesus.

At that very moment, one of Jesus's disciples (Peter) draws his sword and cuts off the ear of the high priest's servant. Jesus rebukes the disciple, explaining that his Father could dispatch an entire host of angels to rescue him if Jesus so desired. Jesus reaffirms that it is God's will that he be arrested and killed in order to fulfill the Scriptures.[435] Once again, this shows Jesus's keen messianic consciousness and awareness that in his life an entire matrix of scriptural predictions are being fulfilled, as Matthew has been diligent to highlight throughout his Gospel. At this, the disciples take flight, and the

---

433. See Aubrey L. Taylor, "In the Garden of Gethsemane: Jesus's Choice to Remain or Run from His Father's Will (Matt 26:36–46; Mark 14:32–42; Luke 22:39–46)," in Beitzel, *Lexham Geographic Commentary*, 476–82.

434. Matthew 26:45–48. On the setting of the arrest and the ensuing events, see Benjamin A. Foreman, "From the Upper Room to the Judgment Seat (Matt 26:47–27:1, 11–26; Mark 14:43–15:15; Luke 22:47–23:25; John 18:2–19:16)," in Beitzel, *Lexham Geographic Commentary*, 483–503.

435. Matthew 26:54–56.

mob takes Jesus to Caiaphas, the high priest, and an assembly of Jewish leaders to stand trial.[436] With these dark spiritual storm clouds gathering on the horizon, the reader wonders: How will it all end? Will Jesus's repeated predictions of his own crucifixion and subsequent resurrection come true?

Jesus's Jewish Trial before the Sanhedrin (26:57–68)

In what follows, Jesus faces two separate yet related sets of interrogation, the first before the Jewish ruling council called the Sanhedrin and the second before Pontius Pilate, the Roman governor. The Jewish trial is cast in all four Gospels as a travesty of justice where numerous legal principles are set aside in order to hasten the "guilty" verdict against Jesus. Thus, the Jewish leaders strenuously look for false witnesses to trump up charges against Jesus. Finally, two individuals come forward, claiming that Jesus promised to destroy the temple and rebuild it in three days.[437] Though their charges are false, Jesus remains silent until the high priest demands that he tell them "if you are the Christ, the Son of God." Quoting two messianic Old Testament passages, Psalm 110:1 and Daniel 7:13, Jesus answers in the affirmative: "You have said so."[438] The high priest promptly charges Jesus with blasphemy; now they have the evidence they need to put Jesus on the cross. The council sentences Jesus to death, and they spit in his face and beat him.

Peter's Threefold Denial (26:69–75)

Adding to the drama, the scene now shifts to Peter sitting in the courtyard, awaiting the results of Jesus's trial before the Jewish leaders. Others there recognize Peter as one of Jesus's followers. At three separate occasions, with increasing exasperation, Peter denies even knowing Jesus. Immediately after the third denial, the rooster crows, signaling the fulfillment of Jesus's prophecy. Peter, for his part, breaks down and dissolves into tears.

---

436. Matthew 26:56–57.
437. Note that this is reminiscent of Jesus's words in John 2:19, though obviously these witnesses totally take Jesus's statement out of context.
438. Matthew 26:63–64.

JESUS'S DEATH, BURIAL, RESURRECTION, AND THE GREAT COMMISSION (26:1–28:20, CONT.)
Jesus's Roman Trial, Crucifixion, and Burial (27:1–66)
Jesus's Roman Trial before Pilate and Judas's Demise (27:1–26)
Making a Mockery of Jesus: The Crucifixion (27:27–56)
Jesus's Burial and the Posting of the Guard (27:57–66)

JESUS'S DEATH, BURIAL, RESURRECTION, AND THE GREAT COMMISSION (26:1–28:20, CONT.)

Jesus's Roman Trial, Crucifixion, and Burial (27:1–66)

Jesus's Roman Trial before Pilate and Judas's Demise (27:1–26)

The next morning, the Jewish leaders take Jesus to Pilate to have him sanction their death sentence.[439] Judas, full of remorse for betraying Jesus, returns the blood money, proclaims Jesus's innocence, and goes and hangs himself.[440] In fulfillment of Old Testament prophecy, the Jewish leaders use the money to purchase a burial plot for foreigners.[441]

When Jesus appears before Pilate, he again remains silent in the face of the Jewish leaders' accusations. The governor, seeing no legitimate reason to put Jesus to death, tries to defuse the situation by appealing to a custom according to which the Roman governor released a prisoner to the people at Passover. The crowd is presented with a fateful choice: "Whom do you want me to release for you: Barabbas [a convicted thief

439. Matthew 27:1–2. On "Pilate, the Governor (A.D. 26–36)," see Wilkins, *Matthew*, 171; Garland, *Mark*, 294–95.
440. Matthew 27:3–5.
441. Matthew 27:6–10. See the discussion at 26:14–16 above. Cf. Zechariah 11:13; Jeremiah 32. Craig Keener (*The Gospel of Matthew: A Socio-Rhetorical Commentary* [Grand Rapids: Eerdmans, 2009], 657) thinks both prophets are in view. Craig L. Blomberg ("Matthew," in *Commentary on the New Testament Use of the Old Testament*, ed. G. K. Beale and D. A. Carson [Grand Rapids: Baker, 2007], 96) sees a typology spanning from both prophets to Matthew.

and murderer] or Jesus who is called Christ?"[442] Incited by the Jewish leaders, the people ask for Barabbas, sealing Jesus's fate. Pilate hypocritically washes his hands in innocence while the Jewish authorities accept full responsibility for Jesus's death, declaring, "His blood be on us and our children!"[443] Travesty of justice, indeed. Pilate releases Barabbas, has Jesus scourged, and delivers him to be crucified.

Making a Mockery of Jesus: The Crucifixion (27:27–56)

Soldiers from Pilate's Roman cohort strip Jesus and ridicule his messianic claims. They put a mock robe on him, place a thorny "crown" on his head, and hand him a reed "scepter."[444] Bowing in fake homage, the soldiers exclaim, "Hail, King of the Jews!" After the series of scourgings and beatings, Jesus is weakened to the point of being unable to carry his own cross to the execution site.[445] The soldiers compel a passerby, a man named Simon from the town of Cyrene, to carry Jesus's cross to Golgotha.[446] Upon their arrival, the soldiers offer Jesus a mixture of wine and gall to dull his senses, but Jesus refuses to drink. They crucify him on a cross between two robbers—graphically depicting Jesus's identification with sinners—and put a sign over his head that reads, "This is Jesus, the King of the Jews."[447] Some even mock Jesus—the "Son of God"—for being impotent to save himself.

Several unusual signs accompany Jesus's death, underscoring its momentous significance. While he hangs on the cross, the sky, as if in solar eclipse, turns black—depicting the darkness of evil—even though it is midday.[448] When Jesus utters a loud cry and gives up his spirit, the heavy curtain separating the Holy of Holies from the rest of the temple—picturing the insurmountable separation between sinful human beings and a holy God—is torn from top to bottom while an earthquake splits rocks and opens tombs in the city.[449] These—literally!—earthshaking miracles convey the vital supernatural reality that, with the substitutionary sacrifice of Jesus, the separation between God and sinners has been removed, the wrath of God has been appeased, and God and sinners have been reconciled. Now believers in Christ can enjoy abundant life, a restored relationship with God and fellow human beings, and numerous other blessings.

---

442. Matthew 27:17.
443. Matthew 27:25.
444. Matthew 27:27–29.
445. See Benjamin A. Foreman, "Locating Jesus's Crucifixion and Burial (Matt 27:32–61; Mark 15:21–47; Luke 23:26–56; John 19:17–42)," in Beitzel, *Lexham Geographic Commentary*, 504–17.
446. On Golgotha, see Wilkins, *Matthew*, 178.
447. Matthew 27:37.
448. Matthew 27:45.
449. Matthew 27:50–53.

If any doubt remains for the reader, the declaration of the Roman centurion and the soldiers overseeing Jesus's crucifixion brings the narrative to a climax: "Truly, this was the Son of God!"[450] This shows that, following Jesus's death, even those closest to the scene—including unbelievers—recognized that this was no ordinary man, nor did Jesus die an ordinary death; he was none other than God's very own Son, suffering not for his own sins but for those of others. In fact, in Mark's Gospel, as we'll see, the Roman centurion's confession forms the climax of the entire narrative, as Mark most likely wrote his Gospel to a predominantly Roman audience.[451]

Jesus's Burial and the Posting of the Guard (27:57–66)

Following Jesus's death, his body is buried in a tomb owned by Joseph of Arimathea, a Sanhedrin member and secret disciple of Jesus, and the tomb is sealed with a large stone. Mary Magdalene, along with several other women, observes the burial. The next day, at the request of the Jewish leaders, Pilate orders a cohort of Roman soldiers to guard the tomb in order to prevent Jesus's disciples from stealing the body and alleging that Jesus rose from the dead.

RECAP

The narrative of Jesus's arrest, trials, and crucifixion is very familiar to us. Perhaps less familiar is reading the passion narrative in the context of an entire Gospel, such as that of Matthew. But this is what we've just done! With the disciples, we can feel the jarring disappointment of seeing the one we've come to love and cherish—the one who has spent three and a half years healing, teaching, and doing good—executed in brutal fashion on a Roman cross. How could this happen? How could it possibly come to this? On a human level, it's hard to explain how such an amazing individual who did nothing but good for countless others could meet such a cruel end. It just isn't right! In fact, what happened to Jesus is absolutely terrible. It's enough to lose faith in any justice, fairness, or goodness in this world. If someone like Jesus could end up on the cross, then nothing in this world still makes sense. It's all wrong.

Or is it? Because, as we'll see shortly, the crucifixion is *not the end*. If the crucifixion had been all that happened, we'd still be in utter disbelief and misery. But at this juncture in the narrative, we must keep faith. We must keep believing that there is a God—a God who is infinitely more concerned about justice, fairness, and goodness than we are. And yet, on a higher plane, this God is also a holy God who must address the problem

---

450. Matthew 27:54.
451. Cf. Mark 15:39.

of sin—humanity's rebellion against its Creator, resulting in every person being born with a fallen, sinful nature—in a way that really deals with sin rather than sweeping it under the rug.

In this way, we can understand that, on a higher, spiritual plane, what happened to Jesus was necessary for our salvation. Jesus volunteered, so to speak, to pay the penalty for our sin by dying on the cross the death we deserved—the God-man, the God-sent Messiah, giving his life for us. When you look at it this way, what at first appears to be a dismal tale of murder and hate, of treachery and misery, turns into a beautiful story of love and sacrifice, of glory and redemption. But we're getting ahead of ourselves. There's one more chapter in Matthew's Gospel. So let's read the rest of the story!

JESUS'S DEATH, BURIAL, RESURRECTION, AND THE GREAT COMMISSION (26:1–28:20, CONT.)
Jesus's Resurrection Appearances and the Great Commission (28:1–20)
The Empty Tomb and Appearances of the Risen Jesus (28:1–15)
The Great Commission to Disciple the Nations (28:16–20)

JESUS'S DEATH, BURIAL, RESURRECTION, AND THE GREAT COMMISSION (26:1–28:20, CONT.)

Jesus's Resurrection Appearances and the Great Commission (28:1–20)

The Empty Tomb and Appearances of the Risen Jesus (28:1–15)

At dawn on the first day of the week—Sunday—the women return to the tomb. By inclusive reckoning (i.e., counting both the first and the last day, Friday as well as Sunday), it has now been three days since Jesus was crucified. As the women arrive, a great earthquake shakes the ground and an angel appears and rolls the stone away from the tomb. Fear grips the guards as they stand in motionless terror before the angel who is dazzling in appearance.

The angel declares to the women, "Do not be afraid, for I know that you seek Jesus who was crucified. He is not here, for he has risen."[452] He sends them to tell the disciples what happened and to go to Galilee, where Jesus will meet them. As they run to do so, they encounter the risen Jesus. They fall to the ground and worship him.

Meanwhile, some of the soldiers assigned to guard Jesus's tomb report back to the chief priests what has happened.[453] The Jewish leaders gather and decide to bribe the guards, urging them to give the false report that Jesus's disciples stole his body while they were sleeping. Parenthetically, Matthew informs his readers that this story has spread among the Jews "to this day" (i.e., the time when he wrote his Gospel)—an ancient instance of "fake news."

452. Matthew 28:5–6.
453. Matthew 28:11–15.

The Great Commission to Disciple the Nations (28:16–20)

The final scene describes Jesus's promised appearance to his disciples in Galilee. Seeing the risen Jesus, many worship, though some doubt. At this, Jesus instructs his disciples to "go and make disciples of all nations," commissioning them to baptize these new disciples and to teach them everything that he himself had commanded them.[454] In so doing, his disciples are to rely on Jesus's continued presence to empower them to fulfill his Great Commission.

The Gospel therefore ends on a high note (literally!)—yet another mountain, on which the risen Jesus commissions the believing Jewish remnant, his new messianic community, to extend his rule to all the nations. Jesus had previously commissioned the Twelve to go, but "only to the lost sheep of the house of Israel";[455] now he tells his followers to go and make disciples of *all* the nations—including, but no longer merely limited to, Israel.

The gospel, the good news of salvation and forgiveness in our crucified and risen Lord and Savior Jesus Christ, has now become the basis for worldwide proclamation, and the new covenant Jesus established with his new messianic community has been enacted in his body and blood given for all—for all, that is, who will believe that Jesus really *is* the Messiah who has come in fulfillment of countless predictions in all the Scriptures (the Law, the Prophets, and the Writings, including the Psalms).

Yet as the conclusion of Matthew's Gospel reminds us, neither the cross nor even the resurrection is the end of the story. At the end of the narrative of Jesus's first coming is the mission given to the believing community to extend the reach of God's kingdom to the farthest corners of the earth. This is the precious privilege granted to believers in the risen Messiah, the Great Commission given to the church, which has never been rescinded and continues to be in effect until this very day.

---

454. The commission to "make disciples of all nations" (Matthew 28:19) forms an *inclusio* with the opening references to Jesus as "son of Abraham" (1:1–2) and signals the fulfillment of God's promise to Abraham that in him "all peoples on earth" would be blessed through him (Genesis 12:3).

455. Matthew 15:24.

CHAPTER 3

The Good News according to MARK

Jesus the Authoritative, Miracle-Working Son of God

JUST THE FACTS

The good news of Jesus Christ, the Son of God

Written by John Mark on the basis of Peter's testimony and preaching[1]

Ministry associate of Paul and Barnabas

WHO WAS MARK?

Mark most likely was the John Mark mentioned in the book of Acts who accompanied Paul and Barnabas on their first missionary journey but deserted them for some unknown reason in order to return home.[2] Apparently, he later became a bone of contention when Barnabas, his cousin, wanted to give him another chance and take him on the second missionary journey but Paul flatly refused, choosing Timothy and Silas instead.[3] Years later, however, Mark's name resurfaces in the company of the apostle Peter.[4] Also, it appears that Paul had use for Mark's services again toward the end of his ministry.[5] In this way, Mark, like Peter, was well acquainted with discipleship failure, which may explain why such is a pronounced emphasis in his Gospel. On a personal level, Mark had a devout mother[6] and a cousin, Barnabas, who was committed to him, which would have been vital in times of failure and discouragement. Mark may

1. A compelling piece of internal evidence in support of Markan authorship is the naming of Peter in both the beginning and the end of the Gospel, signaling him as a major eyewitness (Mark 1:16; 16:7). Richard Bauckham, in his work *Jesus and the Eyewitnesses: The Gospels as Eyewitness Testimony*, 2nd ed. (Grand Rapids: Eerdmans, 2017), 124–27, argues that Mark is using a literary device known as the "*inclusio* of eyewitness testimony." Moreover, Peter refers to Mark as "my son" (1 Peter 5:13). The external evidence is also compelling with a direct reference to Mark as "the interpreter of Peter" by Papias, bishop of Hierapolis (ca. AD 60–130), cited by Eusebius in the early fourth century (*Hist. eccl.* 3.39). For more on authorship, see Andreas J. Köstenberger, L. Scott Kellum, and Charles L. Quarles, *The Cradle, the Cross, and the Crown: An Introduction to the New Testament* (Nashville: B&H, 2009), 276–78; see also Joel F. Williams, *Mark*, Exegetical Guide to the Greek New Testament (Nashville: B&H, 2020), 3–5.
2. Acts 12:25; 13:13.
3. Acts 15:37–40.
4. 1 Peter 5:13.
5. Colossians 4:10; Philemon 24; 2 Timothy 4:11.
6. Acts 12:12.

make a cameo appearance in his own Gospel as the young man who fled naked (or in his undergarments) at Jesus's arrest.[7]

HOW DOES MARK TELL THE STORY OF JESUS?

The Gospel of Mark is the shortest of the four Gospels with the most amount of material shared with the other Synoptic Gospels, Matthew and Luke.[8] Mark's Gospel begins with a remarkable swiftness of movement and a tremendous sense of urgency, highlighted by the frequent use of the word "immediately."[9] Unlike Matthew and Luke, Mark skips any mention of Jesus's birth and infancy, immediately diving into an account of his public ministry. Mark Strauss has referred to Mark as "a gospel narrative on steroids"![10] Like Matthew and Luke, Mark largely tells the story of Jesus, depicting the geographic progression of his ministry.[11] In so doing, Mark emphasizes Jesus's actions, especially his miracles, over some of the longer discourses we find in the other Gospels. He expresses Jesus's character in vivid style and graphic detail.[12] In addition, Mark occasionally orders the events of Jesus's life and ministry topically to highlight important themes.[13] He also utilizes several other literary techniques, such as irony, patterns of three (triads),[14] and "sandwiching" (interpretative intercalation), which refers to placing one event in between another (which constitutes the literary bookends) to provide a framework for interpretation.[15]

---

7. Mark 14:51–52.
8. Many scholars regard Mark as foundational to the other Synoptic Gospels with about 95 percent of its material paralleled in Matthew and Luke. Today, the most widely accepted view is that Mark was written first, a theory known as "Markan priority." Key evidence in support of this theory includes the significant amount of agreement in wording and order with both Matthew and Luke, who may have used Mark as one of their sources (cf. Luke 1:1–4). See Köstenberger, Kellum, and Quarles, *The Cradle, the Cross, and the Crown*, 274–75.
9. Mark uses the word "immediately" (*euthus*) forty-two times. By contrast, the word appears five times in Matthew and only once in Luke.
10. Mark L. Strauss, *Mark*, Zondervan Exegetical Commentary on the New Testament (Grand Rapids: Zondervan, 2014), 17.
11. Williams, *Mark*, 9–10, discerns two major halves each divided into three units, taking place (1) (a) in the wilderness (1:1–13); (b) in Galilee (1:14–3:35); (c) at or near the Sea of Galilee (4:1–8:26); and (2) (a) on the way to Jerusalem (8:27–10:52); (b) at the temple (11:1–13:37); (c) in or near Jerusalem (14:1–16:8).
12. Köstenberger, Kellum, and Quarles, *The Cradle, the Cross, and the Crown*, 286.
13. Mark L. Strauss, *Four Portraits, One Jesus: A Survey of Jesus and the Gospels* (Grand Rapids: Zondervan, 2007), 174.
14. Strauss, *Four Portraits, One Jesus*, 177. For example, three boat scenes illustrate the disciples' lack of faith (4:35–41; 6:45–52; 8:14–21).
15. For example, Jesus's cleansing of the temple is sandwiched between his cursing of a fig tree and the lesson from the withered tree (11:12–25). The two events are meant to be interpreted in view of the other. For more on Mark's literary features, see Strauss, *Four Portraits, One Jesus*, 173–77.

In terms of literary structure, Mark's blueprint is similar to Matthew's, which could be explained by Mark's use of Matthew or (perhaps more likely) Matthew's use of Mark. This is what scholars have termed "the Synoptic problem," though I personally don't like the expression "problem" because it seems to imply that there's an actual problem! The only "problem," however, if there is one at all, is that we don't exactly know what kind of literary relationship there is among the Synoptic Gospels! The available data is insufficient to help us "solve" this conundrum conclusively. Matthew was put first in our Bibles, followed by Mark and Luke, though this doesn't necessarily mean Matthew was *written* first; perhaps more likely, the way Matthew starts his Gospel—with a genealogy of Jesus—makes him the ideal "first Gospel" in our New Testament. The fact that Mark is much more concise makes one wonder (among other things) if he wrote first, and then Matthew and Luke expanded his Gospel by adding more material, as opposed to Mark abbreviating them, which would seem to make less sense: Why compile an abridgment when the fuller story is already available?

In any case, the first half of the Gospel chronicles Jesus's ministry in Galilee and focuses on his authority as the miracle-working Son of God. Following Peter's confession of Jesus, similar to Matthew, Mark turns to Jesus's journey to Jerusalem and his impending sacrificial death on the cross.[16] In the remainder of the Gospel, the meaning of Jesus's suffering and death becomes the focal point of the narrative and shapes the rest of the story. Bearing Mark's focus on the cross in mind, he was likely writing to believers in Rome who needed assurance and encouragement in view of their own suffering.[17] In many ways, Mark's Gospel can therefore be viewed as "an apology [apologetic or defense] for the cross," answering the question "Why was Jesus crucified?"[18] Wouldn't you like to know that too?

WHAT ARE SOME OF MARK'S DISTINCTIVE EMPHASES?

First and foremost, Mark demonstrates that Jesus Christ is the authoritative, miracle-working Son of God. Throughout the Gospel, he places references to Jesus as

16. See Mark 8:29. France notes that there were significant racial, geographical, political, economic, cultural, linguistic, and religious differences between Galilee and Judea in Jesus's day. See R. T. France, *The Gospel of Matthew*, New International Commentary on the New Testament (Grand Rapids: Eerdmans, 2007), 5–6.
17. Scholars continue to debate Mark's specific audience. The internal evidence for a Roman audience includes the frequent use of Latin expressions (Latinisms); the reference to Rufus, who was well known in Rome (15:21); and use of the Roman method of timekeeping. However, the Gospels were widely circulated and written with a broader audience in mind. See Köstenberger, Kellum, and Quarles, *The Cradle, the Cross, and the Crown*, 282–83.
18. Köstenberger, Kellum, and Quarles, *The Cradle, the Cross, and the Crown*, 284.

the Son of God in strategic places, structuring each section of the narrative around this theme.[19] Correspondingly, Mark introduces his Gospel with "Jesus Christ, the Son of God" in the opening verse and concludes with the Roman centurion's climactic confession, "Truly this man was the Son of God."[20] And yet Jesus's identity was not clear to all throughout the entire course of his earthly mission, which leads to another distinctive of Mark's Gospel.

Upon reading Mark's Gospel, you'll notice how Jesus repeatedly commands people to keep silent about his identity. In fact, Mark records Jesus's commands to silence more frequently than any other evangelist.[21] Scholars have referred to this as the "messianic secret."[22] At first, the secrecy surrounding Jesus's identity may seem odd: Why would Jesus not want people to know that he's the Messiah? As the narrative unfolds, however, Jesus's purpose emerges with greater clarity. He is refining, even correcting, Israel's expectations of the Messiah, their long-awaited king. He wasn't going to be a powerful national deliverer but a suffering Savior.

As the story works its way closer to the cross, therefore, Mark zooms in on Jesus's identity as the Old Testament figure of the servant of the Lord.[23] In line with Isaiah's prediction, Jesus came as God's servant "to give his life as a ransom for many."[24] "Ransom" means that Jesus didn't die for his own sins but for those of others—us! However, no one took Jesus's life by force; he gave it willingly, knowing that according to God's plan there was no other way for us to be saved. The price of redemption must be paid, and the God-man must give his life as a sacrifice and shed his blood for others.

Finally, in view of Jesus's vicarious suffering, Mark also paints a portrait of discipleship. As the narrative unfolds, Mark distinctively highlights the frequent failures and misunderstandings of Jesus's earthly followers. Specifically, they fail to understand that the very purpose of Jesus's mission, as mentioned, is for him to suffer and die for sinners. In light of this, contrary to what they think, the nature of true discipleship

---

19. Mark 1:1; 1:11 (introduction); 3:11; 5:7 (Galilean ministry); 9:7; 13:32 (journey to Jerusalem); 14:61; 15:39 (trial and crucifixion). See Köstenberger, Kellum, and Quarles, *The Cradle, the Cross, and the Crown*, 296.
20. Mark 1:1; 15:39.
21. Strauss, *Four Portraits, One Jesus*, 181.
22. *The Messianic Secret* was the title of William Wrede's groundbreaking work in 1901, which proposed that Jesus never claimed to be the Messiah and that the early church identified Jesus as the Messiah only after the resurrection. According to Wrede's proposal, Mark sought to resolve this discrepancy by introducing the secrecy motif into his Gospel. Wrede's conclusions have been rejected by most scholars today. For more on the Markan secrecy motif, see David E. Garland, *A Theology of Mark's Gospel*, Biblical Theology of the New Testament (Grand Rapids: Zondervan, 2015), 368–87.
23. Isaiah 52:13–53:12.
24. Mark 10:45.

involves following Jesus in the way of the cross.[25] The path to glory inexorably leads through suffering—not only for Jesus but for them as well.

WHAT ARE THE MAJOR CONTOURS OF MARK'S ACCOUNT?

Jesus the Messiah and Son of God (1:1–8:26)

- The Beginning of the Gospel of Jesus Christ (1:1–13)
- Jesus's Initial Work in Galilee (1:14–3:6)
- Jesus's Later Work in Galilee (3:7–6:6a)
- Jesus's Work beyond Galilee (6:6b–8:26)

Jesus the Messiah and Suffering Servant (8:27–16:8)

- Jesus's Journey to Jerusalem (8:27–10:52)
- Jesus's Work in Jerusalem (11:1–13:37)
- The Passion Narrative (14:1–16:8)

25. Mark 8:34.

JESUS THE MESSIAH AND SON OF GOD (1:1–8:26)
The Beginning of the Gospel of Jesus Christ (1:1–13)
The Headline (1:1)
The Beginning of the Gospel: Jesus's Forerunner (1:2–8)
The Baptism and Temptation of Jesus (1:9–13)

JESUS THE MESSIAH AND SON OF GOD (1:1–8:26)

We begin our study of Mark's Gospel by exploring what it means for Jesus to be the Messiah and Son of God, before shifting in the second half to Jesus as the Messiah and suffering servant.

The Beginning of the Gospel of Jesus Christ (1:1–13)

The Headline (1:1)

Mark starts his Gospel with the headline, "The beginning of the gospel of Jesus Christ, the Son of God."[26] Unlike the other Synoptic Gospels, Mark doesn't include a genealogy or infancy narrative of Jesus. Rather, he starts at the "beginning of the gospel," which Mark identifies as the appearance and baptizing ministry of Jesus's forerunner, John the Baptist, who, in turn, came in keeping with Old Testament prophecy. As Mark Strauss points out, "Jesus's arrival is no accident of history."[27] Rather, Jesus is "the Christ." He is the long-awaited Messiah, the promised Davidic king who would bring God's salvation to his people.[28] In this, all four Gospels wholeheartedly agree.

26. Mark 1:1. Some early manuscripts don't include the phrase "Son of God," but there is significant support for its inclusion in other key manuscripts. See further Bruce M. Metzger, *A Textual Commentary on the Greek New Testament*, 2nd ed. (Stuttgart: Deutsche Bibelgesellschaft; New York: United Bible Societies, 1994), 62.
27. Strauss, *Four Portraits, One Jesus*, 178.
28. 1 Samuel 7:11–16.

As to his relationship with God, Jesus is the "Son of God." In other words, he is utterly unique! His relationship with God is unlike any other. "Son of God" is a very important title that Mark continues to develop throughout his Gospel.[29] In the first century, the title was understood in a variety of ways. In the Greco-Roman world, Caesar Augustus, following the death of Julius Caesar, claimed the title *divi filius*, "divine son."[30] Increasingly, Roman emperors were deified—declared to be divine—by the senate after they died. The Jewish people took "Son of God" to refer to the messianic descendent of King David, about whom God promised, "I will be his father, and he will be my son."[31] As Strauss observes, "As God's representative before the people, Israel's king was meant to have a special father-son relationship with God. The ultimate Davidic king, the Messiah, would have a unique and unprecedented relationship with God."[32]

From the outset, then, Mark identifies Jesus as Israel's long-awaited king, the God-sent and anointed Messiah and unique Son of God envisioned in the Old Testament. It's very possible, if not likely, that Mark also sets the coming of Jesus in the context of the first-century Greco-Roman world and thus implicitly compares Jesus to the Roman emperors, implying that Jesus was the "Son of God" in a way that was utterly unique and far exceeded any status ascribed to those posthumously deified emperors. Not only did Jesus's power and authority far exceed that of the Roman emperors (contrary to what it might have appeared at the outset), but Jesus also commanded greater allegiance, which, as we'll see below, has all-important implications for what it means to follow Jesus as his disciple.

Mark also characterizes the story of Jesus as "the gospel" or "good news."[33] In the Greco-Roman world of his day, the term "gospel" typically referred to the public declaration of good news, such as that of victory in battle or the bestowal of honor on a worthy individual.[34] In the Old Testament, particularly in the book of Isaiah, the term "gospel" has even greater significance, highlighting the message of a new mighty act of God's deliverance of his people in the form of a "new exodus," followed by the end-time restoration of the world in the form of a new heaven and a new earth.[35] Mark draws on

29. In fact, we can discern a triadic structure. At the beginning, Mark identifies Jesus as the Son of God; in the middle, Peter confesses Jesus as the Christ (8:29); and at the end, a Roman centurion similarly designates Jesus as Son of God (15:39).
30. Strauss, *Mark*, 61.
31. 2 Samuel 7:14. See also Psalms 2:1–12; 89:19–29; Isaiah 9:6–7.
32. Strauss, *Mark*, 61–62.
33. Köstenberger, Kellum, and Quarles, *The Cradle, the Cross, and the Crown*, 274: "A majority believe Mark pioneered the literary genre 'Gospel.' His opening reference to his account as 'the gospel' most likely set the stage for the use of that term as a literary designation for the four distinctive literary works we now call 'Gospels' and contributed to the use of 'Gospel' in a literary sense in the early church."
34. Strauss, *Mark*, 58.
35. Cf. Isaiah 40:9; 52:7; 61:1.

this background to announce the "good news" of Jesus who came to inaugurate God's kingdom—that is, God's rule over all of creation—and demonstrated his divine authority by numerous powerful acts of deliverance, such as healings, demon exorcisms, and even raisings from the dead.

The Beginning of the Gospel: Jesus's Forerunner (1:2–8)

At the very outset, Mark affirms that the gospel began in fulfillment of Scripture and as part of God's plan, in the person of John the Baptist, Jesus's forerunner.[36] Rather than bursting onto the scene unannounced, Jesus was heralded by one whose primary mission was to announce the coming of the Messiah. A contemporary analogy to this would be the role of the Speaker of the House, who, at the beginning of the State of the Union address, announces to Congress, "Ladies and Gentlemen, the president of the United States!" This formal announcement sets the stage for the president's arrival and delivery of his message. Similarly, the Baptist's role was to make formal announcement of the Messiah's imminent arrival.

In characterizing the salvation-historical role of John the Baptist, the second evangelist ties together three interrelated Old Testament passages:

- Exodus 23:20a ("I send an angel before you")
- Isaiah 40:3 ("A voice cries: 'In the wilderness'")
- Malachi 3:1 ("Behold, I will send my messenger, and he will prepare the way before me")[37]

Interestingly, Mark introduces his conflation of these three passages merely by saying, "As it is written in Isaiah the prophet." Most likely, the reason why Mark only mentions Isaiah is that he was the more prominent Old Testament prophet and that the main citation is drawn from him. Following a typical Jewish pattern of Old Testament citation, Mark groups these passages together under a common theme.[38] In addition, as mentioned, Mark may also be using a literary technique known as "sandwiching." In the present instance, he places the passage from Isaiah between Exodus 23:20a and Malachi

36. Mark 1:2–3.
37. See Strauss, *Mark*, 62. Mark follows the text of Exodus 23:20a in the Septuagint (abbreviated LXX, the Greek translation of the Hebrew Old Testament) very closely (note that the Greek word *angelos* can mean either "angel" or "messenger'). Malachi 3:1 follows the Hebrew text closely, except that the phrase "my way" becomes "your way." Strauss comments, "With this change Mark allows for a messianic interpretation and also implies that Jesus is the embodiment of Yahweh himself."
38. Benjamin Gladd, "Mark," in *A Biblical-Theological Introduction to the New Testament*, ed. Michael J. Kruger (Wheaton, IL: Crossway, 2016), 72.

3:1 to emphasize that the latter two passages should be read in light of Isaiah's prophecy in Isaiah 40:3. For its part, Isaiah 40:3 is an important text right at the beginning of the second half of the book of Isaiah that envisions Israel's deliverance from Babylonian exile and return to the Promised Land. In that vein, the second half of the book of Isaiah describes "Israel's release from Babylonian captivity as a second exodus."[39] The "beginning" of the gospel signals to the reader that this new exodus is now at hand. God himself will appear, in the person of the Messiah, to perform a mighty act of deliverance—the crucifixion followed by resurrection—that will save people spiritually and eternally. In this way, the new exodus will serve as the greater corresponding event (antitype) of the original exodus (God's deliverance of his people Israel from bondage in Egypt through Moses); it will be even more powerful, even more definitive, and utterly irreversible. Praise God!

From these three conflated Old Testament passages, we see that there is a key salvation-historical figure heralding this new exodus who signals the "beginning" of the gospel of Jesus Christ, the Son of God—John the Baptist (or Baptizer).[40] This figure, Mark makes clear, is both the "messenger" of Malachi 3 and the "voice" of Isaiah 40. Also significant is the location of John's ministry, the "wilderness," which also was the place of Israel's wanderings on the way to the Promised Land following the original exodus.[41] Often in Old Testament times, the wilderness was a place of testing and preparation for God's work. What's more, John is also depicted as a new Elijah, a powerful prophet proclaiming God's mighty work of deliverance, as made clear by Mark's description of John's outward appearance and attire in terms that are unmistakably reminiscent of those of Elijah.[42]

In typical prophetic style, John's ministry and message convey both warning and comfort: on the one hand, he warns Israel of God's judgment for sin; on the other, he offers hope of forgiveness and restoration. Thus, John's mission is that of preparing the hearts of God's people for the Messiah's arrival by calling them to repentance. This heart change or contrition, in turn, is to be given public expression by submitting to water baptism. In this way, the "way of the Lord" will be made straight, and John's advance mission will have been accomplished.[43] Just like a modern-day evangelist might send an

39. Strauss, *Mark*, 63. See Isaiah 40–66.
40. Strauss, *Mark*, 59. Mark 1:4–8.
41. Note that the "wilderness" is mentioned as many as four times in the introduction to Mark's Gospel (1:3, 4, 12, 13).
42. Cf. 2 Kings 1:8: "He wore a garment of hair, with a belt of leather about his waist."
43. Note that in the original quotation "the way of the Lord" refers to YHWH (God the Father), while in Mark "the way of the Lord" has become the arrival of Jesus, the Messiah and Son of God. It seems, then, that Jesus is here implicitly called "Lord" and thus taken into the identity of YHWH, the Creator of the universe and Redeemer of God's people!

advance team to prepare for a crusade, a scholarly society or company might send an advance team to prepare for a conference, or a political figure might send an advance team to prepare for an upcoming visit, God sent John as an "advance person" to prepare spiritual conditions for the coming Messiah, so that when he would come, the stage would be set for his arrival and mission.

The success of John's ministry is evident as "the entire Judean countryside and all Jerusalem were going out to him and were being baptized by him in the Jordan River as people confessed their sins."[44] John's activity both challenged the thinking and practice of Israel's current institutions and called for the nation's spiritual restoration. As will become increasingly apparent as the Gospel progresses, the contrast between John the Baptist, who administers a baptism of repentance in the wilderness, and the formal, established Jewish religious leadership in Jerusalem could not be more pronounced. Jesus the Messiah will come as an outsider, heralded by a powerful Elijah-like prophet, and will challenge the hegemony of the religious leaders who have usurped their God-given stewardship over his people.

So far we've only been told about John indirectly: by way of Old Testament prophecy and Mark's own characterization of John's baptism, preaching, appeal, and attire. Now, at long last, we hear from John directly, in his own words. This, then, is what John says about himself in relation to the coming Messiah: "After me comes he who is mightier than I, the strap of whose sandals I am not worthy to stoop down and untie."[45] In an ancient context, only slaves would stoop and untie another's dirty sandals. Thus, John is saying here that, in relation to the Messiah, his status is lower than even that of a slave. Compared to Jesus and his exalted status in God's plan of salvation, John is less than nothing! This is an exceedingly humble, hyperbolic statement that impressively draws attention to just how great this coming Messiah is going to be.

John elaborates, "I have baptized you with water, but he will baptize you with the Holy Spirit."[46] Now, it clearly is one thing to dip someone under mere water (in the original Greek, *baptizō*, which we in English simply transliterate as "baptize," means "to dip under or submerge") and something entirely different to be able to "dip" people and "submerge" them in the Holy Spirit! Who has the power to give the Holy Spirit? Again, this clearly identifies the Messiah as exceedingly powerful. In fact, it identifies him as divine and on par with none other than God (YHWH) himself. In Mark's Gospel, this statement by John the Baptist regarding one who would baptize

44. Mark 1:5. Of course, the depiction is hyperbolic: not literally everyone came to John, but his message drew large crowds.
45. Mark 1:7.
46. Mark 1:8.

with the Holy Spirit also has the important narrative function of skillfully shifting the focus of the next scene to Jesus.

The Baptism and Temptation of Jesus (1:9–13)

Just like John the Baptist is introduced in verse 4 with the Greek word *egeneto* (appeared, came, happened), so Jesus is now introduced in verse 9 with the identical Greek word (though it is often untranslated in our English versions). This shows how Mark is an excellent storyteller, introducing his main characters into the narrative one at a time. The way Jesus is introduced in Mark's narrative is reminiscent of Old Testament language: "In those days Jesus came from Nazareth of Galilee."[47] Notice that this is the first time we hear about Jesus directly in this Gospel, and all we're told is that he came from Nazareth in Galilee. Often at this point, we supply what we know from the other Gospels about Jesus's birth and life prior to his public appearance at the age of about thirty. But Mark wants to get straight to the point and is not detained by what he considers unnecessary preliminaries. Let later Gospel writers elaborate on these; in a mere eight verses, Mark has arrived at Jesus's baptism by John, and after a mere fifteen verses, Mark has Jesus call his first disciples. It takes Matthew and Luke until chapter 4 in their respective Gospels to get to that same point. This shows just how condensed Mark's introduction really is.

Jesus's baptism by John itself is recorded by Mark in the tersest of terms. He doesn't even say that Jesus was dipped into the Jordan! He immediately moves on to when Jesus "came up out of the water," at which time he "immediately" saw "the heavens being torn open and the Spirit descending on him like a dove."[48] Not only this, but also a heavenly voice is heard, saying, "You are my beloved Son," echoing Mark's opening words.[49] Mark is not detained by questions such as why Jesus is baptized by John, especially since, as John has just acknowledged, he is not even worthy to untie his sandals. He simply shows additional evidence for the auspicious nature of Jesus's coming. First, he was heralded by a "voice" in the wilderness as the one who would bring about a new exodus. Now, he is heralded by a "voice" from heaven as God's beloved Son with whom God is uniquely pleased. What's more, the Spirit descended on Jesus, showing that both God in heaven and the Spirit were working in tandem with Jesus, the Messiah and Son of God, at the outset of his earthly

47. Mark 1:9.
48. Mark 1:10. "Torn open" (Greek *schizō*) is a striking word; it occurs elsewhere in Mark only at 15:38, where it refers to the tearing of the temple veil from top to bottom, a possible literary *inclusio*. In both cases, the "tearing" is followed by a declaration or confession of Jesus as the Son of God (1:11: a voice from heaven, i.e., God the Father; 15:39: a Roman centurion), a likely joint *inclusio*.
49. Mark 1:11.

ministry, which is about to begin. What later came to be known as the Holy Trinity is jointly at work!

The breathless action in Mark's Gospel continues unabated. Jesus has no time to rest on his laurels or bask in God's commendation. The Spirit (who had just descended onto Jesus at his baptism) "immediately" drives Jesus into the wilderness (previously mentioned as the site of John's preaching and baptizing ministry). The word "drive" in the original Greek is literally to "thrust out," a forceful term describing how the Spirit propelled Jesus into the wilderness to be tempted there by Satan for forty days.[50] The span of forty days, of course, is reminiscent of Israel's forty years of wandering in the desert.[51] Again, Mark's account of the temptation is extremely terse; he doesn't provide any detail whatsoever about the specific nature of the temptation, unlike Matthew and Luke, who each specify three particular temptations. In fact, he doesn't even state explicitly that Jesus successfully resisted these temptations! All he says is that the Spirit drove Jesus into the wilderness, and that Jesus was "with the wild animals, and the angels were ministering to him."[52] Thus, one assumes that Jesus was continually in the Spirit's presence, attended to by angels, and approved by God, so that Satan couldn't touch him in any way. This also gives us an example of how we can resist temptation: by remaining in the Spirit's presence and by resting in the full assurance of God's approval of us in Christ. Jesus's temptation by Satan in the wilderness marks the beginning of the spiritual conflict between Jesus and Satan and the demonic world, which will continue to rage throughout Jesus's earthly ministry, culminating in his death on the cross. Jesus's baptism and testing have prepared him for the colossal spiritual opposition he will face throughout his entire public work, which is about to begin.

---

50. The Greek word is *ekballō*. By contrast, Matthew and Luke merely speak of the Spirit "leading" (*anagō* or *agō*) Jesus into the wilderness (Matthew 4:1; Luke 4:1).
51. Numbers 14:34.
52. Some scholars believe the mention of "wild animals" (Mark 1:13) is an allusion to the garden of Eden, making Jesus's temptation analogous to Adam and Eve. However, the more likely interpretation is that the wild animals indicate the dangers of the wilderness. The angels serve Jesus to protect him (cf. Psalm 91:11–14). See Strauss, *Mark*, 74.

JESUS'S INITIAL WORK IN GALILEE (1:14–3:6)

The Beginning of Jesus's Work (1:14–20)

Again, Mark implies movement or action (just like when he said earlier that Jesus "came up out of the water" without actually narrating that Jesus was dipped *into* the water) when he casually introduces the account of the beginning of Jesus's ministry by saying, "Now after John was arrested." He hasn't actually recorded that John was arrested but is so eager to jump into his account of the beginning of Jesus's ministry that he skips right over John's arrest and moves straight to Jesus's call of his first disciples. (He will narrate John's arrest several chapters later in the form of a historical flashback.)[53] Jesus previously has been said to come from Nazareth in Galilee to the Jordan River. After this he went into the Judean wilderness. Now he goes back to Galilee.

Jesus launches his public ministry by "proclaiming the gospel of God."[54] The expression "gospel *of God*" is striking; the gospel isn't merely a human message—it's the message of God! Specifically, Mark sums up Jesus's message about God's kingdom as follows: "The time is fulfilled, and the kingdom of God is at hand; repent and believe in the gospel."[55] "The time is fulfilled" points to the fulfillment of Old Testament promises regarding the kingdom of God.[56] Since Jesus has come to usher in God's kingdom—

53. Mark 6:14–29.
54. Mark 1:14; cf. Romans 1:1.
55. Mark 1:15.
56. For more on the kingdom of God, see Strauss, *Mark*, 80–82; see also S. M. Baugh, *The Majesty on High: Introduction to the Kingdom of God in the New Testament* (Scotts Valley, CA: CreateSpace, 2017); Nicholas Perrin, *The Kingdom of God: A Biblical Theology*, Biblical Theology for Life (Grand Rapids: Zondervan, 2019); and Patrick J. Schreiner, *The Kingdom of God and the Glory of the Cross*, Short Studies in Biblical Theology (Wheaton, IL: Crossway, 2018). The imminent kingdom of God is central to Jesus's message (cf.

which is terrific news—people must respond by searching their hearts and coming clean of their sins. They must repent and believe in his message, which implies that they also believe in him—that he is the Messiah and Son of God.

The opening two verses of this section thus perfectly encapsulate Jesus's ministry and message by way of a literary *inclusio* bringing the reader back to the way Mark's Gospel started: "The beginning of the gospel of Jesus Christ." This gospel—the gospel of God—we're now told, Jesus came to proclaim. He came to make formal, public announcement that in him God's kingdom was near, in keeping with God's promises in the past. As the presence of God's reign among his people, the kingdom of God had become a present reality with Jesus's arrival. As God's realm—an eternal kingdom on earth—the kingdom is a future hope to be consummated at Christ's return.[57] As mentioned, this good news demands a response; those who hear Jesus's message are called to repent and believe. The same is true today. It's not enough merely to hear the gospel, or even to read this book; you and I must repent in our hearts and believe that Jesus can—and did!—save us from our sins.

From here on out, Mark narrates the launch of Jesus's public ministry in rapid motion. Jesus calls his first disciples, casts out demons, and heals the sick. The story moves quickly from scene to scene, highlighting the magnitude of Jesus's arrival. As Mark Strauss points out, "The purpose of Mark's high-speed narrative is to portray Jesus as the Messiah and Son of God of power and authority, a theme which dominates the first half of the Gospel."[58] Mark's emphasis on Jesus's authority takes center stage throughout Jesus's public work in Galilee. First, Jesus calls his initial disciples—first Simon and Andrew, then James and John, all fishermen.[59] Jesus's call is this: "Follow me, and I will make you fishers of men."[60]

Jesus's practice of calling followers is unique. Old Testament prophets would charge their disciples to follow YHWH, the Lord, not themselves, while first-century disciples would attach themselves to a rabbi of their choice, rather than rabbis calling their own disciples. By calling these men to follow him, therefore, Jesus demonstrates his unique

---

Mark 4:11, 26, 30; 9:1, 47; 10:14–15, 23–25; 12:34; 14:25; 15:43). The verb "is at hand" is "probably intentionally ambiguous" (Strauss, *Mark*, 82). See also Köstenberger, Kellum, and Quarles, *The Cradle, the Cross, and the Crown*, 298: "Mark's use of 'kingdom of God' is synonymous with Matthew's 'kingdom of heaven,' and both of these evangelists view the kingdom as intimately tied to and demonstrated through Jesus's miracles."

57. Cf. Revelation 11:15: "The kingdoms of this world are become the kingdoms of our Lord, and of his Christ; and he shall reign for ever and ever."
58. Strauss, *Four Portraits, One Jesus*, 179.
59. Mark 1:16–20.
60. Mark 1:17.

messianic authority.[61] As they follow Jesus, he will make them "fishers of men." The background of this phrase is found in the Old Testament, where it is used in the context of judgment.[62] Jesus, however, uses this image as one of salvation; to "fish" for people is to rescue them from sin and call them into God's kingdom. Mark will continue to develop this theme of discipleship throughout the Gospel. Here we see that following Jesus entails participating in his mission of rescuing people from sin. In characteristic fashion, Mark tells us that Jesus called his followers, and they "immediately" left their nets and followed him.[63] This doesn't mean, however, that this was the first time Jesus met these men; perhaps more likely, there were previous encounters leading to Jesus's calling of his disciples that Mark narrates here.[64]

Jesus's Power over Demons and Sickness (1:21–34)

Tellingly in a Gospel that stresses the spiritual conflict between God and Satan, Jesus's first act after calling his first disciples is a demon exorcism.[65] This follows the earlier reference to the Spirit leading Jesus into the wilderness and Jesus's being tempted there by Satan.[66] They're still on the shores of the Sea of Galilee where Jesus had called his first disciples. There they enter the well-known synagogue in Capernaum, where Jesus is teaching on the Sabbath where Jews gathered for worship and instruction in the Scriptures. Mark notes that people there "were astonished at his teaching, for he taught them as one who had authority, and not as the scribes."[67] The difference between Jesus's teaching and that of the other Jewish teachers or scribes, as Strauss aptly notes, was that the latter merely handed down traditions while Jesus taught with true spiritual authority.[68] As in Matthew and Luke, the scribes, as well as the Pharisees, serve as a foil for Jesus and present a constant source of conflict throughout his ministry.

---

61. Gladd, "Mark," 74. See also Andreas J. Köstenberger, "Jesus as a Rabbi," in *Handbook of the Jewish Roots of the Christian Faith*, eds. Craig A. Evans and David Mishkin (Peabody, MA: Hendrickson, 2019).
62. Cf. Jeremiah 16:16; Ezekiel 29:4–5; 38:4; Amos 4:2; Habakkuk 1:14–17.
63. As Williams (*Mark*, 32) points out, "In Mark's Gospel, those called by Jesus inevitably leave something behind in order to follow him. In this instance, for Simon and Andrew, it meant abandoning their nets, and therefore their old lives and livelihood (cf. 1:20; 2:14; 10:28). Yet with the cost comes reward, indeed, an abundance in the present age and eternal life in the age to come (10:29–30)."
64. Cf. John 1:35–51. See Andreas J. Köstenberger, "Who Were the First Disciples of Jesus? An Assessment of the Historicity of the Call Narrative (John 1:35–51)," in *John, Jesus, and History*, vol. 3, *Glimpses of Jesus through the Johannine Lens*, eds. Paul N. Anderson, Felix Just, and Tom Thatcher, Early Christianity and Its Literature 18 (Atlanta: SBL Press; Leiden: Brill, 2016), 189–99.
65. Mark 1:21–28.
66. Mark 1:12–13.
67. Mark 1:22.
68. Strauss, *Four Portraits, One Jesus*, 179.

Characteristically, with the phrase "and immediately" Mark swiftly moves on from Jesus's authoritative teaching to his miracle-working activity. Amazingly, there was a demon-possessed man right there in the Jewish synagogue in Capernaum! And it is still the Sabbath, though, unlike at other occasions, Jesus is not given grief by his opponents for breaking the Sabbath here. When the man addresses Jesus, it's not actually the man who is speaking, but an unclean spirit inside of him, using a plural self-reference: "What have you to do with us, Jesus of Nazareth? Have you come to destroy us? I know who you are—the Holy One of God"![69] Remarkably, the demons know both Jesus's human name and origin ("Jesus of Nazareth") and his divine calling ("the Holy One of God"). They also indicate that Jesus and they have vastly conflicting interests ("What have you to do with us?") and are afraid that Jesus has come to destroy them (which is true). In response, Jesus tersely tells the demons to be quiet and commands them to come out of the man—and they comply, with a loud shriek! Mark's summary—given in the narrative by the people who here serve as representative characters voicing the evangelist's desired conclusion for his readers—is to the point: not only does Jesus convey "a new teaching with authority"; he also exerts authority over unclean spirits! Thus, Jesus's powerful deeds impressively back up and validate his powerful teaching. Jesus is the messianic Son of God in both word and deed. His reputation "immediately" spreads like wildfire in the surrounding regions of Galilee.

"And immediately" Jesus leaves the synagogue at Capernaum, apparently still on the Sabbath, and together with James and John enters the home of Simon and Andrew. Simon—clearly not celibate but married—has a mother-in-law who is lying in bed with a fever, "and immediately" they told Jesus.[70] Jesus promptly heals her, and she begins serving them, as I'm sure was her custom.[71] This shows that Jesus isn't merely performing miracles to get public acclaim and attention; he here heals a disciple's mother in a more intimate, private setting. This small incident may also reflect Peter's eyewitness testimony, which, as mentioned earlier, most likely stands behind Mark's Gospel.

Later, at sundown—meaning that now it was no longer the Sabbath—people brought to him numerous sick or demon-possessed individuals (amazing how many people were demon-possessed in that region!).[72] In fact, Mark notes that "the whole

69. Mark 1:24.
70. Mark 1:29–30.
71. Mark movingly narrates that Jesus "came and took her by the hand and lifted her up" (1:31). Beth Moore, in a Twitter post dated February 28, 2019, perceptively notes that Mark repeatedly refers to Jesus taking people by the hand when healing them (see also 5:41; 8:23; and 9:27). She adds, "He's never out of touch. Wherever you are, 'even there [His] right hand will hold [you]' (Ps 139:10)."
72. See the brilliant essay by Dane C. Ortlund, "*History's Dawning Light: 'Morning' and 'Evening' in Mark's Gospel and Their Eschatological Significance,*" *Journal of the Evangelical Theological Society* 61 (2018): 493–511,

city" was gathered outside Peter's house (his mother-in-law most likely stayed in the same house as Peter and his wife as part of an extended household, as was common).[73] Jesus healed "many" more who were sick and cast out "many" more demons, though again he told the demons not to divulge his messianic identity.[74] Thus, we've seen Jesus's steadfast insistence that demons not reveal his identity; he doesn't need citizens of the evil supernatural realm to proclaim he's the Messiah!

This, as mentioned, is an early instance of the "messianic secret" motif that pervades Mark's Gospel. Not that Jesus wanted it to be kept a secret that he was the Messiah and Son of God, but he knew that the concept was open to misunderstanding, and he opted to work patiently with his inner circle—the twelve apostles—until they began to grasp who he truly was rather than accepting the testimony of demons (who in any case merely feared his authority without truly submitting to it).[75] On a narrative level, Jesus's commands to silence add an element of tension and suspense regarding Jesus's true identity, which the second evangelist develops carefully and progressively. Not only this, it also demonstrates Jesus's careful attention to revealing his messianic identity in his own way and at his own time, showing his sovereign control over events and circumstances throughout his public work.[76] What's more, the "messianic secret" motif is counteracted by the fact that Jesus explains the "secrets" or "mysteries" of the kingdom to kingdom insiders—the Twelve! Thus, the messianic secret is not absolute; to the contrary, Jesus discloses his true nature progressively over time to those whom he has called to follow him.[77]

Jesus's Prayer, Preaching, and Healing of a Leper (1:35–45)

The next vignette tells us of a day in Jesus's ministry when he got up early in the morning "while it was still dark" and went to a remote place to pray. It's fascinating to think that even though Jesus was the Son of God, he still regularly prayed! This shows that he acts in tandem with God the Father and in dependence on the Holy Spirit. Jesus's prayer life in general, along with his practice, at least occasionally, of getting up early and getting away to pray by himself, also provides a pattern and example for his followers to emulate. Simon "and those who were with him" (a subtle reference indicat-

who argues that Mark deliberately uses "morning" and "evening" language throughout his Gospel to show that Jesus came at the dawn of a new age of creation. In this regard, the sunset in Mark 1:32 and the sunrise in Mark 16:2 form literary bookends. See also the reference to "very early in the morning, while it was still dark" in 1:35 below.

73. Mark 1:33.
74. Mark 1:34.
75. Cf. James 2:19: "Even the demons believe; and they shudder."
76. Strauss, *Mark*, 114.
77. See the discussion of Mark 4:1–34, esp. 4:1–20, below.

ing that Peter had already emerged as a leader early in Jesus's ministry) track him down and tell him that "everyone" was looking for him.[78] He responds that he must go "to the next towns" to preach there as well, "for that is why I came out."[79] His purpose is to make large-scale proclamation of God's kingdom all over, rather than its being claimed exclusively by people in one location. And so he goes "throughout all Galilee," engaging in his customary twofold activity of preaching and casting out demons.[80]

Next, Jesus is approached by a leper who kneels down in front of him and begs him to make him clean. Jesus is moved with compassion and grants the man's request.[81] "And immediately" the leprosy left the man. Jesus "sternly charged" him not to divulge the healing to anyone but to go through the proper rituals for cleansing from leprosy with the local priest, "for a proof to them."[82] The man cheerfully ignores Jesus's stern charge. He doesn't care; he's just been healed of leprosy and wants everyone to know about it! As a result, Jesus has to withdraw to remote places, but people still track him down from everywhere.

RECAP

The first chapter of Mark's Gospel is an amazing tribute to Jesus's miracle-working power and his growing appeal among the Galilean masses. At this early stage of Jesus's ministry, Jesus is still able to heal and cast out demons relatively freely (though at times, as we've seen, he is forced to withdraw). As regards Jesus's identity as the Son of God, it is most graphically demonstrated through his miracles. Mark chooses to emphasize Jesus's powerful deeds even more than his teaching.[83] Specifically, Jesus's miracles relayed in Mark's Gospel demonstrate his comprehensive authority over both the natural and the supernatural realms.[84] The greater purpose of the miracles, however, is to reveal the "manifestations of the kingdom of God, that is, the powerful presence of God," in and through Jesus, the powerful and authoritative Son of God.[85]

---

78. Mark 1:36–37.
79. Mark 1:38.
80. Mark 1:39. Note that healing is not even mentioned here; the focus is on Jesus's encounters with the demonic realm.
81. Mark 1:41. Some translations (such as the NIV) say Jesus was indignant (Greek *orgizō*), on the basis of an alternate reading in a few ancient manuscripts, though "moved with compassion" has better support (cf., e.g., CSB, ESV, NASB). See Metzger, *Textual Commentary*, 65; Peter J. Williams, "An Examination of Ehrman's Case for ὀργισθείς in Mark 1:41," *Novum Testamentum* 54 (2012): 1–12.
82. Mark 1:42–44.
83. Mark 1:21–28, 29–34, 39–45.
84. See esp. the discussion of 4:35–5:43 below.
85. Craig A. Evans, "Mark," in *The Holman Apologetics Commentary on the Bible: The Gospel and Acts* (Nashville: B&H, 2013), 270, cited in Köstenberger, Kellum, and Quarles, *The Cradle, the Cross, and the Crown*, 298.

JESUS'S INITIAL WORK IN GALILEE (1:14–3:6, CONT.)
Five Controversial Encounters (2:1–3:6)
The Healing of a Paralytic (2:1–12)
The Calling of Levi (2:13–17)
To Fast or Not to Fast (2:18–22)
Eating Grain on the Sabbath (2:23–28)
Healing on the Sabbath (3:1–6)

JESUS'S INITIAL WORK IN GALILEE (1:14–3:6, CONT.)

Five Controversial Encounters (2:1–3:6)

In the next chapter, Jesus continues his healing ministry, which sparks a series of five controversial encounters with the Jewish leaders.[86]

The Healing of a Paralytic (2:1–12)

First, he performs an amazing healing at his return to Capernaum, where he had cast out a demon in the synagogue on a Sabbath.[87] Word quickly spreads that Jesus is "at home," and it is standing room only as Jesus is "speaking the word" to the people there.[88] Four men, carrying a paralyzed man on his mat (a primitive bed), can't get to Jesus because of the large crowd. Undeterred, they remove the roof above him and lower their friend through the opening right above Jesus. Upon seeing their faith, Jesus declares to the paralytic, "Your sins are forgiven."[89] It's unclear whether the man's sins were the cause of his paralysis, but in either case Jesus is able to both heal physically and make whole spiritually.[90]

The scribes who are "policing" Jesus, carefully watching his every move, rightly infer that by claiming to be able to forgive sin, Jesus stakes an implicit claim to deity. They

86. So, e.g., Williams, *Mark*, 45.
87. Mark 2:1; cf. 1:21–34.
88. Mark 2:2. The ESV has "preaching" the word, but the Greek word is simply *laleō*, "to speak."
89. Mark 2:5.
90. Strauss, *Mark*, 121.

think to themselves, "He is blaspheming! Who can forgive sins but God alone?"[91] At once, Jesus perceives what they're thinking and proceeds to engage them. Ironically, even as the scribes question Jesus's claim to divine authority, he knows what's on their minds, displaying supernatural knowledge. In traditional rabbinic style, Jesus responds to the scribes by arguing from the lesser to the greater: "Which is easier, to say . . . 'Your sins are forgiven,' or to say, 'Rise, take up your bed and walk?'"[92] The implied answer, of course, is the former. Words are cheap; anybody can say, "Your sins are forgiven." But not everyone can actually heal a paralyzed man! So Jesus commands the man, "rise, pick up your bed, and go home."[93]

Immediately, the man gets up, picks up his bed, and walks off, so that all are "amazed and glorified God."[94] Jesus has performed this amazing healing so that people "may know that the Son of Man has authority on earth to forgive sins"—an astonishing claim to deity—and Jesus backs it up with action![95] Truly, the chapter starts out with a bombshell, and this is only chapter 2 in the Gospel! Jesus has already staked a strong claim, backed up with action, that he is God. What will he do next? The reader can't help but agree with the crowd (if not even the scribes as well): "We never saw anything like this!" Again, Mark uses representative characters—in the present case, the people present at the healing of the paralytic—to state the conclusion in the narrative that he intends his readers to draw when reading his account.

The Calling of Levi (2:13–17)

In the next scene, Jesus continues to generate controversy through his choice of disciples. He has already called four fishermen to follow him on the shores of the Sea of Galilee.[96] Now he approaches Levi, a tax collector (also called Matthew, the first evangelist), and calls him to follow him. And Matthew gets up and does so. At this, Jesus proceeds to dine with him in his home, which provokes the indignation of the scribes, who ask his disciples, "Why does he eat with tax collectors and sinners?"[97] By way of background, tax collectors were Jews who collected taxes for the hated Romans, which

91. Mark 2:6–7.
92. Mark 2:9.
93. Mark 2:11; cf. Williams, *Mark*, 47: "The claim to forgive sins is easy to make in the sense that it is not verifiable. It would be more difficult for Jesus to command the paralytic to walk, since his words would be open to immediate verification."
94. Mark 2:12.
95. Mark 2:10. The title "Son of Man" is found frequently on Jesus's lips in Mark to convey divers aspects of his earthly mission: his messianic authority (2:10, 28), his impending death and resurrection (8:31), and his glorious return (13:26; cf. Daniel 7:13–14). See Williams, *Mark*, 48.
96. Cf. Mark 1:16–20; see also 1:29–30.
97. Mark 2:16.

made them traitors and extremely unpopular in Jewish eyes (plus, who wants to pay taxes in the first place?). Jesus's response to the scribes was pointed: "I didn't come to call the righteous, but sinners."[98] Jesus continues to amaze by his choice of followers. First, he called simple fishermen, and now a hated tax collector. The Pharisees responded with scathing disapproval. Yet Jesus insisted that only those who humbly received his message were fit to enter God's kingdom.

To Fast or Not to Fast (2:18–22)

The third controversy surrounds the issue of fasting. People observed that both the disciples of John the Baptist and the Pharisees were fasting, but Jesus's disciples were not. Why didn't they? Did they lack piety? Or did they show disregard for the commands of God or the tradition of the elders? Jesus responds with three sets of analogies. First, do wedding guests fast while the bridegroom is with them? Answer: Of course not! They celebrate! Second, do people put a patch of new cloth on an old garment? Again, the answer is no, for if they did, the tear would only grow larger. Third and finally, do people put new wine into old wineskins? Jesus's first-century Jewish audience would again have responded with a resounding no. Nobody put new wine into old wineskins (a wineskin was a bottle-like container in which wine was kept), because, if they did, the wineskins would burst as the wine fermented.

Jesus's point in each of these cases was that he was "inaugurating a new age of salvation that is fundamentally incompatible with the old."[99] The messianic bridegroom had arrived; people needed a new garment; and new wine must be put into fresh containers. As the apostle Paul would later write, "Therefore, if anyone is in Christ, he is a new creation. The old has passed away; behold, the new has come."[100] It was a whole new ballgame! Jesus didn't come merely to patch up the Pharisaic system and make a few minor tweaks. His mission was to establish God's kingdom on earth, a mission that was nothing less than revolutionary. Jesus didn't merely come to engage in the reformation of Judaism; he came to launch a spiritual revolution.[101] Even today, we often don't sufficiently appreciate the revolutionary nature of Jesus's mission and the radical nature of his call to follow him in discipleship.

98. Mark 2:17.
99. Strauss, *Mark*, 137.
100. 2 Corinthians 5:17.
101. See the title of a work by N. T. Wright, *The Day the Revolution Began: Reconsidering the Meaning of Jesus's Crucifixion* (New York: HarperCollins, 2016), though I don't necessarily endorse all of his conclusions in this work.

Eating Grain on the Sabbath (2:23–28)

The last two controversies center on the interpretation of Jewish law, specifically Sabbath laws. In the first instance, the Pharisees accuse Jesus's disciples of working on the Sabbath when plucking heads of grain.[102] In fact, the way the Pharisees saw it, Jesus's disciples' disregard for what was "lawful" on the Sabbath made Jesus himself complicit in Sabbath-breaking. Why didn't he properly instruct his followers? In response, Jesus pointedly questions the Pharisees' understanding of the law by citing an example from the life of King David.[103] While it could be said that David and his men technically broke the law by eating the sacred bread, they didn't violate the *spirit* of the law.[104] As Jesus memorably put it, "The Sabbath was made for man, not man for the Sabbath."[105]

God never meant to put people in bondage by placing heavy, unreasonable religious burdens on them; rather, he instituted the Sabbath as a day of rest and renewal.[106] The Pharisees' zeal for the law was commendable, but their zeal was sorely misguided. They failed to discern the spirit of the law—that is, God's underlying purpose for giving it—and were too rigid in their application. As a result, they accused Jesus himself, the very Son of God, of breaking the Sabbath! This, too, was sorely misguided. In the face of such distortion of God's true, intended purpose for giving the law, Jesus reasserted his authority to rightly interpret the law by declaring, "The Son of Man is lord even of the Sabbath"—again staking a claim to a prerogative reserved for the Creator God alone.[107]

The Pharisees stand as an abiding warning against religious legalism, zealotry, and fundamentalism. Religious zeal, if it becomes rigid and judgmental, leads people to wage moral crusades and incites them to impose their own system of rules and regulations on others, whether by holy war, moral coercion, or other means. Not only is such

102. Note that I've already discussed this same incident as recorded in Matthew's Gospel above (Matthew 12:1–8).

103. Cf. 1 Samuel 21:1–6. See the discussion of Jesus's Sabbath healing at Mark 1:21–28 above. A puzzling element is Jesus's reference (included only in Mark's version) to "the time of Abiathar the high priest," as it was actually Ahimelech, Abiathar's father, who was high priest at the time. This apparent inaccuracy caused Bart Ehrman to become a skeptic; see Bart Ehrman, *Misquoting Jesus: The Story behind Who Changed the Bible and Why* (San Francisco: HarperCollins, 2005), 9–11. However, it is possible that the Greek preposition *epi* (which usually means "upon," which makes no sense here) in the present passage has the force of either "at the time of" (cf. Luke 3:2) or "near the passage referring to" Abiathar (cf. the similar use in Mark 12:26; note that the question "Have you not read?" is found in both places, Mark 2:25 and 12:26). See the detailed discussion in Andreas J. Köstenberger, Darrell L. Bock, and Josh D. Chatraw, *Truth in a Culture of Doubt: Engaging Skeptical Challenges to the Bible* (Nashville: B&H, 2014), 53–55; more succinctly in the book by the same authors, *Truth Matters: Confident Faith in a Confusing World* (Nashville: B&H, 2014), 91–95; and even more briefly, Williams, *Mark*, 54–55.

104. See also Deuteronomy 23:24–25.

105. Mark 2:27.

106. Strauss, *Mark*, 146.

107. Mark 2:28.

an approach misguided as far as these crusaders' own religious ideology is concerned; they also turn others off from pursuing a relationship with God, which is even more deplorable. Jesus did a great job presenting faith in God in a winsome way. Without neglecting to call people to repentance, he focused on grace, love, mercy, and forgiveness, not external rules or religious observance. We desperately need to emulate Jesus in this regard.

Healing on the Sabbath (3:1–6)

On another occasion, Jesus entered the synagogue on the Sabbath and encountered a man with a withered hand. Again, the Pharisees closely watch to see if Jesus will heal the man on the Sabbath (which, in their minds, constituted a violation of the law). Jesus probingly asks, "Is it lawful on the Sabbath to do good or to do harm, to save life or to kill?"[108] Grieved by the hardness of their hearts (as we're about to be told, they're already scheming to kill him), but not intimidated or dissuaded, he heals the man.

This episode, too, is dripping with irony. While Jesus does good in healing the man, the Pharisees promptly "started plotting with the Herodians against him, how they might kill him."[109] One might legitimately wonder who it was who truly broke the Sabbath. These two episodes strike a climactic note in Jesus's early work in Galilee. He has demonstrated his divine authority and messianic identity through his powerful deeds and masterful exposition of the law, even as the religious leaders scoff at his claims.

108. Mark 3:4.
109. Mark 3:6 CSB. The mention of the Herodians is quite curious. The Herodians were pro-Roman supporters of the Herodian dynasty (Herod Antipas ruled Galilee). By contrast, the Pharisees were anti-Roman, hoping for a Davidic Messiah to overthrow Roman rule. Yet both groups perceive Jesus to be a political threat and find common cause to eliminate him.

JESUS'S LATER WORK IN GALILEE (3:7–6:6A)
Realignment: Choosing the Twelve, Opposition from His Own Family (3:7–35)
Jesus's Mass Appeal and the Messianic Secret (3:7–12)
The Calling of the Twelve Apostles (3:13–19)
Opposition from Jesus's Own Family and the Blasphemy against the Holy Spirit (3:20–35)

JESUS'S LATER WORK IN GALILEE (3:7–6:6A)

Realignment: Choosing the Twelve, Opposition from His Own Family (3:7–35)

Jesus's Mass Appeal and the Messianic Secret (3:7–12)

After a series of controversies with the increasingly hostile Jewish leaders, Jesus begins a new phase of ministry in Galilee.[110] Mark begins this section by summarizing Jesus's powerful activity and highlighting his growing popularity, all the way from the Galilean north to Judea and Jerusalem in the south, and extending to Idumea, as well as the region beyond the Jordan, and Tyre and Sidon along the coast.[111] Jesus even has to instruct his disciples to have a boat ready for him because of the large size of the crowd "lest they crush him." All those whom he had healed pressed on him to touch him, and all the demons kept crying out, "You are the Son of God." Once again, he strongly rebuked those spirits and told them not to reveal who he was; he didn't need the witness of demons! This is truly an incredible scene, with crowds growing to almost unmanageable proportions and the spirit world exhibiting an unhealthy fixation on the Son of God without submitting to his messianic authority.[112]

In the present unit, Mark expands on Jesus's teaching ministry and the growing opposition of the Jewish leaders. This stage of Jesus's ministry is characterized by a mounting degree of polarization. Increasingly, what emerges is a sharp spiritual division between

---

110. Cf. Williams, *Mark*, 58: "The story picks up in 3:7 with where it left off in 1:45, before the series of conflicts between Jesus and the religious leaders in 2:1–3:6."
111. Mark 3:7–12.
112. See Perry G. Phillips, "The Crowds That Followed Jesus (Mark 3:7–8)," in *Lexham Geographic Commentary*, ed. Barry J. Beitzel (Bellingham, WA: Lexham, 2017), 117–24.

"insiders" and "outsiders" with regard to his proclamation of God's kingdom. On the one hand, as we'll see momentarily, Jesus appoints the Twelve and sends them out on mission; they are the chosen remnant, though far from perfect, who are given the inside scoop of his messianic mission and message.[113] On the other side of the spectrum in relation to Jesus are the Jewish religious leaders who intensify their efforts to oppose him and make his life difficult at every turn. In addition, as we'll see, even some in Jesus's own family and hometown reject his authority. The key questions Mark wants his readers to ponder, therefore, are "Who is Jesus?" and "Where do you stand in relation to Jesus—are you for him or against him?"[114] This is one case where choosing sides is absolutely essential.

The Calling of the Twelve Apostles (3:13–19)

At this strategic juncture in his ministry, Jesus ascends a mountain and appoints twelve apostles (or "messengers") for the following express purposes: to be with him, and to be sent out to preach and be given authority to exorcise demons. The names of the Twelve are listed, starting with Simon (called Peter) followed by James and John, the sons of Zebedee (called *Boanerges*, "sons of thunder"),[115] then Peter's brother Andrew, Philip and Bartholomew (both of whom are mentioned here for the first time in Mark's Gospel), Matthew and (the not previously mentioned) Thomas, a second James, Thaddaeus, Simon the Zealot, and Judas "who betrayed him."[116] Most likely, the number twelve is designed to establish a connection with the twelve tribes of Israel, constituting the twelve apostles as the new messianic community. While many of the individual apostles play a limited role in the rest of the story, corporately the Twelve represent a believing remnant of Israel.[117] Thus, their appointment signals a critical development in the flow of the Markan narrative as they will constantly be with Jesus,

---

113. This section is framed by the appointment of the apostles (Mark 3:13–19) and their commissioning (Mark 6:6b–13).

114. Strauss, *Mark*, 157.

115. Note that it is only the first three members of the Twelve who are given special names by Jesus; these are the same three who form Jesus's inner circle and witness special events such as the raising of Jairus's daughter, the transfiguration, and Jesus's prayer in the garden of Gethsemane on the night before his crucifixion. *Boanerges* is the first of several Aramaic words or phrases cited (and subsequently translated) in Mark's Gospel. Others include *talitha kum* (5:41), *ephphatha* (7:34), *abba* (14:36), *Golgotha* (15:22), and *Eloi, Eloi lama sabachthani* (15:34). Not only does this practice suggest that Mark did not expect the majority of his readers to understand Aramaic but also that Jesus originally spoke Aramaic and that Mark here replicates his *ipsissima verba* (i.e., the very words of Jesus). This, in turn, most likely reflects eyewitness testimony, whether on the part of Peter (Mark's likely primary eyewitness source) or others.

116. Mark 3:16–19. Thus, while in the original instance the identity of the betrayer wasn't revealed until the very end of Jesus's ministry, for Mark's readers it is an open secret from the very beginning (no "messianic betrayer secret" here!).

117. Strauss, *Mark*, 157–58.

learning from him and participating in his redemptive mission.[118] While plagued by persistent failure and misunderstanding and struggling to fully comprehend his identity and mission, they're given special insight into Jesus's teaching and are apprenticed to continue Jesus's mission following his resurrection and exaltation. With the Twelve in place, Mark draws the lines of division more sharply in the controversies that ensue.

Opposition from Jesus's Own Family and the Blasphemy against the Holy Spirit (3:20–35)

In the next episode, the opposition to Jesus finds unlikely supporters and takes a sharp turn. Upon hearing of his growing ministry, Jesus's family tries to "seize him," having concluded, "He is out of his mind."[119] This is the first time Mark has mentioned Jesus's family. Presumably, they were in Nazareth when they heard the news of Jesus's growing ministry and the increasing scrutiny and opposition he faced. In response, they set out to seize or restrain him, which paradoxically allied them with the religious leaders. Jesus is now facing opposition from multiple sides. To compound the situation, a group of scribes from Jerusalem arrive and accuse Jesus by saying, "He is possessed by Beelzebul" (i.e., Satan), alleging that he casts out demons "by the prince of demons."[120] Some may wonder if Jesus's "insanity" is a sign of demonic influence. This is a serious charge meant to undercut his authority. Thus, ironically, both Jesus's family and the scribes from Jerusalem allege that Jesus has gone off the rails.

In response, Jesus no longer speaks to people in plain language but only in parables (stories invented by Jesus to drive home an important spiritual truth).[121] In this way, he draws a sharp line between insiders and outsiders in God's kingdom. We've already discussed the reference to the "blasphemy against the Holy Spirit" in Matthew's Gospel above.[122] In essence, the point of the ensuing parables is that, through his exorcisms, Jesus has begun to invade Satan's domain. Through his work, God's kingdom "is at

118. Cf. Williams, *Mark*, 60: "In 3:14–15, Mark clarifies why Jesus selected this smaller group of disciples, so that they might be with him and so that he might send them out to continue his work. In a sense, the first—spending time with Jesus—serves as an essential prerequisite for the second—going out on mission for Jesus."

119. Mark 3:21. Mary was certainly aware of Jesus's messianic identity (cf. Luke 1:31–35). At this point, however, Mark highlights his family's concern over Jesus's actions.

120. Mark 3:22. See Garland, *Theology of Mark's Gospel*, 117. He notes that a better translation of "possessed by Beelzebul" is "having Beelzebul," which could mean having an impure spirit under his control (e.g., a sorcerer or spirit-medium). He adds, "This charge is a malicious claim that Jesus has diabolical power and works by a different spirit than the Holy Spirit." See also Mark Strauss, "Beelzebub, the Prince of Demons," in *Luke*, in *Zondervan Illustrated Bible Backgrounds Commentary*, vol. 1, *Matthew, Mark, Luke*, ed. Clinton E. Arnold (Grand Rapids: Zondervan, 2002), 420.

121. Mark 3:23–27.

122. Matthew 12:24–31.

hand."[123] For Jesus to cast out demons, he first needs to overcome Satan, the ruler of demons. There's no way he can cast out demons by the power of Satan, for "a kingdom divided against itself cannot stand." Thus, all other sins people commit can be forgiven, but "whoever blasphemes against the Holy Spirit" is "guilty of an eternal sin."[124] This "blasphemy against the Holy Spirit" is attributing the power of Jesus to Satan, a sin of which some of Jesus's opponents were guilty but which people today can no longer commit as Jesus is no longer physically among us.

THE MARKAN SANDWICH IN MARK 3:20–35

3:20–21 Jesus's family comes to seize him
 3:22–30 Blasphemy against the Holy Spirit
3:31–35 Jesus's family comes and calls for him

The scene closes with yet another reference to Jesus's mother and brothers calling for him.[125] Mark here serves up the first of his tasty "sandwiches."[126] In the present case, the Pharisees' blasphemy is sandwiched between the erroneous conclusions drawn by Jesus's family. Again, Jesus's response is both pointed and powerful: "For whoever does the will of God, he is my brother and sister and mother."[127] As Strauss aptly remarks, "Jesus is not rejecting his own family. He is establishing a new society in which family is defined not by ethnic or national identity but by common allegiance to the kingdom of God and his purpose in the world."[128] Those of us who grew up in non-Christian

123. Cf. Mark 1:15.
124. Mark 3:29. Garland explains the "unforgiveable sin" as follows: "To identify the work of the Holy Spirit as the working of the power of evil with the malicious intent of destroying another's reputation to safeguard one's own sphere of influence is an unforgivable sin" (*Theology of Mark's Gospel*, 117). For further discussion see Strauss, *Mark*, 172–73.
125. Mark 3:31–35. Some versions add "and sisters." See the reference to spiritual sisters in 3:35 below and cf. the reference to Jesus's (half-)sisters in 6:3.
126. This feature is found in the other Gospels as well. In part, the feature simply reflects historical realities, such as when Jesus heals a woman with blood flow en route to raising a girl from the dead. Williams (*Mark*, 63) notes that "3:20–35 is the first example of Mark's sandwich technique, a literary pattern in which he interrupts one story, inserts a second, and then returns to finish the first" (he cites the following later examples: 5:21–43; 6:7–30; 11:12–25; 14:1–11, 53–72). As Williams observes, "By bringing two stories together, Mark draws attention to the similarities and differences between the two events." Cf. James R. Edwards, *The Gospel according to Mark* (Grand Rapids: Eerdmans, 2002), 11–12, 117–18.
127. Mark 3:35.
128. Strauss, *Mark*, 172.

homes and/or were converted later in life will appreciate the important spiritual truth enunciated by Jesus here. Jesus's response acknowledges that many don't understand his message and mission, including even his own natural family. This, too, reveals the radical nature of following Christ, as Jesus's followers too may find themselves opposed by their own natural family, who may even surmise that they are out of their minds.

RECAP

Thus far, Mark has deftly narrated the early stages of Jesus's ministry starting with the ministry of his forerunner, John the Baptist, as well as Jesus's baptism by John and Jesus's temptation. He has told us that Jesus called his first followers and later appointed twelve apostles to be with him and to be sent out as his representatives. At the very outset, Jesus was actively engaged in casting out demons and healing many—a man with an unclean spirit, Peter's mother-in-law, a leper, a paralytic, a man with a shriveled hand—in his adopted hometown of Capernaum. He also spread the news about God's kingdom in many of the villages in Galilee.

When queried by his opponents, Jesus clarified that he had come to bring something entirely new that could not be contained in the "old wineskins" of Judaism. He also resolutely rebuffed charges that he was a Sabbath-breaker and that he cast out demons by the power of Satan. Rather, he asserted messianic authority over the Sabbath and claimed spiritual power over Satan. With this, the stage is set for Jesus's teaching about God's kingdom in the form of a series of parables, most poignantly the parable of the sower, which would provide an important lens for gauging the response (or lack thereof) of many of his contemporaries.

JESUS'S LATER WORK IN GALILEE (3:7–6:6A, CONT.)

Parables of the Kingdom (4:1–34)

The Parable of the Sower (4:1–20)

Chapter 4 consists largely of Jesus's teaching in the form of parables.[129] This is remarkable in a Gospel that generally, as mentioned, focuses more on Jesus's mighty acts than on lengthy discourse portions. Nevertheless, the parable of the sower, which takes up the lion's share of this literary unit, is of strategic and seminal importance (pun intended), as it illustrates the various responses to Jesus's message about God's kingdom. By now, Jesus's disciples are probably wondering why, if Jesus is in fact the Messiah as they've come to believe, some receive him while many (if not most) others reject him. Jesus tells the parable of the sower to answer this question. There are several reasons why people might not be open to Jesus and his message despite the fact that Jesus is the Messiah and his message is true. All of these reasons are rooted in people's sinful human hearts in conjunction with the world in which they live, which is full of distractions, temptations, and persecutions.

The parable goes like this:

> A sower went out to sow. And as he sowed, some seed fell along the path, and the birds came and devoured it. Other seed fell on rocky ground, where it did not have

129. Williams (*Mark*, 69) draws attention to the reference to a boat in 4:1 and frequently throughout the remainder of the first half of Mark's Gospel. While Jesus has previously been mentioned at the Sea of Galilee (1:16; 2:13; 3:7), there was no reference to a boat. Williams continues, "From 4:1 until 8:26, Jesus is in and out of the boat traveling back and forth across the sea. In the final episode in this section (8:22–26), Jesus and his disciples exit the boat, and from that point on in the narrative the boat motif disappears entirely." Structurally, he proposes that "Mark 4:1–8:26 includes three cycles of episodes that portray in order: Jesus's ministry to the crowd, followed by a boat scene, followed by a report of Jesus's healing work."

> much soil, and immediately it sprang up, since it had no depth of soil. And when the sun rose, it was scorched, and since it had no root, it withered away. Other seed fell among thorns, and the thorns grew up and choked it, and it yielded no grain. And other seeds fell into good soil and produced grain, growing up and increasing and yielding thirtyfold and sixtyfold and a hundredfold.[130]

Here Jesus gives us a taxonomy of the human heart and canvases the scope of people's responses to his message about God's kingdom.

Fortunately, we're not left to interpret this parable on our own, because in what follows Jesus's disciples ask him regarding the meaning of the parable and he explains it to them—and thus also indirectly to Mark's readers, including us, as well. The disciples are privileged "kingdom insiders" to whom "the secret of the kingdom of God" has been given, while those who oppose and reject Jesus are "kingdom outsiders" who are given spiritual truth only in the form of parables. The purpose of these parables is thus to reveal the nature of God's kingdom to insiders while concealing it from those outside. In this way, those who are open to hearing Jesus's message can receive it with joy and bear much fruit, while the hearts of those who are resistant are further hardened.

This is an intriguing spiritual dynamic that explains, at least to some extent, why it is that some are more open to spiritual truth than others (though a mystery still remains). According to Jesus, this fulfills the purpose stated by the prophet Isaiah that "they may indeed see but not perceive, and may indeed hear but not understand, lest they should turn and be forgiven."[131] Through Jesus, the "secret" or "mystery" of God's kingdom has been revealed—the mystery being the truth about God's kingdom that was formerly unknown but now has been disclosed.[132] Despite this great revelation, many—including the Jewish leaders—have tragically rejected God's message. Thus, the parable explains "Jesus's lack of success in his mission but also gives the assurance of a successful harvest."[133]

Taking the disciples aside, Jesus speaks to them as insiders and those who have responded to his word.[134] Jesus's gentle rebuke, "Do you not understand this parable? How then will you understand all parables?"[135] makes clear that the parable of the sower is the parable par excellence, serving as the foundation for all other parables, which explains why Mark gives it such prominent coverage in his Gospel: (1) he features it

---

130. Mark 4:3–8.
131. Mark 4:12, citing Isaiah 6:9–10. See the discussion in Williams, *Mark*, 73–74.
132. Garland, *Theology of Mark's Gospel*, 120.
133. Garland, *Theology of Mark's Gospel*, 119.
134. Mark 4:10–20.
135. Mark 4:13.

as one of the few extended discourses of Jesus in a Gospel that is given primarily to a narration of Jesus's powerful miracles; (2) he places the parable in a strategic position early in his Gospel; and (3) he provides not only the parable itself but also its interpretation—by Jesus himself.

Jesus proceeds to explain the parable, which comes close to an allegory where every component part of the story conveys a symbolic meaning and corresponds to a figurative, spiritual equivalent. In the present case:

- The sower is God (or Jesus).
- The seed is God's word—Jesus's message about the kingdom.
- The first type of soil, the area along the *path*, resembles the hardened heart, while the birds represent Satan, who immediately snatches away the truth conveyed by Jesus's teaching.
- The second type of soil, the *rocky ground*, symbolizes a heart that "immediately" receives the message about the kingdom with joy but, when persecution comes, "immediately" falls away. This heart immediately receives the word but then immediately rejects it! There is only a surface response that is sadly short-lived.
- The third type of soil is the *thorns*, symbolizing hearts in which a preoccupation with material possessions chokes out the word so that it proves unfruitful. While there may be a variety of reasons why God's word fails to take permanent root in a person's heart, the first three types of soil all represent hearts that are unregenerate.
- Finally, the fourth type of soil, *good soil*, represents the receptive human heart that bears various multiples of fruit—thirty, sixty, or even a hundredfold. Even a thirtyfold return is nothing to scoff at and far exceeds normal agricultural yields in first-century Palestine. Imagine stocks that have a 3,000 percent return on investment!

Two Sayings and Two More Parables (4:21–34)

Jesus continues his teaching with two sayings[136] and two additional parables.[137] The two sayings extend Jesus's teaching in the parable of the sower. First, Jesus asks, "Is a lamp brought in to be put under a basket, or under a bed, and not on a stand?" The light of God's truth has been revealed, and its recipients must respond accordingly: a lamp's purpose is to shine and give light to others. Second, he says, "Pay attention to

136. Mark 4:21–23, 24–25.
137. Mark 4:26–29, 30–32.

what you hear: with the measure you use, it will be measured to you."[138] We must share what God has given to us generously with others, as the measure by which we give will be the measure God uses to give to us. Thus, those who already have will receive even more, while those who don't have will lose even the little that they have. This, too, is a spiritual law or dynamic revealed by Jesus that may not seem fair to us but reflects the way things work in God's kingdom.

The two ensuing parables describe the nature of the kingdom. In the parable of the seed growing (which, remarkably, is unique to Mark's Gospel), a man scatters seed onto the ground. He goes to sleep while the ground produces grain until it is ripe for harvest. In the parable of the mustard seed, a tiny mustard seed is sown, resulting in a plant so large that birds can nest in the shade of its large foliage.[139] The parables illustrate yet another couple facets of God's kingdom. While starting out inconspicuously, the kingdom will grow gradually but steadily (parable of the mustard seed), not by human effort but by the mysterious inner dynamics of God's spiritual truth doing its work and bearing fruit (parable of the seed growing). Both the sayings and the parables highlight the spiritual hiddenness of God's kingdom. The kingdom has been inaugurated in unexpected ways. Many Jews expected God to establish his rule by overthrowing the Romans. But Jesus has come preaching the good news, healing the sick, and casting out demons. God's work is like a tiny mustard seed that will eventually grow to become "larger than all the garden plants."[140] How wise and spiritually sublime, and yet how different from the way a mere human would go about launching a new movement! The section concludes by reiterating the clear line of demarcation between kingdom insiders and kingdom outsiders. To outsiders, Jesus "did not speak . . . without a parable"; to insiders, he "explained everything."[141]

---

138. Mark 4:24.

139. As Williams (*Mark*, 102, citing the *Theological Dictionary of the New Testament*, 7:228) points out, "The contrast between the size of the mustard seed and the full-grown mustard plant is in fact dramatic, since it can grow to the height of ten to twelve feet."

140. Mark 4:32.

141. Mark 4:33–34.

JESUS'S LATER WORK IN GALILEE (3:7–6:6A, CONT.)
The Fourfold Scope of Jesus's Messianic Authority (4:35–5:43)
The Calming of the Storm (4:35–41)
The Healing of the Gerasene Demoniac (5:1–20)
The Raising of Jairus's Daughter and the Healing of a Woman with Blood Flow (5:21–43)
Rejected in Nazareth (6:1–6a)

JESUS'S LATER WORK IN GALILEE (3:7–6:6A, CONT.)

The Fourfold Scope of Jesus's Messianic Authority (4:35–5:43)

After his account of Jesus's teaching, Mark returns to the theme of Jesus's authority. In a series of miracles, Jesus demonstrates the vast range of his messianic authority over

- the forces of nature (4:35–41),
- demonic spirits (5:1–20),
- chronic disease (5:25–34), and
- even death (5:21–24, 35–43).

This string of units builds on the previous series of miracles, with several themes binding them together.[142] We'll first discuss these common themes and then look at each event individually.

First, death overshadows each of these miracle accounts, yet Jesus comes to bring healing, deliverance, and life. The disciples fear for their lives at sea, yet Jesus comes to the rescue.[143] The Gerasene demoniac lives "among the tombs," yet Jesus casts out the evil spirits and delivers the man from demon possession.[144] A woman suffers from

142. Cf. Mark 1:21–3:6. See Garland, *Theology of Mark's Gospel*, 122.
143. Mark 4:35–41.
144. Mark 5:1–20.

chronic bleeding, which threatens her life, yet Jesus (literally) stops the bleeding.[145] And the young daughter of a synagogue leader dies from sickness yet is miraculously restored to life—one of only three raisings from the dead in all four Gospels combined.[146]

THE MARKAN SANDWICH IN MARK 5:21–34

5:21–24 Jairus's request to heal his daughter
5:25–34 The woman with blood flow
5:35–43 Jesus raises Jairus's daughter from the dead

Second, each of the characters is desperate for help, and, third, the witnesses of Jesus's messianic, powerful, miracle-working authority are overcome by fear and awe. In the calming of the storm, the disciples are "filled with great fear" and ask themselves, "Who then is this, that even the wind and the sea obey him?"[147] In the case of the demoniac, the townspeople witness the man who had been demon-possessed sitting "in his right mind, and they were afraid."[148] The woman who was healed of her bleeding "fell down before" Jesus.[149] And upon seeing the synagogue ruler's daughter get up and walk, the mourners who previously laughed at Jesus "were immediately overcome with amazement."[150] Jesus's power over the forces of nature and even death serves to demonstrate his authority as the unique and powerful Son of God.

The Calming of the Storm (4:35–41)

Jesus's calming of the storm is one of the most famous miracles he performed.[151] While he and the disciples were crossing the Sea of Galilee in a boat, a violent storm arose and waves were breaking into the boat.[152] Meanwhile, Jesus, probably exhausted from a long day of ministry, was in the stern of the boat, asleep on a cushion. The

145. Mark 5:25–34.
146. Mark 5:21–24, 35–43. The other two raisings are those of the widow's son in Nain (only in Luke) and of Lazarus (only in John).
147. Mark 4:41.
148. Mark 5:15.
149. Mark 5:33.
150. Mark 5:42.
151. The calming of the storm is the first of three major boat episodes in this portion of Mark (4:35–41; 6:45–52; 8:14–21).
152. See Gordon Franz, "What Type of Storms Did Jesus Calm: Wind or Rain? (Matt 8:23–27; 14:22–33; Mark 4:35–416:45–52; etc.)," in Beitzel, *Lexham Geographic Commentary*, 175–82.

disciples wake him up, chiding him somewhat incredulously, "Teacher, do you not care that we are perishing?"[153] That storm really did put the fear of God into those rugged fishermen! At this, Jesus wakes up, "rebukes" the wind as one might an unruly person, and tells the sea (again, as one might an obstinate child) to be quiet—and the storm obliges! Instead of the fear-inspiring torrent, "there was a great calm."[154] Jesus looks at the dumbfounded disciples and says, "Why are you so afraid? Have you still no faith?"[155] By this he insinuates that by now they should know who he is—that they don't need to be afraid when a storm arises because he, the Son of God, is with them. In a way, this story can also serve as an acted parable of sorts. We, too, can trust Jesus in the storms of life because he is more than able to calm the waves and turbulences when they arise.[156] We can do better than the disciples and not get so rattled when the elements pound down on us.

The Healing of the Gerasene Demoniac (5:1–20)

Crossing over to "the other side" of the Sea of Galilee with his disciples to the country of the Gerasenes, Jesus has barely stepped out of the boat when "immediately" he is met by a man with an unclean spirit who emerged, forebodingly, "out of the tombs."[157] The man quite clearly was demon-possessed, displayed self-destructive tendencies (he cut himself with rocks), and couldn't be subdued by anyone.[158] Somehow Jesus, like a magnet, regularly seems to have attracted demonic attention wherever he went; the present case is no exception. The story bears testimony to the incredible power Jesus wielded over the spirit world; even an entire horde of demons was no match for him. The man sees Jesus from a distance, runs toward him, falls down before him, and cries out defiantly, in words reminiscent of the earlier incident where Jesus had exorcised a demon, "What have you to do with me, Jesus, Son of the Most High God?"[159] Then he pleads with Jesus not to torment him. Clearly, it was not the man speaking but the demon inside of him. Interestingly, Jesus asks

---

153. Mark 4:38.
154. Mark 4:39. Notice the contrast between the "great calm" in verse 39 and the "great storm" in verse 37 (noted, e.g., by Williams, *Mark*, 84).
155. Mark 4:40.
156. This is not an allegorical or moralistic reading of the passage but (I think) a legitimate point of application.
157. Mark 5:2. Gerasa is a city east of the Jordan River in the region called Decapolis (literally, "ten cities"). Some manuscripts read "Gadarenes"; Gadara is likewise a city east of the Jordan River but is located thirty miles farther north, closer to the Sea of Galilee. See Cyndi Parker, "Crossing to 'The Other Side' of the Sea of Galilee (Matt 8:18–22; Mark 5:1–20; Luke 8:26–39)," in Beitzel, *Lexham Geographic Commentary*, 157–64.
158. Mark 5:3, which reads literally, "No one was able to bind him, not any longer, not even with a chain" (Williams, *Mark*, 87).
159. Mark 5:7.

the demon what his name is, and the demon replies, "My name is Legion, for we are many."[160]

The fact that the man is possessed by a whole horde of demons, however, poses no problem for Jesus. He casts them out of the man and, granting their request, sends them into a herd of pigs feeding on a nearby hillside.[161] As a result, two thousand pigs (!) are drowned in the Sea of Galilee.[162] When the herdsmen see what has happened, just as the demons earlier had "begged Jesus not to send them out of the country," they "beg Jesus to depart from their region."[163] The healed man, for his part, begs Jesus to take him along, but Jesus tells him instead to go home and spread the news among his friends. The begging on the part of the horde of demons as well as the healed man underscores Jesus's supreme authority. The man promptly proclaims (preaches) all over the Decapolis—the area southeast of the Sea of Galilee and east of the Jordan River—what Jesus has done for him. This is a powerful lesson on gratitude. Jesus has done a lot for you and me. Are we gratefully broadcasting his goodness and mercy toward us to the world around us?

The Raising of Jairus's Daughter and the Healing of a Woman with Blood Flow (5:21–43)

What can top Jesus's act of calming a violent storm on the Sea of Galilee and displaying his command over the forces of nature followed by his exorcisms of an entire horde of demons from a violent man "coming out of the tombs" in Gentile territory? How about raising a twelve-year-old girl from the dead—how's that for an encore? And if that weren't enough, sandwiched in between the account of the raising of the daughter of Jairus, the synagogue ruler, is Jesus's encounter with a woman with blood flow whom he heals, literally, *en passant*, on his way to Jairus's house.[164]

This is yet another of Mark's "sandwiches." The story of the synagogue ruler's dying daughter, as mentioned, is interrupted by the bleeding woman (this, incidentally, can teach us a powerful lesson on dealing with interruptions!). The stories are meant to be compared with each other as examples of faith. What's more, the intervening

160. Mark 5:9. A legion was "the largest unit of troops in the Roman army," which "at full strength consisted of approximately 6,000 soldiers, and 25 legions formed the core of the Roman army as a whole (*EDNT* 2:345–46; BDAG 588a)" (Williams, *Mark*, 88).

161. See Chris McKinny, "Pig Husbandry in Israel during the New Testament (Matt 7:6; 8:28–34; Mark 5:1–20; Luke 8:26–39; 15:11–32," in Beitzel, *Lexham Geographic Commentary*, 183–95.

162. See Todd Bolen, "Where Did the Possessed Pigs Drown? (Matt 8:28–34; Mark 5:1–20; Luke 8:26–39)," in Beitzel, *Lexham Geographic Commentary*, 196–218.

163. Mark 5:17; cf. 5:10.

164. Cf. Williams, *Mark*, 94: "The woman's ailment was a chronic condition of vaginal bleeding, a condition that would render her ceremonially unclean (cf. 'flow of blood' in 5:25 with Lev 15:25 LXX and 'fountain of her blood' in 5:29 with Lev 12:7 LXX)."

encounter with the woman with blood flow heightens the drama of the account of the healing of Jairus's daughter as reports reach Jesus that in the interim the girl has died, raising the bar for Jesus considerably. What is required now is not only a healing but a raising from the dead!

You can read the powerful story for yourself; as mentioned, it is one of only three raisings from the dead Jesus performs in any of the Gospels and shows Jesus's tender compassion for a father who has lost his beloved child.[165] Still, Jesus is cautious about revealing his identity. His commands to silence continue; he simply tells people to give the raised girl something to eat.[166] This is an incredibly understated response that shows that, for Jesus, it is not the miracle itself that is the focus but his underlying heart of compassion as God's caring shepherd-healer.

Rejected in Nazareth (6:1–6a)

Just like the previous section on healings, this series of events ends on a note of rejection. Jesus is back in his hometown synagogue in Capernaum, where he teaches on the Sabbath.[167] People there marvel at the depth of his understanding, his wisdom, and his "mighty works."[168] They wonder, "Is this not the carpenter, the son of Mary and brother of James and Joses and Judas and Simon? And are not his sisters here with us?"[169] This is very interesting, for several reasons:

- People acknowledge Jesus's amazing insight and miraculous powers.
- They call him "the carpenter," which means Jesus took up the same trade as his adoptive father Joseph, who had probably taken him under his wings.
- Joseph is not mentioned, only Mary, most likely because he had passed away by that time, being considerably older than Mary.
- The names of Jesus's four half-brothers (same mother, different father) are mentioned, and his sisters (in the plural) are mentioned as well, though not by name.

Mark adds that people in his hometown "took offense" at him. They couldn't reconcile the fact that he was a hometown boy and yet had so much wisdom and did such astounding miracles. How could the Jesus they knew be the messianic Son of God?

165. Mark 5:21–43.
166. Mark 5:43.
167. Cf. Mark 1:21.
168. Mark 6:1–6; cf. 3:6.
169. Mark 6:3. "Carpenter" translates the Greek word *tektōn*, which could refer more broadly to those working with wood, stone, or metal in building construction. See Ken M. Campbell, "What Was Jesus's Occupation?" *Journal of the Evangelical Theological Society* 48 (2005): 501–19.

They couldn't wrap their minds around a truth as unlikely as this. You can hardly blame them, and yet—it was really true! Jesus—who had grown up in their midst, whose family they knew—was also the divine Son of God who taught in their synagogue and cast out demons in their midst.

At this, Jesus coined the well-known saying "A prophet is not without honor, except in his hometown and among his relatives and in his own household."[170] Note that Jesus calls himself a "prophet" here; this is the first time in Mark's Gospel that he identifies himself as standing in the tradition of prophets who were likewise rejected throughout Israel's history.[171] Remarkably, Mark adds that Jesus "could [not merely did] do no mighty work there," except for healing a few sick people.[172] And now it was Jesus's turn to "marvel"—at people's unbelief.[173] He couldn't believe why people wouldn't believe in him! The primary purpose of Jesus's miracles was not to wow people with his amazing powers but to lead them to faith in him;[174] and yet here we see the opposite dynamic: no faith, no miracles. And so Jesus went off to teach in the various adjacent villages.

170. Mark 6:4.
171. Cf. 1 Kings 19:10; 2 Chronicles 36:16; Jeremiah 11:2; 12:6. See further the parable of the wicked tenants in Mark 12:1–12 below.
172. Mark 6:5.
173. Mark 6:6. This is the only place in Mark's Gospel where Jesus is said to be amazed. Everywhere else, people are amazed at him.
174. Garland, *Theology of Mark's Gospel*, 127.

JESUS'S WORK BEYOND GALILEE (6:6B–8:26)
The Sending Out of the Twelve (6:6b–13)
Flashback: The Execution of John the Baptist (6:14–29)
The Feeding of the Five Thousand (6:30–44)
Walking on the Water and Jesus's Expansive Work (6:45–56)

JESUS'S WORK BEYOND GALILEE (6:6B–8:26)

The Sending Out of the Twelve (6:6b–13)

In this next section, we see Jesus's work expand beyond Galilee, drawing crowds from all over the region. First, Jesus summons the Twelve to send them out on mission.[175] He commissions them in pairs and delegates to them authority over unclean spirits. He instructs them to take only minimal supplies and to accept the hospitality of receptive individuals. If anyone rejects them, they are to "shake off the dust that is on [their] feet" as a witness against that house (an ancient custom signifying rejection).[176] The disciples go on their way, casting out many demons and healing many sick people.

As Mark makes clear, the missions of Jesus and his disciples are both linked to John the Baptist.[177] Jesus's mission began after John's imprisonment, while that of his followers commenced as John was executed.[178] This ominously forecasts that Jesus's disciples, following in Jesus's footsteps, will preach the gospel and engage in ministry "in a hostile world" where many will reject them and where the message of the coming of God's kingdom won't be welcomed with open arms.[179] The outcome of the earthly missions of Jesus and John the Baptist teaches us that we should brace ourselves for stiff opposition as we enlist in Jesus's spiritual army.

---

175. Mark 6:7–13.
176. Mark 6:11; cf. Matthew 10:14; Luke 10:10–11; Acts 13:51; 18:6.
177. Garland, *Theology of Mark's Gospel*, 128.
178. Mark 6:14–29; cf. Mark 1:14.
179. Garland, *Theology of Mark's Gospel*, 128.

Flashback: The Execution of John the Baptist (6:14–29)

The account of John's execution—a flashback—foreshadows Jesus's journey to Jerusalem. David Garland notes, "As John was 'handed over' (1:14), so Jesus will be 'handed over' (3:19; 9:31; 10:33)."[180] Again, you can read the sordid story of the Baptist's demise on your own. We've already looked at it in the context of Matthew's Gospel above. Even Herod Antipas, a Gentile ruler, knew John to be a "righteous and holy man," yet he executes him in deference to his wife, who held a grudge against John because he had courageously denounced her illegitimate marriage to Herod as she had previously been the wife of his brother Philip.[181]

Here we have another example of a Markan "sandwich." The story of John's beheading is placed between the commissioning of the Twelve (6:7–13) and their return (6:30). The disciples went out, preaching the good news, driving out demons, and healing the sick. But the news of John's fate is a sober lesson on the cost of true discipleship. John had suffered a gruesome death, not because he had done anything wrong, but because he had done everything right, and done so with great courage. It's not always easy to understand why God allows the righteous to suffer, though through the eyes of faith we can see that ultimately everything works together for good in God's sovereign plan.[182]

THE MARKAN SANDWICH IN MARK 6:7–30

6:7–13 The apostles' mission
    6:14–29 The beheading of John the Baptist
6:30 The apostles' return

The Feeding of the Five Thousand (6:30–44)

After the disciples return from their mission, Jesus takes them away to get some rest (always a good idea in Christian ministry!).[183] But even as they depart in a boat to a "desolate place," many see where they're headed, and a great crowd forms on the shore. Rather than sending people away, Jesus has "compassion on them, because they

180. Garland, *Theology of Mark's Gospel*, 129.

181. Mark 6:17–20. For background, see Josephus, *Jewish Antiquities* 18.5.1 §109; cf. Harold W. Hoehner, *Herod Antipas* (Cambridge: Cambridge University Press, 1972), 131–36.

182. As Paul affirmed in Romans 8:28. Williams (*Mark*, 109) notes how the account of John's burial anticipates that of Jesus: "Both scenes involve the receiving of a dead body (πτῶμα in 6:29; 15:45), which is then placed (ἔθηκαν/ἔθηκεν in 6:29; 15:46) in a tomb (ἐν μνημείῳ in 6:29; 15:46)."

183. Mark 6:30–43.

were like sheep without a shepherd."[184] Mark here plainly alludes to Moses's statement, "Let the LORD, the God of the spirits of all flesh, appoint a man over the congregation who shall go out before them and come in before them, who shall lead them out and bring them in, that the congregation of the LORD may not be as sheep that have no shepherd."[185] In response, God appoints Joshua as Moses's successor.[186] The allusion indicates Mark's understanding that Jesus is the new Joshua who would bring about a new exodus by leading God's people into the Promised Land.

Jesus's care for the people is also reminiscent of Psalm 23, which says, "The LORD is my shepherd."[187] As the messianic shepherd, Jesus makes the people sit down in green pastures beside the water to feed them.[188] He is the good shepherd who cares for his flock. Five thousand men, plus women and children,[189] are fed that day, as Jesus multiplies five loaves of bread and two fish, and twelve baskets are left over. And yet the disciples struggle to grasp the true significance of Jesus's actions. They initially tell Jesus to send the people away to buy food.[190] While their response seems very practical, notice that they had just returned from their mission before which Jesus commanded them to take "no bread" but to trust in God to meet their needs.[191] As Mark Strauss observes, "Here Jesus is challenging them to even greater faith and greater action."[192] Unfortunately, the disciples fail to demonstrate this kind of faith—at least for now.

Walking on the Water and Jesus's Expansive Work (6:45–56)

In the next scene, Jesus dismisses the crowd and sends his disciples by boat to Bethsaida while he prays on a mountain.[193] The scene recalls an earlier event when Jesus calmed the storm.[194] Once again, the disciples face a strong wind on the lake, though

184. Mark 6:34.
185. Numbers 27:16–17.
186. Garland notes several additional Old Testament echoes in this passage, including God's provision of food for Israel in the wilderness (Numbers 11), Elijah feeding the widow of Zarephath (1 Kings 17:8–16), Elisha feeding the company of prophets (2 Kings 4:42–44), and the end-time banquet prophesied by Isaiah (Isaiah 25:6–8; 55:1–2). Garland, *Theology of Mark's Gospel*, 130.
187. Garland, *Theology of Mark's Gospel*, 130.
188. Psalm 23:1–2, 5. Note that, of the evangelists, only Mark records the incidental detail that the grass was "green" (Mark 6:39). Williams (*Mark*, 113) notes the contrast between Jesus's feeding of the five thousand and Herod's banquet in the previous scene. He adds, "The picture is of the crowd sitting down arranged in regular patterns in such a way that the whole scene looked like garden plots."
189. Mark 6:44; cf. Matthew 14:21.
190. Mark 6:36.
191. Mark 6:7–13.
192. Strauss, *Mark*, 275.
193. Mark 6:45–52; cf. Mark 1:35 above.
194. Mark 4:35–41. Again, the story involves a boat (Williams, *Mark*, 115).

this time Jesus had stayed behind on the shore, praying "well into the night."[195] Very early in morning, Jesus "came to them, walking on the sea."[196] By treading the waves, he performs an act that "only God can do."[197] What's more, walking on water, "he meant to pass by them," the language of Old Testament epiphanies.[198] However, the disciples fail to grasp this and react in fear; yet Jesus identifies himself in (likely) divine terms: "It is I" (i.e., "I am").[199] Their failure compounds as they also "did not understand about the loaves" because their hearts were "hardened."[200] It seems as if "the greater the signs, the greater their misunderstanding."[201] The disciples and Mark's readers are left with a deep sense of the "awesome mystery about who Jesus is."[202] A broad summary statement about Jesus's Galilean ministry concludes the chapter.[203]

195. Mark 6:46–47 CSB. See the reference to "very early in the morning" in verse 48; cf. Ortlund, "History's Dawning Light."
196. Mark 6:48b (literally, "the fourth watch of the night," i.e., the period between 3:00 and 6:00 a.m.). Note that Jesus's walking on the water, already discussed in the chapter on Matthew above, is connected in all four Gospels with the feeding of the five thousand, underscoring the probability that these two events are historically linked.
197. Cf. Job 9:8; 38:16; Psalm 77:19; Isaiah 43:16; 51:10; Habakkuk 3:15. See Garland, *Theology of Mark's Gospel*, 130.
198. Mark 4:48c; cf. Exodus 33:19–34:16; 1 Kings 19:11–12. Similarly, the Lord said to Moses, "I will make all my goodness *pass before you*" (Exodus 33:19). As Garland notes, "The purpose of passing by is to allow them to witness his transcendent majesty as a divine being. In the past, God could not be fully seen, but now God can be fully seen in Jesus Christ" (*Theology of Mark's Gospel*, 130). Similarly, Williams, *Mark*, 116, who adds, "For Jesus to want to pass by his disciples, therefore, means that he desired to reveal his glory to them."
199. Mark 6:49–50; cf. Exodus 3:14.
200. Mark 6:52.
201. Bas van Iersel, *Reading Mark* (Collegeville, MN: Liturgical Press, 1988), 88–89, cited in Garland, *Theology of Mark's Gospel*, 131.
202. Garland, *Theology of Mark's Gospel*, 131.
203. Mark 6:45–54; cf. 4:35–5:2; 5:21; 6:32–34.

JESUS'S WORK BEYOND GALILEE (6:6B–8:26, CONT.)

What Truly Defiles a Person (Hint: It's Not Unwashed Hands) (7:1–23)

Following Jesus's healings in Gennesaret, Mark returns to the theme of opposition and draws our attention to a new emphasis in Jesus's mission. The scene opens with a controversy between Jesus and the Jewish religious leaders, including Pharisees and some of the scribes, who resurface after a prolonged absence from the Markan narrative. As mentioned in the previous chapter, it's typically Matthew who provides more extensive coverage of rabbinic disputes about matters of the law involving Jesus. The fact that Mark features the present controversy indicates that he judged this particular matter to be of sufficiently broad relevance, even for his Gentile readers, to include it here.

The dispute is regarding what appears to be a rather petty issue of ritual purity. As "guardians of their tradition," the Pharisees and scribes scrutinized Jesus's disciples who, they alleged, "ate with hands that were defiled, that is, unwashed."[204] In an unusually lengthy aside, Mark informs the reader that this was part of what might be described as the scribes' larger obsession with washings and purification rituals, extending even to objects such as cups, pots, copper vessels, and even dining couches![205] These myopic concerns stand in marked contrast to Jesus's amazing miracles, such as his healings, demon exorcisms, and the feeding of the five thousand recorded in the last chapter.

When approached with these allegations against his disciples, Jesus scathingly denounces his opponents for their hypocrisy and for elevating their tradition above God's word: "Well did Isaiah prophesy of you hypocrites . . . 'This people honors me with their lips, but their heart is far from me; in vain do they worship me, teaching as doctrines the commandments of men.'"[206] With biting irony, Jesus goes on the counterof-

204. Mark 7:2.
205. Mark 7:3–5.
206. Mark 7:6–7; cf. Isaiah 29:13.

fensive, saying, "You have a fine way of rejecting the commandment of God to establish your tradition!" He proceeds to cite the policy of Corban, where the Pharisees declared a given item "dedicated to God" in order to circumvent the command to honor their father and mother. And, Jesus adds, they did many similar things.[207]

In this way, Jesus rejected the Pharisees' entire approach to God's law, which involved focusing on minor details while neglecting "the weightier matters of the law."[208] In a follow-up session with the common people and his disciples, when asked by the latter about the meaning of the illustration (Greek *parabolē*), Jesus notes, "What comes out of a person is what defiles him."[209] God's laws dealt with matters of the heart—our "internal impurity," which "cannot be washed away by external rituals."[210] Jesus, Mark notes in an important aside, therefore declared all foods clean.[211] This prepares the reader for what comes next.

The Faith of a Gentile Woman: Putting the Jews to Shame (7:24–30)

Up to this point, the primary context of Jesus's ministry has been the Jews. However, following Jesus's indictment of the Pharisees, the "Jewish context of Jesus is gradually broken up."[212] From now on, Jesus will engage in frequent withdrawals from Galilee. In the next episode, he withdraws to the region of Tyre.[213] There Jesus encounters a Syrophoenician or Canaanite woman—a Gentile—who pleads with Jesus to cast out a demon from her daughter. Jesus's response, "Let the children be fed first, for it is not right to take the children's bread and throw it to the dogs," is shocking at first glance, as he is referring to Israel as "children" while calling Gentiles "dogs."[214] A closer look at the context, however, reveals that Jesus is speaking about the order of God's plan of salvation.[215] The priority of Jesus's mission is to the Jews first, who are called to be a light of revelation to the Gentiles.[216]

What's more, Jesus seems to use provocative language to arouse the woman's persistence. Without challenging Jesus's statement, she responds with remarkable humility

207. Mark 7:9–13.
208. Garland, *Theology of Mark's Gospel*, 131.
209. Mark 7:17–20. Note that most English translations skip verse 16, "If anyone has ears to hear, let him hear," as it is absent from most of the earliest manuscripts.
210. Garland, *Theology of Mark's Gospel*, 133.
211. Mark 7:19; cf. Acts 10:9–16; 11:5–10; Romans 14:13–23.
212. Köstenberger, Kellum, and Quarles, *The Cradle, the Cross, and the Crown*, 292.
213. Mark 7:24–30. Note that this is the second time Jesus has entered Gentile territory in his public ministry (cf. Mark 5:1–20).
214. Mark 7:27.
215. Cf. Matthew 15:21–28. Matthew explicitly points out that Jesus was sent to the lost sheep of Israel (Matthew 15:24).
216. Cf. Isaiah 42:6; 49:6.

and faith. Impressed by her reply, Jesus grants her request and casts out the demon, even from a distance.[217] As Mark Strauss observes, "While the orderly progress of the gospel remains intact (from Jews to Gentiles), at all times salvation comes by grace through faith for all who believe, not through membership in ethnic Israel."[218] Having already declared all foods clean in the previous scene, Jesus now breaks through the Jewish-Gentile barrier, at least incipiently.[219] Ironically, this Gentile woman is the first character to recognize the universal scope of God's salvation of Jesus's work in Mark's Gospel, serving as a model disciple.[220]

The Healing of a Deaf Man (7:31–37)

Following this important episode, Mark records the second of three miracles performed in Gentile territory. Jesus continues his journey and reaches the city of Decapolis. There he encounters a deaf man (who also has a speech impediment) and heals him. Interestingly, Mark here reproduces the very words of Jesus (his *ipsissima verba*) in Aramaic: *Ephphatha*, "Be opened."[221] Perhaps Peter remembered what Jesus said at this occasion and served as Mark's source? In any case, the reaction to this latest of Jesus's miracles is similar to previous responses. The more Jesus tells people to be quiet, the more they spread the news of his miracle-working powers. And everyone is astonished and recognizes that Jesus is certainly doing the things that Old Testament prophets predicted the Messiah would do.[222]

217. Mark 7:29.
218. Strauss, *Mark*, 313.
219. Garland, *Theology of Mark's Gospel*, 134.
220. Strauss, *Mark*, 317.
221. Mark 7:34; cf. 5:41.
222. Mark 7:37; cf. Isaiah 35:5.

JESUS'S WORK BEYOND GALILEE (6:6B–8:26, CONT.)
The Feeding of the Four Thousand (8:1–10)
The Pharisees' Demand for a Sign (8:11–13)
Warning against the "Leaven" of the Pharisees and Herod (8:14–21)
Healing of a Blind Man (8:22–26)

JESUS'S WORK BEYOND GALILEE (6:6B–8:26, CONT.)

The Feeding of the Four Thousand (8:1–10)

The next miracle in this section is the feeding of the four thousand. Again Jesus, the messianic shepherd, is moved with compassion for the people who have been with him for three days. He even expresses concern that if he were to send them away hungry, some may faint on the way home, as some have come from quite a distance. Undeterred by his disciples who point out the impracticality of procuring bread for all those people in a remote location, Jesus feeds the crowd by multiplying seven loaves and a few fish. Even after all have eaten, seven basketsful are left over.

While the present feeding miracle resembles the first feeding miracle of the five thousand, some of the details differ; also, this second miraculous feeding takes place in Gentile territory. By placing it "in the context of Jesus's interaction with the Gentiles," Strauss points out, "Mark implicitly affirms that the invitation to the messianic banquet is not for Israelites alone, but for all people everywhere."[223] The openness of Gentiles stands in marked contrast to the intransigence of the Jews, at times including even the disciples.[224] How often do you and I miss what God is doing around us, even in our own lives and the lives of those closest to us?

The Pharisees' Demand for a Sign (8:11–13)

This contrast emerges even more clearly in the next scene, which takes place in the district of Dalmanutha on the west side of the Sea of Galilee near Magdala. There, in the final conflict episode during Jesus's Galilean ministry, the Pharisees approach him

223. Strauss, *Mark*, 327.
224. Mark 8:21.

and demand "a sign from heaven" to test him.[225] Jesus sighs at their unbelief and refuses to comply. Just as the Israelites tested God in the wilderness, so this generation of Israelites was testing Jesus.[226]

The Pharisees' request is unmasked as utterly disingenuous, and their motives as insincere. Just like some people don't take no for an answer, so Jesus's opponents appear determined to disregard all the miracles Jesus performs and simply keep asking for more. Nothing is ever good enough for these skeptics! Similarly, there are skeptics today who are determined not to believe the gospel, alleging that the problem is lack of evidence when in fact it is their hard-core skepticism.[227]

Warning against the "Leaven" of the Pharisees and Herod (8:14–21)

What follows is the third and final boat episode in this unit.[228] The scene quickly turns to the disciples, whom Jesus warns to "beware of the leaven of the Pharisees and the leaven of Herod."[229] In another instance of misunderstanding, the disciples think Jesus is chiding them for their failure to bring bread, when in fact he is referring to the corrupting influence of Pharisaic teaching. Similar to Jesus's disciples, we're often blind to God's ways in our lives because we're self-absorbed and caught up in our own way of thinking. We, too, need to set aside preconceived notions of God and shed our preoccupation with our own comparatively minor concerns so we can see the big picture of how God is working in our lives and in the lives of those around us. Fortunately, Jesus was very patient with his original disciples and is still patient with us today.

Healing of a Blind Man (8:22–26)

At the end of their journey, Jesus and his disciples encounter a blind man in Bethsaida, located on the north side of the Sea of Galilee.[230] Jesus proceeds to heal the

---

225. Mark 8:11–21; cf. 7:1–23.

226. Cf. Exodus 17:7; Numbers 14:11; Deuteronomy 6:16; 29:2–6; Psalms 78:11–32; 95:8–10.

227. See Andreas Köstenberger, Darrell Bock, and Josh Chatraw, *Truth Matters: Confident Faith in a Confusing World* (Nashville: B&H, 2014), especially the preface, "Skepticism 101," and chapter 1, "The Skeptical Mystique."

228. Mark 8:14–21; see 8:13. For the first two boat scenes, see Mark 4:35–41 and 6:45–52. What all three boat scenes have in common is the Markan motif of discipleship failure. However, "as the narrative is progressing, the disciples have more and more reason to trust Jesus, and therefore their inadequate response is more and more blameworthy" (Williams, *Mark*, 136).

229. Mark 8:15. Williams (*Mark*, 136) explains, "Leaven refers to old fermented dough, which was thoroughly mixed into a new batch of dough to make the bread rise (*NIDNTTE* 2:362; BDAG 429c)." David Garland adds that, negatively and figuratively speaking, "'leaven' is something that can spoil and spread a dangerous contagion" (*Theology of Mark's Gospel*, 136).

230. Mark 8:22–26. The healing is similar to the one narrated in 7:31–37. See Benjamin A. Foreman, "Jesus Heals a Blind Man Near Bethsaida (Mark 8:22–26)," in Beitzel, *Lexham Geographic Commentary*, 270–77.

man, fulfilling Isaiah's prophecy that, at the coming of the Messiah, "the eyes of the blind shall be opened."[231] What's most intriguing about this episode is the gradual nature of the healing. At first, the man sees only faintly. Yet when Jesus lays hands on him again, "his sight [is] restored, and he [sees] everything clearly."[232] This two-stage healing may function as an "acted parable" for the disciples' spiritual understanding, which similarly emerges in stages and over time. In my experience, too, I often have to do a spiritual double take before I perceive God's powerful work in my life and the lives of those around me.

RECAP

The narrative following the parable chapter (chap. 4) started out with a triple bang: the exorcism of the Gerasene demoniac followed by the raising of a synagogue ruler's daughter and the healing of a woman with blood flow. After this, Jesus is rejected in his hometown of Nazareth and commissions the Twelve. He miraculously feeds the five thousand, and later the four thousand. In between he engages in ministry farther north, healing, among others, the daughter of a Syrophoenician woman, a Gentile. By contrast, Jesus's Jewish opponents are unmasked as hypocrites who are more concerned with religious shenanigans than pursuing a relationship with the living God. Sadly, the disciples too have hardened hearts and fail to understand. The section concludes with the two-stage healing of a blind man. While Jesus progressively reveals himself as the authoritative, miracle-working Son of God, his messianic ministry unfolds against the dark backdrop of unbelieving opposition from everyone he encounters—demons, people in his hometown, his Jewish opponents, and even his own followers.

231. Cf. Isaiah 35:5–6.
232. Mark 8:25.

JESUS THE MESSIAH AND SUFFERING SERVANT (8:27–16:8)

Jesus's Journey to Jerusalem (8:27–10:52)

Peter's Confession of Jesus as the Christ (8:27–9:1)

The Transfiguration and the Aftermath (9:2–29)

Jesus's Second Passion Prediction and Discipleship Struggles (9:30–50)

JESUS THE MESSIAH AND SUFFERING SERVANT (8:27–16:8)

We began our study of Mark's Gospel by exploring what it means for Jesus to be the Messiah and Son of God. Here, in the second half of the Gospel, we transition to Jesus as the Messiah and suffering servant.

Jesus's Journey to Jerusalem (8:27–10:52)

Peter's Confession of Jesus as the Christ (8:27–9:1)

While departing for Caesarea Philippi, Jesus continues to develop his disciples' understanding of his true identity. As they walk along the road,[233] he first asks them, "Who do people say that I am?" When they respond, "John the Baptist; and others say, Elijah; and others, one of the prophets," he follows up, "But who do *you* say that I am?"[234] Having witnessed Jesus's powerful words and deeds for some time now, Peter has come to a settled conviction regarding who Jesus is. Answering for the disciples, he bluntly replies, "You are the Christ."[235] After repeated instances of failing to grasp the

233. Williams (*Mark*, 141) insightfully remarks, "The setting of this episode as 'on the way' marks off the beginning of a new section in the narrative. Throughout this section, Mark provides continuing reminders that Jesus is on the way (8:27; 9:33, 34; 10:17, 32, 46, 52), and 10:32–34 makes it clear that he is traveling to Jerusalem, where he will suffer, die, and rise again. Although Mark uses the word 'way' (ὁδός) elsewhere in his Gospel, he makes the term function as a description for a setting only in 8:27–10:52. This section ends with Bartimaeus, a blind beggar healed by Jesus, following him on the way (10:52)."

234. Mark 8:27, emphasis added.

235. Mark 8:28–29. The Greek title "Christ" (like its Hebrew equivalent, "Messiah") means "the Anointed One," emphasizing Jesus's sacred setting apart for his redemptive mission.

meaning of Jesus's teachings and miracles, the disciples (or at least Peter) have finally arrived at a greater level of understanding of Jesus's true identity. Nevertheless, Jesus "strictly charged them to tell no one about him"; while the Twelve understand at last, for "kingdom outsiders," such as the crowds or the Jewish leaders, the "messianic secret" is still in effect.[236]

From now on, Jesus will increasingly reveal that he, the "Son of Man," must suffer, be rejected by the Jewish leaders, be killed, and rise again after three days.[237] In a surprising twist, however, Peter "rebukes" Jesus, apparently for suggesting that he must be killed. Jesus, in turn, "rebukes" Peter, calling him "Satan" and telling him he is looking at matters from a mere human perspective.[238] This pointed exchange serves to clarify, in climactic fashion, what kind of Messiah Jesus was going to be—not, as widely expected, a national deliverer who would lead Israel to overthrow their foes, but one who would be rejected and crucified and rise again.[239] This has important implications for Jesus's followers. They, too, must deny themselves, take up their cross, and follow him, unashamed and unafraid.[240]

The present episode serves as a watershed in Mark's Gospel.[241] In the first half, Jesus's *messianic authority* took center stage. In the second half, Jesus's *vicarious suffering* becomes the central focus.[242] The first half narrated Jesus's ministry in and around *Gal-*

---

236. Mark 8:30.

237. Mark 8:31. On Jesus's self-identification as the "Son of Man," see the discussion at 2:10 above. In view of the Old Testament background of this expression in the book of Daniel (7:13–14), there is a clear connection between Jesus's impending suffering and the coming of God's kingdom. As Williams (*Mark*, 145) explains, "As the representative for God's people he must fully experience their suffering (Dan 7:19, 21, 23–25), a suffering that necessarily precedes the coming of the kingdom of God (Dan 7:17–18, 22, 26–27)."

238. Cf. Williams, *Mark*, 146: "In Mark's Gospel, Jesus's path of sacrificial service stands at the center of God's plan. Any opposition to this path comes from a limited human perspective, which ultimately has its source in the work of Satan."

239. As Garland notes, "The secret is not that Jesus is the Christ but what he is destined to do as Messiah—or, rather, what will be done to him" (*Theology of Mark's Gospel*, 138).

240. Mark 8:34.

241. For Mark 8:26–27 as the pivot of Mark's Gospel, see, e.g., the commentaries by Robert A. Guelich and Craig A. Evans in the Word Biblical Commentary (WBC) series, which are divided at that very point: in the first volume, Guelich covers 1:1–8:26 (WBC 34A [Dallas: Word, 1989]); in the second volume, Evans covers 8:27 through the rest of the Gospel (WBC 34B [Nashville: Thomas Nelson, 2001]). See also William L. Lane, *The Gospel of Mark*, New International Commentary on the New Testament (Grand Rapids: Eerdmans, 1974), 288, who speaks of the "pivotal importance of this moment" and the "central importance of Peter's confession in the Marcan structure"; and Williams (*Mark*, 141), who identifies 8:27ff. as the "pivot point in the story, one that emphasizes Jesus's suffering more than his power." However, not everyone agrees that 8:26/27 is the pivot in Mark's Gospel. R. T. France, *The Gospel of Mark*, New International Greek Testament Commentary (Grand Rapids: Eerdmans, 2002), for example, starts "Act Two: On the Way to Jerusalem" with 8:22.

242. Garland, *Theology of Mark's Gospel*, 138.

ilee, while the latter half focuses on *Jerusalem*. Peter's acknowledgment of Jesus's messianic identity, followed by the first of a "thrice-repeated pattern of passion prediction, discipleship failure, and instruction regarding true discipleship," thus serves as a segue into the second half of the Gospel.[243] The readers already know who Jesus is, as do the Twelve. The Jewish leaders, on the other hand, will further harden in their opposition to Jesus until they reach a point of no return.[244] This, in turn, will set the stage for the concluding passion narrative.

DISCIPLESHIP FAILURE AND JESUS'S MESSIANIC IDENTITY

At the very outset of Mark's Gospel, Jesus is identified as the "Christ" or "Messiah."[245] As the story unfolds, however, Jesus is reluctant to unveil his full identity as the Messiah. Köstenberger, Kellum, and Quarles note, "Of the four Gospels, Mark most frequently records that Jesus told people not to reveal who he was."[246] As mentioned, scholars have referred to this motif as the "messianic secret." Jesus gives frequent commands of silence to those whom he heals.[247] He even commands the demons to stay silent about his identity.[248] A breakthrough occurs when Peter confesses, "You are the Christ."[249] However, Jesus responds by strictly charging the disciples "to tell no one about him."[250]

Jesus's messianic identity also relates to Mark's "discipleship failure" motif. Mark frequently portrays the disciples as failing to understand the significance of Jesus's words and deeds. This emphasis is unique to Mark.[251] Even after his confession, Peter is cast in a negative light for rejecting the

243. Cf. Mark 8:27–9:1; 9:30–41; 10:32–45. Köstenberger, Kellum, and Quarles, *The Cradle, the Cross, and the Crown*, 293.
244. As Williams (*Mark*, 141) notes, "The focus of this section is clearly on the plot line of Jesus's relationship with the disciples. Even when he casts out a demon or disputes with the Pharisees or talks with a rich man about eternal life, Jesus takes time with his disciples at the end of the event to teach them privately about the significance of what just happened (9:28–29; 10:10–12, 23–31)."
245. Mark 1:1.
246. Köstenberger, Kellum, and Quarles, *The Cradle, the Cross, and the Crown*, 298.
247. Mark 1:44; 5:18–19, 43.
248. Mark 1:25, 34; 3:12.
249. Mark 8:29.
250. Mark 8:30.
251. Köstenberger, Kellum, and Quarles, *The Cradle, the Cross, and the Crown*, 299.

notion of Jesus's impending suffering.[252] The disciples fail to understand Jesus's mission to go to the cross. Mark's point in emphasizing the disciples' failures is not to denigrate them but rather to "highlight the contrast between the masterful, commanding Jesus on the one hand, and the much weaker and less comprehending disciples on the other."[253] Jesus alone is the Messiah.

So why does Mark present Jesus as so reluctant to reveal that he's the Messiah? The answer is twofold. First, Jesus was "wary of accepting the title from Jewish people because of prevailing Christological expectations" that focused on political ramifications.[254] Second, more importantly, Jesus's work would be incomplete until he suffered and died on the cross. As Larry Hurtado remarks, "In Mark's view, no one could understand the true meaning of Jesus and his work until Jesus had actually completed it by his death as a ransom for others (10:45)."[255] The cross is central to Mark's theology. Only after the crucifixion, and as aided by the Holy Spirit, will people truly understand that the Messiah is the suffering servant who gave his life as a ransom for many.

The same is still true for us today. We can truly understand who Jesus is only when we come to terms with his death on the cross as our sinless substitute. He died as a sacrifice for our sins so that we may be forgiven and enter his kingdom.

The Transfiguration and the Aftermath (9:2–29)

Six days after his first passion prediction, Jesus gathers his inner circle of disciples—Peter, James, and John—and leads them up a "high mountain" to be

252. Mark 8:33.
253. Evans, "Mark," 272, cited in Köstenberger, Kellum, and Quarles, *The Cradle, the Cross, and the Crown*, 301.
254. Köstenberger, Kellum, and Quarles, *The Cradle, the Cross, and the Crown*, 299.
255. Larry W. Hurtado, *Mark*, New International Biblical Commentary (Peabody, MA: Hendrickson, 1989), 10, cited in Köstenberger, Kellum, and Quarles, *The Cradle, the Cross, and the Crown*, 299.

alone.[256] The scene recalls the exodus account where Moses was given special revelation from God.[257] On the mountain, Jesus is transfigured to reveal his divine glory to his disciples. In a surreal moment, Moses and Elijah appear, corroborating Jesus's fulfillment of Old Testament prophecy.[258] A heavenly voice confirms that Jesus is God's beloved Son.[259] Significantly, the account of Jesus's transfiguration follows immediately after Jesus's first passion prediction. The Jesus who will suffer at the hands of those who reject him is the same Jesus they see in his radiant splendor. Jesus is the Son of God in both his humble and exalted state.[260]

As Jesus and the three disciples come down the mountain, Jesus charges them to "tell no one what they had seen, until the Son of Man had risen from the dead."[261] At this, the disciples wonder what "risen from the dead" meant. Having just seen Elijah, they also wonder why the scribes say Elijah must come first. Jesus explains that Elijah has already come, by implication, in the form of John the Baptist, though "they did to him whatever they pleased, as it is written."[262]

As Jesus returns to the rest of the disciples, he finds a large crowd and some scribes engaged in a major dispute.[263] Apparently, Jesus's disciples had been asked to cast out a demon from a boy but were unable to do so. Was it due to their lack of power? That's what the consensus seems to be. Jesus, however, makes clear that the issue is rather a lack of faith (an incredibly powerful lesson): "All things are possible for one who believes."[264] At once, the boy's father exclaims, "I believe; help my unbelief!"[265] At this,

---

256. Mark 9:2–13. For an argument that the transfiguration took place on Mount Hermon rather than, as is the traditional view, on Mount Tabor, see Michael S. Heiser, *The Unseen Realm: Recovering the Supernatural Worldview of the Bible* (Bellingham, WA: Lexham, 2015), 285–87.

257. Exodus 24:15–16.

258. Garland, *Theology of Mark's Gospel*, 138. Why Moses and Elijah? As France (*Gospel of Mark*, 351) observes, "Of the many suggestions as to the significance of these two figures in Mark's narrative, probably the least valid is the traditional idea that they represent the law and the prophets." Elijah's name precedes Moses's, and Elijah was not an author of an Old Testament prophetic book. More likely, both embodied end-time messianic hopes. Moses had delivered Israel from bondage in Egypt at the exodus; the Messiah would deliver people from their sins in a new, spiritual exodus (cf. Luke 9:31 where the Greek word for "exodus" is used); also, people expected a new "prophet like Moses" (Deuteronomy 18:15–19). Elijah, of course, never died but was taken by God into heaven, which gave rise to the expectation of the coming of a "new Elijah" (2 Kings 2:11; cf. Mark 1:6; 6:15; see also John 1:21).

259. Mark 9:7.

260. Garland, *Theology of Mark's Gospel*, 138..

261. Mark 9:9. Note that much later Peter recounts the whole story in his second letter, in defending his teaching that Jesus will return (2 Peter 1:16–18).

262. Mark 9:13.

263. Mark 9:14–29.

264. Mark 9:23.

265. Mark 9:24.

Jesus casts out the demon, who comes out of the boy, but not without throwing him into convulsions and leaving him lying on the ground as if dead. But Jesus takes him by the hand, and he gets up.

Later, the disciples ask Jesus why they couldn't exorcise the demon from the boy, and he tells them it was because this kind of demon comes out only with prayer. Not only does this reveal the disciples' prayerlessness and lack of dependence on God; it also shows that Jesus's miracles were undergirded by his relationship with God and his dependence on him, rather than being manifestations of sheer power. It also shows that people, in Jesus's day as well as in ours, often lack faith and fail to pray, which renders them powerless in the spiritual struggle in which we are engaged. If we want spiritual power, we must grow in faith and put a priority on prevailing, persistent prayer.

Jesus's Second Passion Prediction and Discipleship Struggles (9:30–50)

In what follows, they pass through Galilee, though Jesus keeps a low profile. For the second time, he predicts his passion while his followers fail to grasp the meaning of his words.[266] At their arrival in Capernaum, as if to underscore their intransigence, the disciples argue about who is the greatest among them. This display of selfish ambition on their part doesn't bode well for what lies ahead.[267] By placing a child in their midst, Jesus instructs them that true greatness manifests itself in servanthood. This is the intriguing paradox Mark tries to get across in the second half of his Gospel. The first will be last, and the last will be first. (Or, as I sometimes tell my children, the slow lane is the fast lane, and the fast lane is the slow lane!) Jesus is both the powerful Messiah and the suffering servant.

At this, John (the son of Zebedee) tells Jesus, in well-intentioned but, as it turns out, misguided zeal, that someone outside the apostolic circle was performing miracles; does Jesus want John to stop him? Jesus replies, "Do not stop him. . . . For who is not against us is for us."[268] This constitutes an indictment of our denominational tribalism today. I once went to a church where the mantra was "I love my church" but the pastors virtually never prayed for or talked about what God was doing in other churches. Don't just love *your* church; love *the* church as well!

At the same time, Jesus tells his followers that those who cause little children to stumble would be better off if a millstone were hung around their neck.[269] Their judgment

266. Mark 9:30–32, 35–37, 38–45.
267. Garland, *Theology of Mark's Gospel*, 140.
268. Mark 9:38–40.
269. See Cyndi Parker, "Millstones in Capernaum (Matt 17:24–18:14; Mark 9:33–49; Luke 17:1–2)," in Beitzel, *Lexham Geographic Commentary*, 308–13.

will be severe.[270] But the disciples should root out anything that might cause them to sin, so they might not come into judgment. For it is better to enter heaven with only one hand or eye than to enter hell with two![271] This is an interesting stage in the Gospel narrative. No longer do we see Jesus engage in major miracles, or even confrontations. Rather, he instructs his followers about various lessons in ministry.

270. Mark 9:42–50.

271. Williams (*Mark*, 164) notes that hell "came from the Heb. name for Ben Hinnom Valley, a ravine outside of Jerusalem. The reforming king Josiah desecrated the place (2 Kgs 23:10), because it had previously served as a location for offering child sacrifices to the god Molech (2 Kgs 16:3; 21:6; Jer 7:31; 32:35). As a place of evil and defilement outside the city of God's holy temple, Gehenna became a metaphor for the place of final judgment away from the presence of God." See also Gordon Franz, "Gehenna: Jerusalem's Garbage Dump or Place of Eschatological Judgment? (Mark 9:42–50)," in Beitzel, *Lexham Geographic Commentary*, 314–26.

JESUS'S JOURNEY TO JERUSALEM (8:27–10:52, CONT.)
The Question of Divorce (10:1–12)
Jesus's Welcome of Children (10:13–16)
The Rich Young Ruler (10:17–31)

JESUS'S JOURNEY TO JERUSALEM (8:27–10:52, CONT.)

The Question of Divorce (10:1–12)

Jesus now travels to Judea and the region on the other side of the Jordan, where he addresses the topics of marriage and divorce, children's status in the kingdom, and people's possessions.[272] First, as he has done previously, Mark includes an episode in which Jesus engages in dispute over a matter of the interpretation of the law with the Pharisees.[273] This time, the topic is divorce: "Is it lawful for a man to divorce his wife?"[274] In response, Jesus cites both Genesis 1:27 ("God made them male and female") and 2:24 ("Therefore a man shall leave his father and mother and hold fast to his wife, and the two shall become one flesh") and affirms marriage as a divinely instituted, lifelong union: "What therefore God has joined together, let not man separate."[275] Following up with his disciples, Jesus elaborates, "Whoever divorces his wife and marries another commits adultery against her, and if she divorces her husband and marries another, she commits adultery."[276] Jesus's statement is remarkable for its evenhandedness: neither men nor women have a right to divorce. Matthew, in a parallel passage, adds an exception in the case of adultery,[277] but Mark, it seems, is content to focus on Jesus's basic teaching that God instituted marriage as a lifelong union and that divorce is generally not permitted.

272. See Mark 10:1–12, 13–16, and 17–31, respectively.
273. Mark 10:1–12.
274. Mark 10:2–4; for a similar, earlier controversy, see 7:1–15.
275. Mark 10:6–9. Regarding the Bible's teaching on marriage and the family, see Andreas Köstenberger with David W. Jones, *Marriage and the Family: Biblical Essentials* (Wheaton, IL: Crossway, 2012).
276. Mark 10:11–12.
277. Cf. Matthew 19:9.

Jesus's Welcome of Children (10:13–16)

In the next scene, Jesus, despite his disciples' resistance (even "rebuke"!), receives little children to bless them.[278] He declares, "whoever does not receive the kingdom of God like a child shall not enter it."[279] By this he means, among other things, that people need to be open to God's rule in their lives without preconditions. In both of these episodes, Jesus affirms and protects those who are among the most vulnerable in society—women and children. Neither group should be the victim of discrimination or disregard but should be valued and treated as precious and highly esteemed, as God made them and cherishes and values them highly. That said, just like it is wrong for a man to divorce his wife, so it is wrong for a wife to divorce her husband (even though the latter was far less common in ancient Judaism than the former).

The Rich Young Ruler (10:17–31)

The following scene shows Jesus's encounter with someone quite different—a rich young ruler.[280] Though a righteous man, he lacks "one thing."[281] He couldn't turn away from his great wealth to follow Jesus. How hard it is for the wealthy to enter God's kingdom![282] As Jesus has just affirmed, one must receive the kingdom with childlike faith.[283] The disciples, on the other hand, as Peter points out, "have left everything and followed" Jesus.[284] In so doing, they were "sacrificing those things that represent a roadblock to authentic faith."[285] In response, Jesus solemnly assures Peter and the other disciples ("Truly, I say to you") that they'll be amply rewarded both "in this life," in which they will receive a new, spiritual family, and "in the age to come," in which they will receive eternal life.[286] In addition, following Jesus also entails the prospect of persecution. In this way, Jesus encourages his disciples but also prepares them for what lies ahead.[287]

---

278. Mark 10:13–16. You'll recall that earlier Peter had rebuked Jesus (!) (Mark 8:32), which promptly led to Jesus rebuking Peter in front of his fellow disciples (Mark 8:33).
279. Mark 10:15.
280. Mark 10:17–31. See the discussion of the same account in Matthew's Gospel (19:16–30) in the previous chapter.
281. Mark 10:21.
282. Mark 10:23.
283. Mark 10:15.
284. Mark 10:28.
285. Strauss, *Mark*, 444.
286. Mark 10:29–30. See Garland, *Theology of Mark's Gospel*, 145.
287. Williams (*Mark*, 175) drives home the application of the three episodes in this chapter as follows: Jesus expects from his followers "wholehearted obedience" (vv. 1–12), "childlike faith" (vv. 13–16), and "self-denying sacrifice" (vv. 17–31).

JESUS'S JOURNEY TO JERUSALEM (8:27–10:52, CONT.)

The Third Passion Prediction (10:32–34)

In the final cycle of prediction, failure, and teaching, Mark identifies Jesus's destination as Jerusalem.[288] The third cycle parallels the second one closely and functions as the climax of the three.[289] Moreover, it prepares the way for Jesus's entry into Jerusalem. The third passion prediction is the most detailed, including information about to whom Jesus will be handed over ("the Gentiles") and about the way in which he will be treated ("they will mock him and spit on him, and flog him").[290]

James and John's Request (10:35–45)

Despite the astonishment and fear of the disciples, James and John shockingly ask Jesus to be seated at his right and left in glory.[291] They envision an earthly kingdom in which they will share in Jesus's reign. Their request reveals that they've completely misunderstood Jesus's passion predictions.[292] The same is true of the other disciples, who respond with indignation toward James and John. Jesus responds by speaking of the nature of his mission. He will drink the "cup" of suffering.[293] Despite the disciples' repeated failure to comprehend the nature of his mission, Jesus uses the occasion to

288. Mark 10:32.
289. Strauss, *Mark*, 449.
290. Mark 10:33–34.
291. Matthew reveals that it was in fact the mother of the sons of Zebedee who approached Jesus with this request (Matthew 20:20–21). In ancient Israel, the highest place of honor was on a person's right, the second-highest on their left (cf., e.g., 2 Samuel 16:6; 1 Kings 2:19; Psalms 45:9; 110:1; Mark 12:36; 14:62).
292. In fact, there is supreme irony in the fact that, later in Mark's narrative, we learn that two thieves were crucified on either side of Jesus, "one on his right and one on his left" (Mark 15:27). The virtually identical wording makes clear that Mark sees irony in the disciples' question and their failure to understand the true nature of discipleship. Cf. Williams, *Mark*, 177.
293. Mark 10:38; cf. Isaiah 51:17–23.

further explain the nature of true discipleship. He does so by contrasting the world's leaders ("the rulers of the Gentiles") with Jesus's followers. The world's leaders "lord it over" their subjects, while Jesus's followers "must be a slave of all."[294]

The imagery is "graphic and arresting" to Mark's original readers.[295] Up to this point, Jesus has predicted his death three times, but he has yet to reveal *why* he must die. Here, at the end of his warnings to his disciples, we discover the reason: "For even the Son of Man came not to be served but to serve, and to give his life as a ransom for many."[296] This verse can be viewed as the theme verse of Mark's entire Gospel. The concept of ransom in the Old Testament is linked with the notion of substitution and atonement.[297] Jesus's words also recall Isaiah's prophecy of the suffering servant who would be slain as an "offering for guilt" in order to bring forgiveness to many.[298] Jesus the Messiah is the suffering servant who died for our salvation and the forgiveness of sins.

Blind Bartimaeus Healed (10:46–52)

The section closes with the healing of a blind man named Bartimaeus in the city of Jericho.[299] The two accounts of healings of blind men serve as bookends to this section.[300] While James and John have asked for positions of prestige and power, Bartimaeus cries out, "Son of David, have mercy on me!"[301] Jesus tells people to call the man, who (in a touch of eyewitness testimony) throws off his cloak, jumps up, and runs to Jesus, who engages him in conversation and heals him. Immediately, the formerly blind man "followed him [Jesus] on the way" to Jerusalem.[302] Bartimaeus thus stands "in contrast to the spiritual blindness of the religious leaders and blurred vision of the disciples."[303] With this, the road is prepared for the Son of David to enter Jerusalem to fulfill his messianic mission.

294. Mark 10:42–44.
295. Garland, *Theology of Mark's Gospel*, 146.
296. Mark 10:45; cf. Matthew 20:28; 1 Timothy 2:6.
297. Garland, *Theology of Mark's Gospel*, 146; cf. Exodus 30:12. The Greek preposition *anti* (instead of) clearly conveys the notion of substitution (see, e.g., Genesis 22:13 LXX, where Abraham is shown to sacrifice a ram "instead of" his son Isaac).
298. Cf. Isaiah 53:10. "Many" probably is a euphemism for "all" (cf. Mark 1:34; 6:2; 14:24; 1 Timothy 2:6: "ransom given for all").
299. *Bar* means "son of" in Aramaic, while Timaeus is a Greek name (mentioned in the Greek philosopher Plato's writings).
300. Cf. Mark 8:22–26.
301. Mark 10:47–48. On Jesus as the son of David, see the discussion below.
302. Mark 10:52.
303. Strauss, *Mark*, 465.

RECAP

This literary unit of Mark's Gospel started out with Peter's pivotal confession of Jesus as the Christ, which triggered Jesus's passion prediction and instruction of his followers regarding what it means to follow him in committed discipleship. This was followed by the magnificent manifestation of Jesus's future glory at the transfiguration. Immediately after this event, Jesus cast out a demon, an act that required faith and prayer. After Jesus predicted his passion a second time, the disciples argued as to who among them was the greatest, revealing massive misunderstanding.

Following this, Jesus engaged in discussion about divorce, blessed the children, and engaged with the rich young ruler. He followed up with instruction about the difficulty of entering God's kingdom for those who are wealthy and extolled the eternal rewards for following him. After this, Jesus predicted his passion for a third time. Again, the request by James and John to sit on his right and left in glory revealed that they didn't truly understand the nature of discipleship. Jesus himself had come not to be served but to serve and to give his life as a ransom for many. Entering Jericho, Jesus healed a blind man named Bartimaeus, continuing to do the work of Messiah.

JESUS'S WORK IN JERUSALEM (11:1–13:37)

The Triumphal Entry (11:1–11)

The Cursing of the Fig Tree and the Temple Cleansing (11:12–25)

JESUS'S WORK IN JERUSALEM (11:1–13:37)

As mentioned, some, with intentional hyperbole, have called Mark's Gospel a passion narrative with an extended introduction.[304] Their point is well taken: the entire Gospel thus far has been building up to the all-important events surrounding Jesus's death, burial, and resurrection—the gospel. Unlike other world religions, Christianity rises and falls essentially with the truthfulness and historicity of key events in the life of a historical figure—the Lord Jesus Christ. This is why we now enter the most critical phase in Mark's narrative, and not in the narrative only but also in regard to our Christian faith.

As we've seen, Jesus predicted three times in increasing detail to his followers that he would be betrayed and killed and would rise on the third day. The passion narrative shows that Jesus's prediction came literally true. Contrary to the wishes of his followers, Jesus's words would be fulfilled, confirming his credibility and indicating also the kind of Messiah Jesus would prove to be—not a political national deliverer as most Jews expected, but a suffering servant–type of Messiah as the prophet Isaiah had predicted. This shows that Jesus stood in the tradition of the Old Testament prophets culminating in his forerunner, John the Baptist, who had borne witness to Jesus at the inception of his ministry. In contrast, the Jewish leaders who opposed Jesus tooth and nail all the way to the cross were part of an obstinate trajectory of Jews who had resisted God for centuries—both those during the time of Moses (the wilderness generation) and those during the time of Isaiah (the exile generation). This sets Jesus's coming in its proper Jewish and salvation-historical framework.

What's more, Mark—writing to a Gentile, Roman audience—has increasingly surfaced hints that Jesus's coming would ultimately benefit not only believing Israelites but Gentiles as well. While during Jesus's earthly work Gentiles benefited from his healing messianic powers only at their initiative and only as a few representative individuals—Jesus's primary focus during his earthly mission was to come as the Jewish Messiah, as

304. The passion narrative comprises one-third of Mark's Gospel.

the Son of David inaugurating God's kingdom—following the resurrection the scope of the benefits of Jesus's ransom-like death would encompass Gentiles as well as Jews. This will be clear when the Roman centurion—representing Mark's Roman, Gentile audience—utters the conclusion Mark intends all his (Gentile) readers to draw: "This man truly was the Son of God!"

But I'm getting ahead of myself. Let's now read through the last third of Mark's Gospel—his narrative of Jesus's death, burial, and resurrection—and see how these dynamics unfolded historically, literarily, and theologically.

The Triumphal Entry (11:1–11)

Thus far, Mark's narrative has been moving slowly but surely from Galilee to Jerusalem. Upon depicting Jesus's arrival in the Jewish capital, Mark zeroes in on the events leading up to Jesus's death and resurrection. Jesus's arrival in Jerusalem also witnesses a marked shift in his approach. No longer does Jesus perform healing miracles or exorcisms, but rather he focuses on teaching in the temple area. In fact, "all the events in 11:1–13:37 take place either on the way to the temple, in the temple, or on the way out of the temple."[305] Jesus's presence there, in turn, "invites confrontations with his opponents," specifically concerning the temple.[306]

As Williams notes, "Mark structures his narrative in this section around three journeys by Jesus to the temple on three successive days."[307] In fact, the narrative "grows in length with each successive day."[308] Jesus's denunciation of the Jewish leaders and his prediction of the temple's destruction cut to the very heart of Jewish religious and political life.[309] The conflict between Jesus and the authorities escalates until Jesus is betrayed and sentenced to death. At the heart of this gargantuan spiritual battle is the Jewish leaders' rejection of their Messiah.

Traditionally called the "triumphal entry," Jesus's approach to Jerusalem is brimming with messianic overtones.[310] After making proper preparations that reveal God's providence in every detail as he predicted, Jesus enters Jerusalem riding on a colt while people shout, "Hosanna! Blessed is he who comes in the name of the Lord! Blessed is

305. Williams, *Mark*, 186. See the repeated references to the temple area (Greek *hieron*) in this section of Mark's Gospel (11:11, 15, 16, 27; 12:35; 13:1, 3).
306. Garland, *Theology of Mark's Gospel*, 147.
307. Mark 11:1–11; 11:12–19; 11:20–13:37. See Williams, *Mark*, 186.
308. Williams, *Mark*, 186.
309. Garland, *Theology of Mark's Gospel*, 150.
310. Mark 11:1–11. On the setting, see A. D. Riddle, "The Passover Pilgrimage from Jericho to Jerusalem (Matt 21:1–9; Mark 11:1–20; Luke 19:28–40; John 12:12–19)," in Beitzel, *Lexham Geographic Commentary*, 395–407.

the coming kingdom of our father David! Hosanna in the highest!"[311] Jesus's riding on a colt is reminiscent not only of King Solomon's entrance into the Holy City but also recalls the words of the prophet Zechariah:

> Rejoice greatly, Daughter Zion!
> Shout, Daughter Jerusalem!
> See, your king comes to you,
> righteous and victorious,
> lowly and riding on a donkey,
> on a colt, the foal of a donkey.[312]

Notice that the emphasis is not merely on the fact that Jesus enters the city of Jerusalem as king but more specifically on *what kind of king* Jesus proved to be: "righteous and victorious," yet "lowly and riding on a donkey." Jesus didn't come on a war horse but on a lowly beast of burden, showing that the purpose of his coming was not military conquest but humble service—giving his life as a ransom for sinners. In this sense, Jesus is the Son of David, Israel's long-awaited king.[313]

THE MARKAN SANDWICH IN MARK 11:12–25

11:12–14 Jesus curses the fig tree
11:15–19 Jesus cleanses the temple
11:20–25 The fig tree has withered

The Cursing of the Fig Tree and the Temple Cleansing (11:12–25)

On the next day, Jesus returns from Bethany, a village less than two miles outside Jerusalem,[314] and engages in a rather curious action that constitutes the last-recorded miracle in Mark's Gospel: he curses a barren, fruitless fig tree, rendered even more curious because, as Mark himself mentions, "it was not the season for figs."[315] Apparently, Jesus expected that the leaves might conceal at least some indication that the tree would

311. Mark 11:9–10. "Hosanna!" echoes Psalm 118:25; it originally was a cry to God for help ("Save now!") but in New Testament times had simply become a joyful shout (see the discussion in Williams, *Mark*, 188–89).
312. Zechariah 9:9 NIV.
313. Cf. Mark 10:47–48.
314. Cf. John 11:18.
315. Mark 11:12–14, esp. v. 13.

bear fruit in season, but he discovers no sign of life. Thus, he declares, "May no one ever eat fruit from you again!"

This is more than the frustrated reaction of a hungry, disappointed fig lover! A closer look reveals that the next scene—the temple cleansing—is followed by a second reference to the fig tree (its withering). This "Markan sandwich" points to the mutually interpreting nature of the cursing of the fig tree and the temple cleansing. The barren fig tree symbolizes unfaithful Israel and its failure to keep its covenant with God, while Jesus's "condemnation" of the tree symbolizes God's judgment on Israel.[316]

Later, when Jesus enters the temple, he similarly condemns the profiteering taking place there as he drives out the merchants and overturns both the money changers' tables and the dove sellers' seats.[317] In so doing, he cites Isaiah's prophecy, "My house will be called a house of prayer for all nations."[318] The temple was meant to be a place where everyone, including Gentiles, could pray to God. Clearly, the presence of these merchants in the Court of the Gentiles made worship there all but impossible.[319]

What's more, in keeping with Jeremiah's prophecy, Jesus called the temple in its current condition a "den of robbers."[320] This stood in marked contrast to God's intended purpose for the temple to be a "house of prayer" not merely for Israel but, in keeping with Isaiah's prophecy, "for all nations"! This means that Jesus's denunciation pertains not only to profit-hungry merchants but also to the "priestly aristocracy" that permitted such travesty and "under whose authority the temple has become a defiled place."[321]

As Jesus enters Jerusalem, therefore, he acts with compelling messianic authority, calling the Jewish leaders to account for their corruption of the temple. God had intended for the sanctuary to be holy ground devoted to spiritual worship, yet Israel had profaned and defiled it, which made a mockery of the worship of God and showed any religious activities to be nothing but a charade. Like the barren fig tree, Israel looked good from a distance but at closer scrutiny proved to be spiritually barren and devoid of genuine fruit.

---

316. Cf. Jeremiah 8:13; Isaiah 28:3–4; Hosea 9:10, 16; Micah 7:1; Joel 1:7, 12. Note that Matthew says the fig tree withered "immediately" (Matthew 21:19), while Mark says the disciples noticed that the fig tree had withered the next morning (Mark 11:20). Cf. France, *Gospel of Mark*, 447: "In Matthew the death of the fig tree is instantaneous. . . . In Mark its destruction is complete . . . , but is visible only on their next visit. Either is of course equally miraculous." He continues, "It is not easy, and perhaps not important, to decide whether Matthew has telescoped an originally more extended event . . . or whether Mark has stretched out a previously single incident in order to fold it around the protest in the temple."
317. Mark 11:15.
318. Isaiah 56:7; cf. Mark 11:17.
319. Cf. Isaiah 2:3.
320. Mark 11:17; cf. Jeremiah 7:11.
321. Strauss, *Mark*, 495.

In the original instance, this marks a pivotal, chilling moment in salvation history. Yahweh, in the person of the Messiah, visits his temple and confronts the travesty of worship perpetrated there. How convicting! In a derivative sense, the account of Jesus's cleansing of the temple also constitutes a sobering challenge to each one of us and to our respective churches as well: When we worship, are we merely going through the motions? Are we putting on a good show but failing to truly worship God in our hearts?

After Jesus has cleansed the temple with unmistakable messianic authority, he and his followers make the short trek back to Bethany where they stay for the night. Upon returning to the fig tree the next morning, the disciples notice that it has "withered away to its roots."[322] Jesus seizes the teachable moment by impressing on his followers the importance of believing, "mountain-moving" prayer. "Therefore I tell you," Jesus says, "whatever you ask in prayer, believe that you have received it, and it will be yours."[323]

Jesus adds that, as his followers pray, they should forgive others so that they, too, will be forgiven by their heavenly Father. How much time do you and I spend in prayer? And when we pray, do we believe that God will answer our prayer? Do we believe that by praying we can move spiritual mountains, overcoming obstacles that are insurmountable by mere human effort? This is the challenge Jesus here puts before his disciples, both to his original followers and to us today as well.

322. Mark 11:20–26.
323. Mark 11:24.

JESUS'S WORK IN JERUSALEM (11:1–13:37, CONT.)

Six Controversies (11:27–12:37)

- Who Gave You Authority to Do These Things? (11:27–33)
- What Will the Vineyard Owner Do with the Wicked Tenants? (12:1–12)
- Is It Lawful to Pay Taxes to Caesar? (12:13–17)
- Whose Wife Will a Remarried Widow Be in Heaven? (12:18–27)
- What Is the Greatest Commandment? (12:28–34)
- How Can the Messiah Be Both David's Son and His Lord? (12:35–37)

JESUS'S WORK IN JERUSALEM (11:1–13:37, CONT.)

Six Controversies (11:27–12:37)

Who Gave You Authority to Do These Things? (11:27–33)

Jesus returns to the temple and is confronted by the chief priests, scribes, and elders.[324] This episode is the first of six controversy stories, each of which depicts the escalating conflict between Jesus and the Jewish leaders. Jesus has just asserted his authority by cleansing the temple; but who gave him the authority to do this? Jesus cleverly turns the table on them—figuratively, this time—and asks, "Was the baptism of John from heaven or from man?"[325] The leaders are at a loss on how to answer Jesus's question, so Jesus declines to answer theirs as well.

What Will the Vineyard Owner Do with the Wicked Tenants? (12:1–12)

And so Jesus speaks to them again in parables. After the parable of the sower and several other related parables in chapter 4, this marks the other major instance in Mark's Gospel where Jesus speaks in the form of parables. The parable of the tenants, a masterful salvation-historical allegory alluding to Isaiah's Song of the Vineyard, depicts Israel's

324. Mark 11:27–33.
325. Mark 11:30.

leaders as wicked tenant farmers.[326] In the parable, God, the owner of the vineyard, sends a series of servants—symbolizing the Old Testament prophets—who are mistreated or even killed. At last, he sends his own son, thinking the tenants will respect him. Yet, shockingly, they kill him, thinking that if they kill the heir, the vineyard will be theirs.

At the conclusion of the parable, Jesus asks the provocative question, "What will the owner of the vineyard do?" Answering his own question, he replies, "He will come and destroy the tenants and give the vineyard to others," quoting a well-known Old Testament passage that predicted that "the stone that the builders rejected [would] become the cornerstone."[327] The Jewish leaders continue to be conflicted. They have enough spiritual perception to realize that the parable was directed against them. Yet their hearts are hardened, so rather than relent and repent, they are dead set on arresting Jesus and putting him to death. For the moment, though, they desist from arresting Jesus out of fear of the ordinary people with whom Jesus was very popular.

Is It Lawful to Pay Taxes to Caesar? (12:13–17)

In the next several confrontations, Jesus answers his questioners' challenge to reveal "his divine authority to interpret the law."[328] In each case, Jesus silences his detractors and amazes the people. First, some Pharisees and Herodians (sympathizers with the Herodian dynasty) approach Jesus and seek to trap him by asking, "Is it lawful to pay taxes to Caesar, or not?"[329] They think Jesus is caught, because either way he answers he will incriminate himself. If he says people should pay taxes to Caesar, he is un-Jewish and cannot be the national deliverer people are expecting. If he says people shouldn't pay taxes, they can report him to the Romans as a rebel. How hypocritical! How will Jesus wriggle out of this no-win situation? Easy—in response, Jesus asks for a denarius, queries whose image is on the coin (Caesar's), and distinguishes between different realms of authority: "Render to Caesar the things that are Caesar's, and to God the things that are God's."[330] People should honor the Romans as God-given civil authorities by paying taxes to them, and at the

---

326. Mark 12:1–12; cf. Isaiah 5:1–7.
327. Mark 12:9–11, citing Psalm 118:22.
328. Garland, *Theology of Mark's Gospel*, 152. As Williams (*Mark*, 197) notes, "The rest of Jesus's teaching in the temple appears in two sets of three encounters. In the first set of three passages (12:13–17, 18–27, 28–34), Jesus answers questions brought to him by religious leaders, with the third passage portraying the positive example of the wise scribe. In the second set of three passages (12:35–37, 38–40, 41–44), Jesus takes the initiative to state his own perspective as it stands in opposition to the teaching and behavior of the scribes, with the third passage portraying the positive example of the poor widow."
329. Mark 12:14.
330. Mark 12:17. A denarius was a silver coin minted by the Romans that was the typical wage for a day's work (Matthew 20:2). The image on the coin in Jesus's day was most likely that of Tiberius (reigned AD 14–37), who would have been identified (in abbreviated form) as "son of the divine Augustus."

same time honor God in the spiritual realm by worshiping him. By answering the trick question in this way, Jesus not only sidesteps an apparent dilemma; he also confronts the Pharisees once again for failing to worship God the way he deserves.

Whose Wife Will a Remarried Widow Be in Heaven? (12:18–27)

Now the Sadducees take their turn. As Mark informs his readers, they "say there is no resurrection."[331] On this point, they and the Pharisees disagreed.[332] Historical records show that the Sadducees only held to the authority of the five books of Moses (the Pentateuch). They claimed that there was no clear reference to resurrection there and therefore denied it. This explains why Jesus pointedly referred to "the book of Moses" in his response, noting that, in the account of Moses and the burning bush, God identified himself (in the present tense!) as being "the God of Abraham, Isaac, and Jacob." This shows how Jesus held the Scriptures in very high regard. In the present case, he derived significance even from the use of the present rather than past verb tense!

In the narrative that follows, Mark tells his readers how Jesus's opponents concoct a hypothetical (and, one might add, rather implausible) scenario designed to put Jesus on the spot. A woman has had multiple husbands (seven!): Whose wife will she be at the final resurrection (in which, of course, the Sadducees didn't believe in the first place!)? Again, the trick question poses no problem for Jesus. He replies, rather intriguingly, that in heaven people won't marry at all but sustain an angel-like existence! What's more, God is not the God of the dead but of the living, so the Sadducees' denial of the final resurrection was quite wrong. Another gotcha moment had failed to materialize. In fact, it was Jesus's challengers who stood exposed as engaging in an erroneous interpretation of Scripture.

What Is the Greatest Commandment? (12:28–34)

The Pharisees, the Herodians, and the Sadducees have all taken turns in challenging Jesus—who's next in line to trip him up with an "unanswerable" question? This is rapidly turning into a "stump the teacher" exercise. One of the scribes is next. He seems less bent on exposing Jesus as a fraud, having overheard some of the previous challenges and witnessed Jesus's apt responses. Rather, he simply asks Jesus, "Which is the most important commandment?"

Without hesitation, Jesus responds that the greatest commandment is to love God, and the second, related commandment is to love other people.[333] The scribe concurs, at which Jesus replies that he is "not far from the kingdom of God." Sadly, however, this particular

331. Mark 12:18.
332. Cf. Acts 23:6–8.
333. Cf. Deuteronomy 6:4–5; Leviticus 19:18.

scribe was the exception; Jesus's verdict on the scribes in general was not nearly as kind.[334] At this point in the narrative, Mark informs his readers, "no one dared to ask him [Jesus] any more questions."[335] Where have all the challengers gone? They've all disappeared. We've gone from militant opposition, even mockery, to polite inquiry. What will happen next?

How Can the Messiah Be Both David's Son and His Lord? (12:35–37)

As it turns out, with Jesus's challengers having run out of questions, Jesus goes on the counteroffensive and raises a question of his own: "How can the scribes say that the Christ is the son of David" when David himself, "in the Holy Spirit," said that "the Lord said to my Lord, 'Sit at my right hand, until I put your enemies under your feet'"?[336] How can the Messiah be both David's Lord and his son? The scribes have no answer. The reader sees that Jesus here makes the keen point that the fact that David called the Messiah both his Lord and his son meant that the Messiah would be both his descendant (his "son") and his superior (his "Lord"). But since the term "Lord" in the Old Testament regularly refers to Yahweh, this suggested that David believed the Messiah would also be divine! Thus, the Messiah would be both human in his physical, human ancestry of David and divine as the Son of God—a sublime point Jesus's opponents utterly failed to appreciate but which Mark, as we've seen, has consistently sought to establish throughout his Gospel.

At this, the evangelist again notes the contrast between the common people who heard Jesus "gladly" and the scribes—the Jewish religious establishment—who held positions of privilege in society ("the best seats in the synagogues and the places of honor at feasts") and who "for a pretense" uttered "long prayers" but who "devour[ed] widows' houses." That is, they were long on prayers but short on actual piety expressed in active concern for those who were poor, lowly, and in desperate need of help.[337] As one such example, Jesus noted a poor widow who humbly put two small coins worth a fraction of a day's wage in the offering box in the temple area.[338] In terms of proportionate giving, Jesus pointed out, this widow had given infinitely more than those who "contributed out of their abundance": she, out of her poverty, had given "everything she had"![339] Similar to the Canaanite woman before her, this poor widow, through her sacrificial giving, emerges as an unlikely example of true devotion to God. The lesson is that it's not what you *know* about God that matters; it's what you *do* with what you know that makes you either a hypocrite or a true worshiper.

---

334. See Mark 12:38–40 below.
335. Mark 12:34.
336. Mark 12:35–37; cf. Psalm 110:1.
337. Mark 12:38–40.
338. Williams (*Mark*, 212) notes that two *lepta* were worth a *quadrans*, "the smallest Roman coin, which in turn was worth one-sixty-fourth of a denarius (*EDNT* 2:349–50)."
339. Mark 12:44.

JESUS'S WORK IN JERUSALEM (11:1–13:37, CONT.)
The Olivet Discourse (13:1–37)
Jesus's Prophecy and the Disciples' Question (13:1–4)
Possible Signs Preceding the End in Palestine and Beyond (13:5–13)
The "Abomination of Desolation" and Destruction of Jerusalem (13:14–20)
Imposters, Cosmic Upheaval, and the Coming of the "Son of Man" (13:21–27)
This Generation and the Timing of Jesus's Return (13:28–37)

JESUS'S WORK IN JERUSALEM (11:1–13:37, CONT.)

The Olivet Discourse (13:1–37)

Jesus's Prophecy and the Disciples' Question (13:1–4)

As Jesus leaves the temple for the last time, one of his followers draws his attention to the beauty of the temple building. In response Jesus predicts, shockingly, that the temple will soon be utterly destroyed—a prediction that came true about forty years later in the year 70, when the Romans laid siege to Jerusalem and razed the temple. Shortly thereafter, Jesus sits down on the Mount of Olives overlooking the temple and is asked by Peter, James, John, and Andrew to elaborate on the prophesied destruction of the Jewish sanctuary: "When will these things be, and what will be the sign when all these things are about to be accomplished?"[340] In response, Jesus delivers what is commonly called the Olivet Discourse, which in Mark's Gospel serves as a transition from the temple controversies to the passion narrative and takes up the remainder of the chapter.

340. Mark 13:4.

In our book *Jesus and the Future*, we outline the Markan Olivet Discourse as follows:[341]

I. Jesus's Prophecy and the Disciples' Question (13:1–4)
II. Possible Signs Preceding the End in Palestine and Beyond (13:5–13)
III. The "Abomination of Desolation" and Destruction of Jerusalem (13:14–20)
IV. Imposters (13:21–23)
V. Cosmic Upheaval and the Coming of the "Son of Man" (13:24–27)
VI. This Generation (13:28–31)
VII. The Timing of Jesus's Return (13:32–37)

Throughout the discourse, Jesus repeatedly exhorts his disciples to "watch out" in light of the staggering events to come.[342] The discourse deals with events leading up to the destruction of Jerusalem in the year 70 as well as the more distant future return of Christ.[343] In interpreting the Olivet Discourse, it's important to keep three audiences in mind: Jesus's original listeners, believers at the time of the writing of Mark's Gospel, and readers today. First, Jesus is addressing his disciples, who must be vigilant in view of the destruction of Jerusalem, which would occur in their lifetime ("this generation"). Second, Mark is addressing believers in his day (remember, Mark wrote about twenty to thirty years after the events originally took place) who were similarly confronting (potential or real) persecution if not actual martyrdom.

Possible Signs Preceding the End in Palestine and Beyond (13:5–13)

In dealing initially with the second part of the question posed by Jesus's disciples as to the sign preceding the temple's destruction, both audiences—Jesus's original listeners and believers at the time of the writing of Mark's Gospel—need to be aware that messianic pretenders will appear; there'll be wars and rumors of wars; and earthquakes and famines will occur—yet none of these will constitute the actual sign about which Jesus's disciples were inquiring.[344] In addition, there will be persecution.[345]

---

341. See Andreas J. Köstenberger, Alexander E. Stewart, and Apollo Makara, *Jesus and the Future: Understanding What He Taught about the End Times* (Bellingham, WA: Lexham, 2017), 33–79. I'll combine some of the headings in the discussion below.
342. Mark 13:5, 9, 23, 33.
343. See Köstenberger, Stewart, and Makara, *Jesus and the Future*, 31–86. See also Alan S. Bandy and Benjamin L. Merkle, *Understanding Prophecy: A Biblical-Theological Approach* (Grand Rapids: Kregel, 2015), 171–90.
344. Mark 13:5–8; cf. 13:4.
345. Mark 13:9–13.

The "Abomination of Desolation" and Destruction of Jerusalem (13:14–20)

Jesus continues, "But when you see the abomination of desolation standing where he ought not to be (let the reader understand), then let those who are in Judea flee to the mountains."[346] The sign, therefore, is "the abomination of desolation," the desecration of the temple predicted in the book of Daniel. Initially, this prophecy was fulfilled at the inception of the Maccabean period in the second century BC, but, as Jesus explains here, there would be a second fulfillment of Daniel's prophecy in the near future at which the temple would once again be desecrated. This would be a time of great distress and tribulation for the inhabitants of Jerusalem and Judea, as proved to be the case when the Romans laid siege to and conquered Jerusalem and put down the Jewish rebellion in AD 66–73.[347] In addition, as we'll see below, the events surrounding the year 70, in turn, would foreshadow the events surrounding the second coming of Christ at the end of human history.

Imposters, Cosmic Upheaval, and the Coming of the "Son of Man" (13:21–27)

Finally, there are warnings and exhortations that apply to later generations of believers, including us today as well, which highlight the "need for spiritual diligence, warnings against false teachers, the danger of eschatological fervor, and the reality of persecution."[348] The crucial transition from the more immediate to the more distant future in Mark's version of the Olivet Discourse is found in verse 24 with the phrase "But in those days, after that tribulation." This is where the scene shifts from the destruction of Jerusalem and the temple in the year 70 to the second coming of Jesus. Amid cosmic upheaval, "they will see the Son of Man coming in clouds with great power and glory. And he will send out the angels and gather his elect."[349]

This Generation and the Timing of Jesus's Return (13:28–37)

Having discussed the second part of the disciples' question regarding the sign preceding the temple's destruction, which in turn would serve as a portent of Jesus's eventual return, Jesus now turns to the first part of their question regarding the timing of these events. In this regard, he urges his disciples to learn the lesson of the fig tree—when the branch becomes tender and the fig tree puts out its leaves, the summer, and thus the tree's bearing of ripe fruit, is near—and tells them that no one

346. Mark 14:14.
347. Mark 13:14–23. For primary sources, see Köstenberger, Stewart, and Makara, *Jesus and the Future*, 58. The closest Old Testament antecedent for an urgent flight from destruction is the imminent destruction of Sodom and Gomorrah (Genesis 19:16–17; cf. Luke 17:28–32).
348. Strauss, *Mark*, 584.
349. Mark 13:26.

knows the exact time of his return: "not even the angels in heaven, nor the Son, but only the Father."[350]

In a mini-parable, Jesus explains that his coming will be like the return of a master whose servants are left in charge of the estate. They don't know when their master will come back, but they must be ready whenever he finally returns. The bottom line, therefore, is this: Be on guard, keep awake. For you do not know when the time will come.[351] This admonition applies to both present and future believers: we must be vigilant, because none of us knows the exact time when Jesus will return.

350. Mark 13:32.
351. Mark 13:33.

THE PASSION NARRATIVE (14:1–16:8)
The Plot against Jesus, the Anointing of Jesus, and the Betrayal of Jesus (14:1–11)
The Last Supper (14:12–25)
Jesus Predicts Peter's Denials and Prays in Gethsemane (14:26–42)
Jesus Is Betrayed and Arrested (14:43–52)
Jesus's Jewish Trial before the Sanhedrin and Peter's Denial of Jesus (14:53–72)

THE PASSION NARRATIVE (14:1–16:8)

It's now only two days before the Passover.[352] The Jewish leaders are plotting to arrest Jesus by stealth, but not during the festival, in order to avoid any undue commotion. The Romans could be very sensitive to that, as they wanted to avoid any public unrest that could spiral out of control. This is why the Roman governor, who otherwise spent his time in the lush and posh Caesarea Maritima on the coast, came to the capital during feast times just to make sure everything stayed calm and under control. The Jews had a certain measure of political and religious autonomy but were on a short-enough leash that they could not execute capital punishment (which would become an issue with Jesus). Nor did they want to stir up the crowds so as to attract undue attention from the Romans lest they crack down violently to quell any possible popular uprising. Also, the Romans were hardly familiar with internal Jewish religious matters (nor did they care to be). In addition, if you were Roman, Palestine wasn't exactly the most exciting place to be. It was far away from Rome, a sort of political backwater, and not the most desired post for government officials—not even close. An ambassadorship to Paris, being stationed in Jerusalem was not!

352. "Passover" in Mark and the other Gospels can refer to the Passover feast (as it does in 14:1), the Passover meal (14:12, 14, 16), or the Passover lamb (14:12).

Throughout the passion narrative, Mark makes clear that it was God's sovereign purpose to accomplish the work of salvation through Jesus's vicarious suffering and substitutionary sacrifice on the cross. As incredible as it may seem, Jesus is betrayed, rejected, abandoned, condemned, and executed according to God's sovereign purpose! As Mark Strauss aptly notes, "Despite all appearances, the dreadful events about to unfold in Jerusalem represent the sovereign purposes of God, the good news of salvation, and the inauguration of the kingdom of God."[353] One of the primary ways in which Mark expresses this is by demonstrating that the final events of Jesus's life occur in fulfillment of Scripture. Everything happens according to God's preordained plan—just as the Old Testament writers envisioned and predicted it would. This is at the heart of Mark's apologetic for the cross—his explanation that, even though both Jews and non-Jews couldn't see how a crucified criminal could be the Messiah and Savior of the world, the cross was a central plank in God's plan, because Jesus would give his life as a ransom for sinners.

THE MARKAN SANDWICH IN MARK 14:1–11

14:1–2 The plot against Jesus
14:3–9 The anointing of Jesus
14:10–11 The betrayal of Jesus

The Plot against Jesus, the Anointing of Jesus, and the Betrayal of Jesus (14:1–11)

As mentioned, the narrative begins with yet another reference to the plot to arrest Jesus.[354] The three opening scenes in the passion narrative form another "Markan sandwich," in which the anointing of Jesus at Bethany—the place outside Jerusalem where Jesus and his followers typically lodge for the night—is framed by the Jewish leaders' plot and Judas's betrayal.[355] The sandwich contrasts the treacherous character of Judas and the religious leaders with the pure devotion of the woman who remains unnamed here, though from John's account we know it was Mary of Bethany, sister of Martha and Lazarus, whom Jesus raised from the dead.

When Jesus dined at the house of a man named Simon the Leper (presumably a leper healed by Jesus), a woman appeared with a bottle of very expensive perfume and

353. Strauss, *Mark*, 601.
354. Mark 14:1–2.
355. Mark 14:1–11.

proceeded to pour its contents over Jesus's head (probably not like a bucket of water over the head of a victorious college football coach, but more gently). Some of those present objected to the extravagant "waste" (John tells us it was Judas), but Jesus rises to the woman's defense and says she has done a "beautiful thing" to him.[356] In fact, she has acted prophetically by anointing his body for burial even prior to the crucifixion.[357] In addition, her story would be told wherever the gospel was preached and be included in three of the four Gospels.[358]

With this pronouncement, Jesus is implicitly predicting his death once again.[359] While the woman was likely unaware that Jesus would soon have to die, there's no doubt that Jesus's mind was firmly fixed on the cross-death he would shortly have to endure. Like the poor widow,[360] the woman serves as a model of true discipleship and devotion in contrast to the greedy, self-seeking religious leaders (not to mention Judas the traitor). The disciples have a choice to make as to whom they will emulate—the woman's devotion or the leaders' devious scheming. Tragically, Judas would cast his lot with the latter. From that point forward, "he sought an opportunity to betray him."[361]

The Last Supper (14:12–25)

In the next episode, Jesus celebrates the final Passover with his disciples. This is a moment pregnant with meaning, as Jesus simultaneously commemorates the Passover that originated on the eve of Israel's exodus from Egypt and institutes the new covenant with his new messianic community, the Twelve. In each scene, Jesus demonstrates his foreknowledge of what is about to happen. As David Garland perceptively notes, "His foreknowledge underscores that what happens is not some tragic miscarriage of justice."[362] Jesus foreknows

- the details for the meal's preparations,
- Judas's betrayal,
- Peter's denials,
- the disciples' falling away, and
- his imminent death.

356. Mark 14:6.
357. Mark 14:8.
358. Mark 14:9. That is, Matthew, Mark, and John; Luke features a different anointing by another woman earlier in Jesus's ministry.
359. Cf. Mark 8:31; 9:31; 10:33–34.
360. Cf. Mark 12:41–44.
361. Mark 14:11.
362. Garland, *Theology of Mark's Gospel*, 162.

Jesus proceeds "as it is written of him" in fulfillment of God's foreordained plan.[363] His submission to the Father's will is contrasted with the disciples' ignorance. They boldly claim that they'll never deny Jesus. Peter (Mark's likely eyewitness source) even emphatically declares, "If I must die with you, I will not deny you."[364] Mark adds, "And they all said the same." In stark contrast, Jesus prays in the garden of Gethsemane (an olive grove at the outskirts of Jerusalem), "not what I will, but what you will."[365] While the disciples fall asleep in their spiritual dullness, Jesus remains alert and trusts in the Father even in the face of suffering and death.

During the supper, Jesus takes the bread and wine that represent his body and blood. By this symbolic gesture, Jesus illustrates the purpose of his vicarious sacrifice, as both elements jointly point to his atoning death on the cross. He first prays, breaks the bread, and says, "Take; this is my body."[366] After this, he takes the cup, again gives thanks, and gives it to the disciples, saying, "This is my blood of the covenant, which is poured out for many."[367] Jesus's words here hark back to Moses's sealing of God's covenant with Israel through the blood of animal sacrifices, through which atonement was made for the sins of God's people.[368]

The phrase "for many" echoes Isaiah's prophecy, according to which the suffering servant "bore the sin of many."[369] In the context of Mark's Gospel, Jesus's words build on the previous reference to Jesus giving his life as a ransom "for many."[370] Just like these animal sacrifices in the old covenant, only with infinitely greater effectiveness, Jesus's blood would be poured out "for many" as he died on the cross as God's suffering servant.[371] In this way, Jesus would effectively die for others, paying the penalty for their sins by dying in their place.

Jesus Predicts Peter's Denials and Prays in Gethsemane (14:26–42)

At this, they sing a hymn, leave the upper room, and head toward the Mount of Olives. No doubt with a heavy heart, Jesus tells his followers that, in fulfillment of Scripture, they will all fall away: "I will strike the shepherd, and the sheep will be scattered."[372] Nevertheless, after the resurrection, he will go before them to Galilee. This is

363. Mark 14:21.
364. Mark 14:31.
365. Mark 14:36.
366. Mark 14:22.
367. Mark 14:24.
368. Cf. Exodus 24:8.
369. Isaiah 53:11–12.
370. Mark 10:45.
371. Mark 14:24.
372. Mark 14:27; cf. Zechariah 13:7.

an important forward-looking reference in Mark's Gospel, as the narrative ends with the angel's words to the women at the empty tomb following the resurrection, "He has risen; he is not here. See the place where they laid him. But go, tell his disciples and Peter that he is going before you to Galilee. There you will see him, just as he told you."[373] In this way, the present reference constitutes a bookend, together with the penultimate verse in the Gospel, enveloping the account of Jesus's arrest, trials, crucifixion, burial, and resurrection that is about to follow.

Following Jesus's prediction that "all" will fall away, Peter tells Jesus, "Even though they all fall away, I will not."[374] Peter's words here stand as an abiding warning against undue confidence in one's ability to resist temptation in one's own strength. While his love for Jesus and his resolve to remain loyal to him are moving and commendable, his best intentions will carry him only so far. Instead, Jesus predicts that Peter will deny him three times. Nevertheless, he takes Peter, along with James and John (his inner circle), as he prays in the garden of Gethsemane. There, he agonizes over the imminent prospect of his death: "Abba, Father, all things are possible for you. Remove this cup from me. Yet not what I will, but what you will."[375] Prior to his threefold denial, Peter (as well as the other two) are caught napping three times by Jesus upon his return from praying. Jesus urges them on: "The hour has come. The Son of Man is betrayed into the hands of sinners."[376]

Jesus Is Betrayed and Arrested (14:43–52)

"Immediately," while Jesus is still declaring that he will be "betrayed into the hands of sinners," Judas the traitor arrives on the scene with an unruly crowd from the Jewish leaders.[377] Somewhat ridiculously, and completely unnecessarily, they carry "swords and clubs," as if they've come to arrest a common criminal who is likely to resist arrest. Judas the betrayer steps up to Jesus and gives the crowd the agreed-upon sign. With deep irony, and as he had likely done many times before, he greets Jesus with "Rabbi" and kisses him, presumably on both cheeks.[378] At this, they arrest Jesus. Yet "one of those who stood by" (from the other Gospels we know it is Peter, Mark's primary eyewitness) draws his sword and cuts off the ear of the high priest's servant.

We know from the other Gospels that Jesus intervened and healed the ear, but Mark only tells us that Jesus says, "Have you come out as against a robber, with swords and

373. Mark 16:6–7.
374. Mark 14:29.
375. Mark 14:36.
376. Mark 14:41.
377. Mark 14:41–43.
378. Mark 14:45.

clubs to capture me? Day after day I was with you in the temple teaching, and you did not seize me. But let the Scriptures be fulfilled."[379] In this way, Jesus exposes the cowardly covert operation Judas and the Jewish leaders were performing. It also shows that quiet assertiveness is appropriate for Christians when they're unjustly treated. Then, in keeping with Jesus's prediction, "they all left him and fled."[380] In all this adversity, Jesus is in no way caught off guard but retains his composure, as each event transpires according to God's predetermined purpose that "the Scriptures be fulfilled."[381]

One unique and in fact curious feature of Mark's account of Jesus's arrest is the reference to a young man who followed Jesus—remarkable because Mark has just said that "they all left him and fled"—dressed with "nothing but a linen cloth."[382] Those who had arrested Jesus take him into custody as well, but, leaving the linen garment behind, the young man apparently breaks free and runs away—stark naked![383] What a bizarre scene! And why did Mark even include it? It's possible that here the author of the Gospel—Mark himself—makes a cameo appearance, though it's impossible to verify this conclusively. This would be as good a reason as any I could think of why the second evangelist would include an event that otherwise strikes one as thoroughly innocuous and inconsequential as far as the main plotline of the narrative is concerned.[384]

Jesus's Jewish Trial before the Sanhedrin and Peter's Denial of Jesus (14:53–72)

With his disciples scattered, Jesus is first led to a hearing before the Sanhedrin—the Jewish highest court—and subsequently to Pontius Pilate, the Roman governor, who, as mentioned, alone can pronounce the death sentence.[385] Throughout the latter half of Mark's Gospel, the Jewish leaders were "seeking a way to destroy," "arrest," and "kill him."[386] The mischievous plan they hatched is at last moving forward. Nevertheless, while Jesus is crucified according to God's will and in fulfillment of Scripture, the

379. Mark 14:48–49.
380. Mark 14:50; cf. Mark 14:27, citing Zechariah 13:7.
381. Mark 14:49.
382. Mark 14:51–52. Williams (*Mark*, 246–47) favors the translation "linen garment" (NIV) and points out that "nothing but" is not in the original Greek.
383. Though Williams (*Mark*, 247) notes that "naked" could also mean the young man was wearing only an undergarment or was otherwise not fully clothed (cf. John 21:7).
384. In addition, as Williams (*Mark*, 247) points out, "Mark 14:51–52 offers yet another example of failure, a picture of a 'would-be' disciple, dressed in an expensive garment and therefore perhaps unfamiliar with sacrifice, who chose to follow Jesus even after his arrest but was unprepared for the cost. He was badly beaten and ran off in shame."
385. Mark 14:53–65; 15:1–22.
386. Mark 11:18; 12:12; 14:1.

Jewish leaders, as well as Judas, and the Roman governor are clearly the human agents responsible for Jesus's suffering and death.

David Garland highlights three vital aspects of Mark's depiction of Jesus's passion in the unfolding narrative. He records

- what happens to Jesus;
- the titles ascribed to Jesus (prophet, king of the Jews, Savior, Messiah, king of Israel, and Son of God); and
- the response of the witnesses.[387]

The trial scene opens with the reference to Peter following Jesus "at a distance, right into the courtyard of the high priest."[388] Peter's timid presence at the scene is juxtaposed with Jesus's bold testimony before the high priest.[389] From a safe distance outside, Peter warms himself by the fire, while Jesus is "under fire" from the Jewish leaders inside.[390] Though falsely accused, Jesus chooses to remain silent, just as Isaiah's suffering servant "opened not his mouth."[391] Jesus's only words are uttered in response to the high priest's question as to whether he is "the Christ, the Son of the Blessed."[392] Strikingly in a Gospel that up to now has been pervaded by the "messianic secret,"[393] Jesus boldly acknowledges that, yes, "I am," and adds, in an affirmation that he surely knew would prove to be exceedingly provocative to the high priest's ears, "and you will see the Son of Man seated at the right hand of Power, and coming with the clouds of heaven."[394] Sure enough, the high priest at once tears his robes (a cultural expression of outrage) and exclaims, "What further witnesses do we need? You have heard his blasphemy!"[395]

The entire scene is dripping with irony. By sentencing Jesus to death, the Jewish leaders are advancing his mission of dying for people's sins as God's suffering servant-Messiah.[396] What's also ironic is that some of the Jewish leaders mock and spit on Jesus,

387. Garland, *Theology of Mark's Gospel*, 167.
388. Mark 14:54.
389. We may have here another "Markan sandwich," with the mention Peter at the outset (vv. 53–54), Jesus's Jewish trial (vv. 55–65), and Peter's denials of Jesus (vv. 66–72). The device here frames Jesus's trial by references to Peter's discipleship failure.
390. Garland, *Theology of Mark's Gospel*, 167.
391. Cf. Isaiah 53:7.
392. Mark 14:61. The Jewish high priest is careful not to pronounce the name of God and so uses the euphemism "the Blessed," yet he has no scruples about crucifying the Son of God!
393. Cf. Mark 1:25, 34, 44; 3:12; 5:43; 7:36; 8:30.
394. Mark 14:62; cf. Psalm 110:1; Daniel 7:13–14.
395. Mark 14:63–64.
396. Garland, *Theology of Mark's Gospel*, 168.

calling on him to prophesy.[397] As Mark's readers know perfectly well, yet as has apparently escaped the Jewish leaders' attention, Jesus has in fact predicted repeatedly that he would be delivered into their hands in order to be killed.[398] He even predicted that Judas would betray him, that all his disciples would be scattered, and that Peter would deny him three times on that very night![399] In the very next scene, Peter fulfills Jesus's words and "broke down and wept" after denying Jesus three times.[400] In all these ways, Jesus proves to be a true prophet whose "words will never pass away."[401] The mockery and travesty of justice that unfolds is hard to fathom and put into words.

How do you adequately write about the Son of God being put on the cross by sinners who are motivated by nothing but self-interest, envy, and hatred? One wants to halt the narrative and put a stop to the madness. *Stop!!!* If anyone didn't deserve to die, it was Jesus! Jesus, we're so sorry you had to endure this for us! And yet we're so glad you did. What great mercy! What amazing love! What unfathomable forgiveness! Words are woefully inadequate to express all that would need to be said in the face of the atrocious sin that was committed toward Jesus. Yet, as all of us know, even though we weren't on the scene when all of this happened, if we had been there, we would have done the same thing. Like all the characters in the narrative, we, too, are sinners who fail to appreciate just how deep the fall has affected us. As Isaiah put it, "All our righteous acts are like filthy rags."[402]

---

397. Mark 14:65.
398. Cf. Mark 9:31; 10:33–34.
399. Cf. Mark 14:30.
400. Mark 14:66–72. Mark mentions in verse 68 that "a rooster crowed." Then, in verse 72, he says the rooster "crowed a second time," in keeping with Jesus's prediction (cf. v. 30). In this, Mark's account is more detailed than that of the other Gospels (reflecting Peter's recollection), which only mention one crowing (e.g., Matthew 26:74–75). The fact that the rooster crowed once after Peter's first denial and Peter went on to deny Jesus two more times may further accentuate Peter's discipleship failure (so, e.g., Williams, *Mark*, 252).
401. Garland, *Theology of Mark's Gospel*, 169; cf. Mark 13:31.
402. Isaiah 64:6 NIV.

THE PASSION NARRATIVE (14:1–16:8, CONT.)
The Ratification of the Sanhedrin's Verdict and Jesus's Roman Trial (15:1–15)
The Crucifixion (15:16–41)
The Burial (15:42–47)
The Women at the Tomb (16:1–8)

THE PASSION NARRATIVE (14:1–16:8, CONT.)

The Ratification of the Sanhedrin's Verdict and Jesus's Roman Trial (15:1–15)

The nighttime meeting of the Sanhedrin has resulted in a "guilty" verdict on account of blasphemy. In the early morning hours, the entire council meets to ratify the verdict and sends Jesus on to Pontius Pilate, the Roman governor, who alone can legally approve capital punishment. While Jesus's Jewish trial before the Sanhedrin, as we've seen, was marked by false testimony and a rejection of his affirmation of deity, Jesus's Roman trial before Pilate is crippled by the governor's cowardly indecision. While the Sanhedrin leveled the religious charge of blasphemy against Jesus, Pilate frames his identity in political terms: "Are you the king of the Jews?"[403] The term "king" appears repeatedly in the remaining passion narrative;[404] the irony, of course, is that while Pilate conceives of kingship in political terms, Jesus is king in a broader sense that transcends mere human politics. For this reason, as we've seen, from the very beginning of his earthly ministry Jesus has consistently proclaimed the coming of the "kingdom of God"—understood primarily as God's reign in repentant, believing human hearts, manifested both individually and in the believing community.

Jesus's response to Pilate's question resembles his conduct at the Jewish trial. He simply says, "You have said so."[405] He doesn't take the bait and refuses to incriminate himself by his words. From John's Gospel we know that, at some point in the conversation, Jesus told Pilate that his kingdom was "not of this world" (i.e., it was nonpolitical and posed

403. Mark 15:2.
404. Cf. Mark 15:2, 9, 12, 18, 26, 32.
405. Mark 15:2.

no threat to Roman interests).[406] The Jewish leaders (who are apparently right there with Jesus and Pilate) keep accusing Jesus "of many things."[407] When Pilate asks Jesus to respond, he says nothing. Pilate is amazed; why would Jesus not defend himself? One reason I can think of is that a person's testimony regarding himself was inadequate. The witness of at least two or three others was required. Thus, one reason why the entire proceedings against Jesus are a travesty of justice is that he was refused proper legal representation. This unmasks any pretense at fairness as hollow and makes Jesus's "trial" nothing but a charade. In any case, Jesus remains composed and stays above the fray, dignifying neither Pilate's nor the Jewish leaders' charges with a response. If they want to condemn him unjustly, he is not going to supply them with further ammunition to do so.

Rather than taking control of the proceedings, Pilate, in a weak move of shirking and shifting responsibility on his part, puts the matter into the hands of the Jewish crowd, presumably thinking they will exonerate Jesus "the king of the Jews," whom he considers not guilty.[408] As a result, Pilate invokes an apparent custom according to which the Roman governor would release a prisoner at the festival. Yet when faced with the fateful decision on whether to ask for Jesus's release or that of Barabbas, a murderous rebel, the people inexplicably choose Barabbas, having been incited by the envious chief priests.[409] When Pilate asks the crowd what he should do with Jesus, they cruelly shout, "Crucify him"![410] Believing Jesus to be innocent, Pilate asks the crowd, "Why? What evil has he done?"[411] But they merely repeat their call for Jesus's crucifixion. Incredible! Where did the crowd go that acclaimed Jesus only a few days earlier as the Messiah at his triumphal entry into Jerusalem?[412] Where are they now? Lacking the moral fortitude to stand up to the Jewish leaders and the raucous mob, and "wishing to satisfy the crowd," Pilate accedes to their demand.[413] He releases Barabbas and sentences Jesus to be scourged and crucified. Justice served? Emphatically not.

The Crucifixion (15:16–41)

When Jesus arrives at the governor's headquarters—the so-called Praetorium—the soldiers call together their entire battalion. As was common for those rough Ro-

406. John 18:36.
407. Mark 15:3.
408. Mark adds in an aside, "For he perceived that it was out of envy that the chief priests had delivered him up" (Mark 15:10).
409. The irony is palpable: the people choose Barabbas, which in Aramaic means "son of the father" (cf. Mark 10:46; 14:36), rather than Jesus, the Son of (God) the Father (Mark 15:6–15)!
410. Mark 15:13.
411. Mark 15:14.
412. Mark 11:1–11.
413. Mark 15:15.

man soldiers in the first century, they don't miss the opportunity to amuse themselves at Jesus's expense. They drape a purple coat around Jesus, mocking his royal claim, and put a crown made of thornbush branches woven together on his head (no doubt that hurt a lot!). After this, they prostrate themselves in mock homage and salute him: "Hail, king of the Jews!"[414] While doing so, they strike his head with a reed, spit on him, and keep prostrating themselves. After a while, they get bored, take off the robe, and put Jesus's own clothes back on. Then they lead him away to be crucified. Again, one shudders at the sight of such callousness directed toward anyone, much more so the Son of God. Whatever happened that people can be so cruel toward a fellow human being?

Throughout Mark's passion narrative, as mentioned, his depiction of Jesus's crucifixion highlights the theological significance of Jesus's death. Unable to carry his own cross, Jesus is helped by a man identified as Simon of Cyrene who is pressed into service.[415] As other Markan characters before him, Simon is depicted as a model disciple who bears the cross as Jesus had instructed (though he carries Jesus's cross, not his own).[416] When they arrive at Golgotha (Aramaic for "Place of a Skull"[417]), they crucify Jesus. An inscription states the charge: "The King of the Jews." Jesus is crucified at the third hour (about nine o'clock in the morning) between two robbers, "one on his right and one on his left."[418] This expression recalls James and John's ungranted request to sit at Jesus's right and left in glory.[419] Certainly, dying on crosses on Jesus's side—being crucified with Christ—is not what they had in mind.[420]

While dying on the cross, Jesus is mocked as the "king of Israel."[421] Passersby wag their heads and say, with deep Markan irony, "Aha! You who would destroy the temple and rebuild it in three days, save yourself, and come down from the cross!"[422] The Jewish leaders, too, join in the mockery, saying to one another, "He saved others; he cannot save himself. Let the Christ, the King of Israel, come down now from

414. Mark 15:16–18.
415. Mark 15:21.
416. Cf. Mark 8:34; Garland, *Theology of Mark's Gospel*, 172. Bauckham suggests that Simon is mentioned because he is the eyewitness behind this account. His sons (Alexander and Rufus) are also known in the early Christian movement (see Romans 16:13). See Richard Bauckham, *Jesus and the Eyewitnesses: The Gospels as Eyewitness Testimony*, 2nd ed. (Grand Rapids: Eerdmans, 2017), 51–52.
417. Mark 15:22.
418. Mark 15:27. In keeping with common convention in his day, Mark counts the hours of the day as starting with sunrise at six o'clock in the morning and counting in increments of three hours.
419. Cf. Mark 10:37.
420. Though, as Paul would later write, spiritually speaking, all true believers have been crucified with Christ (Galatians 2:20).
421. Mark 15:32.
422. Mark 15:29–30.

the cross that we may see and believe."[423] That's so infinitely sad. Talk about stepping on someone when he's already down (and almost dead)! How cowardly! The Jewish leaders gloat in their "victory" and mock Jesus for his impotence in saving others. Even the robbers who were crucified at Jesus's side hurl abuse at him![424] How ironic that Jesus is in the very process of procuring salvation by dying on the cross! Tragically, this spiritual truth is utterly lost on the Jewish leaders. They entirely miss the significance of Jesus's cross-death. In this, they serve as negative examples in Mark's Gospel. May none of his readers commit the same tragic mistake and miss the meaning of the cross! Just like understanding the meaning of Jesus's parables or discerning the underlying significance of Jesus's miracles, this takes eyes of faith and spiritual understanding.

Then, at the sixth hour (around noon), darkness falls over the land until the ninth hour (approximately three o'clock in the afternoon).[425] At the ninth hour, having hung on the cross for an excruciating six hours, Jesus cries out, citing the opening line of Psalm 22, "My God, my God, why have you forsaken me?"[426] Psalm 22 is a well-known psalm of David, recalling his fate as a prototype of the righteous sufferer. Throughout the passion, Jesus has been identified as the "king of Israel"—albeit in ironic, even mocking, ignorance. By citing Psalm 22, Jesus further identifies himself both as Israel's anticipated Davidic king and as God's righteous sufferer. As Benjamin Gladd remarks, "David's experiences prophetically anticipate Jesus's own experiences throughout his earthly ministry, especially here at the crucifixion."[427] In this way, Jesus's anguished "cry of dereliction" (as it is customarily called) corresponds to David's cry of abandonment. This doesn't mean Jesus was actually separated from God; as the Son of God, he was one with the Father. It does mean, however, that in his humanity Jesus identified with us in our sin and thus bore the full weight of God's wrath upon sin.[428]

423. Mark 15:31–32.

424. Mark 15:32. Mark doesn't mention that one of them later repented (cf. Luke 23:40–43).

425. Mark 15:33.

426. Mark cites Jesus's actual words in the original Aramaic (Mark 15:34). See the diagram of "Mark's Account of Jesus's Crucifixion" below. As Williams (*Mark*, 263) points out, "By referring to the third hour in 15:25, the sixth hour in 15:33, and the ninth hour in 15:33–34—a precise pattern with three-hour intervals—Mark leaves the impression that all the events surrounding Jesus's death took place on schedule, according to a divinely ordered plan." He also notes, "This is the first time that Jesus's name is directly mentioned in the crucifixion scene. . . . From that point on, Jesus has nothing else to say to anyone for the rest of Mark's Gospel, except for this one question to God in v. 34" (*Mark*, 265).

427. Gladd, "Mark," 89.

428. As Paul wrote to the church at Corinth, "He who knew no sin became sin on our behalf, so that we might become the righteousness of God in him" (2 Corinthians 5:21).

MARK'S ACCOUNT OF JESUS'S CRUCIFIXION

Hour	*Time*	*Event*	*Mark*
Third hour	Nine in the morning	Jesus is crucified	15:25
Sixth hour	Around noon	Darkness falls over the land	15:33
Ninth hour	Three in the afternoon	Jesus dies, quoting Psalm 22	15:34

Some of the bystanders think that when Jesus speaks the opening words of Psalm 22, *Eloi, Eloi* ("My God, my God"), he is actually calling for Elijah, yet another instance of misunderstanding. Mark's entire account of the crucifixion is an almost incessant string of grotesque, tragic, and ironic misunderstandings reflecting people's spiritual incomprehension, obduracy, and dullness. So, people say, mockingly, "Wait, let's see whether Elijah will come to take him down."[429] That's the last mockery Jesus has to endure. With a loud cry, he dies. The Son of God dies!

Mark records two remarkable things that happen as soon as Jesus breathes his last. First, the curtain of the temple is torn in two.[430] As Mark Strauss observes, the tearing of the curtain marks the end of temple sacrifices, and a "new way" is now "open for all into the presence of God."[431] By Jesus's death, the sin barrier between God and humanity has forever been removed for those who recognize Jesus as Messiah and trust in his sacrifice on their behalf. No more offerings are needed, because Jesus brought the once-for-all sacrifice! In fact, Jesus is the substitute for the temple, because people can now enter God's presence through the body of Christ, which has been broken for them, and his blood, which has been shed for them.

Second, upon witnessing Jesus's death, a Roman centurion confesses at the climax of Mark's Gospel, "Truly this man was the Son of God!"[432] You may remember that at Jesus's baptism the voice from heaven declared, "You are my beloved Son."[433] Then, in a pivotal moment halfway through the Gospel, Peter, speaking for the Twelve—representing the Jewish believing remnant—confessed Jesus as "the

429. Mark 15:36.

430. Mark 15:38. "Torn" echoes the heavens being "torn" open at Jesus's baptism (Mark 1:10).

431. Strauss, *Mark*, 705.

432. Mark 15:39. For a detailed discussion of this climactic reference, see Williams, *Mark*, 267–68. Williams concludes, "The context of Mark's Gospel as a whole certainly suggests that υἱὸς θεοῦ in the centurion's confession should be regarded as a def[inite] expression, since it is def[inite] elsewhere in Mark (e.g., 3:11; 14:62) and since God's own perspective is that Jesus is 'the Son' (1:11; 9:7)."

433. Mark 1:11.

Christ."[434] Now, a Roman soldier, a Gentile, comes to the identical conclusion: Jesus is the Son of God.[435] What's more, while Peter called Jesus "the Christ" (i.e., the Messiah), this is the first time in Mark's Gospel that Jesus is acknowledged as the "Son of God" by a human voice; so far, in an unwelcome witness, it had only been demons cast out and silenced by Jesus.[436] The Jewish leaders were blind to this truth, but outsiders such as the Gentile centurion perceive it by faith. The "messianic secret" has now been lifted, even for the Gentiles: Jesus is the Son of God![437] The gospel is now ready to be proclaimed to all nations.[438]

Not only does the centurion's confession serve as the climax of Mark's Gospel; it also, as mentioned, forms a bookend with the identical earlier declaration at Jesus's baptism.[439] Both heaven and earth proclaim that Jesus is the Son of God! Thus, the two passages frame Mark's entire Gospel, which serves as "the explanation of these two great acclamations."[440] The heavens are open because Jesus the Son of God gave his life as a ransom for many. What's more, at the pivotal midpoint of the Gospel stands Peter's watershed confession of Jesus as the Christ. As literary scholars tell us, every good story has a beginning, a middle, and an end. Thus, Mark turns out to be a storyteller par excellence who has crafted his account of Jesus with great literary skill. With Jesus as the indisputable main character, and the Twelve as other significant characters (especially corporately as Jesus's new messianic community), Mark has given us a rich and colorful cast of characters, including John the Baptist, Jesus's forerunner, and the Pharisees and scribes, Jesus's main antagonists, not to mention many ordinary people whom Jesus encountered and (in many cases) healed. Mark has also given us a compelling plotline with tremendous drama, suspense, and a fitting climax. Anything after the Roman centurion's confession would be anticlimactic; perhaps it is for this reason that Mark doesn't include any resurrection appearances of Jesus, as we'll briefly discuss below. And while talking about Mark's literary art, who could forget the "sandwiches" he served up numerous times throughout the narrative?

434. Mark 8:29.
435. "Christ" and "Son of God" are roughly equivalent; both are messianic titles.
436. See Mark 3:11; 5:7; cf. Garland, *Theology of Mark's Gospel*, 175; and see the sidebar "Son of God" below.
437. Cf. Mark 1:1. See Köstenberger, Kellum, and Quarles, *The Cradle, the Cross, and the Crown*, 295.
438. Cf. Mark 13:10.
439. Cf. Mark 1:11.
440. Strauss, *Four Portraits, One Jesus*, 192.

SON OF GOD

Jesus's most prominent title in Mark's Gospel is "Son of God." This title frames the entire Gospel from the first verse to the Roman centurion's confession. At every critical junction in Jesus's life and ministry, he is identified as the Son of God:

MARKAN REFERENCE	PERSON CONFESSING JESUS
• Introduction	
◦ 1:1 ("Jesus Christ, the Son of God")	◦ Mark the evangelist
◦ 1:11 ("You are my beloved Son")	◦ Voice from heaven at Jesus's baptism
• Galilean ministry	
◦ 3:11 ("You are the Son of God")	◦ Demons
◦ 5:7 ("Son of the Most High God")	◦ Demons
• Journey to Jerusalem	
◦ 9:7 ("This is my beloved Son")	◦ Voice from heaven at transfiguration
◦ 12:6; 13:32 ("the Son")	◦ Self-reference of Jesus
• Passion narrative	
◦ 14:61 ("the Christ, the Son of the Blessed")	◦ Caiaphas, the Jewish high priest
◦ 15:39 ("Truly this man was the Son of God")	◦ Roman centurion

Jesus is declared to be the Son of God by the voice from heaven both at Jesus's baptism (1:11) and at the transfiguration (9:7). In addition, Jesus twice refers to himself as the Son (12:6; 13:32), and Caiaphas the Jewish high priest references the title in his interrogation of Jesus, though of course disapprovingly (14:61). Apart from these references, the only characters to recognize Jesus's identity as the Son of God are demons (3:11; 5:7)!

Except for demons, no one recognizes Jesus as the Son of God until the Roman centurion's confession at the crucifixion (though Peter, at a pivotal juncture, does confess Jesus as "the Christ" at 8:29, while rebuking Jesus shortly thereafter for suggesting that he would have to suffer and die, showing his limited understanding of what Jesus's messianic ministry would entail). Similarly, the disciples repeatedly fail to understand Jesus, while both the Jewish leaders and the Roman authorities consistently reject his claims.

Part of the reason for this failure is that Jesus didn't conform to Jewish or Roman expectations as to what it meant to be the Son of God. The Jewish people referred to the royal Son of David as God's Son, whom they understood to be human.[441] In the Roman world, emperors were increasingly deified after they died.[442] Yet Jesus inaugurated God's kingdom by suffering and dying on a Roman cross! It's easy to see that "Mark's presentation of Jesus as the Son of God is profoundly countercultural."[443]

What's more, in his depiction of Jesus's identity as the Messiah and Son of God, Mark features both Jesus's powerful miracles and his humble service. In the first half of Mark's Gospel, Jesus is depicted primarily as the Son of God who demonstrates his divine authority by performing a variety of striking miracles. In the latter half, he is cast as the lowly servant who suffers on our behalf. Both depictions combine to show what kind of Son of God Jesus is, clarifying and correcting popular misconceptions.

Speaking of Markan sandwiches, a final such sandwich closes out the Gospel. It depicts the presence of several women at the cross, followed by Jesus's burial and the women's visit to the tomb on Sunday morning.

---

441. Cf. 2 Samuel 7:14; Psalms 2:7; 110:1.
442. Köstenberger, Kellum, and Quarles, *The Cradle, the Cross, and the Crown*, 297.
443. Köstenberger, Kellum, and Quarles, *The Cradle, the Cross, and the Crown*, 297.

THE MARKAN SANDWICH IN MARK 15:40–16:8

15:40–41 The women at the cross
15:42–47 The burial of Jesus
16:1–8 The women at the tomb

In some ways, as mentioned, the remainder of the Gospel is almost anticlimactic: How do you follow the Roman centurion's confession of Jesus as the Son of God? At first, Mark briefly mentions the presence of several women at the cross who were looking on from a distance, including Mary Magdalene, Mary the mother of James, and Salome. These are the same women who "followed him and ministered to him"(!) in Galilee. In addition, Mark notes, "there were also many other women who came up with him to Jerusalem."[444] These are the very same women who set out for Jesus's tomb on Sunday morning.[445]

By featuring these women, Mark makes clear that Jesus had a very large contingent of committed, devoted female followers. It may even be possible to detect a contrast between Jesus's male disciples, all of whom fled at Jesus's arrest, and those women who faithfully followed Jesus amid all his adversity and gruesome death. In our churches today, women often are not esteemed highly enough or recognized for their faithful service. We would do well to look for ways to show female church members and servants of Christ the respect and appreciation they so amply deserve.

The Burial (15:42–47)

In between the sections on the women at the cross and at the tomb, Mark tersely and solemnly records the burial of Jesus's body by Joseph of Arimathea, "a respected member of the council" (i.e., the Sanhedrin), "who was also himself looking for the kingdom of God."[446] This shows, remarkably, that the Sanhedrin was not unanimous in its rejection of Jesus but that there were notable exceptions. (John also tells us about another Sanhedrin member, Nicodemus, who likewise took part in securing a proper burial for Jesus.)[447] This Joseph apparently went to Pilate, which would have taken quite a bit of courage, and asked for Jesus's body.

444. Mark 15:40–41.
445. Compare Mark 15:40 with 16:1.
446. Mark 15:43.
447. Interestingly, none of the other Gospels (including Mark) mentions Nicodemus.

After verifying with a centurion that Jesus is dead, Pilate releases the body.[448] Apart from its immediate purpose in narrating how Jesus's death and burial historically took place, this also serves an important apologetic purpose: it confirms that Jesus actually died! When he came back to life, therefore, this was not merely a resuscitation but a resurrection! Joseph has Jesus's body taken down from the cross and has it wrapped in a linen shroud and laid in a new tomb, and a rock is rolled against the entrance, sealing the tomb.

Mark is careful to note that Mary Magdalene and the other Mary saw where Jesus was put. This is important, as it ensures that both women know where to go Sunday morning to finish Jesus's burial. In addition, it serves to verify that they went to the right tomb. This confirms that the empty tomb they found was in fact the same tomb as the one in which Jesus was buried. Mark's narrative is concise, even terse, and yet subtle. He is clearly very deliberate in what he records and why he does so. It's also interesting to note that Mark could have recorded several ways in which Jesus's burial fulfilled Scripture (such as that he was laid in a rich man's tomb), but Mark omits such references, perhaps because he is writing to Gentiles.

The Women at the Tomb (16:1–8)

When Sabbath is over—Mark reasonably assumes his readers know that people weren't supposed to do any work on the Jewish Sabbath—Mary Magdalene and the other women set out for the tomb to finish what had been left undone at Jesus's burial owing to sunset and the beginning of the Sabbath. On their way to the tomb, they worry how they'll be able to roll away the "very large" stone at the entrance of the tomb, but their concerns are allayed when they arrive and the stone has already been rolled back. As if this was not startling enough, as they enter the tomb, they're "alarmed" at the sight of an angel dressed in a white robe who announces to them that Jesus has risen![449] "See the place where they laid him," the angel says; the reader knows that Jesus is no longer there.

What's more, the angel commissions the women, "But go, tell his disciples and Peter that he is going before you to Galilee. There you will see him, just as he told you."[450] This, as mentioned, harks back to Jesus's earlier prediction that after the resurrection he would go ahead of the disciples to Galilee and meet them there.[451] It was also at that time that Jesus predicted that Peter would deny him three times.[452] Perhaps this is why the angel now adds "and Peter." Of all the disciples, Peter would be particularly glad

---

448. Note that two Greek words are used here. In verse 43 the word is *sōma*, "body," while in verse 45 the word is *ptōma*, "corpse." Jesus has died; he is now a corpse (at least until he rises again)!

449. Mark 16:6.

450. Mark 16:7.

451. Mark 14:28.

452. Mark 14:29–30.

to hear that Jesus rose from the dead and that he would see him again (though he may have been slightly apprehensive meeting Jesus again in light of his denials). The Gospel closes with the women trembling in fear and astonishment. And while the angel had told them to "go tell his disciples," the Gospel closes with Mark telling his readers that the women "said nothing to anyone, for they were afraid"![453]

Thus, the Gospel ends on a massive cliffhanger. We know that Jesus has risen (though we haven't seen him appear in the narrative yet). We also know that the centurion acknowledged that Jesus truly was the Son of God, just as Mark had asserted at the beginning of his Gospel and Peter had confessed halfway through. Like the women, we're left to ponder what it all means. The Son of God has risen from the dead just like he said he would! If so, everything he said as recorded in the Gospel is true, and his miracles really did attest him to be the Messiah and Son of God. This also means, therefore, that the disciples would see him again, and that their decision to follow Jesus was the right one. Beyond the grave, beyond the brutal cross, is the triumphant resurrection, and the suffering servant is now the glorious Lord whom some of Jesus's disciples saw at the transfiguration.

Mark leaves us with a lot to think about. But one thing is clear: Jesus has risen, and we must follow him, no matter the cost, for he is worthy to be followed. Do you agree?

EXCURSUS: HOW DOES MARK'S GOSPEL END?

Most English translations continue with several additional verses.[454] However, they include a footnote at 16:8 stating that the external evidence reveals that the oldest and most reliable manuscripts don't include the longer ending. The internal evidence also supports the ending at verse 8, as the longer ending contains different vocabulary and style, including questionable references to drinking poison and handling snakes.[455] Both the external and the internal evidence thus seem to favor the ending at verse 8.[456] Yet one wonders: Why would Mark end his Gospel so abruptly?[457] Here are a few considerations to keep in mind.

First of all, Mark has a right to write the Gospel he chooses to write. Remember that Luke, for example, cuts off the book of Acts with Paul arriving in Rome. The reader is left

453. Mark 16:8.

454. Mark 16:9–20.

455. Mark 16:18.

456. On Mark's ending, see Köstenberger, Kellum, and Quarles, *The Cradle, the Cross, and the Crown*, 285; Garland, *Theology of Mark's Gospel*, 535–59; Metzger, *Textual Commentary*, 104–6; Williams, *Mark*, 271–72, 274–76.

457. The ending is even more unusual in the Greek original, where the last word in verse 8 is the postpositive coordinating conjunction "for" (Greek *gar*).

wondering: What happened after that? Was Paul released from house arrest? Did he ever make it to Spain as he had planned? These and other questions go unanswered. Yet Luke's purpose for writing has been accomplished: he has shown how the gospel spread all the way from Jerusalem to Rome. Also, consider the fact that Mark starts his Gospel immediately with John the Baptist, rather than, like Matthew and Luke, with a birth narrative of Jesus or even a genealogy (not to mention John, who starts his Gospel in eternity past!). One surmises that, for Mark's purposes, starting with Jesus's forerunner was sufficient, as he was trying to chronicle Jesus's mission from his baptism to his death on a cross.

Similarly, I believe, while the reader may wonder what happened after verse 8 of chapter 16 of Mark's Gospel, Mark's purpose has already been accomplished. Our curiosity may cause us to ask: Did Jesus meet his followers in Galilee? What about the Great Commission? In fact, it is in order to answer such questions that a later copyist most likely added a longer ending, perhaps on the basis of the endings of the other Gospels (such as Matthew's).

Rightly understood, therefore, Mark's Gospel is coherent and compelling as it stands (i.e., with the shorter ending). Although there are no resurrection appearances in Mark's passion narrative, the angel has announced that Jesus has risen and that his disciples will see him in Galilee. So Mark is fully aware of Jesus's resurrection appearances; otherwise, the angel's command to go to Galilee would be inexplicable.

What's more, Mark tells us that, in response to the resurrection announcement, the women were "trembling and astonishment had seized them."[458] As David Garland notes, "The description of their fear combined with their 'alarm,' 'trembling,' and 'bewilderment' all serve to accentuate the overpowering mystery of this news of the resurrection."[459] This is the same kind of mystery and awe that has characterized Jesus's ministry throughout Mark's Gospel. The women's fear and awe accord well with Mark's presentation of Jesus.

Finally, the command to go to Galilee is unique to Mark. If you remember, Galilee is where the disciples initially heard Jesus's call to follow him.[460] So Mark brings us back to the beginning, but now the disciples will see Jesus with fresh eyes and follow him anew.[461] The story will continue as the disciples proclaim the good news that Jesus is "the Messiah, the Son of God."[462] And the gospel will come to a climax when the Son of Man comes "in clouds with great power and glory" to "gather his elect from the four winds, from the ends of the earth to the ends of heaven."[463]

458. Mark 16:8.
459. Garland, *Theology of Mark's Gospel*, 555.
460. Cf. Mark 1:16–20; 2:13–14.
461. Garland, *Theology of Mark's Gospel*, 558–59.
462. Mark 1:1.
463. Mark 13:26–27.

CHAPTER 4

The Good News according to LUKE

Jesus the Compassionate Healer and Savior for All People

JUST THE FACTS

The good news of salvation for all people written by Luke

Not one of the Twelve but a physician and travel companion of Paul

The only Gospel with a sequel: the book of Acts[1]

WHO WAS LUKE?

Luke was a medical doctor; the apostle Paul calls him "the beloved physician."[2] As such, he was highly educated, as his elegant Greek and the careful research underlying his Gospel and the book of Acts amply attest. As he candidly admits, Luke was not an eyewitness of Jesus's earthly ministry.[3] At the same time, he was an eyewitness of portions of Paul's missionary exploits and participant in the early church's mission, as can be seen in the so-called "we" passages in the book of Acts, where Luke switches from the third-person plural (they) to the first-person plural (we).[4]

Luke is not only an evangelist and theologian; he is also a careful historian. As such, he presents the origins of Christianity and the early Christian mission within the compass of world history, in particular Roman history. Luke's Gospel, for example, includes references to Caesar Augustus, Emperor Tiberius, Herod Antipas, Pontius Pilate, Quirinius, and others.[5] Luke may have had time to work on his Gospel in Caesarea during Paul's two-year imprisonment there (ca. AD 55–57). He also was with Paul during his

1. While Luke and Acts share a close literary and theological relationship, they can also stand alone as individual books. For further details on the unity of Luke and Acts, see Darrell L. Bock, *A Theology of Luke and Acts*, Biblical Theology of the New Testament (Grand Rapids: Zondervan, 2012), 55–61, who notes, "The idea is that Luke wrote his gospel with the goal of writing Acts later in order to tell one basic story" (55).
2. Colossians 4:14. There are places in the Gospel where Luke's medical background seems to shine through, such as when only he speaks of Peter's mother-in-law having a "high fever" and describes her healing more graphically than do the other evangelists (Luke 4:38–39; cf. Matthew 8:14–15; Mark 1:30–31). Luke is mentioned elsewhere in Paul's writings in 2 Timothy 4:11 and Philemon 24. For a thorough introduction to Luke and his Gospel, see Andreas J. Köstenberger, L. Scott Kellum, and Charles L. Quarles, *The Cradle, the Cross, and the Crown: An Introduction to the New Testament* (Nashville: B&H, 2009), 308–21; more succinctly, see Alan J. Thompson, *Luke*, Exegetical Guide to the Greek New Testament (Nashville: B&H, 2016), 3–8.
3. Luke 1:1–3.
4. Acts 16:10–17; 20:5–15; 21:1–18; 27:1–28:16.
5. Luke 2:1; 3:1.

first Roman imprisonment.[6] Thus he could have completed the Gospel in Caesarea, Rome, or anywhere in between.

HOW DOES LUKE TELL THE STORY OF JESUS?

Luke is unique among the Gospels in having a sequel—the book of Acts—which continues the story of Jesus with an account of the early Christian movement. Luke's is also the longest of the four Gospels, beginning earlier (with the announcement of John's birth) and ending later (with the ascension of Jesus into heaven) than the other Synoptic Gospels. By and large, Luke follows a geographical pattern in his presentation of Jesus's work. As you can see from the outline below, he presents Jesus's story in three parts: (1) his initial work in Galilee, (2) his lengthy journey from Galilee to Jerusalem, and (3) his final work in Jerusalem.[7]

Like Matthew and Mark, Luke starts by tracing the initial stages of Jesus's teaching and healing ministry in Galilee.[8] Luke's distinct contribution, however, comes with his extensive "travel narrative,"[9] which shows Jesus "set[ting] his face to go to Jerusalem."[10] Over the span of ten chapters, Luke narrates Jesus's journey to Jerusalem, which highlights his mission "to seek and save the lost."[11] This section also includes many parables unique to Luke.[12] At last, Jesus arrives in Jerusalem, culminating in Luke's passion

---

6. See Colossians 4:14.
7. Note that commentators differ on how to outline Luke's Gospel. Darrell L. Bock, *Luke 1:1–9:50*, Baker Exegetical Commentary on the New Testament (Grand Rapids: Baker, 1996), 43–48, and *Theology of Luke and Acts*, 64–65, presents the following outline: I. Luke's Preface and the Introduction of John and Jesus (1:1–2:52); II. Preparation for Ministry (3:1–4:13); III. Galilean Ministry (4:14–9:50); IV. Jerusalem Journey (9:51–19:44); V. Jerusalem (19:45–24:53). David E. Garland, *Luke*, Zondervan Exegetical Commentary on the New Testament (Grand Rapids: Zondervan, 2011), 38–41, delineates the structure as follows: I. Prologue and Infancy Narrative (1:1–2:52); II. Preparing for Ministry (3:1–4:13); III. Jesus's Ministry in Galilee (4:14–9:50); IV. Jesus's Journey to Jerusalem (9:51–19:28); V. Jesus in Jerusalem (19:29–21:38); VI. Jesus's Suffering and Death (22:1–23:49); VII. Jesus's Resurrection and Ascension (23:50–24:53). I. H. Marshall, *The Gospel of Luke*, New International Greek Testament Commentary (Grand Rapids: Eerdmans, 1978), 7–11, provides the following outline: Preface (1:1–4); The Birth and Childhood of Jesus (1:5–2:52); John the Baptist and Jesus (3:1–4:13); The Ministry in Galilee (4:14–9:50); Progress towards Jerusalem (9:51–19:10); The Ministry in Jerusalem (19:11–21:38); The Passion and Resurrection of Jesus (22:1–24:53). The outline below takes these proposals into consideration while seeking to track as closely as possible with transitional phrases in Luke's Gospel.
8. Luke 4:14–9:50.
9. Luke 9:51–19:27. This section makes up nearly 38 percent of the Gospel, with much of the material unique to Luke. For further details, see Köstenberger, Kellum, and Quarles, *The Cradle, the Cross, and the Crown*, 327.
10. Luke 9:51.
11. Luke 19:10.
12. Most of these are found in chapters 13–18. There are thirty-three parables in Luke's Gospel, fourteen of which are unique to Luke.

narrative.[13] Jesus suffers and rises from the dead to fulfill the Scriptures so that forgiveness of sins "should be proclaimed in his name to all nations."[14]

WHAT ARE SOME OF LUKE'S DISTINCTIVE EMPHASES?

The most prominent theme in Luke's Gospel is arguably that of salvation.[15] Luke highlights this theme in several ways. First, he uses the language of salvation more than any other Gospel writer.[16] Jesus's mission is summarized by the programmatic declaration: "For the Son of Man came to seek and to *save* the lost."[17] Luke includes many unique parables that highlight this theme, such as the parables of the lost sheep, the lost coin, and the prodigal son.[18]

Luke also portrays the life of Jesus as fulfilling God's promises to Israel as recorded in the Old Testament and as the culmination of God's purposes in salvation history.[19] Everything that takes place in the life of Jesus, including his death on the cross, his burial, and his resurrection, is necessary and happens according to God's plan.[20] God's plan entails that, in addition to believing Jews, the Gentiles will be recipients of salvation as well.[21]

Last but not least, Luke highlights Jesus's concern for those of low status in society, such as women, children, the poor, the sick, and other "outsiders." Contrary to the expectations of the Jewish leaders, Jesus is a "friend of sinners" who came to call them to repentance and faith in him for the purpose of salvation.[22] As you read the Gospel, keep an eye on how this idea of a "great reversal" of expectations plays out through the characters highlighted by Luke (e.g., Zacchaeus).

---

13. Luke 22:39–24:51.
14. Luke 24:44–47.
15. Luke's treatment of salvation is focused on the forgiveness of sins (e.g., 1:77; 7:50; 18:26; 24:47) but is also multidimensional, including personal and spiritual dimensions. For further details, see Bock, *Theology of Luke and Acts*, 239–77.
16. Luke uses the word "save" seventeen times (also used frequently in Matthew and Mark). The word "Savior" is used twice, and "salvation" six times; these words appear only once in John and never in Matthew and Mark. In addition, there is a similar emphasis in Acts, with "salvation" terms appearing six times.
17. Luke 19:10, emphasis added.
18. Luke 15:3–7, 8–10, 11–32.
19. Luke 22:44–49. See I. I. du Plessis, "Once More: The Purpose of Luke's Prologue (Lk I 1-4)," *Novum Testamentum* 16 (1974): 271: "[Luke's] purpose was not to draw important lessons from history, as it was the case with other Greek historians, but to serve Christianity with a true report of *God acting in history*."
20. The Greek word *dei*, translated "must" or "it is necessary," is used eighteen times in Luke, often in the context of salvation.
21. Luke 2:32; 3:6; 24:47.
22. Luke 5:32; 7:34.

WHAT ARE THE MAJOR CONTOURS OF LUKE'S ACCOUNT?

Preface: Luke's Purpose (1:1–4)

Introduction: Jesus's Birth and Preparation for His Work (1:5–4:13)

- "In the Days of Herod, King of Judea": Announcement of Two Special Births (1:5–80)
- "In Those Days a Decree Went Out from Caesar Augustus": The Birth and Childhood of the Messiah (2:1–52)
- "In the Fifteenth Year of . . . Tiberius Caesar": Beginning of John's Ministry and Jesus's Preparation for Ministry (3:1–4:13)

Jesus's Work in Galilee (4:14–9:50)

- Work in Galilee, Part 1 (4:14–7:50)
- Work in Galilee, Part 2 (8:1–39)
- Work in Galilee, Part 3 (8:40–9:50)

The Lukan Travel Narrative: Jesus's Journey to Jerusalem (9:51–19:27)

- Lessons on Discipleship (9:51–11:54)
- Further Lessons on Discipleship (12:1–13:9)
- Healings and Additional Teachings on Discipleship (13:10–15:32)
- Additional Parables and Teachings on Discipleship (16:1–17:10)
- Closing in on Jerusalem (17:11–19:27)

Jesus's Work in Jerusalem (19:28–24:49)

- The Triumphal Entry and Final Work in Jerusalem (19:28–21:38)
- The Last Supper, Jesus's Arrest, Crucifixion, and Resurrection (22:1–24:49)

Epilogue: The Ascension (24:50–53)

PREFACE: LUKE'S PURPOSE (1:1–4)
INTRODUCTION: JESUS'S BIRTH AND PREPARATION FOR HIS WORK (1:5–4:13)
"In the Days of Herod, King of Judea": Announcement of Two Special Births (1:5–80)
Background to John the Baptist's Birth (1:5–25)
Background to Jesus's Birth (1:26–38)
The Stories of the Two Births Converge: The Mothers Meet and Mary's Magnificat (1:39–56)
The Birth of John the Baptist and Zechariah's Song (1:57–80)

PREFACE: LUKE'S PURPOSE (1:1–4)

Luke's is the only Gospel that begins with a preface that sets out the purpose of writing—that his readers might have "certainty" concerning the truth of the gospel.[23] Luke seeks to achieve this through his presentation of an "orderly account" of the life of Jesus from his birth to his ascension.[24] The word "orderly" most likely doesn't refer so much to chronological sequence as to a coherent arrangement enabling the reader to comprehend the material.[25]

Both Luke's Gospel and its sequel, the book of Acts, are addressed (or at least dedicated) to a man named Theophilus. This Theophilus most likely was a Roman government official who may have served as the patron sponsoring the publication of Luke's work.[26] Beyond this, Luke clearly had a broader audience in mind, including in his purview Gentile Christians who required solid information regarding the things they had been taught.[27]

---

23. Luke 1:4.
24. Luke 1:3.
25. See Garland, *Luke*, 55.
26. Luke 1:3; Acts 1:1. Scholars debate the exact identity of Theophilus (whose name means "lover of God"). In his Gospel, Luke addresses him as "most excellent" (1:3), the same expression used to address the Roman governors Felix (Acts 23:26; 24:2) and Festus (Acts 26:25).
27. See Garland, *Luke*, 56.

The word "certainty" carries the nuance of stability.[28] Through his Gospel, Luke intends for his readers—whether recent or prospective converts—to see the reliability of the good news of Jesus.[29] In view of this, he stresses the historical accuracy of his material. As he candidly admits, he himself was not an eyewitness to the events, but he carefully researched the life of Jesus through eyewitness sources, whether written or oral, to ensure the veracity of his work.[30]

INTRODUCTION: JESUS'S BIRTH AND PREPARATION FOR HIS WORK (1:5–4:13)

In Luke 1:5–4:13 we read about Jesus's origins and preparation for ministry. There are three parts to Luke's presentation, each of which begin with reference to a ruler. In 1:5 Luke refers to "Herod, king of Judea," in 2:1 he mentions "Caesar Augustus," and in 3:1 he refers to "Tiberius Caesar." In this way, Luke frames his narrative in the context of Roman history for the benefit of Theophilus, who, as mentioned, most likely was a Roman government official.

"In the Days of Herod, King of Judea": Announcement of Two Special Births (1:5–80)

Luke begins narrating the story of Jesus imitating the style of the Greek translation of the Old Testament called the Septuagint. He intends for the reader to draw parallels between the characters in the story of Jesus's birth and prominent figures in the Old Testament who were righteous and faithful to God. The central theme of the birth narrative is the arrival of God's salvation, which fulfills his promise of redemption for Israel.[31] Highlighting this theme are two noteworthy features in Luke's literary presentation.

First, Luke records the birth accounts of John the Baptist and Jesus in parallel fashion. The two stories are artfully intertwined as their births are both foretold by the angel Gabriel and elicit songs of praise by (one of) their parents. This is part of the intriguing theme of two in Luke-Acts, which frequently presents a pair of witnesses or events side by

28. Köstenberger, Kellum, and Quarles, *The Cradle, the Cross, and the Crown*, 318.
29. The word "taught" (Luke 1:4) suggests that Luke's intended audience needed further instruction in the faith.
30. The word "eyewitnesses" (Luke 1:2) refers to firsthand observers of events. In addition, these eyewitnesses were "from the beginning," which indicates a group of people that had been present during the time of events being narrated. This group of eyewitnesses included the Twelve and likely other followers of Jesus. For further details on Luke's Gospel as historiography, see Richard Bauckham, *Jesus and the Eyewitnesses: The Gospels as Eyewitness Testimony*, 2nd ed. (Grand Rapids: Eerdmans, 2017), 116–24.
31. Mark L. Strauss, *Four Portraits, One Jesus: An Introduction to Jesus and the Gospels* (Grand Rapids: Zondervan, 2007), 264.

side, possibly as part of the witness theme in Luke's two-volume work. This, in turn, may hark back to the requirement of two or three witnesses in the book of Deuteronomy.[32]

JOHN THE BAPTIST	JESUS
Prophecy regarding John (1:5–25)	Prophecy regarding Jesus (1:26–28)
	Mary's song (1:46–56)
John's birth and circumcision (1:57–66)	
Zechariah's song (1:67–79)	Jesus's birth and circumcision (2:1–21)

Background to John the Baptist's Birth (1:5–25)

When sketching the background of the story of John the Baptist's birth, Luke notes that his parents were childless, Elizabeth was barren, and both Zechariah and Elizabeth were well advanced in years (reminiscent of Abraham and Sarah!). Thus, humanly speaking, there was no chance they would still conceive in their old age. This underscores the miraculous nature of John's birth. What's more, when Zechariah ministers in the temple, an angel of the Lord suddenly appears "standing on the right side of the altar of incense" and delivers the news that Zechariah and Elizabeth would have a son whom they are to name John. He would be filled with the Holy Spirit, turn many Israelites to the Lord, and minister in the spirit of Elijah, the powerful Old Testament prophet.[33] When Zechariah expresses doubt, the angel identifies himself as Gabriel and says that Zechariah will be unable to speak because of his unbelief. In keeping with Gabriel's words, Elizabeth conceives and is five months along in her pregnancy when the section ends.

Background to Jesus's Birth (1:26–38)

At this, the third evangelist skillfully weaves the second birth story into his narrative. Again, God dispatches the angel Gabriel, this time to Nazareth in the Galilean

32. Deuteronomy 17:6; 19:15.
33. Luke 1:11–17.

north. He appears to a young woman named Mary, a virgin betrothed (engaged) to a man named Joseph, a descendant of David. Gabriel tells Mary that she will conceive a son whose name will be Jesus. He will be the Son of God and the Son of David who will inherit God's promise to David of an eternal kingship and royal dynasty.[34] When Mary inquires as to how she, a virgin, will conceive, Gabriel explains that the Holy Spirit will impregnate her! Thus, while John the Baptist's birth was miraculous in that God has enabled barren old Elizabeth to conceive, Jesus's birth will be even more miraculous in that his conception will bypass a human father altogether! In exemplary faith and humility, Mary responds, "Behold, I am the servant of the Lord; let it be to me according to your word."[35]

The Stories of the Two Births Converge: The Mothers Meet and Mary's Magnificat (1:39–56)

The births of Jesus and John the Baptist are tied together even further when Mary visits Elizabeth. In a moving recognition scene, Elizabeth greets Mary her relative and tells her that she is blessed among women to carry the Messiah and blessed also because she believed that the angel's words would be fulfilled.[36] In fact, the child in her own womb—John the Baptist—leapt for joy at the sight of Mary! And Elizabeth humbly adds, "And why is this granted to me that the mother of my Lord should come to me?"[37] Both birth stories signal that God is visiting his people once again. Nevertheless, John's role is quite distinct from that of Jesus. John will "prepare the way" for the Lord's salvation as the Messiah's herald. Thus Zechariah, his father, quotes the prophet Malachi in his song, which speaks of an Elijah-like forerunner to the Messiah.[38] Yet, while John is to be a prophet, Jesus is to be both Savior and king. The angel Gabriel tells Mary that Jesus will be called the "Son of the Most High" who will sit on the "throne of his father David."[39]

A second noteworthy feature is the series of hymns or songs of praise offered by Mary, Zechariah, and Simeon. The two birth narratives are structured around and intercalated with the following hymns:[40]

34. Luke 1:26–33.
35. Luke 1:38.
36. Luke 1:42, 45.
37. Luke 1:43.
38. Luke 1:17; cf. Malachi 4:5–6.
39. Luke 1:32–33.
40. The traditional titles derive from the first word of the respective hymn in the Latin version of the Bible, the Vulgate: "Magnifies" (Magnificat), "Blessed" (Benedictus), and "Now dismiss" (Nunc Dimittis).

- Mary's Magnificat (1:46–55) highlights God's exaltation of the lowly and humiliation of the proud at the coming of Jesus the Messiah and descendant of Abraham, in keeping with Luke's emphasis on the reversal of earthly status Jesus came to bring.[41]
- Zechariah's Benedictus (1:68–79) focuses on John the Baptist's role in preparing the way for God's salvation through the Messiah and Son of David, which would include the preaching of forgiveness, in keeping with Luke's emphasis on the social implications of the gospel.
- Simeon's Nunc Dimittis (2:29–32) extols God's salvation and the Messiah's coming as a light to the Gentiles, in keeping with Luke's emphasis on the implications of Jesus's coming not only for Jews but also for Gentiles.

These hymns are reminiscent of Old Testament psalms reciting the story of God's coming salvation. Especially pronounced are parallels between Hannah's song when conceiving the prophet Samuel and Mary's song.[42] The hymns also continue parallels between John and Jesus. Clearly, both are key participants in God's plan, but Jesus is the Messiah whose coming John heralds.[43]

The Birth of John the Baptist and Zechariah's Song (1:57–80)

John's birth narrative is sandwiched between Mary's and Zechariah's hymns. After some back and forth regarding John's name—unusual because none of his relatives is called John—there is amazement and a sense of excited anticipation as to what kind of ministry John would have. The chapter closes with John's coming of age and his appearance in the wilderness prior to his public work, which is paralleled by a similar reference to Jesus's growth in wisdom and stature at the end of chapter 2.[44]

---

41. For a more detailed discussion, see Andreas J. Köstenberger and Alexander E. Stewart, *The First Days of Jesus: The Story of the Incarnation* (Wheaton, IL: Crossway, 2015).
42. See 1 Samuel 2.
43. As Bock observes, "John is the forerunner who announces fulfillment's approach, but Jesus is the fulfillment" (*Theology of Luke and Acts*, 100).
44. Luke 1:80; cf. 2:52. See also Luke 2:40.

INTRODUCTION: JESUS'S BIRTH AND PREPARATION FOR HIS WORK (1:5–4:13, CONT.)

"In Those Days a Decree Went Out from Caesar Augustus": The Birth and Childhood of the Messiah (2:1–52)

The Birth of Jesus (2:1–20)

Name-Giving and Dual Recognition of the Infant Jesus (2:21–40)

Twelve-Year-Old Jesus in the Temple (2:41–52)

INTRODUCTION: JESUS'S BIRTH AND PREPARATION FOR HIS WORK (1:5–4:13, CONT.)

"In Those Days a Decree Went Out from Caesar Augustus": The Birth and Childhood of the Messiah (2:1–52)

The Birth of Jesus (2:1–20)

John's arrival sets the stage for the birth of Jesus. On account of a census during the reign of Caesar Augustus (reigned 31 BC–AD 14) when a certain Quirinius was governor of (literally, "leading") Syria in the north, Joseph returns to his hometown of Bethlehem.[45] Remarkably, Augustus's decree becomes the providential means by which Jesus's parents are induced to travel from Nazareth to Bethlehem, where Jesus would be born in keeping with Old Testament messianic prophecy. Emperor Augustus presided over the Golden Age in Roman history, which was characterized by political stability, the Roman Peace (*Pax Romana*), and the flourishing of Roman culture, politics, and the arts. Placing the birth of Jesus within the context of Augustus's reign, beyond serving as a historical reference, also makes the point that Jesus's birth would eclipse even the Golden Age and the Roman Peace over which Augustus presided. Jesus would be the Prince of Peace and the harbinger of the Kingdom of the Ages—the kingdom of God.

There is no independent historical verification in extrabiblical sources for a Roman census in the years 5–1 BC, during which Jesus likely was born, but since Luke's historical data is regularly confirmed where corroborating evidence is available, we can

45. Luke 2:1–5.

surely trust his account here as well.[46] Significantly, Bethlehem is called "the city of David," and Joseph is said to be "of the house and lineage of David."[47] In these ways, Luke is careful to point out that Jesus stood firmly in the lineage of David, both by being born in Bethlehem and by his adoptive father Joseph being of Davidic ancestry. Thus, Jesus comes to earth as a human infant, as Mary's firstborn, implying she had later children, as attested later in the Gospels (Jesus had four half-brothers and at least two half-sisters, for a total of at least seven children including Jesus).

Yet the circumstances surrounding Jesus's birth don't seem fitting for a king. He is born in the humble town of Bethlehem rather than in Jerusalem, Judea's religious and political capital.[48] Upon his birth, he is laid in a manger, or feeding trough for animals, because there was no room for him in the inn.[49] This may signify the rejection Jesus is later to experience. Moreover, news of Jesus's birth is first announced to a group of lowly shepherds: an angel announces that Jesus is the "Savior" and "Christ [or Messiah] the Lord."[50] These shepherds, in turn, become the first messengers of the good news of salvation.[51] Yet, while humble in his human origins, Jesus's birth is hailed in the heavenly realm by a host of angels who appear and break out in praise, saying, "Glory to God in the highest, and on earth peace among those with whom he is pleased!"[52]

Name-Giving and Dual Recognition of the Infant Jesus (2:21–40)

Just like John, Jesus is given his name and is circumcised on the eighth day.[53] The offering brought by his parents—"a pair of turtledoves or two young pigeons"—marks them as poor.[54] The first ones to recognize God's activity are a devout man named Simeon

46. For detailed, even technical, discussions, see Köstenberger and Stewart, *First Days of Jesus*, 234–39, and Köstenberger, Kellum, and Quarles, *The Cradle, the Cross, and the Crown*, 319–21. The Jewish historian Josephus speaks of a census taken by Quirinius in AD 6, but he may have gotten the date wrong, as he demonstrably does elsewhere; see John H. Rhoads, "Josephus Misdated the Census of Quirinius," *Journal of the Evangelical Theological Society* 54 (2011): 65–87. Alternatively, Quirinius may have taken an earlier census that is not otherwise attested. Another possibility is that the word commonly translated "first" in Luke 2:2 here means "before" (though admittedly this would be an uncommon meaning). If so, the census would have been taken *before* Quirinius became governor of Syria. There are other options as well.
47. Luke 2:4; repeated in Luke 2:11. The story of how David conquered Jerusalem when becoming king of Israel and called it the "city of David" is found in 2 Samuel 5:1–10.
48. Cf. Micah 5:1–2.
49. Luke 2:7.
50. Luke 2:8–15; see esp. v. 11.
51. Luke 2:18, 20.
52. Luke 2:13–14.
53. Luke 2:21; cf. 1:59.
54. Luke 2:24; cf. Exodus 13:2, 12; Leviticus 5:11; 12:8.

and an elderly widow named Anna, part of Luke's "two theme" featuring two witnesses—one man and one woman—to Jesus's circumcision and appearance in the temple area.[55] This is hardly the kind of reception you would expect for the Davidic king and Messiah: a largely unheralded birth in a small Judean village, in a manger and of humble parents, off the mainline Jewish religious aristocracy and political establishment. As German scholar Martin Hengel rightly comments, "For Luke, the manger expresses the contrast between the world-ruler Augustus and the hidden and lowly birth of the world-redeemer."[56] And yet there is a marked contrast between worldly fanfare and spiritual significance, as here is one born who would change world history like no one else.

THE MESSIAH IN LUKE

At the arrival of Jesus, the angel of the Lord announced to the shepherds, "For unto you is born this day in the city of David a Savior, who is *Christ the Lord*."[57] The title "Christ" refers to Jesus as the promised Anointed One or Messiah who is at the center of God's promises in the Old Testament. This is Luke's most frequent title for Jesus and serves as a foundation for our understanding of his identity.[58] Expectations of the Messiah can be traced back to God's covenant with King David.[59] There was hope that God would restore his kingdom through a regal Davidic descendent. At the outset of Luke's Gospel, we're told that Jesus is born from the line of David and will be given the throne of David by God.[60] In addition, John the Baptist is clearly designated as a prophet who would prepare the way of the Lord.[61] Conscious of his calling, John refused to accept the title "Christ" for himself.[62] Instead, he revealed that a distinguishing mark of the Messiah would be his full possession of the Spirit. Significantly, the Holy Spirit descended on Jesus at his baptism.[63] However, Jesus's identity as the Messiah was veiled to many. While Jesus

55. Luke 2:25–38.
56. Martin Hengel, "φάτνη," in *Theological Dictionary of the New Testament*, eds. Gerhard Kittel and Gerhard Friedrich, trans. Geoffrey W. Bromiley (Grand Rapids: Eerdmans, 1984), 9:54.
57. Luke 2:11.
58. Bock, *Theology of Luke and Acts*, 185–86.
59. 2 Samuel 7:1–17.
60. Luke 1:26–33.
61. Luke 1:76.
62. Luke 4:15–17.
63. Luke 4:21–22.

performed the acts of the Messiah—healing the sick, casting out demons, preaching good news to the poor—most rejected his authority, most notably the Jewish leaders. An interesting usage of the title, unique to Luke, occurs when the demons "knew that [Jesus] was the Christ."[64] Even the demons recognized Jesus's authority as the Messiah! Despite this fact, many people struggled to grasp Jesus's messianic identity.

The breakthrough doesn't come until chapter 9 when the disciples are questioned by Jesus about who they say he is. Peter responds by identifying Jesus as "the Christ of God."[65] It's hard to emphasize just how pivotal this moment is in Luke's Gospel. It's exactly at this point that Jesus begins to divulge some of the finer points of his messianic identity to his disciples. Most significantly, he reveals that he will suffer and die and be raised on the third day.[66] This grave prospect stood in stark contrast to the common Jewish expectation that the Messiah would reclaim Israel's throne and overthrow the Roman overlords.[67] For the Jews, the concept of a suffering messiah was "incongruous, an impossibility."[68] The issue of Jesus's messianic identity came under full scrutiny during his trials before the Sanhedrin and Pilate. The chief priests and scribes asked Jesus point-blank, "If you are the Christ, tell us."[69] Jesus's claim to be the Messiah became the central issue leading up to his death. Even on the cross, the leaders scoffed at him: "Let him save himself, if he is the Christ of God, his Chosen One!"[70]

As the narrative unfolds, Luke expands our understanding of the Messiah by incorporating other crucial aspects of Jesus's identity. As the Messiah, Jesus is also God's *servant* and a *prophet* powerful in word and deed. In Mary's Magnificat, Israel is called God's "servant," alluding to Isaiah 49:3 and the special role that Israel played as his representative.[71] This servant imagery is picked up later in Jesus's inaugural sermon, in which

64. Luke 4:41.
65. Luke 9:20.
66. Luke 9:22.
67. Bock, *Theology of Luke and Acts*, 186.
68. Bock, *Theology of Luke and Acts*, 186.
69. Luke 22:67.
70. Luke 23:35.
71. Luke 1:54.

he quotes Isaiah 61:1–2 in declaration of his mission. Jesus fulfills Isaiah's prophecy of the Spirit-anointed servant who would preach good news to the poor, set the captives free, and give sight to the blind. This passage also reveals the prophetic dimension of Jesus's mission. Jesus is the servant-like prophet who proclaimed God's word and performed miracles. When Jesus raised the widow's son at Nain, the people cried out, "A great prophet has arisen among us!"[72] The disciples on the road to Emmaus recognized Jesus as "a prophet mighty in deed and word before God and all the people."[73] What's more, Jesus identified himself as standing in the lineage of Israel's prophets (e.g., Elijah and Elisha). And like the prophets of old, Jesus would be rejected and suffer.[74] If Israel chose to reject Jesus's prophetic message, people would face God's judgment.[75] Jesus's role as a servant and prophet further corroborates his identity as the Messiah.

Moving forward in the story, Jesus will continually challenge people's expectations of the kind of Davidic ruler and Messiah who would come to lead the Jewish nation and bring deliverance and redemption. What's more, as Luke—the only Gentile evangelist—is careful to point out, not only does Jesus come as "the consolation of Israel"; he also appears as "a light for revelation to the Gentiles."[76] In keeping with the reversal of popular messianic expectation, Simeon tells Mary on an ominous note that her child would "cause the falling and rising of many in Israel" and that a sword would pierce her own soul as well, referring to Mary's grief at Jesus's rejection and ultimate crucifixion.[77] Can you imagine how Mary must have felt during the excruciating hours of Jesus's death on the cross? Seeing her son brutally executed must have been almost too much to bear.

At this, Luke records the infant Jesus's return with his parents to Nazareth in Galilee. A summary statement notes that "the child grew and became strong"; he was "filled with wisdom" and God's favor rested upon him.[78]

72. Luke 7:16.
73. Luke 24:19.
74. Luke 4:24–27; 11:47–52.
75. Luke 6:24–26; 10:13–16; 11:37–52.
76. Luke 2:25, 32; cf. Isaiah 42:6; 49:6.
77. Luke 2:34–35 NIV.
78. Luke 2:40, 52; cf. the description of the Messiah who would be endowed with wisdom from the Spirit in Isaiah 11:2.

Twelve-Year-Old Jesus in the Temple (2:41–52)

Jesus's parents, as was customary, went up to Jerusalem every year at Passover. At this point, Luke skips over a decade and recounts the twelve-year-old Jesus's visit to Jerusalem. At the end of Passover, Jesus's parents set out on their return trip, presumably as part of a caravan, but after a day's journey realized that Jesus wasn't with them (truly every parent's nightmare!). They hurry back to Jerusalem and search for him among their relatives. After three days, they finally find him in the temple, sitting among the teachers and amazing them with his grasp of Scripture. When Mary addresses him as any concerned mother would have, Jesus responds that she should have known he was going to be "in his Father's house" (i.e., the temple)![79] This provides a fascinating glimpse into Jesus's messianic identity and awareness of his unique relationship with God the Father, a bond that transcended his relationship with his earthly parents. The account of the twelve-year-old Jesus—the only such account anywhere in the Gospels—serves as a transition to his public work; it may well have Mary herself as the source.[80]

79. Strauss notes, "At an early age, Jesus demonstrates his messianic credentials through an awareness of a unique father-son relationship with God and through his extraordinary God-given wisdom" (*Four Portraits, One Jesus*, 267).

80. See the reference to Mary as "treasur[ing] up all these things in her heart" in Luke 2:51. The account stands in marked contrast to several "Infancy Gospels" that speculate about Jesus's childhood and growing-up years.

INTRODUCTION: JESUS'S BIRTH AND PREPARATION FOR HIS WORK (1:5–4:13, CONT.)

"In the Fifteenth Year of . . . Tiberius Caesar": Beginning of John's Ministry and Jesus's Preparation for Ministry (3:1–4:13)

The Messiah's Forerunner, John the Baptist (3:1–22)

The Messiah's Ancestry: Jesus the Son of Adam (3:23–28)

The Messiah's Threefold Temptation (4:1–13)

INTRODUCTION: JESUS'S BIRTH AND PREPARATION FOR HIS WORK (1:5–4:13, CONT.)

"In the Fifteenth Year of . . . Tiberius Caesar": Beginning of John's Ministry and Jesus's Preparation for Ministry (3:1–4:13)

The Messiah's Forerunner, John the Baptist (3:1–22)

Picking up where he left off with John the Baptist in chapter 1, Luke returns to John in preparation for narrating Jesus's ministry. As in the case of Old Testament prophets, "the word of God came to John."[81] The fact that God's call came to John "in the wilderness" prepares for the reference to the words of Isaiah that in the last days a "voice of one crying in the wilderness" would be raised in order to "prepare the way of the Lord."

Luke highlights three vital features of John's ministry. First, he sets it in historical context by providing the actual names and dates of those in authority.[82]

- John's ministry began in the fifteenth year of the reign of the Roman emperor Tiberius, which began in AD 14 following the death of Caesar Augustus.[83]

---

81. Luke 3:2.
82. Luke 3:1–2.
83. Cf. Luke 2:1. This provides a secure historical anchor that allows us to date the beginning of John's ministry, and later of Jesus's ministry, in AD 29 (14 + 15). This, incidentally, assuming a three-and-a-half-year ministry of Jesus, means that Jesus was most likely crucified in the year 33. Others believe that Jesus died in AD 30, but this is hard to reconcile with a start date of AD 14 for Tiberius's reign. Those holding to AD 30 must posit a two-year co-regency between Caesar Augustus, Tiberius's predecessor, and Tiberius, for which

- Pontius Pilate was already governor of Judea, having started his tenure in AD 26 (his tenure would last until AD 36).
- Herod Antipas, one of Herod the Great's sons, was tetrarch of Galilee; he was the one who would eventually have John beheaded.
- Antipas's brother Philip was tetrarch of Iturea and Trachonitis in the north in the area of today's Lebanon.
- The lesser-known Lysanias was tetrarch of Abilene in the Syrian north near Damascus.[84]
- Caiaphas was the actual high priest, having been appointed in AD 18 (there was supposed to be a new high priest every year, but this was often not observed).
- Annas had served as high priest for ten years (AD 6–15) but continued as the patriarch whose family supplied several high priests in the first half of the first century.

In all these ways, Luke, as an excellent historian, takes great care to locate the beginning of John the Baptist's ministry in world, Roman, and Jewish history.

Second, similar to Matthew and Mark, Luke cites the opening words of the second half of the book of Isaiah with reference to John's role in preparing the way for the Lord. He would be the herald of a new exodus at which God's servant would lead his people through the wilderness as Moses did with regard to Israel of old. What's more, in a fascinating move, Luke doesn't end the quotation where the other Gospel writers do but continues to cite the Isaianic passage, which points out that this new exodus would be not only for Israel but for all people, with the result that "*all* flesh" would "see the salvation of God."[85] This, along with tracing Jesus's genealogy all the way back to Adam (see below), makes the important point that Jesus's messianic mission has universal entailments beyond the nation of Israel. In Luke's day, this was important, as Roman government officials such as (possibly) Theophilus would be made to realize that Christianity was not merely another Jewish sect but a religion in its own right (albeit deeply rooted in Old Testament messianic predictions and expectations).

Third, Luke is the only Gospel writer to include special details of John's preaching regarding right relationships.[86] He warned his fellow Jews against presuming on their Abrahamic descent, asserting that God could raise up children for Abraham "from these stones."[87] In other words, God didn't need the Jews—but they needed him! In

there is little secure (i.e., sufficiently early) historical evidence. See "The Date of Jesus's Crucifixion," in *ESV Study Bible* (Wheaton, IL: Crossway, 2008), 1809–10.

84. Josephus mentions an earlier ruler named Lysanias, but an inscription supports this second later figure.
85. Luke 3:6, emphasis added; cf. Isaiah 40:3–5.
86. Luke 3:10–14.
87. Luke 3:8.

their smug complacency, they resembled the Israelites centuries earlier who thought that surely God couldn't renege on his covenant and allow the nation to be carried into exile. Well, guess what? He could! And he did! Judgment was at hand. The Jews' ethnic presumption would have dire consequences unless people repented and turned to the Messiah in contrition and humble faith. What's more, John's baptism of repentance must result not merely in outward expressions of faith but in a radically transformed life that was characterized by integrity in one's dealings with others. Jesus himself, most notably in the Sermon on the Mount/Plain—and later, James his half-brother in his epistle—would make the same point.[88]

The impact of John's ministry led some to wonder whether he was the Messiah.[89] However, John affirmed that his baptism was only with water while the Messiah would baptize with the Holy Spirit.[90] At this, Luke notes parenthetically that Herod Antipas threw John into prison for publicly chastising him for taking his brother Philip's wife, a woman named Herodias.[91] Almost casually, Luke mentions that Jesus was baptized, along with "all the people."[92] Yet at Jesus's baptism, several supernatural manifestations occurred that indicated his unique identity: "the heavens were opened"; "the Holy Spirit descended on him in bodily form, like a dove"; and a heavenly voice was heard affirming, "You are my beloved Son; with you I am well pleased."[93] Throughout his Gospel, Luke will emphasize the vital role of the Holy Spirit in connection with Jesus's messianic mission. Here, the Spirit's descent represents the formal installment and anointing of Jesus for his messianic work at the dawn of God's salvation, and the divine voice confirms Jesus as the Davidic Messiah and servant of the Lord.

The Messiah's Ancestry: Jesus the Son of Adam (3:23–38)

Noting that Jesus was "about thirty years of age" when he began his public ministry, Luke includes Jesus's genealogy at this point in the Gospel rather than at the very beginning as does Matthew.[94] As Matthew does, Luke traces Jesus's ancestry back to David and Abraham; yet going beyond Matthew, Luke goes all the way back to Adam. That is to say, Jesus is not just Israel's Messiah but the Savior of all people. Also, in terms of chronological and literary structure, Matthew moves forward from Abraham to (infant)

88. See Matthew 7:21–27; James 1:22–25.
89. Luke 3:15.
90. Luke 3:16.
91. Luke 3:19–20. Both Matthew and Mark tell the whole story by way of a flashback.
92. Luke 3:21. Luke doesn't include any justification as to why Jesus's baptism "fulfills all righteousness."
93. Luke 3:21–22; cf. Psalm 2:7; Isaiah 42:1.
94. Luke 3:23–38. If Jesus was born in 2/1 BC and started his ministry in AD 29, he would have been about thirty years old at that time (no year zero).

Jesus, while Luke backtracks from (the adult) Jesus to Adam. In this way, Matthew presents his genealogy as a prelude to his account of the virgin birth (remember his inclusion of five women and his distinction between Mary as Jesus's mother and Joseph as merely his adoptive father); Luke, on the other hand, starts with Jesus and shows that Jesus is not merely the son of David and descendant of Abraham—though he is that—but a true human being descended all the way from Adam. This qualifies him, together with his divine credentials made apparent at his baptism, to serve as the Savior of all humanity, Jew as well as Gentile. Jesus is Savior of all!

The Messiah's Threefold Temptation (4:1–13)

The conclusion of Luke's genealogy, which identifies Adam as "son of God," sets up the final stage of Jesus's preparation for his work, where *the* Son of God is tempted by the devil.[95] Fresh from being baptized by John, Jesus returns from the Jordan River, "full of the Holy Spirit," and is led by that same Spirit into the wilderness to be tempted by the devil for forty days (note Luke's characteristic emphasis on the Holy Spirit and his depiction of Jesus as the Spirit-anointed Messiah).[96] This sets Jesus's messianic mission within the context of intense spiritual warfare, pitting Jesus, the Holy Spirit, and God the Father against the devil and his demons. In the temptation narrative, Jesus is contrasted with Adam and the nation of Israel, both of which are referred to as "sons of God" in Scripture.[97] God's son Adam failed his test of obedience at the original temptation of humanity; he ate the fruit from the forbidden tree that his wife gave him after succumbing to the serpent's deception.[98] Likewise, God's son Israel failed when tested in the wilderness for forty years, being barred from entering the Promised Land because of persistent unbelief.[99]

In response to each of the devil's temptations, Jesus cites passages from Deuteronomy that relate directly to wilderness Israel's failures:

- "It is written: 'Man shall not live on bread alone.'"[100]
- "It is written: 'Worship the Lord your God and serve him only.'"[101]
- "It is said: 'Do not put the Lord your God to the test.'"[102]

---

95. Luke 4:1–13. The order of the temptations in Luke's account is different from that of Matthew's, with the last two temptations being reversed. Luke ends the narrative with Jesus in Jerusalem, which is consistent with his emphasis on the city as a focal point in his Gospel. See further Strauss, *Four Portraits, One Jesus*, 268–69.
96. Cf. Luke 4:18–19 citing Isaiah 61:1 below.
97. Cf. Luke 3:38; Exodus 4:22–23.
98. Genesis 3:1–19.
99. Psalm 95:8–11.
100. Luke 4:4 NIV; cf. Deuteronomy 8:3.
101. Luke 4:8 NIV; cf. Deuteronomy 6:13.
102. Luke 4:12 NIV; cf. Deuteronomy 6:16.

Incredibly, Satan, too, cites Scripture—a psalm that says, "He will command his angels concerning you to guard you carefully; they will lift you up in their hands, so that you will not strike your foot against a stone"![103] In each case where Adam and Israel failed, Jesus the true Son resisted temptation and succeeded. Jesus refused to eat when doing so would have transgressed God's command. He affirmed that God alone must be worshiped and rejected idolatry and worshiping Satan. And unlike Israel, which repeatedly put God to the test during the wilderness wanderings, Jesus rebuffed the devil's challenge to treat God presumptuously. Jesus, the perfect Israelite and sinless Son of God, lived the perfect life in perfect obedience to God so that those who trust in him can enjoy a righteous standing before God.[104]

RECAP

We've come a long way since Luke's elegant preface, in which he assured us that he carefully investigated all the events related to Jesus's coming "from the beginning." In his opening chapters, Luke carefully sets the stage for the beginning of Jesus's work in Galilee. He starts out by narrating the intertwined miraculous births of John the Baptist, Jesus's forerunner, and Jesus himself. He then briefly recounts Jesus's upbringing in Nazareth and Jesus's visit to the Jerusalem temple as a twelve-year-old. In a huge jump, Luke fast-forwards to the beginning of John the Baptist's ministry culminating in Jesus's baptism by John. Luke narrates how at that occasion the Spirit of God descended on Jesus and a voice from heaven (God the Father) declared that Jesus was his beloved Son with whom he was well pleased. At this point, Luke backtracks from the approximately thirty-year-old Jesus to trace his ancestry all the way back to Adam. The final preparatory event is Jesus's temptation by the devil. Here Luke stresses both that Jesus was "full of the Holy Spirit" and that it was the Spirit himself who led him into the wilderness to be tempted. This highlights the cosmic battle surrounding the Messiah's mission, which is about to begin.

In all this, Luke is careful to present his narrative within the framework of Roman history. Every major portion of the unfolding story of Jesus is related to a ruler: Herod the Great in 1:5, Emperor Augustus in 2:1, and Emperor Tiberius in 3:1. These references mark successive stages in salvation history: (1) the announcement of the births of Messiah's forerunner, John the Baptist, and of Jesus the Messiah; (2) the messianic birth and childhood of Jesus; and (3) the beginning of John the Baptist's public ministry and Jesus's preparation for ministry, including his baptism by John and his temptation by the devil.

---

103. Psalm 91:11–12 NIV.

104. This is often referred to as the "imputation" of Jesus's righteousness to believers.

JESUS'S WORK IN GALILEE (4:14–9:50)

Work in Galilee, Part 1 (4:14–7:50)

Jesus's Inaugural Address: Rejected at Nazareth (4:14–30)

Capernaum: Casting Out Demons, Healing Many, and Further Work (4:31–44)

JESUS'S WORK IN GALILEE (4:14–9:50)

After emerging triumphant and victorious over the devil's threefold temptation, Jesus returns to Galilee in the "power of the Spirit," poised to formally begin his public ministry.[105] Luke mentions that word about Jesus spread throughout the entire region, and that he taught in many synagogues, "being glorified by *all*."[106]

Work in Galilee, Part 1 (4:14–7:50)

Jesus's Inaugural Address: Rejected at Nazareth (4:14–30)

On one such Sabbath, he preached in the synagogue at Nazareth, his hometown.[107] In a scene pregnant with meaning, he is given the scroll of Isaiah, unrolls it, and finds the place where it said, "The Spirit of the Lord is upon me, because he has anointed me to proclaim good news to the poor. He has sent me to proclaim liberty to the captives and recovering of sight to the blind, to set at liberty those who are oppressed, to proclaim the year of the Lord's favor."[108] At this, he rolls the scroll back up, gives it to the person who handed it to him (the synagogue attendant), and sat down. Everyone's gaze in the synagogue is fixed on him, and he says, "Today this Scripture has been fulfilled in your hearing"!

105. Luke 4:14. Note again the emphasis on the Holy Spirit's agency in Jesus's ministry (cf. Luke 4:1 above). On the geography of Galilee, see the discussion at the parallel passage in Matthew 4:13–16 above.

106. Luke 4:14–15, emphasis added.

107. Luke 4:16–21. See Elaine A. Phillips, "On the Brow of the Hill at Nazareth (Luke 4:16–20)," in *Lexham Geographic Commentary*, ed. Barry J. Beitzel (Bellingham, WA: Lexham, 2017), 100–107.

108. Luke 4:18–19; cf. Isaiah 61:1–2.

This is truly a remarkable moment in salvation history and an incredible climactic exclamation point in Luke's Gospel. In Matthew's Gospel, Jesus's inaugural address is the Sermon on the Mount. In Luke's Gospel, it is his reading of the passage in Isaiah that refers to a coming Messiah, the suffering "servant of the Lord," who would be anointed with God's Spirit in order to proclaim the good news of healing, liberty, and grace to those who were poor, blind, and oppressed. Strikingly, Jesus proclaims that that prediction had now been fulfilled—in him! *Jesus* is the Spirit-anointed Messiah! Fittingly, Jesus makes this announcement in his hometown of Nazareth, which, in keeping with Isaiah's prediction, served as his base for ministry. This climactic moment is distinctive to Luke's Gospel. It uniquely presents Jesus as the liberator of the oppressed, the friend of the poor, and the healer of the sick and weak. This is the kind of Messiah Jesus is, according to Luke. Great news! Great news, that is, if you know yourself to be poor, weak, and needy. These are the people for whom Jesus came. That's the Jesus Luke portrays in his Gospel.

At first, all speak well of Jesus and commend his gracious words. And yet they wonder: "Is not this Joseph's son?" Implied is doubt that Jesus is more than a mere human. Jesus picks up on their skepticism by saying, "Doubtless you will quote to me this proverb, 'Physician, heal yourself.'"[109] And he anticipates their demand that he do in Nazareth what he had done in Capernaum (though these works are not recorded in Luke's Gospel). He goes on to point out that in the days of Elijah and Elisha there was great famine and sickness, and many people were in need. Yet God sent his prophets only to two Gentiles—the widow of Zarephath and Naaman the Syrian, unlikely recipients of his grace.[110]

Upon hearing this, the people of Nazareth are enraged and drive Jesus out of the city. In fact, they bring him to the edge of a cliff so they can throw him down! Yet he passes through their midst and goes away. Can you imagine how Jesus must have felt? What a gut-wrenching experience! Where were those people who had "glorified" Jesus and only a short while ago were amazed at his gracious words? The crowds were fickle, especially those who thought they knew him best, in his own backyard. Yet they didn't know him for who he truly was: the Spirit-anointed Messiah who worked compassionate wonders—yet not among them, because they rejected him out of spiritual blindness. This story underscores two important emerging themes in Luke's Gospel—God's salvation extending to the Gentiles and the rejection of the Messiah.[111]

109. Luke 22:22–23.

110. Luke 4:24–27; cf. 1 Kings 17:8–16; 2 Kings 5:1–14.

111. Cf. Luke 2:28–32, 34.

Capernaum: Casting Out Demons, Healing Many, and Further Work (4:31–44)

The fulfillment of Isaiah's messianic prophecy is further confirmed by the actions that follow Jesus's rejection in Nazareth. He next goes to his adoptive hometown of Capernaum, where he preaches in their synagogue and all are astonished at his evident authority. He sternly casts out a demon from a man right there in the synagogue by directly addressing the demon: "Be silent and come out of him!" The demon, speaking in the plural, had previously addressed him as "Jesus of Nazareth" and continued, "I know who you are—the Holy One of God."[112] Ironically, what the people of Nazareth failed to realize, thinking he was merely Joseph's son, demons know full well: Jesus is God's set-apart Messiah, the Holy One of God. In this way, Jesus shows himself to be the Messiah with commanding authority in both word and deed, preaching good news to the poor, healing the sick, and setting captives free from demonic bondage.[113]

After a brief intermezzo where Jesus, after leaving the synagogue, enters Peter's house and heals his mother-in-law, who had come down with a fever, people at sunset brought all their sick and even demon-possessed to Jesus, "and he laid hands on every one of them and healed them."[114] Those are incredible scenes! Demons came out of many people at Jesus's command, exclaiming, "You are the Son of God!" Yet Jesus didn't need their witness. He told them to be quiet because "they knew that he was the Christ" (proving that the Markan "messianic secret" is the "Lukan secret" as well, and in fact may be better called the "Jesus secret"!).[115] At this, Jesus tries to withdraw, but people attempt to keep him from leaving. Yet he tells them that he must preach "the good news of the kingdom of God" to people in other towns as well.[116] And he goes on to preach in synagogues in Judea.

112. Luke 4:34–35.

113. Luke 4:31–39; cf. 5:12–26.

114. Luke 4:40.

115. Luke 4:41. Here "Son of God" and "the Christ" are used interchangeably, indicating that both are messianic titles referring to Jesus (cf., e.g., John 20:30–31).

116. Luke 4:43.

JESUS'S WORK IN GALILEE (4:14–9:50)

Work in Galilee, Part 1 (4:14–7:50, cont.)

Calling His First Disciples (5:1–11)

During the first stage of his Galilean ministry, Jesus also calls his first disciples: Simon Peter; James and John, Peter's fishing partners; and a little later Levi (Matthew), a tax collector.[117] Luke narrates the stories of their calling. In Peter's case, he had fished all night and come up empty-handed. When Jesus tells him where to cast his nets, he takes him at his word despite his skepticism and catches so many fish that the nets are breaking. They call on the others to help and fill both boats with fish, and the boats begin to sink. Another incredible scene! Peter is deeply struck by Jesus's authority, so much so that he tells him to depart from him, for he is nothing but a sinful man.[118] Yet this is exactly where Jesus wants him. He calls him to follow him and tells him that from now on he will no longer be catching fish but people, a reference to the powerful preacher of the Christian gospel Peter would one day become. You can hardly blame Peter, James, and John for leaving everything behind to follow Jesus.

117. Luke 5:1–11, 27–32. See Carl J. Laney, "Fishing the Sea of Galilee (Matt 13:47–50; Luke 5:1–11; John 21:6)," in Beitzel, *Lexham Geographic Commentary*, 165–74.

118. Note the progression from Peter calling Jesus "Master" in verse 5 to calling him "Lord" in verse 8 (different words in the original Greek).

Cleansing a Leper, Healing a Paralytic (5:12–26)

Beginning here, a series of events in Jesus's ministry incite the growing opposition of the Jewish leaders.[119] First, "in one of the cities," Jesus cleanses a leper, telling him to be quiet about the healing and to show himself to the local priest and bring the required offering for the cleansing. It doesn't work—word about Jesus spreads everywhere; great crowds gather to hear him teach and to be healed. Jesus, for his part, withdraws to pray.[120] Second, "on one of those days," Jesus heals a paralyzed man, in a scene memorably told by Mark at the outset of his Gospel.[121] The man's friends creatively lower him through the roof, and Jesus promptly pronounces the man's sins forgiven, exercising authority reserved for God alone. The scribes and Pharisees promptly accuse Jesus of blasphemy. Inciting their anger even further, Jesus tells the man to get up, take his mat, and go home, which he does. All are amazed, yet one senses Jesus's opponents are seething; they are not amused.

Calling Levi and Questions about Fasting (5:27–39)

At this, Jesus calls another disciple, Levi (Matthew) the tax collector, expressing his mercy toward sinners and his concern for outcasts in society.[122] Tax collectors—even more so than the IRS in our day—were despised by all, because they, being Jews, were collecting taxes for the hated Romans. In effect, they had sold out to the other side. Consequently, they were considered to be traitors, and no one wanted to be associated with them. No one, that is, except for Jesus! In a remarkable reversal of the world's values, he was willing to forgive sinners such as these and in Levi's case even called them to join his apostolic circle. This too is the kind of Jesus Luke portrays—a Messiah who called those whom the world rejected and who forgave those who repented of their sins while rejecting those who were proud of their standing in society, such as the scribes and Pharisees.

In fact, Luke says that Levi had a huge party at his house, celebrating Jesus's calling with many of his tax collector and "sinner" friends, with Jesus right in their midst. The Pharisees and scribes, unsurprisingly, voice their disdain and disapproval, but Jesus retorts that it is the sick who need a doctor and that he, consequently, had come not to call the righteous but sinners to repentance. It's hard to overstate just how iconoclastic and revolutionary Jesus's approach was when compared to other Jewish religious teach-

119. The references to "one of those cities" or "one of those days" show that Luke merely uses certain events for illustrative purposes. Jesus did many other things, which Luke covers only by broad summary statements. As John writes, there was no way anyone could have written down everything Jesus did (John 21:24–25).
120. Luke 5:12–16.
121. Luke 5:17–26; see the discussion at Mark 2:1–12.
122. Luke 5:31–32.

ers of his day. After criticizing Jesus's association with tax collectors and sinners, Jesus's opponents go on to question his disciples' failure to fast.[123] By ways of response, Jesus says that you can hardly blame the disciples for rejoicing while the bridegroom (Jesus) is with them! Plus, new wine—the gospel about Jesus—must be put into fresh wineskins. Luke doesn't record any rebuttal by the Pharisees. The reader surmises they didn't understand the true meaning of Jesus's words.

123. Luke 5:33–39.

JESUS'S WORK IN GALILEE (4:14–9:50, CONT.)

Work in Galilee, Part 1 (4:14–7:50, cont.)

Jesus's Authority over the Sabbath (6:1–11)

Finally, in an account also featured in Matthew's and Mark's Gospels, the Pharisees object to Jesus's disciples plucking out and eating some heads of grain, rubbing those in their hands on the Sabbath. Apparently, this offended the Pharisees' sensibilities and violated one of their numerous regulations of what constituted work on the Sabbath. In response, Jesus pointedly defends his disciples' conduct by citing a scriptural precedent where David and his men did something similar.[124] This makes the point that the disciples didn't violate any biblical command but only Jewish tradition. Then Jesus adds, "The Son of Man is lord of the Sabbath."[125] By this Jesus claimed authority to interpret the Sabbath command in Scripture, ultimately on the basis that he was one with Yahweh, the Creator and covenant God of Israel. No response on the part of the Pharisees is recorded.

Continuing the topic of the Sabbath, on another Sabbath Jesus is teaching in a synagogue (no location is mentioned) in the presence of a man with a limp right hand. Despite the Pharisees' opposition, Jesus heals the man in plain view of them,

124. Luke 6:3–4; cf. 1 Samuel 21:7.
125. Luke 6:5.

knowing this would only exacerbate their antagonism toward him. Sure enough, Luke tells us they were "filled with fury" and plotted how to take action against Jesus.[126] Why were they so strongly opposed to him? As Jesus repeatedly said, they had built an entire system of regulations on top of Scripture and increasingly failed to distinguish between what was directly stated in Scripture and their own interpretations and applications.

This is a dangerous mistake to commit in any age. Every preacher, scholar, and ordinary Christian must be keenly aware of the distinction between what Scripture explicitly teaches and what is merely one's own interpretation. While Scripture is authoritative and infallible, our interpretation of Scripture is fallible and subject to revision and correction. Even where it may be appropriate for us to apply Scripture in a certain way, we should be careful not to absolutize our application and make it normative for everyone else, as individual circumstances may differ. Yet this is exactly where the Pharisees in Jesus's day had gone astray; and because Jesus was unwilling to bow to their dictates, he became a nuisance and rubbed them the wrong way to such an extent that they determined the only effective way to deal with Jesus was to get rid of him. It's deeply ironic, even tragic, that people such as the Pharisees, who prided themselves on their religious piety and devotion, hated Jesus so much that they ended up killing him, the Messiah and Son of God—supposedly out of love for God's Word, when in fact what they really were trying to protect was their own religious position and authority.

Calling the Twelve Apostles (6:12–16)

"In these days" when opposition to him was gradually mounting, Jesus goes "to the mountain" to pray all night before appointing his twelve apostles the next morning.[127] The list is equivalent to that in the other Gospels and Acts, including the aforementioned Peter, James, John, and Matthew, plus the other members of the Twelve, with Judas Iscariot listed last and identified as "a traitor."[128] There are two men each named Simon, James, and Judas on the list, distinguished by various family or other designations.

Leadership is vitally important in any human organization. Jesus's mission is no exception. Especially in leaving a legacy, it is critical that one selects the right successors and mentors them diligently. The care Jesus devotes to calling his disciples and prayerfully choosing the Twelve reinforces the importance of having others continue our mission when we depart from the scene. Of course, in Jesus's case his mission is irreplaceable and foundational, but his followers will proclaim the gospel of salvation and

126. Luke 6:11.
127. Luke 6:12.
128. Luke 6:16.

forgiveness through Jesus's substitutionary death on the cross and will represent him as they crisscross the globe as his ambassadors.

In the specific men he chose, Jesus made some interesting choices that fly in the face of conventional wisdom. Yet he discerned the condition of people's hearts and knew that he could always train them in ministry skills and the performance of various tasks. He also knew that over time they would grow in understanding their own sinfulness and need for spiritual enablement. Yet what cannot be learned as easily is the willingness to leave everything behind to follow Jesus and to put him first in all things. The Twelve (except for Judas) were prepared to do that out of true love for and devotion to him and at least an incipient understanding of who Jesus was. In due course, they all (except for John, and Judas, of course) would give their lives for him and die a martyr's death. This proves that, while not conforming to the world's criteria of what a good résumé looks like, Jesus chose well.

The Sermon on the Plain (6:17–49)

After this, Jesus descends to a "level place" to engage in an extended period of teaching, often referred to as the Sermon on the Plain.[129] Unlike Matthew and the distinct Jewish background of the Sermon on the Mount,[130] Luke seems to appeal to a Gentile audience by making no mention of the Mosaic law. The sermon begins with the Beatitudes, a series of blessings highlighting the present condition of the disciples: poor, hungry, weeping, and rejected.[131] Conversely, Jesus pronounces four woes on those who are presently rich, full, laughing, and popular.[132] As mentioned earlier, a great reversal is taking place with the arrival of Jesus. Throughout his Gospel, Luke is careful to show how social and economic realities go hand in hand with spiritual ones.[133] The Sermon on the Plain serves as an example of the Messiah's mission to preach good news to the poor.[134] It also summarizes Jesus's ethical message, emphasizing the radical values of God's kingdom, including the call to love one's enemies.[135] Jesus also calls his followers to be merciful even as God is merciful, to forgive so that they will be forgiven, and to give generously to others.[136] He cautions them to be careful to confront sin in their own lives before confronting others. Otherwise, in a humorous picture, Jesus says we'll be

129. Luke 6:20–49.
130. Cf. Matthew 5:1–8:1.
131. Luke 6:20–22.
132. Luke 6:24–26.
133. Strauss, *Four Portraits, One Jesus*, 270.
134. Cf. Luke 4:18–19.
135. Luke 6:27–35.
136. Luke 6:36–38.

like people who fault others for a speck in their eye while having a huge log in our own! That would be absurd, yet all too often we're guilty of that very thing. In fact, we tend to recognize a particular sin in others because we ourselves have committed it or are even committing it right now.

Jesus's teaching is as compelling as it is convicting. "Can a blind man lead a blind man?" he asks. "Will they not both fall into a pit?"[137] Just imagine this literally happening! Jesus's point here is that, spiritually, we need to make sure we ourselves see clearly if we want to guide others in the truth and confront them with their sin. Similarly, Jesus makes the compelling point that just as a tree is known by its fruit, and it is impossible for a bad tree to bear good fruit, so—whether we like to face up to this or not—our hearts are revealed and reflected in our words and actions: "The good person out of the good treasure of his heart produces good, and the evil person out of his evil treasure produces evil, for out of the abundance of the heart his mouth speaks."[138] This is as simple as it is profound. There's no escaping the logic of Jesus's argument here. Sin is never merely outward; it always has an inward aspect that must be rooted out if our external actions are to be corrected. Dealing merely with outward symptoms fails to address the root cause, as any good biblical counselor will be quick to point out. In yet another powerful illustration, Jesus drives his message home by comparing those who act on its truth or fail to do so to two men who respectively build a house on a proper foundation (rock) or on ground without a proper foundation.[139] Again, the message is obvious: only those who build their lives on the foundation of Jesus's teaching will withstand the final day of judgment; all others will be swept away.

137. Luke 6:39.
138. Luke 6:45.
139. Luke 6:46–49.

JESUS'S WORK IN GALILEE (4:14–9:50, CONT.)

Work in Galilee, Part 1 (4:14–7:50, cont.)

Healing a Centurion's Servant (7:1–10)

So, how will people respond to Jesus's radical message? Luke devotes the rest of the early ministry in Galilee to highlight various *responses* to Jesus. Contrary to the expectations of some, the outsiders and lowly receive forgiveness and healing, while the proud and self-righteous are left out. The transitional phrase "After he had finished all his sayings" is similar to phrases Matthew uses in his Gospel to transition from Jesus's teaching to his healing ministry.

In the present case, Luke tells his readers that Jesus went back to Capernaum, his Galilean headquarters. There, in a story also included in Matthew's Gospel, Jesus encounters a Roman centurion who pleads with Jesus to heal his servant. While those who know the centurion tell Jesus that "he is worthy," for he "loves our nation" and "built us our synagogue," the centurion himself tells Jesus he is "not worthy" to have him come to his house.[140] Instead, he asks Jesus just to say the word so that his servant might be healed. As a military commander, he is well aware of the compelling power of

140. Luke 7:4–6.

a command spoken by a person in authority; Jesus could just "say the word, and let my servant be healed."[141]

What incredible faith! Here was someone who believed in the power of Jesus's word. This is one of the rare occasions in Luke's Gospel where it is not people who marvel at Jesus's words or deeds but *Jesus* who marvels at the centurion's faith and promptly does as he requested. Jesus exclaims, "I tell you, not even in Israel have I found such faith"![142] In this way, Luke again highlights that now Gentiles have come under the orbit of Jesus's salvation. In fact, they surpass the Jewish people by their receptivity to Jesus and his word.

PARALLEL ACCOUNTS IN THE SYNOPTIC GOSPELS

We've already discussed Matthew's account of the healing of the centurion's servant; now we have arrived at a similar account in Luke's Gospel. Quite clearly, the two accounts are parallel; that is, they describe the same historical encounter between Jesus and a Roman centurion who pleaded with Jesus to heal his servant.

While the story told by the two evangelists is congruent and essentially the same, there are some interesting differences in detail. This has led skeptics to allege that Matthew and Luke here contradict each other and thus that Scripture contains error. However, such a conclusion is highly premature, for the differences can be plausibly explained.

Thus, these accounts provide an excellent case study on how to deal with parallel pericopes in the Gospels. There is large agreement between Matthew and Luke with regard to the basic narrative sequence and even word-for-word correspondence:

1. Jesus enters Capernaum.
2. He is told about a centurion's servant who needs healing.
3. He goes to heal the servant.
4. The centurion tells Jesus he is not worthy for Jesus to come to his house.
5. Jesus marvels at the man's faith.
6. He heals the servant.

141. Luke 7:7.
142. Luke 7:9.

We know what happened. It's essentially the same story. The one difference is that in Matthew the reader is led to believe that the interaction between Jesus and the centurion was *direct*, while in Luke it is depicted as being transacted *through intermediaries* sent to Jesus.

What happened here? This is one of the stories included in Matthew and Luke but not in Mark. Matthew may have been an eyewitness, while Luke consulted the accounts of others.[143] In addition, both evangelists may have used various sources. Matthew may have abbreviated his source,[144] or Luke may have added this detail.

In any case, as a Jew, Matthew would have known, and expected his Jewish readers to know, that messengers were thought to represent the person who sent them. According to an often-quoted maxim in first-century Palestine, "A man's messenger is as the man himself."

In fact, there are other places in Scripture where accounts are condensed by omitting the mention of intermediaries who carried out actions on behalf of others:

- Elijah probably didn't personally kill each of the 450 prophets of Baal, though the text indicates that "Elijah brought them down to the brook Kishon and slaughtered them there."[145]
- Likewise, Pilate wouldn't have scourged Jesus personally.[146] Rather, soldiers would have administered the scourging.
- Similarly, Pilate probably didn't personally write the inscription and put it on Jesus's cross.[147]
- Joseph of Arimathea and Nicodemus most likely didn't take Jesus's body and prepare it for burial by themselves, and Nicodemus hardly carried the seventy-five pounds' worth of spices personally.[148]

143. Luke 1:2.
144. See, e.g., Matthew 8:28–34; 9:2, 18–26; 11:2–3; and parallels.
145. 1 Kings 18:40.
146. Though this is what Matthew 27:26 and Mark 15:15 imply.
147. John 19:19, 22.
148. John 19:39–40.

The bottom line, therefore, is that Matthew *assumed* that the centurion sent messengers, while Luke explicitly *narrated* this minor detail. No big deal for their original readers, who would have known that intermediaries were often omitted because they were simply representing those who sent them.

If we keep the author's intent in mind and know the cultural background, we won't jump to the conclusion that we have a contradiction here, but will understand that the accounts in Matthew and Luke are complementary.

Raising a Widow's Son (7:11–17)

Next, Jesus, approaching a town called Nain, learns of a poor widow's only son, who had died and was being carried away.[149] Jesus has compassion on her and raises her son from the dead, one of only three such events recorded in all four Gospels.[150] As Luke tells the story, "the dead man sat up and began to speak, and Jesus gave him to his mother"![151] Again, this is an absolutely stunning scene, and details such as "And He came up and touched the coffin; and the bearers came to a halt" reflect eyewitness testimony.[152] The episode is brimming with Jesus's messianic authority to raise the dead, intermingled with moving compassion for weak and needy people, in this case a poor widow and her deceased son, who likely was her only means of support. At the sight of this amazing miracle, people are seized by fear and give glory to God, saying, "A great prophet has arisen" and "God has visited his people!"[153] This is nice but still falls short of understanding who Jesus truly is—the Messiah and Son of God, a fact of which the supernatural world is fully cognizant but which humans tragically are exceedingly slow to grasp.[154] Again, Jesus's amazing miracles provide powerful advertising, and the news about him is broadcast far and wide all over Judea and its vicinity.[155]

Messengers from John the Baptist (7:18–35)

Jesus's identity continues to be a central focus in the Gospel when news of his work reaches John the Baptist.[156] The last we heard of John was that he was thrown in jail by

149. See Emily J. Thomassen, "Shared Memories of Resurrection on the Hill of Moreh (Luke 7:11–17)," in Beitzel, *Lexham Geographic Commentary*, 149–56.
150. The other two being the raising of Jairus's daughter and the raising of Lazarus.
151. Luke 7:15.
152. Luke 7:14 NASB.
153. Luke 7:16; cf. Deuteronomy 18:15. For a similar earlier reaction, see Luke 5:26.
154. Cf. Luke 4:41, where demons address Jesus as "the Son of God" because they knew he was "the Christ."
155. Luke 7:17; cf. 4:37.
156. Luke 7:18–30.

Herod Antipas.[157] Now Luke tells us that John's disciples report to John the feats Jesus performed in his ministry. Upon receiving the news, John sends some of his followers to Jesus to inquire, "Are you the one who is to come?"[158] This is both sad and surprising, as John was Jesus's forerunner who had heralded him as the Messiah. Now apparently, languishing in a dark dungeon, John is plagued by lingering doubts. The Baptist's followers relay his question to Jesus, who, rather than giving a direct yes or no answer, responds by saying, "The blind receive their sight, the lame walk, lepers are cleansed, and the deaf hear, the dead are raised up, the poor have good news preached to them."[159] In other words, Jesus points to the messianic manifestations he has provided and allows John himself to draw the inexorable conclusion: anyone who did the works of the Messiah was in fact the Messiah![160] This conclusion further reinforces Jesus's inaugural message in the synagogue at Nazareth that he was the Spirit-anointed servant of the Lord envisioned by the prophet Isaiah. As Mark Strauss observes, Jesus's "messiahship is revealed not through a war of conquest with the Romans but by inaugurating the signs of the kingdom age predicted by Isaiah the prophet."[161]

Upon sending the messengers back to John, Jesus talks to the crowds about him, affirming that he indeed was the one of whom it was written, "Behold, I send my messenger before your face, who will prepare your way before you."[162] As the forerunner of the Messiah, John is second to none; and yet every citizen of God's kingdom is greater than he. At this, the tax collectors and sinners rejoiced because they had been baptized by John as a sign of their repentance while the Pharisees and experts in the law cringed as they had "rejected the purpose of God for themselves" and refused John's baptism.[163] The stubborn refusal of "this generation" is a sign of the rise and fall of many in Israel.[164] Jesus compares people to children on the playground who can't agree on which game to play. They didn't like John's asceticism, and they didn't like Jesus's gregariousness either! No matter what Jesus did, it seems, they were going to reject him. Yet wisdom would be vindicated by all her children who would listen to her.

Anointed by a "Sinful Woman" (7:36–50)

Jesus's comment on wisdom is further illustrated in the story of the Pharisee and the sinful woman. This is a different account from the one found in the other three Gospels

157. Luke 3:19–20.
158. I.e., the Messiah; Luke 7:20.
159. Luke 7:22.
160. Isaiah 26:19; 29:18–19; 35:5–6; 60:1–2; cf. Luke 4:18–19.
161. Strauss, *Four Portraits, One Jesus*, 272.
162. Luke 7:27; cf. Malachi 3:1.
163. Luke 7:28–30.
164. Luke 7:31–35; cf. 2:34. See Garland, *Luke*, 319.

about an anointing of Jesus.[165] The Pharisee invites Jesus for a meal in his home. As they recline, a woman anoints Jesus's feet with expensive ointment. At this, the Pharisee thinks to himself that Jesus must not be a true prophet or else he would have known that this was a "sinful woman." Jesus, knowing the Pharisee's thoughts, tells him a story about a moneylender with two debtors, one who owed a small amount and the other who owed a large amount. Neither was able to pay, so the moneylender canceled their debt. Which of them will love him more?

The obvious answer: the one with the large debt! Similarly, Jesus argues, those who are forgiven much will have much greater love for the one who forgave them. In this way, he provides a fitting commentary on what had just transpired: the woman had loved Jesus by anointing his feet, while the Pharisee had criticized him. At this, Jesus turns to the woman and tells her that her sins are forgiven. Her faith had saved her; she could go in peace. The Pharisee, on the other hand, had failed to acknowledge his need for forgiveness, expressed by his critical stance toward Jesus. The sinful woman had proven herself a true child of wisdom, while those with him at table posed the poignant question: "Who is this, who even forgives sins?"[166]

RECAP

Jesus's ministry in Galilee began with his inaugural address in his hometown synagogue in Nazareth. There he introduced himself as the Spirit-anointed servant of the Lord who would proclaim the good news to the poor and liberty to the captives. After this he called his first disciples, performed several healings, and fielded questions about his disciples' lack of fasting. He also asserted his authority over the Sabbath, called his twelve apostles, and delivered the Sermon on the Plain. He healed a centurion's son and raised a widow's son from the dead, in striking displays of his compassionate messianic mission.

Thus, when messengers arrive from John the Baptist asking if Jesus in fact was the one who was to come, Jesus is able simply to point them to the works he had performed in keeping with Old Testament prophetic passages regarding the coming Messiah. The initial cycle of ministry in Galilee concludes with Jesus's anointing by a "sinful woman," which occasions his instruction that those who have been forgiven much love much. All in all, we see that Jesus backs up his claims with action. His heart goes out to the many people he encounters, and he meets their needs out of mercy and compassion. Jesus's messianic mission is off to a great start!

---

165. Cf. Matthew 26:6–13; Mark 14:3–9; John 12:1–8.
166. Luke 7:49.

JESUS'S WORK IN GALILEE (4:14–9:50, CONT.)
Work in Galilee, Part 2 (8:1–39)
Jesus's Female Followers (8:1–3)
The Parable of the Sower (8:4–15)
Truth Brought to Light (8:16–18)
True Family Relationships (8:19–21)
Calming the Storm (8:22–25)
The Gerasene Demoniac (8:26–39)

JESUS'S WORK IN GALILEE (4:14–9:50)

Work in Galilee, Part 2 (8:1–39)

Jesus's Female Followers (8:1–3)

In the last chapter, we witnessed several vastly different responses to Jesus. Some of Jesus's followers may have wondered why this was the case if Jesus was truly the Messiah. At the beginning of the second part of his Galilean ministry, Jesus addresses these questions by teaching the parable of the soils.[167] But first, Luke is keen to mention a group of female followers of Jesus who sacrificially supported him in his work and served as examples of "good soil": Mary Magdalene, Joanna, Susanna, and many others.

Some of these women "had been healed of evil spirits and sicknesses"; in Mary Magdalene's case, Jesus had cast out seven demons.[168] One of these women, Joanna, was the wife of Herod Antipas's steward. And many of these women even supported Jesus and the Twelve financially, giving sacrificially from their own means so Jesus and the

167. Luke 8:4–15.
168. Luke 8:2 CSB.

apostles could go about their mission. In this way, these women exhibited true gospel partnership with the leaders of the early Jesus movement.

The Parable of the Sower (8:4–15)

I've discussed this important parable previously, as it is also found in Matthew's and Mark's accounts. Each of the four types of soil portrays a heart condition that yields a certain response to Jesus's message. Yet only the "good soil" is responsive to God's word and produces a rich crop through perseverance and obedience, while the other types of soil prove unfruitful. Jesus explains the meaning of the parable at the request of his disciples.[169]

Truth Brought to Light (8:16–18)

At the end of his explanation of the parable of the sower, Jesus spoke of an "honest and good heart"[170] that produces spiritual fruit upon hearing the word of God. He continues by urging his followers to let their light shine, because eventually the truth will come to light. Therefore, Jesus warns them to "take care how you listen."[171] It may not seem fair, but according to a spiritual law enunciated by Jesus, those who have will receive even more, while those who don't have will lose even what they think they have.

True Family Relationships (8:19–21)

At this, Jesus's mother and brothers come to see him. When Jesus is told that his family is waiting for him outside, wanting to see him, he declares, "My mother and my brothers are those who hear the word of God and do it."[172] This may seem harsh, as some may wonder why Jesus wouldn't go out to see his mother and brothers, who may have come from some distance. But rather than being rude, Jesus is seeking to drive home the point that those who follow him make up a new, spiritual family that is even closer than natural family ties.

Calming the Storm (8:22–25)

Jesus's parable and his interaction regarding his mother and brothers are followed by a series of encounters. Each of these encounters demonstrates his divine power and authority.[173] First, while on a boating trip with his disciples, Jesus calms a fierce storm by his mere word. In awe, the disciples ask one another, "Who then is this, that he com-

169. Luke 8:9–15.
170. Luke 8:15.
171. Luke 8:18 CSB.
172. Luke 8:21.
173. Cf. Thompson, *Luke*, 137, who notes that 8:22–56 features "four miracles that demonstrate Jesus's power."

mands even winds and water, and they obey him?"[174] The question of Jesus's identity continues to loom large in the minds of his followers.

The Gerasene Demoniac (8:26–39)

In the final scene of this portion of Luke's narrative, the disciples meet a demon-possessed man from the region of Gadara. Again, the account is also found in Matthew and Mark. The demon-possessed man who charges at Jesus is naked and roams among the tombs. The demons inside the man challenge Jesus, "What have you to do with me, Jesus, Son of the Most High God?"[175] Jesus proceeds to cast the "legion" of demons out of the man and into a herd of pigs which rush down a steep bank into the Sea of Galilee and drown.

Not only does Jesus wield power over creation; demons submit to his authority as well. As Darrell Bock remarks, "This A to Z exercise of power shows Jesus's comprehensive authority."[176] Is there anything Jesus can't do? The answer is no; he shows comprehensively and compellingly that he acts with messianic authority because he is in fact the Messiah.

At the conclusion of the account of the Gadarene demoniac, Luke strikingly hints at Jesus's divine nature by referring to him in the same vein as God. When the man begs Jesus to allow him to follow him, Jesus instead tells him to go home and "declare how much *God* has done for you." At this, Luke tells us that the man "went away, proclaiming throughout the whole city how much *Jesus* had done for him."[177] It's not hard to put two and two together: Jesus is God, and God has done amazing things through Jesus!

RECAP

Luke's account of the second phase of Jesus's Galilean ministry commenced with a reference to the group of women who followed Jesus and supported him and the Twelve financially. In his parable of the sower, Jesus explained the different responses to him. He also made clear that those who believe in him constitute a new, spiritual family that overrides flesh-and-blood ties. After this, Jesus continued his messianic firework display of dazzling feats when he calms a fierce storm on the Sea of Galilee and casts out a legion of demons from the Gadarene demoniac.

174. Luke 8:25.
175. Luke 8:28.
176. Bock, *Theology of Luke and Acts*, 71.
177. Luke 8:38–39.

JESUS'S WORK IN GALILEE (4:14–9:50, CONT.)

Work in Galilee, Part 3 (8:40–9:50)

Raising Jairus's Daughter and Healing a Woman with Blood Flow (8:40–56)

Jesus Sends Out the Twelve and Herod Is Perplexed (9:1–9)

Jesus Feeds the Five Thousand (9:10–17)

JESUS'S WORK IN GALILEE (4:14–9:50, CONT.)

Work in Galilee, Part 3 (8:40–9:50)

Raising Jairus's Daughter and Healing a Woman with Blood Flow (8:40–56)

The third part of Jesus's Galilean ministry picks up where the second part left off. Jesus has previously raised a widow's *son* from the dead; now, in typical Lukan fashion, he raises a man's *daughter*, as it were, to even the score. Upon Jesus's return from his excursion with his disciples, he is met by a synagogue leader named Jairus, whose twelve-year-old daughter is deathly ill. While on his way to Jairus's home, Jesus encounters a woman who has been suffering from bleeding for twelve years. Despite Jairus's urgent need, Jesus attends to the suffering woman and heals her. He then proceeds to the girl despite news of her death, brushing aside the comment from a messenger not to "trouble the Teacher [Jesus] any more."[178]

When he enters the house, taking only his inner circle (Peter, James, and John) with him, the parents are heartbroken and everyone is weeping and mourning for the girl who had died. When Jesus tells the bystanders that she isn't dead but only asleep, they laugh at him because they know she is dead. Yet Jesus tenderly takes her by the hand and says, "Child, arise."[179] At this, her spirit returns, she immediately gets up, and Jesus gives instructions to give her something to eat. This is an extremely rare instance

178. Luke 8:49.
179. Luke 8:54.

of a raising from the dead. Jesus's tender compassion for the girl and her parents shines through the entire story. It is deeply moving how his heart goes out to them and his messianic authority over life and death enables him to bring the girl back to life.

The conclusion is obvious: this is no mere human! Jesus has divine authority over sickness and even death. While it makes sense to call a doctor or healer when a person is sick or even close to dying, people intuitively realize that once a person has died, even a doctor is no longer able to help. Yet Jesus is no mere physician. He is the divine physician who can bring people back to life even when they've died. Jesus only did this a few times literally during his time on earth, but he did so as a sign that, as God, he has the power to bring people back to life in the resurrection from the dead. This is our hope as Christians: that when we die, he will raise us up again on the last day, and we will spend eternity with him in the new creation.

Jesus instructs the girl's parents to "tell no one what had happened."[180] Tell no one that someone has just raised their daughter from the dead? No response is recorded, but one wonders if the parents obliged and kept the story to themselves. In any case, Peter, James, and John were eyewitnesses, and Luke included this amazing feat of Jesus in his Gospel, as did Matthew and Mark.[181] If Mark wrote first, he may have heard this story from Peter; and Matthew and Luke, using Mark as a source, may have chosen to include this account in their Gospels as well. Jesus's instructions to the girl's parents, incidentally, are in sharp contrast to his directive to the Gadarene demoniac.[182] This shows that Jesus can't be put in a box; he responds to people individually depending on varying circumstances, just as God's Spirit directs each of us personally today.

Jesus Sends Out the Twelve and Herod Is Perplexed (9:1–9)

Having established Jesus's messianic authority, Luke shifts the focus onto the Twelve, Jesus's new messianic community. Having trained his followers for a considerable amount of time, Jesus now grants them authority over demons and diseases and commissions them to proclaim the kingdom of God and to heal (note the dual focus on verbal proclamation and active demonstrations of power).[183] By commissioning his followers and putting them to work, Jesus demonstrates that following him involves participating in his mission. News of their mission even reaches Herod Antipas, who asks, "John I beheaded, but who is this about whom I hear such things?"[184] Luke tantalizingly mentions that Herod even sought to see Jesus, though apparently his efforts

180. Luke 8:56.
181. Matthew 9:18–26; Mark 5:21–43.
182. Cf. Luke 8:39.
183. Luke 9:1–6.
184. Luke 9:7–9.

were unsuccessful, at least at that time. At this, Jesus's followers return and report back to Jesus what they had done (though Luke provides no details).

Jesus Feeds the Five Thousand (9:10–17)

Next, Jesus takes his followers aside and they go to Bethsaida, a town on the north shore of the Sea of Galilee and hometown of several of Jesus's disciples (Peter, Andrew, Philip, and possibly also John and James).[185] Again, Jesus tells them about the kingdom of God—the universal reign of God, which in Jesus had already cast its shadow forward—and cures those in need of healing. This is followed by the familiar feeding of the five thousand, the final miracle of this section. Again, Jesus's authority is shown to be comprehensive, extending to both word and deed, and providing for physical needs of various kinds, whether feeding or healing, or even (as in the case of the girl Jesus raised from the dead) the giving or restoring of life itself. In all these ways, Luke shows Jesus to be a certain kind of Messiah: a gentle healer, a compassionate shepherd whose heart goes out to the needs, frailties, and weaknesses of people in the variety of human struggles they are facing.

185. Cf. John 1:44; 12:21.

JESUS'S WORK IN GALILEE (4:14–9:50, CONT.)
Work in Galilee, Part 3 (8:40–9:50, cont.)
Peter Confesses Jesus as the Messiah and Jesus Predicts His Passion (9:18–27)
The Transfiguration, the Aftermath, and Jesus's Second Passion Prediction (9:28–45)
True Greatness in the Kingdom (9:46–50)

JESUS'S WORK IN GALILEE (4:14–9:50, CONT.)

Work in Galilee, Part 3 (8:40–9:50, cont.)

Peter Confesses Jesus as the Messiah and Jesus Predicts His Passion (9:18–27)

The stage is set for two climactic moments in Luke's narrative, similar to Matthew's and Mark's: Peter's confession of Jesus as the Messiah at Caesarea Philippi and Jesus's glorious transformation on the Mount of Transfiguration. Paradoxically, Luke tells us that Jesus was praying "alone," yet the disciples "were with him." Jesus could almost never be completely alone; even when he was "alone," his closest followers were observing in close company. Apparently as an outflow of his praying (which may have centered on his desire that those around him might finally come to realize who he truly was), Jesus asks the Twelve who the crowds say that he is. When they indicate that there is no consensus among the masses, Jesus follows up with the even more important question: "But who do *you* say that I am?"[186] Peter, speaking for the Twelve, replies, "The Christ of God."[187]

This is truly a watershed in the narrative and in salvation history. It marks the moment when Jesus's revelation of himself broke through and one of his closest followers truly understood who he was—the Messiah sent by God in keeping with the

186. Luke 9:18–20, emphasis added.
187. Köstenberger, Kellum, and Quarles, *The Cradle, the Cross, and the Crown*, 327.

prediction of various Old Testament prophets. This is what people had intimated when Jesus was born (remember the hymns of Jesus's mother Mary and John's father Zechariah, as well as that of Simeon in the temple?). This is also what Jesus's entire earthly ministry up to this point had indicated—he's the Messiah! It's almost as if after all this pent-up tension, struggle, and hopeful expectation, Peter's confession breaks the ice and erupts as an exclamation point to what the entire Gospel has been building toward.

Peter's confession also serves as a significant pivot in Jesus's ministry. Jesus now shifts his attention to preparing his disciples even more intensely for their future mission as followers of the soon-to-be crucified, risen, and ascended Messiah.[188] It's at this point—now that Peter has confessed him as "the Christ of God"—that Jesus predicts that he, "the Son of Man," must suffer and be rejected, killed, and raised on the third day.[189] This is the first of three passion predictions.[190] Contrary to the prevailing expectation in Jesus's day of a powerful national deliverer, Jesus reveals that he is a *suffering* Messiah. His mission involves being rejected and even killed, taking up a cross and dying for the forgiveness of sinful humanity. In the same vein, he calls every disciple to "take up his cross daily and follow me."[191]

This call to follow Jesus in his sacrifice and suffering is at the very heart of biblical discipleship. Don't gloss over this too quickly! Jesus doesn't identify himself merely as a religious leader or national hero. He's not just another prophet, rabbi, or charismatic figure. As C. S. Lewis famously noted, he is either a lunatic, a liar, or Lord! And no, he is no mere legend! As those who have carefully read Luke's Gospel thus far, witnessing Jesus's sane yet strikingly transcendent spiritual authority, we are compelled to conclude that this is no lunatic and certainly no liar.

Rather, he is the "Christ of God," God in the flesh who came to identify with the plight of frail, sinful humanity in desperate need of healing, forgiveness, and salvation. He is the divine Christ and compassionate Savior of the world. And yet he will accomplish salvation most unexpectedly by suffering and dying on a Roman cross, rejected by the Jewish religious leaders and abandoned by those he came to save. What's more, the rejection won't stop even when Jesus has been nailed to a cross. Following the resurrection and ascension of Jesus, people's rage, rebellion, and rejection will turn toward his followers, who, like their Master, must suffer as they continue his redemptive mission and proclaim the arrival of God's kingdom in both word and deed.

188. As we'll see below, the focus on Jesus's ascension is distinctive for Luke-Acts.

189. Luke 9:21–22.

190. "Passion" (from the Latin *passio*) in the context of the story of Jesus's life and ministry means "suffering." Cf. Luke 9:43–45; 18:31–34.

191. Luke 9:23.

Speaking of God's kingdom, as the story continues, we witness the second climactic moment in Jesus's earthly ministry thus far narrated in Luke's Gospel.[192] Following his convicting, powerful words that "whoever is ashamed of me and of my words, of him will the Son of Man be ashamed when he comes in his glory and the glory of the Father and of the holy angels," Jesus adds, "there are some standing here who will not taste death until they see the kingdom of God."[193] This is indeed a stirring prospect, which no doubt left the disciples at a loss as to what Jesus meant.

The Transfiguration, the Aftermath, and Jesus's Second Passion Prediction (9:28–45)

The reader of Luke's Gospel doesn't have to wait long to find out. As at the outset of the previous episode, Jesus goes off to pray. And as at the raising of Jairus's daughter, he takes only Peter, James, and John with him. As he is praying on the mountain, his inner circle is given a tantalizing glimpse of Jesus's glory as the appearance of his face changes and his clothes turn radiant white. All of a sudden, Moses and Elijah appear, also in a glorious state, and speak with Jesus about his "departure" in Jerusalem. Tellingly, the word translated "departure" is the Greek word *exodos*: while Moses served as Israel's deliverer from physical bondage in Egypt at the original exodus, Jesus's death would provide deliverance for God's people from spiritual bondage to sin.[194] As if all these supernatural manifestations—Jesus's transfiguration, the appearance of Moses and Elijah—were not enough, the disciples hear a heavenly voice reiterating what was said at Jesus's baptism: "This is my Son, my Chosen One," with the additional charge, "listen to him!"[195] Truly, Jesus's inner circle had just witnessed an unforgettable mountaintop experience—literally and figuratively! In fact, Peter would write about this in his final letter more than thirty years later.[196]

In the ensuing event following Jesus's descent from the Mount of Transfiguration, Luke focuses on the theme of discipleship. Now that his followers have seen Jesus's glory, what does it mean for them to follow the suffering Messiah? And how are they to reconcile the fact that Jesus is both a glorious and a suffering Messiah? Truly, this is a lot to process for them in a short amount of time. At first we see several examples of discipleship failure. We learn that while Jesus and the three disciples were on the mountain,

192. Luke 9:28–36.

193. Luke 9:26–27.

194. Köstenberger, Kellum, and Quarles, *The Cradle, the Cross, and the Crown*, 328.

195. Luke 9:35; cf. Deuteronomy 18:18–19. We'll skip Peter's bizarre offer to build three tents, one each for Jesus, Moses, and Elijah (Luke 9:33). He was understandably confused and overwhelmed!

196. 2 Peter 1:16–18.

the other disciples had been unable to cast out a demon from a young boy.[197] How quickly the scene shifts from the mountaintop of excitement and exhilaration to the valley of darkness and despair! It has at times been my experience that striking successes are often followed by unexpected challenges, at times as a result of spiritual warfare. Satan knows that we're rarely more vulnerable than when relishing in a remarkable victory. Precisely when we have tasted success, we must be guarded and take precautions lest we be vulnerable to spiritual attack.

In the present case, Jesus chastises his disciples for being part of a "faithless and twisted generation."[198] Then he promptly casts out the demon and gives the boy back to his father. As might be expected, all were amazed at the "majesty of God" on display in Jesus.[199] At this point in the narrative, it's hard to see how the remarkable displays of Jesus's majesty won't inexorably lead to his messianic victory. At present, at least, Jesus's prediction that he must be rejected and killed seems unduly pessimistic and counterintuitive. In view of such widespread amazement and acclaim, how could the tide turn so drastically that the Messiah would end up forsaken? Yet Jesus reiterates the prediction of his imminent demise for a second time: "Let these words sink into your ears: The Son of Man is about to be delivered into the hands of men."[200] Yet Luke tells us they didn't understand what Jesus was saying and they were too afraid to ask him—continuing the theme of discipleship failure.

True Greatness in the Kingdom (9:46–50)

As if their incomprehension, impotence, and intimidation were not enough, the disciples proceed to argue with one another as to who among them is the greatest.[201] How out of it can you be? Jesus has just reminded them that he'll soon be killed, and they respond by jockeying for position! It's evident that they didn't believe a word Jesus was saying and instead continued to presumptuously divide the spoils of Jesus's conquests that, they were sure, would follow in short order. One can only imagine Jesus's exasperation at his followers' intransigence. With astonishing forbearance and patience, Jesus challenges their selfish attitudes and instructs them that "he who is least among you all"—devoid of any formal status like a little child—"is the one who is great."[202]

Apparently changing the topic, John tells Jesus that the disciples had witnessed someone cast out demons in Jesus's name and had tried to stop him. In some ways,

197. Luke 9:37–43.
198. Luke 9:41.
199. Luke 9:43.
200. Luke 9:44.
201. Luke 9:46–48.
202. Luke 9:48.

the disciples' reaction is understandable. Yet, again, Jesus rebukes them and tells them that "whoever is not against you is for you."[203] It seems that, at this juncture in Jesus's ministry, the disciples can't do or get anything right! Despite Peter's confession, it's clear that Jesus's followers don't fully grasp what it means to follow him. They still have a long way to go. True discipleship is inextricably tied to grasping the truth of Jesus's identity as the suffering Messiah. The disciples indulge in delusions of grandeur while Jesus is thinking about the cross. Luke emerges as a masterful guide trying to help his readers understand what kind of Messiah Jesus proved to be and what it means to follow him.

RECAP

The third and final phase of Jesus's Galilean work according to Luke started with his raising of a synagogue ruler's daughter, followed by his miraculous feeding of the five thousand. In a stunning declaration, Peter then confesses Jesus as the Messiah. This triggers Jesus's prediction of his passion. As in the other Synoptic Gospels, Jesus's first passion prediction is followed by his glorious transfiguration. A second passion prediction follows, accompanied by the disciples' discussion of who was the greatest among them. This triggers Jesus's instruction about true greatness in God's kingdom.

In many ways, this third and final cycle of ministry in Galilee is a highlight reel. It's hard to imagine more climactic manifestations of Jesus's messianic nature than raising a person from the dead or feeding a multitude. In addition, Peter's confession is unquestionably a major breakthrough in Jesus's revelation of his messianic identity to his followers, which sets in motion Jesus's repeated prediction of his passion and a series of instructions on the nature of true discipleship. What does it mean to follow a Messiah who is on the way to his death on a cross? This is the question that will occupy Luke in the major section that follows next.

203. Luke 9:50 CSB.

THE LUKAN TRAVEL NARRATIVE:
JESUS'S JOURNEY TO JERUSALEM (9:51–19:27)

Lessons on Discipleship (9:51–11:54)

Rejected by a Samaritan Village (9:51–56)

Three Would-Be Followers (9:57–62)

THE LUKAN TRAVEL NARRATIVE: JESUS'S JOURNEY TO JERUSALEM (9:51–19:27)

A little more than a third into his Gospel, Luke writes that Jesus, with steely determination and in certain expectation of his rejection by the Jewish leaders, "set his face to go to Jerusalem." Not only this; Luke also refers, at this still relatively early stage in his narrative, to Jesus's future ascension to heaven ("the days drew near for him to be taken up").[204] This underscores the pivotal nature of this passage in his narrative. From a literary standpoint, the references to Jesus's resolute determination to head toward Jerusalem and to his ascension introduce the remainder of Luke's Gospel and form bookends with the conclusion of the Lukan narrative.[205]

This section is often called the "Lukan travel narrative," as the third evangelist devotes more space to Jesus's journey to Jerusalem than any other Gospel writer—ten long chapters made up of mostly unique material.[206] In many ways, this is the Lukan equivalent of the Markan motif of Jesus and his followers being "on the way."[207] You'll notice the phrase "as they were traveling" appear repeatedly as a way of keeping the narrative moving.[208] However, the travel narrative doesn't read like a travel log. Rather, it records a large amount of Jesus's teaching, most notably several unique Lukan parables, such as the parable of the good Samaritan and the parable of the prodigal son.[209]

204. Luke 9:51.
205. Cf. Luke 24:50–53.
206. This section makes up more than a third (38 percent) of Luke's Gospel. See Köstenberger, Kellum, and Quarles, The *Cradle, the Cross, and the Crown*, 327. Thompson (*Luke*, 163) notes that "there is a notable shift in emphasis with fewer miracles (four) and more teaching (seventeen parables)." He also notes the repeated references to Jerusalem (9:53; 13:22, 33; 17:11; 18:31; 19:28) which provide the backdrop for "what Jesus will accomplish in Jerusalem" and the repeated predictions of Jesus's suffering, death, and resurrection (12:50; 13:33; 17:25; 18:31–33).
207. Cf., e.g., Mark 8:27; 9:33, 34; 10:17, 32, 46, 52.
208. See, e.g., Luke 9:57; 10:38.
209. Luke 10:25–37; 15:11–32.

Most importantly, the travel narrative highlights an intensified focus on the cross and the salvation it would accomplish in Jesus's ministry. Mark Strauss puts it well: "The journey is not a straight-line trip to Jerusalem but a period of Jesus's heightened resolve to reach his Jerusalem goal."[210] Jesus is "determined" or "resolved" to fulfill his mission as the suffering Messiah. It's impossible to fully grasp who Jesus is without grappling with the purpose of his impending death. So Luke casts the rest of his Gospel in the shadow of the cross. This is symbolized by the emphasis on Jerusalem, where previous prophets such as Isaiah and Zechariah were put to death.[211] But it's also the place where Jesus will accomplish humanity's salvation.[212]

Lessons on Discipleship (9:51–11:54)

Rejected by a Samaritan Village (9:51–56)

As Jesus moves closer to his goal of reaching Jerusalem, what will this mean for his followers?[213] In answering this question, the first section of the travel narrative builds on Jesus's previous teaching on discipleship. First is another instance of discipleship failure. Jesus sends an advance team to a Samaritan village, but the people there don't receive him (note that it doesn't say receive "them," his disciples, but "him"). The reason Luke gives for the Samaritan rejection of Jesus, strikingly, is that "his face was set toward Jerusalem"![214] This ties in the account with the just-mentioned Lukan reference to Jesus "set[ting] his face to go to Jerusalem." On one level, this may simply mean that the Samaritans were engaged in their long-standing feud with the Jews who considered them a mixed race and looked at their rival sanctuary on Mount Gerizim with disdain.[215] At a deeper level, Luke shows that the Samaritans are seeking to obstruct the very purpose for which Jesus came: to die on the cross for the sins of all people.

Nevertheless, when James and John (the sons of Zebedee) ask him if he wants them to call down fire from heaven and consume the Samaritans, he rebukes them at once. One admires their self-confidence (could they really call down fire from heaven?) and their zeal for Jesus (they're obviously outraged that the Samaritans rejected him), but

---

210. Strauss, *Four Portraits, One Jesus*, 273.

211. See, e.g., Matthew 23:35, 37; Luke 13:34; cf. 2 Chronicles 24:20–22. "Sawn in two" in Hebrews 11:37 may refer to the fate of Isaiah. At the same time, it should be acknowledged that not all, or even most, prophets were killed in Jerusalem.

212. Luke 13:32–35.

213. See Chris McKinny, "The Words and Teachings of Jesus in the Context of Judea (Luke 10:29–37; etc.)," in Beitzel, *Lexham Geographic Commentary*, 338–55.

214. Luke 9:53; cf. 9:51.

215. John 4:9, 20.

their over-the-top reaction shows that they've misunderstood the nature of Jesus's mission. He has come not to exact wrath and revenge on humanity but rather to save it.[216] One thinks of Sodom and Gomorrah, Elijah, or Jonah's stance toward Nineveh.[217] While there will be a time for God to judge the world, this is the time of his salvation.

Three Would-Be Followers (9:57–62)

"As they were going along the road" reinforces the Lukan travel narrative: Jesus and his followers are on the road to Jerusalem.[218] As they're on their way, Jesus is approached by three potential disciples. In each case, Jesus reveals the radical cost of following him—a willingness to leave behind the comforts of home, occupation, and loved ones. "Foxes have holes, and birds have nests," Jesus tells the first, "but the Son of Man has nowhere to lay his head."[219]

In the second instance, it is Jesus who calls a man to follow him, but the man asks Jesus for time to first go and bury his father. This would seem like a reasonable request if his father had already died; yet it is possible that the man is saying he wants to wait until his father dies at some undetermined point in the future, and then he will follow Jesus. Jesus tells him to let the dead bury the dead, but he must proclaim God's kingdom. This man, too, one assumes, desists from following Jesus.

Yet a third would-be follower asks Jesus to allow him to say goodbye to his loved ones. Jesus says, "No one who puts his hand to the plow and looks back is fit for the kingdom of God."[220] Here one thinks of Lot's wife, who looked back toward Sodom and Gomorrah and turned into a pillar of salt.[221] Following Jesus and proclaiming the arrival of God's kingdom require wholehearted devotion and dedication to this task. Anyone who thinks he can focus simultaneously on both serving Jesus and attending to his family has divided interests.

This is illustrated by the call narratives in the Gospels that show that Jesus's disciples left their families and sources of livelihood to follow Jesus. They didn't look back; their interests weren't divided; they put it all on the line for Jesus. If he went down, they would go down with him. By gathering these three vignettes and joining them together at the outset of Jesus's travel narrative, Luke skillfully highlights what it means to follow Jesus. It requires radical commitment and must be one's top priority. Nothing is more important than one's commitment to follow Jesus.

216. Cf. John 3:17.
217. Cf. the reference to Sodom at Luke 10:12 below; the reference to Elijah at the transfiguration at Luke 9:30, 33 above; and to Jonah at Luke 11:29–32 below.
218. Luke 9:57.
219. Luke 9:58.
220. Luke 9:62.
221. In fact, Jesus says later in Luke's Gospel, "Remember Lot's wife" (Luke 17:32).

THE LUKAN TRAVEL NARRATIVE: JESUS'S JOURNEY TO JERUSALEM (9:51–19:27, CONT.)

Lessons on Discipleship (9:51–11:54, cont.)

Jesus Sends Out the Seventy(-two) (10:1–20)

In the next scene, Jesus sends out seventy(-two) other disciples to highlight the importance of mission.[222] As noted at the sending out of the Twelve, following Jesus entails participating in his mission, which will continue after his departure.[223] In fact, that's when it'll kick into high gear fueled by the power of his resurrection and energized by the Holy Spirit! The fact that Jesus sends out not only the Twelve but now also a larger circle of followers shows that Jesus's mission is expanding. Jesus prepares his disciples for this vital mission, instructing them to travel light, heal the sick, announce the arrival of God's kingdom, and expect rejection. The number seventy (or seventy-two) carries symbolic significance and represents all the nations of the earth.[224] As John Nolland explains, "Luke is fond of anticipations and almost certainly uses the number here to anticipate later mission to all the nations of the earth."[225]

---

222. Luke 10:1–12. This account is unique to Luke's Gospel. The manuscript evidence is split between "seventy" and "seventy-two" disciples. The numbers are interchangeable in Jewish tradition. See Garland, *Luke*, 425.
223. See Luke 9:1.
224. Cf. Genesis 10:2–31.
225. John Nolland, *Luke*, Word Biblical Commentary 35B (Dallas: Word, 1993), 2:549. Note also that Luke's account of the first Pentecost in Acts 2 is reminiscent of the tower of Babel incident, reversing the confusion of languages there by recounting how at Pentecost people were able to hear strangers speak in their own language (Acts 2:6–11).

The Seventy return in amazement, having experienced the same kind of success as the Twelve.[226] Indeed, in a striking image, Jesus tells his followers, "I saw Satan fall like lightning from heaven."[227] However, Jesus instructs them that their joy should be grounded not in their success in ministry but in the certainty of their eternal destiny.[228] The disciples' ability to cast out demons is part of the inbreaking of God's kingdom and Jesus's conquest and triumph over evil supernatural forces arrayed against God's reign. As David Garland explains, "What is happening is not simply the expulsion of random demons that they might come across in their travels but the beginning of the complete overthrow of Satan's rule."[229] Jesus helps his disciples see that, from a heavenly perspective, they're engaged in a cosmic conflict and mortal combat with the forces of evil, and that in the power of Jesus they can and will prevail.

The Privilege of Knowing Jesus (10:21–24)

Jesus rejoices in the Holy Spirit because God the Father has revealed his true identity to his disciples. He contrasts the disciples with the Galilean cities that rejected this revelation—Chorazin, Bethsaida, and Capernaum—and praises God that he chose to hide these spiritual truths from those who pride themselves in their wisdom and understanding while revealing them to those who know they're ignorant and spiritually blind. In a flash of Johannine language, Luke quotes Jesus as saying, "All things have been handed over to me by my Father, and no one knows who the Son is except the Father, or who the Father is except the Son and anyone to whom the Son chooses to reveal him."[230]

Then Jesus tells the disciples that they're blessed to see and hear what many Old Testament prophets and kings desired to witness but didn't.[231] The disciples are in a

---

226. Luke 10:17–20.

227. Most commentators take Luke 10:18 as a reference to the defeat of Satan in the ministry of Jesus's disciples (e.g., Bock, *Luke 1:1–9:50*, 1006–7; Stein, *Luke*, New American Commentary [Nashville: B&H, 1993], 309–10; Morris, *Luke*, rev. ed., Tyndale New Testament Commentaries [Grand Rapids: Eerdmans, 1988], 202). Beyond this, some also see a reference to the ultimate demise of Satan (e.g., Simon J. Gathercole, "Jesus's Eschatological Vision of the Fall of Satan: Luke 10:18 Reconsidered," *Zeitschrift fur die neutestamentliche Wissenschaft und die Kunde der älteren Kirche* 94 [2003]: 143–63; Nolland, *Luke*, 2:564; Joel B. Green, *Luke*, New International Commentary on the New Testament [Grand Rapids: Eerdmans, 1997], 418–19). In addition, there may be an echo of the original fall of Satan. The New Testament also teaches that Satan was defeated at the cross (e.g., Colossians 2:14–15; cf. Bock, *Luke*, NIV Application Commentary [Grand Rapids: Zondervan, 1996], 296; Frank Thielman, *Theology of the New Testament* [Grand Rapids: Zondervan, 2005], 690). See also the discussion in Garland, *Luke*, 428–29.

228. Luke 10:20; cf. 9:40.

229. Garland, *Luke*, 429.

230. Luke 10:22; cf. Matthew 11:27. Scholars commonly call this passage "the bolt from the Johannine blue." Cf., e.g., Jesus's language in his final prayer in John 17.

231. Cf. Luke 10:13–16.

privileged position to catch a glimpse of God's revelation at this extraordinary juncture in human history. While we no longer live during Jesus's earthly ministry or the apostolic period, we're still engaged in spiritual combat with Satan and the forces of evil. In waging spiritual warfare, we should wield spiritual weapons—faith, our assurance of salvation, truth, prayer, the Word of God—and proceed in the confidence that the victory, *Jesus's* victory, has already been won.[232]

The Parable of the Good Samaritan (10:25–37)

In the next scene, Jesus is tested by an expert in the law who asks, "Teacher, what shall I do to inherit eternal life?"[233] Notice that this is not a question by someone who really wants an answer and is open to follow Jesus. Rather, Luke tells us that this Jewish "legal expert" was "putting Jesus to the test." This is both sad and tragic, as Jesus's coming required a response at a much deeper spiritual level than playing "stump the teacher" or catching him in some contradiction! Clearly, this scribe had totally missed the point. For him, interpreting Scripture was like playing a game where you outhustle or outmaneuver your rabbinic opponent and show how clever you are. Did this scribe think he was smarter than Jesus? One thinks of Jesus's just-uttered prayer in which he praised his Father in heaven for having "hidden these things from the wise and understanding and revealed them to little children."[234] God doesn't give us information in order to inflate our egos and boost our pride!

In response, Jesus coolly asks the scribe a counter-question: "What is written in the Law? How do you read it?"[235] The scribe replies by quoting two well-known passages from Deuteronomy and Leviticus: "You shall love the Lord your God with all your heart and with all your soul and with all your strength and with all your mind, and your neighbor as yourself."[236] Jesus responds, "You've answered correctly. . . . Do this and you will live."[237] This is both very astute and deeply ironic because Jesus knows that loving God with all one's heart and loving one's neighbor as oneself is a lot easier said than done! Sure enough, the scribe tightens up and gets defensive. In fact, Luke tells us that he "desir[ed] to justify himself," once again trying to involve Jesus in a rabbinic squabble: "And who is my neighbor?"[238]

Rather than responding with a straight answer or definition, Jesus tells the scribe a story—the famous parable of the good Samaritan. To reap the full benefits, please read

232. Cf. Luke 10:18; John 16:33; 2 Corinthians 10:4–6; Ephesians 6:10–18; 1 John 5:4.
233. Luke 10:25.
234. Luke 10:21.
235. Luke 10:26.
236. Luke 10:27; cf. Deuteronomy 6:5; Leviticus 19:18.
237. Luke 10:28 CSB.
238. Luke 10:29.

the entire parable for yourself; it can't be adequately summarized or reduced to a simple lesson or proposition (though I'll try anyway below!). Essentially, the parable is answering the scribe's question of who his neighbor is. As the story goes, a man is robbed on his way from Jerusalem to Jericho. Both a priest and a Levite pass by without helping him; then a despised Samaritan comes along, who movingly cares for the man. At the end of the parable, Jesus asks the scribe, "Which of these three, do you think, proved to be a neighbor to the man who fell among the robbers?" The scribe is forced to admit, "The one who showed him mercy" (though he can't get himself to pronounce the word "Samaritan"!). At this, Jesus simply tells him is to "go, and do likewise."[239] Love is validated by action, and being a true neighbor is expressed by charitable action toward a person in need.

This is one of several parables unique to Luke included in the travel narrative. Many of these parables, in continuity with Old Testament law, illustrate God's deep concern for outcasts in society and the great reversal taking place through Jesus's ministry: humble outsiders are welcomed and blessed, while arrogant insiders are rebuked and left out.[240] Throughout this section, we see the following parables reinforce and resonate with this theme of reversal:

- The parable of the good Samaritan (10:29–37): While a priest and Levite pass by, a despised Samaritan helps a dying man, illustrating true obedience to the law by loving his neighbor.
- The parable of the rich fool (12:13–21): A rich man who stores up wealth for himself but not toward God proves to be a fool.
- The parable of the great banquet (14:16–24): A man throws a large banquet, but his guests make excuses and decline his invitation. In response, the man invites the poor, physically challenged, blind, and lame to enjoy his feast.
- The parables of the lost sheep, lost coin, and lost (or prodigal) son (15:1–32): A shepherd leaves ninety-nine sheep to find the one lost sheep; a woman diligently searches for and rejoices over finding her lost coin; and a father rejoices over the return of his wayward son, while the oldest son challenges his father's generosity.
- The parable of the rich man and Lazarus (16:19–31): A rich man named Lazarus (the only named character in all of Jesus's parables) and a beggar experience a dramatic reversal in the afterlife.
- The parable of the persistent widow (18:1–8): The poor widow receives justice from an indifferent judge on account of her persistence.
- The parable of the Pharisee and the tax collector (18:9–14): The repentant tax collector is justified by God, while the outwardly pious Pharisee is not.

239. Luke 10:36–37.

240. The travel narrative has sometimes been called "The Gospel for the Outcast."

THE LUKAN TRAVEL NARRATIVE: JESUS'S JOURNEY TO JERUSALEM (9:51–19:27, CONT.)

Lessons on Discipleship (9:51–11:54, cont.)

Mary and Martha (10:38–42)

After Jesus has told his parable, he and his followers, "as they went on their way" in Luke's travel narrative,[241] enter a village where a woman named Martha welcomes him. In this episode, Luke further clarifies the nature of discipleship. Mary, Martha's younger sister, takes the posture of a disciple, humbly sitting at Jesus's feet and listening to him. You'll recall the Father's words to Peter, John, and James at the Mount of Transfiguration: "Listen to him!"[242] This is exactly what Mary does. Also, her example stands in contrast to the lack of compassion shown by the priest and the Levite in the parable of the good Samaritan, not to mention the scribe who questioned Jesus, all of whom failed to understand and heed God's word.

What's more, in the immediate story, Mary's quiet, devoted listening stance toward Jesus stands in contrast to her action-oriented older sister Martha, who asks Jesus to

241. Luke 10:38; see also Luke 9:57 above and Luke 13:22 and 17:11 below.
242. Luke 9:35.

tell Mary to help her serve. This may seem like a reasonable request, and Martha seems certain Jesus will join her in shaming Mary for not helping, but again, there is an unexpected reversal of expectations. Jesus refuses to rebuke Mary but instead commends her for doing the "one thing" that was truly "necessary."[243] Martha wasn't wrong for serving, but she was wrong for chiding Mary for listening to Jesus! Listening has priority over serving; and serving must flow out of listening rather than being a substitute for it.

Teaching on Prayer (11:1–13)

The story of Martha and Mary is followed by yet another reference to Jesus's life of prayer: "Now Jesus was praying in a certain place."[244] Luke previously mentioned how Jesus

- was praying at his baptism when the heavens opened, the Spirit descended on him, and the Father commended him as his beloved, well-pleasing Son (3:21–22);
- would regularly "withdraw to desolate places and pray" (5:16);
- went to a mountain to pray, and "all night he continued in prayer to God" before appointing the Twelve the following morning (6:12);
- told his followers to pray for those who abused them, something Jesus certainly did himself (6:28);
- prayed alone before asking his disciples who the crowds and they thought he was (9:18); and
- took Peter, James, and John with him to the Mount of Transfiguration to pray (9:28), and as he was praying, his face shone and his clothes became dazzling white (9:29).

This is an impressive, even convicting, list of Jesus's commitment to prayer throughout his earthly ministry, especially before making important decisions such as appointing the Twelve or asking them concerning his true identity. We also see how he prayed at his baptism and transfiguration. What is truly impressive is that Jesus was the Son of God and yet felt an acute and consistent need to pray. This shows that Jesus in his humanity went about his messianic mission with a keen sense of dependence on God, which drove him to prayer. Prayer thus became an important means by which Jesus overcame spiritual challenges and opposition and by which he achieved significant milestones and breakthroughs in his ministry. He knew that it was God who had to reveal his true identity to his followers, and he continually and persistently prayed for God to do so until they understood that he was the suffering *and* glorious Messiah

243. Luke 10:42.
244. Luke 11:1.

who would give his life on the cross so sinners could be saved and lost people could be found.

In keeping with Luke's theology of prayer centered on Jesus, the next three units all deal with prayer:

1. The Lord's Prayer (11:1–4)

2. The parable of the reluctant neighbor (11:5–10)

3. The parable of the father who gives what his child needs (11:11–13)

In contrast to the religious leaders who were long on talk and short on action, Jesus was just the opposite. He lived by example, and his prayer life was no exception. Jesus was praying apparently within earshot of his disciples, and when he finished, his disciples asked him, "Lord, teach us to pray, as John taught his disciples."[245] That's interesting, as we have no record of what John (the Baptist) taught his followers about prayer. Elsewhere, Jesus told the disciples not to make many words or offer flowery prayers like pagans are wont to do. In keeping with this maxim, the so-called Lord's Prayer is a model of concision.

In Luke's version of Jesus's prayer, the first two petitions focus on God, plainly addressing him as "Father":

- May your name be glorified.
- May your kingdom come.[246]

This teaches us to be God-centered rather than self-centered. Rather than frame our prayers in terms of *self*-interest, as is all too common in many prayer meetings, we're called to frame them in terms of *God's* interests, which are bound up with the greater glory of his name and the advancement of his kingdom. In this way, Jesus teaches his followers to discipline themselves to think about their needs in the context of God's larger purposes in this world. Within this context, they can trust God to supply whatever they need to carry out their God-given mission.

Only after making these God-centered requests, Jesus directs, should his followers humbly ask God:

245. Luke 11:1.

246. God as Father is highlighted at both the beginning and end of the unit on prayer (Luke 11:2, 13). Luke does not include the third petition, "Your will be done on earth as it is in heaven" (cf. Matthew 6:10).

- to supply their daily needs (material provision);
- to forgive their sins as they forgive the sins of others; and
- to deliver them from temptation (spiritual protection).

These three requests fittingly describe human existence in this fallen world, which entails a concern for material provision, a need for forgiveness, and a recognition of human sinfulness and weakness that render us susceptible to temptation. Notice how this threefold prayer expresses humble dependence on God, for it is God to whom we prayerfully look to provide for our needs; it is also God to whom we look to forgive our sins; and it is God to whom we look, with longing and even desperation, to deliver us from the devil as he incites our sinful nature to yield to worldly temptation. Thus, in this model prayer, Jesus teaches us to look to God to meet all our needs so that he may be glorified and his spiritual reign may be advanced on this earth.

Earlier we learned about the Father's role in entrusting all things to the Son; here we learn about God's goodness and graciousness toward all his children.[247] Jesus drives this truth home through the illustration of a man and his friend who knocks at his door at midnight and asks him to lend him three loaves of bread. At first, the man tries the excuse that his children are with him in bed, but eventually he gets up and grants his friend's request simply to get rid of him because he is so persistent!

One can hardly accuse Jesus of lack of candor when he says, "If you then, who are evil [!], know how to give good gifts to your children, how much more will the heavenly Father give the Holy Spirit to those who ask him!"[248] The Holy Spirit is the Father's most precious gift. Throughout Luke's Gospel, we've already seen the prominent role of the Holy Spirit in carrying out God's work in the world by resting on and empowering the work of Jesus, the Messiah.[249] The presence of the Holy Spirit in the disciples will be a further sign of the coming of God's kingdom in this present evil age. In addition, the promise of the Holy Spirit foreshadows what will happen in the sequel to Luke's Gospel, the book of Acts.[250]

The True Source of Jesus's Power (11:14–26)

As we saw earlier, part of Jesus's ministry entails exercising divine authority by casting out evil spirits. Jesus's authority over the demonic realm demonstrates the inbreaking of God's kingdom. However, many people fail to understand this. They wonder:

247. Cf. Luke 10:22.
248. Luke 11:13.
249. Cf. Luke 1:15, 35; 3:16; 4:18; 10:21.
250. Cf. Acts 1:8; 2:1–4, 38; 9:31; 11:15; 13:52.

What is the source of Jesus's power? In the next scene, Jesus drives out a demon, which triggers a series of controversies regarding his ministry.[251] While the crowds marvel at Jesus's authority, there are some who allege that the source of his power is none other than Satan![252] Perhaps he is some sort of medium of spirits, they speculate. Jesus masterfully parries the argument and shows its flawed logic. A kingdom divided against itself cannot stand. If Satan is divided against himself, how can he prevail? Anyone wanting to plunder a house must first overcome the one who guards it. With compelling logic, Jesus concludes, "But if it is by the finger of God that I cast out demons, then the kingdom of God has come upon you."[253]

True Blessedness and the Sign of Jonah (11:27–32)

At this, a woman in the crowd calls Jesus's mother blessed; but Jesus retorts that blessed rather are those who hear God's word and keep it.[254] This continues Jesus's emphasis on discipleship that transcends flesh-and-blood ties.[255] As the crowds were swelling, Jesus excoriated this "evil generation" for seeking a sign from him to prove the legitimacy of his messianic claim.[256] He flatly refuses to give any sign "except the sign of Jonah," a reference to Jonah's preaching.[257] Ironically, people have already received the sign they were seeking.[258] As it is, both the queen of Sheba, a Gentile ruler who came to pay homage to King Solomon, and the people of Nineveh who repented at Jonah's preaching will rise up to testify against Jesus's contemporaries at the final judgment. People should recognize that "something greater than Jonah is here."[259]

What Truly Defiles a Person (11:33–54)

Jesus's teaching on the eye being the lamp of the body sets up the next scene, where he denounces the Jewish leaders.[260] When a Pharisee asks him to dine with

---

251. Luke 11:14–54.
252. Luke 11:15. "Beelzebul" is an alias for Satan.
253. Luke 11:20. "Finger of God" likely is an emblematic way of referring to the Holy Spirit (cf. the parallel passage, Matthew 12:28, where "*Spirit* of God" is used). See Gregg R. Allison and Andreas J. Köstenberger, *The Holy Spirit*, Theology for the People of God (Nashville: B&H, 2020).
254. Luke 11:27–28.
255. Cf. Luke 9:59–62.
256. Luke 11:29; cf. 11:16.
257. Luke 11:29–32. Cf. Jonah 3:4–10. Luke seems to focus on the sign as Jonah's preaching to the unbelieving Ninevites, whereas Matthew references Jesus's future resurrection (cf. Matthew 12:38–42). The "sign" doesn't need to be miraculous in nature but must correspond to phenomena that signal the deliverance of God's elect and judgment of his enemies. See Garland, *Luke*, 481–82.
258. Joseph A. Fitzmyer, *The Gospel according to Luke*, Anchor Bible 28A (New York: Doubleday, 1985), 2:933.
259. Luke 11:32.
260. Luke 11:37–54.

him, he is astonished that Jesus doesn't wash his hands before dinner. At this, Jesus denounces the Pharisaic preoccupation with external appearances while neglecting their inner lives. They attempted to clean house through religious reforms, but in the end the house's condition was worse than before.[261] They were full of darkness, not light.[262] Consequently, Jesus pronounces a series of woes against them for their hypocrisy. After the first three woes, a lawyer tells Jesus he is offended, at which Jesus pronounces three more woes![263] This predictably does little to ease the growing tension between Jesus and the Jewish leaders.[264] They begin to apply added pressure, hoping to trap him by his own words.

261. Cf. Luke 11:24–26.
262. Cf. Luke 11:33–36.
263. Read the whole account here: Luke 11:42–52.
264. Luke 11:53–54.

THE LUKAN TRAVEL NARRATIVE: JESUS'S JOURNEY TO JERUSALEM (9:51–19:27, CONT.)

Further Lessons on Discipleship (12:1–13:9)

Be Guarded but Not Afraid (12:1–12)

Luke begins the next phase of the journey with the opening phrase "in the meantime," linking the following sayings to the growing antagonism of the Pharisees.[265] Incredibly, Jesus's popularity is still growing; Luke tells us that "so many thousands" gathered "that they were trampling one another"![266] In view of the Pharisees' hostility, Jesus warns his followers to be on their guard and to face opposition with faith rather than fear. This section alternates between Jesus addressing his disciples[267] and the large crowd.[268] He warns his followers of three specific obstacles to hearing and keeping his word: religious hypocrisy, greed, and sluggishness.[269]

265. Thompson (*Luke*, 199) notes that "an overall characteristic of this section [12:1–13:9] is the constant reference to the final judgment and the significance of that for present priorities."

266. Luke 12:1.

267. Luke 12:1–12, 22–48.

268. Luke 12:13–21, 49–59; 13:1–9.

269. Luke 12:1–12; 12:13–34; and 12:49–59, respectively.

Avoid Improper Attachments and Don't Be Anxious (12:13–31)

When asked to mediate in an inheritance dispute, Jesus teaches that "one's life does not consist in the abundance of his possessions."[270] This is at the heart of Luke's message on what it means to follow Jesus; any disciple of Jesus must renounce improper flesh-and-blood ties and worldly possessions and hold these with an open hand. In keeping with the humble request in the Lord's Prayer asking God to provide for one's daily bread, his disciples should not be anxious about material needs such as food, clothing, or shelter. If God feeds the birds and clothes the grass, he will certainly care for his people! If people seek God's kingdom, they can trust him to provide for all their needs. This is how simple, dependent trust in God expresses itself in the life of the disciple. Jesus's followers put God and his interests first, even though this means putting self-interest aside: "Fear not, little flock, for it is your Father's good pleasure to give you the kingdom."[271]

Be Alert and Be Ready (12:32–59)

At the same time, Jesus's followers must remain faithful—acknowledging him before others, trusting in God's providential care, and remaining vigilant until the end. This need for continual vigilance Jesus seeks to impress on his followers through a lengthy parable in which servants are put in charge of a household and their master's return is delayed. Faithful servants will be rewarded in the end, while faithless ones will be "cut . . . in pieces."[272] There is a pronounced sense of urgency in Jesus's tone in this chapter. He must undergo a "baptism" (i.e., his crucifixion) and is in great distress until it is accomplished.[273] Rather than bring peace, his coming has divided entire families, in keeping with the words of the prophet Micah.[274] Sadly, while Jesus's hearers can forecast the weather, they're unable to discern the significance of his coming.[275]

The Importance of Repentance and Bearing Fruit (13:1–9)

In what follows, some tell Jesus about an otherwise unattested incident about "Galileans whose blood Pilate had mingled with their sacrifices," a cruel act that left many with raw emotions questioning God's sovereignty.[276] How could God allow this kind of suffering? Did these people somehow deserve to meet such an ignominious end? Jesus

---

270. Luke 12:15.
271. Luke 12:32.
272. Luke 12:46.
273. Luke 12:50.
274. Luke 12:49–53; cf. Micah 7:6.
275. Luke 12:54–56.
276. Luke 13:1.

is quick to dispel such baseless speculation: "Do you think that these Galileans were worse sinners than all the other Galileans, because they suffered in this way? No, I tell you; but unless you repent, you will all likewise perish."[277] He also mentions a similar incident where eighteen people were killed when the tower in Siloam fell on them.[278] Rather than speculate about sin causing suffering, such reports should put the fear of God into people and cause them to repent. This holds powerful lessons for us today as well when natural disasters or terminal illnesses strike. What's more, as John the Baptist pointed out, people must produce fruit in keeping with repentance, as Jesus makes clear by telling a mini-parable about a barren fig tree.[279]

277. Luke 13:2–3.
278. Luke 13:4.
279. Luke 13:6–9; cf. 3:9.

THE LUKAN TRAVEL NARRATIVE:
JESUS'S JOURNEY TO JERUSALEM (9:51–19:27, CONT.)

Healings and Additional Teachings on Discipleship (13:10–15:32)

Healing on the Sabbath (13:10–17)

Jesus's Teaching in Parables and Additional Healings (13:18–15:32)

THE LUKAN TRAVEL NARRATIVE: JESUS'S JOURNEY TO JERUSALEM (9:51–19:27, CONT.)

Healings and Additional Teachings on Discipleship (13:10–15:32)

Healing on the Sabbath (13:10–17)

The next phase of the journey contains a long thread of Jesus's teachings.[280] Another round of controversies ensues, triggered by Jesus's healing ministry. This time the dispute surrounds the timing of the healings—on the Sabbath.[281] Just as the Sabbath recalls God's deliverance from the bondage of slavery, so Jesus sets a woman free on the Sabbath who has been disabled for eighteen years.[282] Similarly, we can be released from our affliction after years of struggle. Yet, in their hypocrisy, the Jewish leaders fail to recognize the work of God in their midst, and the synagogue ruler objects: "There are six days in which work ought to be done. Come on those days and be healed, and not on the Sabbath day."[283]

Jesus pointedly replies, "You hypocrites! Does not each of you on the Sabbath untie his ox or his donkey from the manger and lead it away to water it? And ought not this woman, a daughter of Abraham whom Satan bound for eighteen years, be loosed from this bond on the Sabbath day?"[284] Jesus's words expose that, in their maze of Sabbath

280. Cf. Thompson (*Luke*, 220), who lists several "thematic connections throughout 13:10–35 and 14:1–35 [that] tie this unit together": (1) Sabbath healings (13:10–17; 14:1–6); (2) kingdom parables (13:18–21; 14:7–14); (3) descriptions of those present at the end-time banquet (13:22–30; 14:15–24); and (4) Jesus's travel toward Jerusalem to die, a pattern followed by his disciples (13:31–35; 14:25–35).

281. Luke 13:10–17; 14:1–6.

282. Cf. Deuteronomy 5:12–15.

283. Luke 13:14.

284. Luke 13:15–16.

traditions, the Jewish leaders had no heart. They cared more about upholding their oral tradition than about helping this poor woman and alleviating her desperate condition. Jesus's adversaries were "put to shame," while the crowds rejoiced at all the "glorious things" Jesus did.[285] Looks like Jesus is winning the battle for public opinion!

Jesus's Teaching in Parables and Additional Healings (13:18–15:32)

At this, Jesus resumes his teaching on the nature of God's kingdom by telling people several parables:

1. The parable of the mustard seed (13:18–19)
2. The parable of the leaven (13:20–21)
3. The parable of the wedding guest (14:7–11)
4. The parable of the great banquet (14:12–24)
5. The parables of the lost sheep, lost coin, and prodigal son (15:1–32)

In between these parables, Jesus provides other instructions to his followers, as discussed below.

The parables of the mustard seed and the leaven (13:18–21). The parable of the mustard seed makes the simple point that the kingdom will grow from inconspicuous beginnings until it is expansive. In the spiritual realm, even mighty movements of God may have inconspicuous beginnings; such is the case with God's kingdom. The parable of the leaven similarly asserts that the kingdom will gradually grow until it fills the entire world. In this way, phenomena in the natural world, whether farming or baking, can be used to demonstrate spiritual truths to men (farming) and women (baking) alike.

Enter through the narrow gate (13:22–30). Luke's introductory remark, "He went on his way through towns and villages, teaching and journeying toward Jerusalem," reminds the reader that Jesus is still on his way to Jerusalem; the Lukan travel narrative continues.[286] The reader wonders: When will Jesus finally get there? Yet Luke savors the process and features several additional encounters and parables as the cross casts its shadow forward on the soon-to-be-suffering Messiah. The question by an unidentified individual, "Lord, will those who are saved be few?" causes Jesus to affirm that those who would be saved must enter through the "narrow door."[287] Jesus hints that many Gentiles will dine in God's kingdom with Abraham, Isaac, Jacob, and all the prophets,

285. Luke 13:17.
286. Luke 13:22. See previously Luke 9:57; 10:38; and see Luke 17:11 below.
287. Luke 13:23–24.

while many of his Jewish contemporaries will be shut out.[288] As David Garland observes, "Stubborn Israel is in peril of being excluded from salvation."[289] Thus, some who are last will be first (Gentiles), and some who are first will be last (Jews).[290] At this, some warn Jesus that Herod Antipas is out to kill him. He replies that they should go tell "that fox" that he will continue to cast out demons and to heal because no prophet should perish outside Jerusalem.[291] The fact, of course, is that Jesus is much more than a mere prophet; he is the Messiah and Savior—not only of Israel but of the entire world.

Jesus's lament over Jerusalem (13:31–35). At this, Jesus breaks out in lament, "O Jerusalem, Jerusalem, the city that kills the prophets and stones those who are sent to it!" In this way, Jesus reiterates his resolve to go to Jerusalem to finish his work.[292] This shows that the cross was Jesus's destiny all along and that Jerusalem, represented by its leaders, was bent on rejecting its Messiah. They rejected Jesus not only when putting him on the cross at the very end but throughout his ministry with ever-escalating hostility. This is sobering because it shows the extent to which human hearts were hardened toward God's Messiah and his salvation, and there was really nothing Jesus could have done to overcome this hardened opposition. The cross was inevitable.

Another Sabbath healing (14:1–6). Jesus performs another Sabbath healing.[293] His argument is almost identical to the previous one.[294] His opponents have no reply, though one senses that their hearts harden even further.

The parables of the wedding guest and the great banquet (14:7–24). The parables of the wedding guest and of the great banquet continue Jesus's instruction about the nature of God's kingdom. The parable of the wedding guest makes the point that humility is prized highly in the kingdom, so people should choose to take the lower place. Whoever humbles himself will be exalted, but whoever exalts himself will be humbled. In the parable of the great banquet, those who were invited all make excuses, so servants are sent out to invite "the poor and crippled and blind and lame" and even people from the "highways and hedges" to fill the banquet hall for the feast.[295]

288. Luke 13:28–29.
289. Garland, *Luke*, 554.
290. Luke 13:30.
291. Luke 13:32–33.
292. Luke 13:34–35.
293. Luke 14:1–6; cf. 13:10–17.
294. Luke 14:5; cf. 13:15.
295. Luke 14:23; 14:21.

Again, Luke strikes the note of reversal in God's kingdom. The tables will be turned; those exalted in society will be brought low, and the lowly will be exalted. This is tremendously encouraging for those who are powerless and lack recognition in this world, yet it poses an enormous challenge to the rich and powerful. It is no wonder that Luke's Gospel has been a favorite among advocates of justice. While socioeconomic and political justice does matter, however, this must be balanced with the recognition that ultimately it is only believing in Jesus and the gospel that saves.

The cost of discipleship (14:25–35). Great crowds continue to follow Jesus, so he takes the opportunity to teach them another lesson on discipleship: "If anyone comes to me and does not hate his own father and mother and wife and children and brothers and sisters, yes, and even his own life, he cannot be my disciple. Whoever does not bear his own cross and come after me cannot be my disciple."[296] This is an incredible shot across the bow for anyone who thinks following Jesus is easy. It also puts to shame much of shallow gospel proclamation in our day, which is virtually silent on the cost of following Jesus. Jesus had no such scruples. No one can accuse him of sugarcoating the gospel and of luring people into following him without having them read the fine print first.

Following Jesus is hard! Therefore, Jesus urges people to count the cost before making their decision, just like the builder of a tower or a king sending his army into war. If they don't have the resources and the stomach to complete what they've finished, they'll be everybody's laughingstock and suffer great loss: "So therefore, any one of you who does not renounce all that he has cannot be my disciple."[297] Tasteless salt is good for nothing except for the trash heap. These are stern words, but they're true. At least Jesus is telling us the truth! Also, although Luke doesn't say so here, it is equally true that while following Jesus is hard, it's also infinitely rewarding in the end; conversely, not following Jesus comes at a terrible price—a Christless eternity.

The parables of the lost sheep, the lost coin, and the prodigal son (15:1–32). The parables of the lost sheep, lost coin, and prodigal son continue the banquet theme, each ending with a joyful feast. The three parables form a single unit, emphasizing the lesson "from the lesser to the greater."[298] Notice that the value of what is lost increases exponentially with each parable—one of ninety-nine sheep, one of ten coins, and one of two sons. If a shepherd, woman, and father will search assiduously for what they've lost, how much more will God seek after lost people! This is exactly what God is doing through Jesus's ministry.

296. Luke 14:26–27.
297. Luke 14:33.
298. Garland, *Luke*, 609.

However, some are too self-righteous to recognize their need for God's grace. The parables are specifically directed toward the Pharisees and scribes who, like the older brother in the parable of the prodigal son, are unable to rejoice in Jesus's gracious welcome of sinners.[299]

The Pharisees' opposition to Jesus's fraternizing with so-called sinners (as if they weren't sinners too!) triggers this unique trilogy of parables. The three parables are mutually reinforcing, packing a triple punch in Jesus's powerful response to the Pharisees' objections. In this way, this trilogy of parables, which as mentioned is unique to Luke's Gospel, reinforces his message that Jesus was a friend of sinners who showed solidarity with the lowly in society while rejecting the wealthy, status-conscious, and proud.

Jesus opens the first parable with a question: "What man of you, having a hundred sheep, if he has lost one of them, does not leave the ninety-nine in the open country, and go after the one that is lost, until he finds it?"[300] This is a great way to engage his audience. I'd venture to say that most people in Jesus's audience would have agreed with his premise that the shepherd who left the ninety-nine sheep to go search for the lost sheep did the right thing. Sure enough, when the lost sheep is found, the man calls his friends and neighbors together to tell them the joyful news. The clincher is this: "Just so, I tell you, there will be more joy in heaven over one sinner who repents than over ninety-nine righteous persons who need no repentance."[301] Of course, those persons who need no repentance don't exist; Jesus merely posits this for the sake of the argument. Alternatively, Jesus affirms that there is greater joy in heaven over the repentance of those who are perceived as sinners (the outsiders and outcasts) than over those who perceive themselves to be righteous (echoing the Lukan "reversal motif"). In either case, his main point is that there is great joy in heaven over even one sinner who repents. The joyless, even reproachful, attitude of the Pharisees regarding Jesus's efforts to seek and save the lost stands exposed and corrected.

The second parable in the trilogy of lost things (or people)—the shortest of the three—has a woman as the main character, showcasing Luke's special concern for women and his consistent pattern of balancing his presentation so as to show that the gospel is good news for both men and women. Who cannot relate to losing one's wallet, or glasses, and looking everywhere to find them? So, Jesus tells the story of a woman who has lost a coin. She lights a lamp, sweeps the house, and searches diligently until she finds it. As in the previous parable, the focus is on the joy that accompanies finding what was lost. Similarly, "there is joy before the angels of God over one sinner who repents."[302] Just like in the previous parable, where the lost sheep represented a lost sinner

299. Luke 15:1–2.
300. Luke 15:4.
301. Luke 15:7.
302. Luke 15:10.

who repented, so in this parable it is a lost coin that represents a repentant sinner. And in both cases there is great joy in heaven. Salvation is what it's all about! Meanwhile, the Pharisees were playing shell games and jockeying for position while laying religious burdens on people and caring little for their spiritual well-being.

Finally, Jesus tells the third parable in the trilogy, which is so well developed that it seems to relegate the first two parables to mere preambles for the third one. This parable is also unique in that we expect the parable to end with the lost son's return and the joyful feast in keeping with the pattern of the first two parables, but then, surprisingly, the parable isn't over yet! Instead, it continues with the older brother, supplying an additional lesson that hits the Pharisees who had objected to Jesus's company with so-called sinners right between the eyes.

The opening of the parable is innocuous enough: "There was a man who had two sons."[303] Now remember that parables are made-up, albeit realistic, stories. In other words, all the characters in the parable were invented by Jesus in order to convey a vital spiritual lesson. It is a tribute to the mastery of Jesus's storytelling that the characters are so true to life that one almost thinks there really was such a father, and a prodigal son, and an older brother. Yet the truth of the spiritual lessons Jesus seeks to impart by telling this parable is not dependent on the historicity of the characters, plotline of the story, or other incidental details. The characters and the plot are mere vehicles to conveying the spiritual truth Jesus aims to impart.

So, in the story, the younger son comes to his father and brazenly asks for his inheritance. I say "brazenly" because normally, like today, people don't receive their inheritance until the person from whom they receive it has actually died. Yet here we have a son who asks his father for his inheritance during the father's lifetime! The father in the story, however, is very gracious and does as his son has requested, and soon the young man is off with his share of the inheritance to a faraway country. There, he "squandered his property in reckless living."[304] At this, a famine arises (notice that all of this is fictional, though the story is so well told that by now we're completely engrossed in it), so the young man takes a job feeding pigs. He longs to eat the pods he is feeding the pigs, but "no one gave him anything."[305] Life can be very harsh sometimes! And rebelliousness hardly ever pays in the long run. We can live on borrowed funds only for so long.

Then the miracle happens, and the story turns around radically: the young man comes to his senses and repents! This represents his spiritual conversion, which causes him to return to his father's house. He swallows his pride and decides to go back to the father and

303. Luke 15:11.
304. Luke 15:13.
305. Luke 15:16.

admit his mistake. For those of us who had to do something similar, we know that's hard. So here we must give the young man a lot of credit. The emotional high point of the story comes when the son approaches the father's house, and "while he was still a long way off, his father saw him and felt compassion, and ran and embraced him and kissed him."[306]

It's hard not to be moved by this scene and identify with the son, who expected a stern rebuke and instead is met with love and compassion. He says to his father, "Father, I have sinned against heaven and before you. I am no longer worthy to be called your son."[307] Wow! This is what true repentance looks like. The father, though, cuts the son's apology short (notice that when the son previously rehearsed his apology, he added, "Treat me as one of your hired servants"[308]) and honors him with a big feast celebrating his return: "For this my son was dead, and is alive again; he was lost, and is found."[309] The parable has a happy ending. But wait! The story isn't over yet.

When the older son arrives at the scene, hears the music and dancing (again, the story is told so well we almost forget it's just a story), and inquires what all the fuss is about, he is told that this was a party to celebrate the return of his (previously) rebellious younger brother. At this, he is filled with self-righteous indignation and bitterly complains to his father: "It's not fair!" "I've never done anything wrong," he says, in effect, "and yet you never even gave me a young goat to celebrate with my friends! And yet, when my brother returns, you slaughter the fattened calf so he can have a feast!"[310] The father gently tries to console his son and pleads with him to join in the festivities: "Son, you are always with me, and all that is mine is yours. It was fitting to celebrate and be glad, for this your brother was dead, and is alive; he was lost, and is found."[311]

In many ways, this parable is the emotional high point of the entire Gospel. It is here that we see Jesus's heart on display, which in turn is a reflection of the very heart of God. It is a heart full of love for wayward sinners, with a gracious willingness to forgive and to celebrate true repentance and conversion. What's more, not only does Jesus through this parable plead with the Pharisees to join in his joy over lost (Gentile) sinners; he tries to reassure them that they continue to be welcome in the Father's house. Despite Jesus's gentleness in issuing this invitation, it falls on deaf ears with the Pharisees, who further harden in their opposition (though Luke records no response from them whatsoever). We'll have to catch our breath after such an emotional conversion story that reveals the heart of God toward sinners before moving on.

306. Luke 15:20.
307. Luke 15:21.
308. Luke 15:19.
309. Luke 15:24.
310. See Luke 15:29–30.
311. Luke 15:31–32.

THE LUKAN TRAVEL NARRATIVE: JESUS'S JOURNEY TO JERUSALEM (9:51–19:27, CONT.)

Additional Parables and Teachings on Discipleship (16:1–17:10)

The Parable of the Dishonest Manager (16:1–13)

In the next scene, Jesus tells his disciples the parable of the dishonest manager.[312] A manager is fired by his master because of mismanagement of funds. Before his employment ends, however, he summons his master's debtors and reduces their debts so as to ingratiate them to him for the time when he'll be out of a job. The twist comes when the master commends the dishonest manager for his shrewdness! The lesson, according to Jesus, is this: "Make friends for yourselves by means of unrighteous wealth, so that when it fails they may receive you into the eternal dwellings."[313] In other words, realize that money is a tool rather than an object of worship; therefore, use that tool effectively and even shrewdly. As Jesus points out, "For the sons of this world are more shrewd in dealing with their own generation than the sons of light."[314]

312. This is his second warning on the issue of wealth (cf. Luke 12:13–34). Thompson (*Luke*, 250) identifies the present unit as reaching from 16:1 to 18:8. He observes that the focus of this section is on "the need to live by faith in anticipation of that day"—that is, the final day of judgment triggered by Jesus's return.

313. Luke 16:9.

314. Luke 16:8.

To be clear: Jesus doesn't commend dishonesty here; he simply advocates dealing shrewdly with "unrighteous wealth."[315] His charge for his followers is therefore to be faithful in little things. Otherwise, they won't be entrusted with spiritual wealth of their own. What's more, they must make up their mind about whom they will serve, God or money, because no one can serve two masters. This speaks to the heart attitude of a disciple when it comes to stewardship. No matter is too small for a man or woman to handle with integrity. Also, we are managers for God and others. Can they trust us with the way we handle their property? Or are we dishonest in small things when it works to our advantage? Finally, do we use our possessions wisely, even shrewdly, for the advancement of God's kingdom? Do we realize that what we own is just a tool to accomplish his purposes?

Addressing the Pharisees (16:14–18)

Again, the Pharisees serve as a foil in the story because they were "lovers of money."[316] And Luke tells us that they ridiculed Jesus for his teaching! Yet, as Jesus is quick to point out, God knows their hearts: "For what is exalted among men is an abomination in the sight of God."[317] I recently had an experience where someone presented something they did as noble-minded and subsequently was praised for it by others. Problem is, I happened to know that the reason they did this was for financial self-interest, while those other people presented it as having been done out of pure altruism. Naturally, this irked me, but it's comforting to know that, as Jesus said, God knows our hearts. He even knows that people may ignorantly and falsely praise those who act out of greed presented as generosity! In his kingdom, hearts will be revealed, and God will effect a dramatic reversal of the injustices and patterns of pretense that run rampant in this world.

The Parable of the Rich Man and Lazarus (16:19–31)

After a brief intermezzo, Jesus continues his teaching on wealth and poverty (a major theme in Luke's writings) with another remarkable story, the parable of the rich man and Lazarus. This parable, too, is found only in Luke's Gospel. It is the only parable in all the Gospels with a named character, Lazarus (not to be confused with the Lazarus Jesus raised from the dead), not to mention that Abraham, the Old Testament patriarch, is featured in the parable as well.[318] Jesus paints a vivid picture of the rich man feasting

315. Luke 16:9, 11.
316. Luke 16:14.
317. Luke 16:15.
318. The fact that this parable has a named character is the exception that proves the rule (that, typically, parable characters are unnamed). What's more, the presence of a named character in this parable in no way casts legitimate doubt on this being a genuine parable. Who says that parable characters can't occasionally be

every day, while poor Lazarus languishes miserably at the rich man's gate, longing "to be fed with what fell from the rich man's table."[319] Both men die and are transported to their eternal destiny. In Hades (hell) the rich man catches a glimpse of Lazarus, who now is at the side of Abraham, the patriarch.

Now the roles are strangely reversed, with the rich man in deep anguish, begging Lazarus to dip the end of his finger in water to cool his tongue. Yet Abraham informs him that a great chasm has been fixed between them that no one can cross. This is yet another powerful parable by Jesus that impresses on his listeners the importance of fearing God in this life because one's eternal destiny depends on it. What's more, as in the parable of the prodigal son, there is a sort of epilogue to this parable. The rich man asks Abraham to send Lazarus to warn his five brothers who are still living, lest they end up in the same horrible place he did. Abraham refuses, saying they have Moses (the Law) and the Prophets. They have the Scriptures! Not taking no for an answer, the rich man insists, "No, father Abraham, but if someone goes to them from the dead, they will repent."[320] Abraham retorts, "If they do not listen to Moses and the Prophets, they will not be convinced even if someone rises from the dead."[321]

With this, Jesus predicts his own resurrection and once again highlights the stubborn unbelief of the Jewish leaders, for whom no evidence is compelling enough to change their mind about the identity of Jesus. While we should take care not to build our entire theology of the afterlife on this parable (e.g., there probably won't be conversations across the divide between heaven and hell, C. S. Lewis's classic *The Great Divorce* notwithstanding), this fictional story conveys powerful spiritual truths. We must respond to the ample evidence we have about Jesus rather than always demanding more. Lack of evidence won't be a sufficient excuse when we have to give an account for our unbelief on judgment day before God. Also, our wealth can't save us. If we live our lives for the sake of accumulating material possessions and enjoying life in the present apart from God, we'll die and our wealth will rot, and our only prospect will be spending eternity apart from God in hell. And no one can say Jesus didn't warn us. Because he did.

And if anyone were to object that God should provide clearer manifestations of his presence, or his power, to convey his reality to people, I believe Jesus would have the

---

named? This is similar to the reference to the road from Jerusalem to Jericho in the parable of the good Samaritan. It's possible that Lazarus is named because Abraham is named as well; in this way, Abraham doesn't have to carry on a conversation with an unnamed character. Contra Elmer L. Towns and Ben Gutiérrez, *The Essence of the New Testament* (Nashville: B&H, 2012), 86: "The story of the rich man and Lazarus is sometimes thought to be a parable (16:19–31). However, this is a true story about two individuals."

319. Luke 16:21.

320. Luke 16:30.

321. Luke 16:31 NIV.

same answer Abraham gave in the parable of the rich man and Lazarus: "If they do not listen to Moses and the Prophets, they will not be convinced even if someone rises from the dead." Virtually anyone can read the Bible (except for the few dialects that still await translation, an urgent task). Just check out any bookstore (I know, a dying breed) or online retailers; the Bible is available in many shapes, colors, and translations. Take your pick and read the Bible!

The Need for Faith and Humble Servanthood (17:1–10)

With the self-righteous Pharisees still in the back of his mind, Jesus continues to instruct his followers. "Temptations to sin are sure to come," he says, striking a note of realism, "but woe to the one through whom they come!"[322] In other words, you'll be tempted, but make sure you're not the source of temptation for others. In fact, as Jesus illustrates with a powerful metaphor, it would be better for such a person "if a millstone were hung around his neck and he were cast into the sea" than for him to "cause one of these little ones to sin."[323] The disciples doubtless realize that Jesus is talking about the Jewish leaders who, rather than gently leading their flock, have put unbearable religious burdens on the backs of their weary followers. By contrast, Jesus's disciples must forgive those who sin against them if they genuinely repent.[324] They sense that they can't do what Jesus commands apart from growing in faith and ask him to increase it.[325]

Jesus responds that all they need is the tiniest amount of faith (like a mustard seed). He goes on to tell a story of a servant who is working in the field or tending sheep. When he returns to the house, does his master invite him to join him at the dinner table? No! Rather, he tells him to go prepare supper! He may not even thank the servant for the work he did, because it is expected of him. In the same way, Jesus tells his followers to be content with being God's servants. They should be humble and obedient and let their privilege of working for their Master be enough.[326] This doesn't mean that we shouldn't say "thank you" when someone does something nice for us. Nor does it mean that we should exploit people in the church and take advantage of their sacrifice of time and money spent in serving. Rather, Jesus here talks about proper attitude. Our motivation for serving shouldn't be to be recognized and praised by others.[327]

322. Luke 17:1.
323. Luke 17:2.
324. Luke 17:3–4.
325. Luke 17:5.
326. Luke 17:7–10.
327. The complementary truth is that those who serve God faithfully should be honored. Cf., e.g., 1 Timothy 5:17. As Jesus himself said, "The worker is worthy of his wages" (Luke 10:7 CSB; cf. Leviticus 19:13; Deuteronomy 24:15; 1 Corinthians 9:14; 1 Timothy 5:18).

THE LUKAN TRAVEL NARRATIVE: JESUS'S JOURNEY TO JERUSALEM (9:51–19:27, CONT.)

Closing in on Jerusalem (17:11–19:27)

An Attitude of Gratitude: The Cleansing of Ten Samaritan Lepers (17:11–19)

The Arrival of the Kingdom (17:20–37)

THE LUKAN TRAVEL NARRATIVE: JESUS'S JOURNEY TO JERUSALEM (9:51–19:27, CONT.)

Closing in on Jerusalem (17:11–19:27)

An Attitude of Gratitude: The Cleansing of Ten Samaritan Lepers (17:11–19)

In case some of his readers forgot, Luke again reminds them that Jesus was "on the way to Jerusalem."[328] The final portion of his journey to Jerusalem (no surprise here) focuses on the topics of faith and the kingdom. These are the topics that Jesus tried to hammer home to his followers throughout his entire ministry, and he continues to do so in order to impress on them the importance of faith and the preeminence of God's kingdom. While Jesus has told several powerful parables, Luke now shifts to narrative to impress on his readers some of the same lessons.

As Jesus passes through the region between Samaria and Galilee, he enters a village and heals ten lepers. He tells them to go to the priests, which they do, but only one—a Samaritan—thanks Jesus for healing him. Jesus's response is deeply convicting: "Where are the other nine?"[329] Did only the one Samaritan return to give thanks? As in the parable of the good Samaritan, this mixed race that was hated by the Jews supplies the hero of the story, indicating the great reversal taking place in God's kingdom. Jesus goes on to tell the Samaritan who returned to thank him, "your faith has made you well."[330] The other nine lepers were merely cleansed physically; the Samaritan who had faith was made whole spiritually as well.

---

328. Luke 17:11. See previously Luke 9:57; 10:38; 13:22.
329. Luke 17:17 NIV.
330. Luke 17:19.

The Arrival of the Kingdom (17:20–37)

When asked by the Pharisees when the kingdom of God would come, Jesus declares that the kingdom is already in their midst![331] Clearly, he is speaking about himself, the King who has already come to proclaim the good news of the arrival of God's kingdom. Tragically, by refusing the King, the Jewish leaders would also be shut out of God's kingdom. Turning to his disciples, Jesus goes on to predict a time when he, the "Son of Man," will no longer be in their midst—even though messianic pretenders will arise and false alarms will sound—until, one day, he will return "as the lightning flashes and lights up the sky from one side to the other."[332] No one will be able to miss Jesus's second coming! It will be highly public and visible: "But first he must suffer many things and be rejected by this generation" by divine necessity.[333]

Conditions at Jesus's return will be as in the days of Noah (the flood) and Lot (Sodom and Gomorrah).[334] People will go about their daily lives, unsuspecting that "today is the day." Yet "in that night" two will be sleeping in one bed; one will be taken, and the other left behind.[335] Most likely, this refers to Jesus's second coming at the end of the "Great Tribulation," at which believers who are alive at the time will be caught up and meet the Lord in the air (the so-called rapture).[336] Jesus's teaching here instructs his followers that there are two aspects of his kingdom. On the one hand, the kingdom is a *present* reality, even though many are oblivious to the signs of its arrival. On the other hand, the kingdom has a *future* dimension, which climaxes in Jesus's second coming and the judgment that will ensue.

331. Luke 17:20–21.
332. Luke 17:24.
333. Luke 17:25.
334. Luke 17:27–30; cf. Genesis 6:9–22; 19:1–26.
335. Luke 17:34–35. Note that verse 36 is a later scribal addition omitted in our modern English versions.
336. Cf. 1 Thessalonians 4:13–17.

THE LUKAN TRAVEL NARRATIVE: JESUS'S JOURNEY TO JERUSALEM (9:51–19:27, CONT.)
Closing in on Jerusalem (17:11–19:27, cont.)
The Parable of the Unrighteous Judge and the Persistent Widow (18:1–8)
The Parable of the Pharisee and the Tax Collector (18:9–14)
Little Children and the Rich Young Ruler (18:15–30)
Jesus's Third Passion Prediction (18:31–34)

THE LUKAN TRAVEL NARRATIVE: JESUS'S JOURNEY TO JERUSALEM (9:51–19:27, CONT.)

Closing in on Jerusalem (17:11–19:27, cont.)

The Parable of the Unrighteous Judge and the Persistent Widow (18:1–8)
Jesus continues to highlight the issues of faith and the kingdom by the parable of the persistent widow. Luke states the moral of the parable at the outset. Jesus was trying to impress on his followers that "they ought always to pray and not lose heart."[337] The parable features an unrighteous judge and a persistent widow. While the judge didn't care about the justice the widow was seeking, in the end he gave in to her persistent pleas simply to get her off his back! In an argument from the lesser to the greater, Jesus concludes, if this unrighteous judge gave the widow the justice she was persistently seeking, "will not God give justice to his elect, who cry to him day and night? Will he delay long over them? I tell you, he will give justice to them speedily." Jesus concludes the parable by asking, "When the Son of Man comes, will he find faith on earth?"[338] Jesus's return will be preceded by a period of great tribulation in which believers' faith will be severely tested and many will be martyred for their faith. This is a great challenge to pray persistently and to not give up, because in the end God will vindicate those who put their faith in him and answer their prayers for justice.

337. Luke 18:1.
338. Luke 18:7–8.

The Parable of the Pharisee and the Tax Collector (18:9–14)

One vital ingredient of Jesus's parables is that they often aimed to address heart attitudes that were in need of correction. The next parable, Luke tells us, Jesus told "to some who trusted in themselves that they were righteous, and treated others with contempt."[339] One cannot help but wonder if Jesus here has the Pharisees in mind. Sure enough, in the parable of the Pharisee and tax collector, Jesus pits a self-righteous Pharisee who is proud of all his religious accomplishments against a humble tax collector who cries out to God for mercy. Only the latter goes home justified. Again, we see a stunning reversal in common expectations; nothing could have been more shocking to Jesus's listeners in his day. As Jesus concluded, "Everyone who exalts himself will be humbled, but the one who humbles himself will be exalted."[340] Pride comes before the fall, while humility will result in exaltation.

Little Children and the Rich Young Ruler (18:15–30)

Jesus reinforces his lesson on humility by welcoming little children who are brought to him. In the process, he rebukes his own disciples who had rebuked those who were trying to bring the children to Jesus! "Let the little children come to me," Jesus tells them, "for the kingdom of God belongs to such as these."[341] In fact, "whoever does not receive the kingdom of God like a child shall not enter it."[342] In other words, those who would enter God's kingdom must admit that they themselves have nothing to offer to him. They must realize that they come to God with empty hands and must be willing to humble themselves to receive his free gift of salvation in the Messiah.

The episode featuring little children is juxtaposed with the story of the rich young ruler in the following scene.[343] He had obeyed all of God's commandments from his youth but was unwilling to give away his wealth to the poor. In contrast to the children who receive God's kingdom, Jesus points out, "How difficult it is for those who have wealth to enter the kingdom of God!"[344] At the same time, he reassures Peter and the other disciples, "There is no one who has left house or wife or brothers or parents or children, for the sake of the kingdom of God, who will not receive many times more in this time, and in the age to come eternal life."[345] Following Jesus has great spiritual rewards, not only in the life to come, but already in this life as well!

---

339. Luke 18:9.
340. Luke 18:14; cf. Luke 14:11.
341. Luke 18:16 NIV.
342. Luke 18:17.
343. Luke 18:18–30.
344. Luke 18:24.
345. Luke 18:29–30.

Jesus's Third Passion Prediction (18:31–34)

Momentum continues to build as Jesus is getting ever closer to the goal of his journey, the city of Jerusalem. At this juncture in Luke's narrative, Jesus predicts his suffering for the third and last time. In this final prediction, he emphatically declares his purpose for going to Jerusalem: to be handed over to the Gentiles, to be beaten, killed, and rise on the third day, in keeping with the message of the Old Testament prophets.[346] In this way, Jesus is going to Jerusalem to accomplish God's predetermined plan of salvation. He is a man on a mission—a messianic, saving mission—and is in the process of executing his mission in faithfulness to God and in fulfillment of Old Testament expectations (though not those of his contemporaries!). In fact, as Luke is careful to note, the disciples still don't grasp the meaning of Jesus's words. Did they at least have a glimpse of what Jesus was trying to say and understand some of it? No; as Luke categorically states, "they understood none of these things." They still didn't understand that Jesus, the Messiah, must die, because this spiritual truth "was hidden from them."[347]

In this regard, Luke is in complete alignment with the other Gospel writers, all of whom go to great lengths to show that it didn't enter the minds of Jesus's human followers that the Messiah must suffer and be crucified to accomplish the work of salvation. This furnishes powerful proof that the story of Jesus could never have been invented by his followers. To the contrary, they fought it tooth and nail. The only reason why Jesus's story is so compelling is not because it is so cleverly invented, or because it is so logical or rational, but because it is historically and spiritually true. The series of Jesus's three passion predictions in Matthew, Mark, and Luke (not to mention similar passages in John) serves this very purpose: to show that Jesus knew what would happen to him and repeatedly predicted it, while his followers steadfastly refused to believe that the Messiah would need to be crucified. The reason for this is that they didn't understand the substitutionary atonement—the need for Jesus, the sinless God-man, to give his life for the sins of the people on the cross.

346. Luke 18:31–32.
347. Luke 18:34.

THE LUKAN TRAVEL NARRATIVE: JESUS'S JOURNEY TO JERUSALEM (9:51–19:27, CONT.)
Closing in on Jerusalem (17:11–19:27, cont.)
Healing a Blind Man on the Road to Jericho (18:35–43)
Zacchaeus the Tax Collector (19:1–10)
Your Best Kingdom Now? The Parable of the Ten Minas (19:11–27)

THE LUKAN TRAVEL NARRATIVE: JESUS'S JOURNEY TO JERUSALEM (9:51–19:27, CONT.)

Closing in on Jerusalem (17:11–19:27, cont.)

Healing a Blind Man on the Road to Jericho (18:35–43)

Undaunted, Jesus continues on his way, misunderstood by those closest to him, yet confident in God's plan and assured of his presence and approval. As Jesus approaches Jericho, now within striking distance of Jerusalem, a blind man sitting by the road wonders what the commotion is he is hearing. When told that "Jesus of Nazareth is passing by," he cries at top of his lungs, "Jesus, Son of David, have mercy on me!"[348] As in the case of the little children brought to Jesus earlier, people tell him to be quiet and not to bother Jesus. After all, Jesus was a celebrity (perhaps a prophet) embarking on an important mission! Yet the blind man is desperate enough to cry even louder: "Son of David, have mercy on me!"[349]

At this, the reader's heart stops as Jesus stops and asks that the blind man be brought to him. He speaks a word of healing and tells him that his faith has made him well, similar to his words to the Samaritan leper earlier. Immediately, the man is healed and follows Jesus, praising God, as do all those who saw the amazing miracle. In this way, Jesus continues to furnish proofs of his messianic identity, which included the ability to perform amazing healings such as restoring sight to the blind. We also see once again that it is those who are desperate for healing—those who come to Jesus with empty

348. Luke 18:37–38.
349. Luke 18:39.

hands, crying out for mercy, and recognizing him as the Son of David, the messianic King—who receive healing. Conversely, others continue to misconstrue Jesus's identity because it doesn't conform to their own misguided expectations of who the Messiah would turn out to be.

Zacchaeus the Tax Collector (19:1–10)

Next, Jesus enters Jericho on his way to Jerusalem.[350] There he encounters a man named Zacchaeus, the chief tax collector, who had used his position to enrich himself greatly. No doubt drawing on eyewitness testimony, Luke tells us that Zacchaeus wanted to catch a glimpse of Jesus passing through town but couldn't because he was too short! So he runs ahead and climbs onto a sycamore tree (that's pretty specific information!). When Jesus notices him, he tells him to come down. Not only had Jesus previously called a tax collector named Matthew to join the ranks of the Twelve; he had recently told a parable about a Pharisee and a tax collector. Now he is calling another tax collector to salvation! Predictably, Jesus's opponents grumble once again, but he doesn't care. Zacchaeus shows active repentance by giving away half of his fortune to the poor (a major concern for Luke) and by promising to repay fourfold those whom he defrauded.

In this way, Luke upholds Zacchaeus as a fitting role model for the rich, who can repent and make amends for their past exploitation of the poor. When the rich young ruler had come to Jesus in the previous chapter and been unwilling to part with his great wealth, Jesus had pointed out how difficult it was for rich people to be saved; yet all things were possible with God. The example of Zacchaeus in the present chapter demonstrates that Jesus's words were true: all things are indeed possible with God.[351] Following Zacchaeus' act of repentance, Jesus declares, "Today salvation has come to this house."[352] Jesus's words in the next verse encapsulate the core message of Luke's entire Gospel: "For the Son of Man came to seek and to save the lost."[353] Here we see how Luke uses real-life characters—Zacchaeus and the rich young ruler—to teach vital spiritual lessons to his readers right alongside parables (stories invented by Jesus), which impart some of these very same lessons.

---

350. Jesus has previously featured the road from Jerusalem to Jericho in the parable of the good Samaritan (Luke 10:30). The alert reader will therefore realize that now that Jesus has arrived in Jericho, the long journey to Jerusalem is almost over. You can just hear the disciples asking Jesus, as our children always do on a long trip, "Are we almost there?" In the present instance, the answer is "Yes, almost there!"
351. Cf. Luke 18:27.
352. Luke 19:9; cf. 4:21.
353. Luke 19:10.

Your Best Kingdom Now? The Parable of the Ten Minas (19:11–27)

Finally, as "he was near to Jerusalem," Jesus again seized the need of the moment because he knew that his followers expected him to usher in the kingdom of God upon his entrance into Jerusalem. Note that, as Luke records in the book of Acts, even after the resurrection, Jesus's disciples asked him, "Lord, will you at this time restore the kingdom to Israel?"[354] All of this reflects widespread Jewish messianic expectations that the Messiah would come as a national deliverer for Israel to restore David's kingdom and overthrow Israel's political enemies, in the present case the Romans. Luke writes to correct such expectations, both in terms of the scope of God's kingdom (it would not merely be for Israel but include believing Gentiles as well) and in terms of the kind of king Jesus was (not a national, earthly messiah but the suffering and risen Savior and Son of God). In the parable of the ten minas, therefore, Jesus addresses the expectations of those who thought the kingdom would appear immediately upon his entrance into Jerusalem.

You can read the entire parable on your own to receive the full impact.[355] The story revolves around a nobleman (representing Jesus) who goes away to receive a kingdom. Upon his return, he calls his servants to account for their stewardship, rewarding those who had been faithful while punishing the servant who made excuses for failing to invest his money. The bottom line is this: what matters most is that Jesus's followers be faithful with what they've been entrusted; they can safely trust God to bring about his kingdom at his appointed time! Remember that Jesus told many kingdom parables throughout his ministry; none teaches everything there is to know, but every one of them imparts one small, specific spiritual truth about the kingdom. Therefore, we shouldn't expect teaching about the kingdom in its totality to be found in any one parable but rather engage in a comprehensive study of all of Jesus's kingdom parables and teachings about God's kingdom to attain a composite sketch of what God's kingdom will be like.

RECAP

Whew! We've just completed a fairly thorough run-through of the entire Lukan travel narrative, which depicts Jesus's lengthy journey toward Jerusalem, the setting of the passion narrative that is about to follow. If you've plowed through this entire section, I'm sure you've learned a lot about what God's kingdom is like and what it means to be Jesus's disciple. Luke had started out by saying, "When the days drew near for him

354. Acts 1:6.
355. Luke 19:11–27. On the setting, see Aubrey L. Taylor, "The Historical Basis of the Parable of the Pounds (Luke 19:11–27)," in Beitzel, *Lexham Geographic Commentary*, 385–94.

to be taken up, he set his face to go to Jerusalem."[356] After this, Jesus was rejected by a Samaritan village. Also, he was approached by three prospective disciples, all of whom he turned away because they were unwilling to pay the price for following him. The sending out of the Seventy (or Seventy-two) frames Jesus's denunciation of the Galilean cities that had rejected him. Characteristically, Jesus praised the Father for revealing himself to the humble while concealing himself from the proud. Next, he told the parable of the good Samaritan to a lawyer who wanted to test Jesus and then tried to justify himself, implying it was unclear what "neighbor" meant.

The following vignette showed Jesus enjoy the hospitality of two sisters, Mary and Martha; Mary was commended for taking a learning, listening posture toward Jesus—that of a disciple. At his disciples' request, Jesus taught them how to pray (the Lukan version of the Lord's Prayer). Jesus's opposition once again reared its ugly head by accusing him of casting out demons by the power of Satan. Jesus warned them against committing the sin of blasphemy against the Holy Spirit. He also rebuffed demands for signs other than the "sign of Jonah." The Ninevites (Nineveh was the capital of Assyria, Israel's enemy) had repented at Jonah's preaching, and they would pronounce judgment on unbelieving Israelites on judgment day. Jesus denounced the Pharisees and scribes in a series of withering woes and warned his own followers against the "leaven" of the hypocritical Pharisees.

He proceeded to tell the parable of the rich fool and instructed his disciples not to be anxious but rather to be ready for his return. He had come to bring division, not peace, dividing entire families depending on their allegiance (or lack thereof) to Jesus. Jesus taught many additional parables, such as the parable of the barren fig tree, the parables of the mustard seed and the leaven, as well as the parables of the wedding guest and of the great banquet. Each of these added a precious piece to the composite mosaic depicting the beauty, truth, and sublime spiritual nature of God's kingdom. Jesus's teaching in parables continued unabated and reached an emotional high point in the trilogy of parables of lost things: the lost sheep, the lost coin, and the lost (or prodigal) son. God's heart is full of compassion toward lost sinners, and if they repent, he welcomes them with open arms. What a great God and merciful Savior we have!

In what follows, Jesus continues to instruct his followers regarding the nature of God's kingdom by way of parables. This includes the parable of the dishonest manager and the parable of the rich man and Lazarus. People should use money wisely and for kingdom purposes. They should also be aware that God's kingdom will witness a radical reversal of values and positions: the wealthy and socially exalted will be brought low, while the poor and disenfranchised will be exalted. Along the way, Jesus cleanses

356. Luke 9:51.

ten lepers, but only one—a Samaritan—returns to give thanks. When asked by the Pharisees about when God's kingdom would come, Jesus tells them it is already in their midst! Then Jesus tells still more parables: the parable of the persistent widow and the parable of the Pharisee and the tax collector. God's people should persistently cry out to God for justice, and he will not delay to intervene on behalf of his elect. He gives grace to the humble but opposes the proud.

Along the way, Jesus also has several memorable encounters with various individuals: the rich young ruler (who cannot part with his wealth), a blind beggar on the side of the road near Jericho (whom he heals), and, perhaps most memorably, Zacchaeus the tax collector. In the context of Luke's narrative, Zacchaeus serves as a powerful example of how the rich can be saved: by genuinely repenting and making proper amends for having exploited the poor in the past. The travel narrative concludes, fittingly, with yet another parable, the parable of the ten minas. Jesus's followers must be faithful so they can give an account to God on the last day, even though it may be a while before their Master returns. Luke's narration of Jesus's long journey toward Jerusalem has provided a rich set of instructions for his followers regarding the nature of discipleship. At long last, he has arrived at the holy city. What will happen next?

JESUS'S WORK IN JERUSALEM (19:28–24:49)

The Triumphal Entry and Final Work in Jerusalem (19:28–21:38)

The Triumphal Entry into Jerusalem and the City's Future Destruction (19:28–44)

Cleansing the Temple (19:45–48)

JESUS'S WORK IN JERUSALEM (19:28–24:49)

After the lengthy buildup in Luke's Travel Narrative, we now enter the final, decisive phase in Jesus's mission. Preparations are made for his final Passover, and he enters Jerusalem hailed by the crowds. But he laments the city's fate and cleanses the corrupt temple. In response to a challenge to his authority, he tells a parable which presages his imminent rejection by the Jewish authorities. Various other disputes follow, showing the rising degree of animosity toward Jesus by the leaders. Now in greater detail, Jesus predicts the destruction of Jerusalem and the temple in the "Olivet discourse." The Last Supper and the final events of Jesus's earthly ministry ensue in rapid succession, culminating in his resurrection, final commission, and ascension.

The Triumphal Entry and Final Work in Jerusalem (19:28–21:38)

The Triumphal Entry into Jerusalem and the City's Future Destruction (19:28–44)

In Jesus's preparations for his arrival, we're given the first of many indications that everything is taking place in keeping with God's sovereign, predetermined plan. Everything turns out to be exactly as Jesus told his disciples who are to fetch a colt and bring it to Jesus so that he can mount it and ride into Jerusalem as the humble King and Savior.[357] As Jesus approaches the holy city, his disciples are brimming with messianic hope. Descending from the Mount of Olives, Jesus arrives in Jerusalem in humility and peace, in fulfillment of Zechariah's messianic prophecy.[358]

Luke's account focuses on the reaction of the crowd of disciples who recognize the significance of the event by announcing: "Blessed is the King who comes in the name of

357. Luke 19:28–32.

358. Zechariah 9:9; cf. 14:4. The Mount of Olives is also the place where the Messiah was expected to arrive.

the Lord! Peace in heaven and glory in the highest!"[359] Luke's reader has no trouble recognizing the allusion to Jesus's birth narrative, in which a multitude of angels hailed the infant Messiah by exclaiming, "Glory to God in the highest, and on earth peace among those with whom he is pleased!"[360] Note, however, that the rejoicing "multitude" of angels is now replaced by a rejoicing "multitude" of Jesus's disciples![361]

The exuberant reception by the disciples contrasts with the disparaging reaction of the Pharisees who urge Jesus (calling him a mere "teacher") to rebuke his disciples.[362] Jesus's response is pointed: if his followers were silent, the very stones would cry out![363] In many ways, therefore, Jerusalem epitomizes the polarized response to Jesus. As Mark Strauss explains, "Again we see the paradox of Jerusalem, representing both God's salvation and Israel's rejection."[364] Fully aware of what will happen to him, Jesus mourns Jerusalem's fate.[365] At the very beginning of Luke's Gospel, Zechariah spoke of God "visiting" his people to provide redemption.[366] Several decades later, Jesus begins his final approach to the holy city and laments because, as he says, "you [Jerusalem] did not know the time of your visitation."[367]

In entering Jerusalem, Jesus again displays great prophetic foresight, declaring that Jerusalem failed to recognize him as its messianic king. As a result, the city wouldn't know peace, but instead its enemies would lay siege to it and raze it to the ground, decimating the population of Jerusalem, men and women and children alike. The city's destruction would be utterly complete and devastating. Jesus presents these future events (which would take place about forty years later in the year 70) as God's judgment on the city and its people for rejecting him as their God-sent messianic king. This broke Jesus's and God the Father's heart as it represented a heart-wrenching failure to recognize God's good, saving purposes for his people. It's like when, as a parent, you go through great expense and trouble to give one of your children a precious gift and they throw it in the trash.

Similarly, God's people, represented by their religious leadership, would treat the Messiah with contempt and trample God's magnificent gift underfoot. Notice that Jesus is saying these things when a multitude of disciples hails him as the messianic king

359. Luke 19:38; cf. Psalm 118:26.
360. Luke 2:14.
361. See Luke 2:13 and Luke 19:37, respectively. In each case, the Greek word for "multitude" is the same (*plēthos*).
362. Luke 19:39.
363. Luke 19:40.
364. Strauss, *Four Portraits, One Jesus*, 276.
365. Luke 19:41–44.
366. Luke 1:68.
367. Luke 19:44.

who was foretold in the Psalms and presaged by the prophets. This makes clear that even his disciples didn't truly understand who Jesus was (another instance of discipleship failure) and that their acclaim was not to be trusted. Jesus knew that he would end up on the cross in just a few short days. Ironically, therefore, when we celebrate Palm Sunday, we reenact the disciples' misunderstanding on a yearly basis! Hopefully we understand that Jesus's followers spoke better than they knew and Jesus really was the Davidic king—and yet he was a different kind of Messiah than they expected. And in a blessed irony and paradox, God used their rejection of Jesus to bring about his saving, substitutionary cross-death on their and our behalf.

Cleansing the Temple (19:45–48)

In the next scene, in a fairly terse account, Jesus enters the temple and drives out the merchants there.[368] He had just predicted the destruction of Jerusalem; now, in prophetic style, he acts out God's judgment on the temple by cleansing the temple area. Explaining the significance of his action (which no doubt was puzzling to many), Jesus told the merchants—conflating the words of the prophets Isaiah and Jeremiah—"It is written, 'My house shall be a house of prayer,' but you have made it a den of robbers."[369] In other words, Jesus acted with prophetic, even messianic, authority in keeping with the words of Israel's premier prophets. The merchants, sanctioned by the corrupt, ungodly religious leadership, have utterly perverted the God-intended purpose of Israel's central sanctuary. Rather than being a site of spiritual worship, the temple had become a place of greedy commerce—a robber's den. After thus cleansing the temple of activities unworthy of the true God, Jesus sets up shop (so to speak) in the temple area himself and begins "teaching daily in the temple."[370] Luke is diligent to note that Jesus continues to be a thorn in the side of the religious leaders—the chief priests and the scribes—who are tragically out to destroy him; but there was as of yet nothing they could do because the people were hanging on his every word.[371]

368. Thompson (*Luke*, 311) starts the final major unit here in Luke 19:45 rather than in Luke 19:28, calling it "The Lord Accomplishes the Salvation of the Kingdom (19:45–24:53)."

369. Luke 19:46.

370. Luke 19:47.

371. Luke 19:47–48.

JESUS'S WORK IN JERUSALEM (19:28–24:49, CONT.)
The Triumphal Entry and Final Work in Jerusalem (19:28–21:38, cont.)
A Challenge to Jesus's Authority (20:1–8)
The Parable of the Wicked Tenants and Various Controversies (20:9–47)
The Widow's Mite (21:1–4)
The Lukan Olivet Discourse (21:5–38)

JESUS'S WORK IN JERUSALEM (19:28–24:49, CONT.)

The Triumphal Entry and Final Work in Jerusalem (19:28–21:38, cont.)

A Challenge to Jesus's Authority (20:1–8)

In what follows, Luke elaborates on Jesus's teaching "and preaching the gospel" (!) in the temple area.[372] In so doing, he also directs our attention to the escalating opposition of the Jewish leaders as representative of Israel's rejection of Jesus. First up, the Jewish leaders challenge his authority to cleanse the temple. This is a pointed challenge, as they're in charge of what happens in the temple area! In effect, therefore, by cleansing the temple, Jesus invaded and infringed on what they considered to be their turf. Jesus, of course, as the Messiah and Son of God, has a higher spiritual authority, conferred on him by God the Father himself, which transcends any human authority such as that of the Jewish leaders and temple authorities.

In his response, interestingly (you can never predict what tack Jesus will be taking when responding to a given challenge or question posed to him), Jesus poses a counter-question. Aligning himself with John the Baptist, he asks his opponents whether they think John's baptism is "from heaven" (i.e., divinely authorized) or "from man" (i.e., self-appointed). Since people commonly thought John was a prophet (a spokesman for God), the Jewish leaders know that they're between a rock and a hard

372. Luke 20:1.

place: if they say "from heaven," they concede Jesus's point that he stands in the prophetic tradition of John the Baptist; if they say "from man," they find themselves in conflict with the common people.[373] So they say they don't know. Jesus replies, "Neither will I tell you by what authority I do these things."[374] The reader knows that Jesus's authority is from heaven.

The Parable of the Wicked Tenants and Various Controversies (20:9–47)

As a sort of allegorical commentary, Jesus goes on to tell people the parable of the wicked tenants. Again, please read the entire parable on your own to gauge the full impact.[375] We've seen that the parable occupies a pivotal place in both Matthew and Mark, and it does in Luke as well, as a climactic indictment of the Jewish leaders who are about to kill Jesus their Messiah. The owner of a vineyard rented it out to tenant farmers and at harvest time sent a series of servants to collect on the harvest. The tenants abuse them all, until at last the owner sends his beloved son, thinking that "perhaps they will respect him."[376] It's easy to see that the owner of the vineyard represents God, the series of servants the Old Testament prophets, and the beloved son Christ, while the tenants represent Israel, which is frequently in the Old Testament depicted as God's vineyard, most famously in Isaiah's Song of the Vineyard.[377]

Outrageously, the tenants kill the son, surmising that now the inheritance will be theirs. Jesus poignantly asks, "What then will the owner of the vineyard do to them?"[378] The answer is obvious: he'll destroy the wicked tenants (the Jewish religious leaders, and even Jerusalem and the temple) and give the vineyard to others (Jesus's new messianic community, i.e., the Twelve, the believing Jewish remnant, a group that would eventually also include believing Gentiles). The people who hear this story are aghast, but Jesus looks straight at them and cites a well-known passage from the Psalms: "The stone that the builders rejected has become the cornerstone."[379] Jesus—the stone the builders (Israel) rejected—had become the cornerstone in God's plan of salvation, and those who rejected him would themselves be destroyed and "be broken to pieces" and utterly crushed.[380] Just as they had persecuted the prophets, they were about to kill God's beloved Son and thus bring God's judgment on themselves.

373. Cf. Luke 3:7–9.
374. Luke 20:8.
375. Luke 20:9–18.
376. Luke 20:13.
377. Isaiah 5.
378. Luke 20:15.
379. Luke 20:17; cf. Psalm 118:22.
380. Luke 20:18.

In response, the scribes and chief priests were enraged and brazen in their opposition. They "sought to lay hands on him," as they knew full well that the parable was directed at them.[381] They put him under constant surveillance and even "sent spies" to catch him in something he might say so they could report him to the Roman governor (Pontius Pilate).[382] In the next few scenes, they attempt to corner Jesus by questioning him on now-familiar controversial issues, such as paying taxes to Caesar[383] and marriage in the resurrection.[384] In each case, Jesus responds impeccably and silences his opponents,[385] demonstrating his superior wisdom and unmatched authority. The chapter closes with Jesus's counter-challenge to his opponents—how can the Messiah be both David's son and his Lord?—and Jesus's warning to his disciples concerning the pride and hypocrisy of the scribes.[386]

The Widow's Mite (21:1–4)

The warning is accentuated in the next scene where Luke narrates that Jesus observed a poor widow who put two small copper coins into the offering box in the temple area. While the scribes "devour widows' houses,"[387] Jesus commends this poor widow for her generosity, which allows Luke to highlight the theme of reversal in God's kingdom once again. Caring for widows and orphans was expected of God's people as these groups were particularly needy and potentially vulnerable. To take advantage of such weak and vulnerable individuals was particularly heinous and despicable. And here Jesus draws attention to a widow who, by her sacrificial giving, put those to shame who put on a pious facade but whose hearts were far from God.

The Lukan Olivet Discourse (21:5–38)

With the time of his departure quickly drawing near, Jesus instructs his disciples concerning the end times. This unit, which is found in all three Synoptic Gospels (but not in John, who stresses the present fulfillment of end-time expectations), is commonly known as the Olivet Discourse.[388] This is now the third time that Jesus has spoken of end-time events, with each passage providing additional detail.[389] Luke's version of

381. Luke 20:19.
382. Luke 20:20.
383. Luke 20:20–26. Cf. Matthew 22:15–22; Mark 12:13–17.
384. Luke 20:27–40. Cf. Matthew 22:23–33; Mark 12:18–27. See the discussion of these two challenges in the previous two Gospels.
385. Luke 20:26, 40.
386. Luke 20:41–47; cf. Psalm 110:1.
387. Luke 20:47.
388. Cf. Matthew 24; Mark 13.
389. Cf. Luke 12:35–40; 17:20–37.

the Olivet Discourse is similar to the accounts found in Matthew and Mark in its basic structure but places greater emphasis on the imminent destruction of the temple and Jerusalem. The discourse gradually moves from the destruction of the temple to the demise of Jerusalem and from there to Christ's return:

I. Setting and Destruction of the Temple
   A. Jesus's Prophecy and the Disciples' Question (21:5–7)
   B. Possible Signs Preceding the End (21:8–19)
II. The Abomination of Desolation and the Destruction of Jerusalem (21:20–24)
III. The Return of Christ
   A. Cosmic Upheaval and the Coming of the Son of Man (21:25–28)
   B. This Generation (21:29–33)
   C. The Timing of Jesus's Return (21:34–38)[390]

In this discourse, Jesus prepares his disciples for the persecution that will take place in the decades following his ascension, still during their lifetime, as well as instructing them regarding the circumstances of his more distant return—the second, glorious coming of "the Son of Man." Perhaps most gripping is the uniquely Lukan reference, "When you see Jerusalem surrounded by armies, then you will know that its [the temple's] desolation is near."[391] In this way, Luke provides more specific details about the coming demise of Jerusalem than any of the other Gospels. In vintage prophetic fashion, the more imminent cataclysmic events surrounding the destruction of the temple and Jerusalem serve as a sort of lens through which to view the more distant events accompanying Jesus's return. Clearly, tumultuous times lay ahead, so Jesus exhorts his disciples to be discerning through the parable of the fig tree.[392] They must constantly stay alert, so they'll be able "to escape all these things" and "to stand before the Son of Man."[393]

390. The following outline is adapted from Andreas J. Köstenberger, Alexander E. Stewart, and Apollo Makara, *Jesus and the Future: Understanding What He Taught about the End Times* (Bellingham, WA: Lexham, 2017), 31–86. Alternatively, the discourse can be divided into two periods: the present age with the destruction of the temple (envisaging the Romans' destruction of the temple and Jerusalem in the year 70) and the end of the age with Jesus's glorious return to earth. Please consult *Jesus and the Future*, 31–86, for a much more detailed discussion of Luke's version of the Olivet Discourse.

391. Luke 21:20 NIV.

392. Luke 21:29–33.

393. Luke 21:36.

JESUS'S WORK IN JERUSALEM (19:28–24:49, CONT.)

The Last Supper and Jesus's Arrest, Crucifixion, and Resurrection (22:1–24:49)

The Plot against Jesus and Judas's Betrayal (22:1–6)

Luke opens the second major subsection of Jesus's work in Jerusalem with the following solemn declaration: "Now the Feast of Unleavened Bread drew near, which is called the Passover."[394] In what follows, Luke narrates the events leading up to Jesus's crucifixion in three parts: preparation, confrontation, and crucifixion.[395] The opening scene, as mentioned, is framed by the approach and arrival of the Passover feast. The chief priests and scribes continue to seek an opportune time to put Jesus to death (with the help of the Romans), though such an occasion had yet to present itself. At this, Judas the betrayer, one of the Twelve, arrives on the scene; chillingly, we're told

394. Luke 22:1; cf. 22:7. As mentioned above, the Greek verb *engizō* (come near) occurs at the beginning of both major subunits in this section, in Luke 19:29 and here in 22:1. In 22:1, Luke uses the terms "Feast of Unleavened Bread" and "Passover" interchangeably, though in verse 7 he makes clear that, within the week of the festival, there was a specific day, the day of Passover in a narrow sense, on which the Passover lamb must be sacrificed.

395. Köstenberger, Kellum, and Quarles, *The Cradle, the Cross, and the Crown*, 331.

that Satan enters him,[396] and he confers with the chief priests. Now, at last, the Jewish leaders have the breakthrough they've long been looking for. They've penetrated Jesus's inner circle, which will enable them to nab him discreetly without attracting undue attention. In this way, they would avoid stirring up a riot, which would rile the Roman authorities, especially during the Passover when Jerusalem's population would swell to massive proportions. Passover was one of the "pilgrim festivals," and many made the trek to the Jewish capital to celebrate the feast there. The chief priests seal the deal with Judas by promising him money for his treachery. Now it is no longer solely they who seek to arrest Jesus, but Judas too is looking for an opportune moment to hand Jesus over to the authorities.[397]

In this way, Luke shows that there is more in play than what appears on the surface—petty partisan politics, jockeying for position, or conflicting commercial, religious, and socioeconomic interests. As the time of Jesus's suffering draws near, Luke highlights the cosmic significance of Jesus's journey to the cross by pointing out that Satan himself is actively working behind the scenes to bring about Jesus's demise. Judas's act of betrayal is ultimately orchestrated by Satan himself, who hatches his wicked schemes to destroy Jesus.[398] Later, when predicting Peter's denials, Jesus will reveal that Satan asked to "sift you like wheat."[399] At his arrest, Jesus will tell his opponents, "this is your hour, and the power of darkness."[400] Jesus's impending death is not the result of mere human ploys but rather the outcome of a cosmic struggle between God and Satan.

The Last Supper (22:7–38)

At one level, things are proceeding almost perfectly. The preparations for celebrating the Passover are marked by God's providential ordering of even the smallest detail. As earlier when rounding up the donkey on which Jesus rode into Jerusalem, the disciples line up the Upper Room and prepare the Passover just as Jesus instructed them to do.[401] When the hour comes and Jesus reclines at table with the twelve apostles, the solemnity

396. Luke is alone among the Gospel writers in saying Satan entered Judas. Note that this is not just any demon (as in Jesus's previous encounters with demon-possessed individuals) but Satan himself. And he is "entering" Judas, which implies Satan taking control of Judas's will and actions. It's important to realize that Judas was not a believer (i.e., he was not saved or regenerate), which is why Satan could enter him. Satan cannot enter true believers.

397. Luke 22:5–6.

398. Luke 22:3.

399. Luke 22:31. The Greek for "you" in verse 31 is plural, referring to the disciples including but not limited to Peter; in verse 32, however, the pronouns shift to the singular, focusing on Peter (emphasis added): "but I have prayed for *you* that *your* faith may not fail. And when *you* have turned again, strengthen *your* brothers."

400. Luke 22:53.

401. Luke 22:13.

of the occasion is palpable: "I have earnestly desired to eat this Passover with you before I suffer. For I tell you I will not eat it until it is fulfilled in the kingdom of God."[402] Jesus's last Passover with his disciples is also the first Lord's Supper, which marks the new covenant Jesus is establishing with them as a believing Jewish remnant and representatives of the new messianic community. At Pentecost, they would be constituted as the New Testament church, to which soon thereafter believing Gentiles would be added as well.[403]

In the context of Luke's narrative, the Last Supper represents the culmination of Jesus's ministry with his disciples. At this festive, solemn occasion, so pregnant with meaning, Jesus reveals to his disciples the purpose of his now-imminent death. His sacrifice will serve as an atonement for the forgiveness of sins, establishing a new covenant through the broken body and shed blood of Christ.[404] In this way, the Passover meal is transformed from a commemoration of God's deliverance of the Israelites from bondage in Egypt to a memorial of Jesus's death for humanity's sins as God's ultimate Passover lamb. As Paul would later write, "For Christ, our Passover lamb, has been sacrificed."[405] The Last Supper is also the culmination of a long series of meals highlighted by Luke that represent tangible signs of Jesus's mercy, forgiveness, and acceptance of sinners.[406]

In his depiction of the Passover, Luke is careful to note that all the events surrounding Jesus's suffering are taking place according to God's plan. As David Garland observes, "Jesus is not being swept away by events but is in command and is accomplishing his divine mission."[407] Preparations for the Passover unfold "just as he [Jesus] had told" Peter and John.[408] During the meal, Jesus predicts Judas's betrayal. He also forecasts Peter's threefold denial before the rooster would crow early the next morning.[409] Yet Jesus is not a mere victim of circumstances; everything unfolds "as it has been determined,"[410] so that "what is written about [him] has its fulfillment."[411] In all of this, Luke makes clear that Jesus's ordeal for our salvation was no accident; it happened in keeping with God's predetermined plan.

402. Luke 22:15–16.
403. See the book of Acts, esp. chapters 2 and 10.
404. Luke 22:20.
405. 1 Corinthians 5:7.
406. Cf. Luke 5:27–32; 7:36–50; 9:11–17; 14:15–24; 15:2; 19:5–7.
407. Garland, *Luke*, 849.
408. Luke 22:13.
409. Luke 22:21, 34. Crazily, in between these predictions, the disciples have another go at arguing who among them is the greatest (Luke 22:24–30). It's hard to believe that they would have this kind of argument right between the Last Supper and Gethsemane!
410. Luke 22:22.
411. Luke 22:37.

GOD'S PLAN OF SALVATION

Luke is very careful in composing his Gospel with a sensitivity to *theology* and *history*, presenting his theology in the form of a historical narrative. With this in mind, he sets forth Jesus's story as the continuation of Israel's story. Together they form "one unfolding plan" that continues in the story of the church in the book of Acts.[412] That plan centers on the arrival of God's salvation in Christ. Luke draws our attention to God's plan of salvation in several ways.[413] First, Luke emphasizes that this salvation is not limited to the redemption of Israel but also includes the Gentiles. In the infancy narrative, Simeon reveals that Jesus will be "a light for revelation to the Gentiles, and for glory to your people Israel."[414] From the outset, the reader anticipates God's universal mission. This culminates in Luke's Great Commission, when Jesus declares that "repentance for the forgiveness of sins should be proclaimed in his name to all nations."[415] Luke distinctly presents Jesus as the Savior for all people.

Second, Luke presents Jesus as the *fulfillment* of God's *promises*. "Fulfillment" language is used throughout the Gospel from the first line to the last scene. The Gospel opens with the words "Inasmuch as many any have undertaken to compile a narrative of the things that have been accomplished [fulfilled] among us. . . ."[416] And the Gospel closes with Jesus telling his disciples that "everything written about me in the Law of Moses and the Prophets and the Psalms must be *fulfilled*."[417] Jesus proceeds to tell his disciples how the Hebrew Scriptures have been fulfilled—through his death and resurrection, the message of forgiveness and repentance, and the message's universal proclamation.[418] As Mark Strauss sums up, "As predicted in the prophets, God has acted through Jesus the Messiah to save his people Israel, and this salvation is now going forth to the whole world."[419]

412. Garland, *Luke*, 975.
413. For a fuller treatment of God's plan of salvation in Luke-Acts, see Bock, *Theology of Luke and Acts*, 122–48.
414. Luke 2:32.
415. Luke 24:47.
416. Luke 1:1.
417. Luke 24:44.
418. Luke 24:46–47.
419. Strauss, *Four Portraits, One Jesus*, 284.

Third, Luke stresses the point that Jesus "must" fulfill God's plan. His life, death, and resurrection are matters of divine *necessity*, expressed through the repeated use of the Greek word *dei* ("must" or "it is necessary").[420] Jesus *must* be in his Father's house.[421] He *must* preach the good news of the kingdom of God.[422] He asks the Emmaus disciples, "Was it not *necessary* that the Christ should suffer these things and enter his glory?"[423] As David Garland explains, "The divine necessity shows that the history of Jesus (through Acts) is rooted in God's plan. These are divinely authorized events."[424] Everything that takes place in the story of Jesus is directed by God and unfolds according to his divine design.

Lastly, Luke emphasizes that the events that fulfill God's plan of salvation happen *today*. This expression appears several times with "a force that points to special acts of God in the program."[425] The angels announce the birth of Jesus the Savior "today."[426] In his inaugural sermon, Jesus declares that the Scripture he has read has been fulfilled "today."[427] In his programmatic declaration to Zacchaeus, he announces, "*Today* salvation has come to this house."[428] The emphasis on "today" highlights "the immediacy and availability" of God's salvation.[429] As Darrell Bock points out, "Right now God makes available such blessings and promises. . . . Salvation is here and now."[430]

Luke wants you to know that God's promises have been fulfilled in Christ and that his salvation is available to you *today*. This is terrific news! God has been faithfully working in history despite human sinfulness. He has kept his word by sending his Son for the forgiveness of our sins. All that's required to receive this salvation is repentance and faith. You don't have to come from a religious background or earn God's favor. In fact, Luke

420. The Greek word *dei* is used ninety-nine times in the New Testament, of which forty are in Luke-Acts.
421. Luke 2:49.
422. Luke 4:43.
423. Luke 24:26.
424. Garland, *Luke*, 975.
425. Bock, *Theology of Luke and Acts*, 135.
426. Luke 2:11.
427. Luke 4:21; cf. Isaiah 61:1–2.
428. Luke 19:9.
429. Bock, *Theology of Luke and Acts*, 135.
430. Bock, *Theology of Luke and Acts*, 135.

makes it unmistakably clear that Jesus welcomes those who are outsiders. Like Zacchaeus, you can know that, through Jesus, today salvation has come, not only to the people of Israel but to everyone who responds to the good news of salvation and forgiveness in the Lord Jesus Christ in repentance and faith.

Jesus's Prayer and Arrest and Peter's Denials (22:39–65)

After the meal, Jesus leads his disciples to the Mount of Olives where he agonizes in prayer—in his humanity dreading the impending suffering, yet resolved to do God's will.[431] Jesus and his disciples have come to the end of a long road, both literally and figuratively. The stage has been set for Jesus's death, burial, and resurrection, the climax of Luke's Gospel. As the passion narrative unfolds, two significant themes emerge: (1) Jesus is in full control of the circumstances surrounding his death; and (2) Jesus suffers while being innocent of all the charges brought against him. We see these two themes running throughout the narrative like two pearls on a string, with Jesus's innocence shining brightly.[432]

In scriptural terms, Luke portrays Jesus as Israel's righteous servant.[433] The scene opens with the Jewish authorities coming to arrest him, armed with swords and clubs as if he were a criminal.[434] Judas the traitor is leading them, betraying Jesus with the famous "Judas kiss." A disciple (John tells us it was Peter) draws his sword and cuts off the ear of the high priest's servant. Jesus stops the nonsense, quickly puts the ear back

431. Luke 22:39–46. Note that Luke, unlike Matthew and Mark, does not specifically mention the garden of Gethsemane by name but instead speaks of the Mount of Olives (v. 39; cf. Matthew 26:36; Mark 14:31; John 18:1 simply speaks of "a garden"). Darrell L. Bock conjectures that the reason may be that Luke often omits Semitic terms (in addition to Gethsemane, Luke also omits Golgotha); see *Luke 9:51–24:53*, Baker Exegetical Commentary on the New Testament (Grand Rapids: Baker, 1996), 1756. Note, however, that Matthew and Mark do mention the Mount of Olives as the place where Jesus and his disciples are headed following the Last Supper (cf. Matthew 26:30; Mark 14:26). On a different matter, note that verses 43–44 (which contain a reference to Jesus's sweat becoming "like great drops of blood falling down to the ground") are likely not original to Luke as they're not found in some early manuscripts such as 𝔓[75] and Codex Alexandrinus (A). While noting that it is a later addition, the verses are included in square brackets in the standard Greek text because of their antiquity and importance in the textual tradition. See Bruce M. Metzger, *A Textual Commentary on the Greek New Testament*, 2nd ed. (Stuttgart: Deutsche Bibelgesellschaft; New York: United Bible Societies, 1994), 151.

432. As Bock (*Luke 9:51–24:53*, 1698) observes, "The main theme is Jesus's righteous suffering as an innocent martyr."

433. Cf. Isaiah 53. Strauss, *Four Portraits, One Jesus*, 277.

434. Luke 22:47–53.

on (!), and asks the arresting officers why they would come to seize him like a common criminal. Any unbiased reader of Luke's narrative will realize that treating Jesus in this way is grotesque, to say the least.

As Jesus himself points out, he was teaching daily in the temple area in a very public forum. There was no need to track him down like this and insinuate he was eluding the authorities and would resist arrest! Nevertheless, Jesus hands himself over to the authorities because this is their "hour."[435] Peter follows at a distance; he ends up denying Jesus three times, just as Jesus predicted.[436] The men guarding Jesus proceed to mock and beat him.[437]

The Jewish Trial (22:66–71)

The early morning witnesses a formal assembly of the Sanhedrin, the Jewish council. Jesus is formally tried and asked point-blank if he is the Messiah. He refuses to answer their question directly, saying only that if he were to tell them, they wouldn't believe, as they've amply demonstrated by rejecting his claims throughout his entire ministry. Then, strikingly, Jesus identifies himself as "the Son of Man" who "shall be seated at the right hand of the power of God," referring to his vindication and enthronement at God's right hand.[438]

At this, the Sanhedrin asks Jesus, "Are you the Son of God, then?" But he only replies, "You say that I am."[439] Jesus doesn't throw his pearls before swine, so to speak. He doesn't openly identify himself as the Messiah only for the Jewish authorities to reject his claim. Yet they can easily read between the lines that, despite Jesus's evasive answers, he really does claim to be the Son of God, as well as the exalted, authoritative Son of Man. This is more than sufficient for them to charge him with blasphemy. In their eyes, Jesus must die.

RECAP

In the previous unit, Luke has narrated Jesus's arrival in Jerusalem, starting with his "triumphal entry," his lament over the city, and the cleansing of the temple. When the Jewish leaders challenge his authority, Jesus responds by telling them the parable of the

435. Luke 22:53.
436. Luke 22:54–62.
437. Luke 22:63–65.
438. Luke 22:69. See Strauss, *Four Portraits, One Jesus*, 287: "Both Matthew and Mark include an allusion to Daniel 7 ('and coming on the clouds of heaven'), but Luke again stresses Jesus's present heavenly reign over his future return in glory."
439. Luke 22:70.

wicked tenants. In this masterful allegorical parable, Jesus threatens that God would give his "vineyard" to others. Jesus, the stone over which they stumbled, is the cornerstone in God's plan of salvation in keeping with Old Testament messianic prophecy. The Jewish authorities now pursue a strategy of catching Jesus in saying something they can use against him. Should we pay taxes to Caesar? Whose wife will a woman who has had multiple husbands during her lifetime be in the eternal state? Nothing works; Jesus proves himself to be more than a match for their trickery. Jesus asks them a counter-question: How can the Messiah be both David's son and his Lord? He warns his disciples against the scribes while commending a poor widow who has given a most generous offering.

At this, Jesus foretells the future destruction of Jerusalem that would serve as a sign of God's judgment and prepare for the glorious return of the "Son of Man." Jesus's final Passover has now arrived. The plot against Jesus achieves a major breakthrough when Judas decides to defect and betray Jesus; Satan enters him to pull the strings behind the scenes. More than party politics or religious controversies are at work; at root, this is a struggle between the forces of God and Satan. As ominous spiritual storm clouds gather, Jesus celebrates the Passover with his apostles. In keeping with Passover symbolism, Jesus establishes a new covenant with them in anticipation of his upcoming death on their behalf. Just as Passover commemorated God's deliverance of the Israelites on the basis of blood smeared on their doorposts in Egypt, so God would deliver believers through Jesus's broken body and shed blood. After this, Jesus engages in agonizing prayer and is arrested. Peter would deny Jesus three times as Jesus had predicted. The section closes with a succinct account of Jesus's Jewish trial.

LORD

The title "Lord" appears in key passages at the beginning and end of Luke's Gospel. Apart from its use as a term of respect, Luke highlights the title to elevate our understanding of Jesus's messianic identity. Upon his birth, the angels announce that Jesus is "Christ *the Lord*."[440] Here, the title is associated with Jesus's identity as Christ and Savior. However, the title is not developed any further until Jesus's final ministry in Jerusalem and the passion narrative. At a critical juncture of his final ministry, Jesus uses the title himself when confronted by the scribes. He quotes Psalm 110:1 (a psalm of David): "The Lord said to my Lord, 'Sit at my right

440. Luke 2:11, emphasis added.

hand, until I make your enemies your footstool.'"[441] He then raises the question: "How can they say that the Christ is David's son?"[442] In other words, how can the Messiah be called David's *son* if David called him *Lord*? Essentially, Jesus is asking which title is more appropriate to use for the Messiah—"Son of David" or "Lord"? Darrell Bock explains, "This text shows Luke as moving the reader from seeing Jesus just as the promised Anointed One to seeing him as Lord."[443]

This comes into even sharper focus during Jesus's trial before the Sanhedrin. When asked if he is the Christ, Jesus responds, "But from now on the Son of Man shall be seated at the right hand of the power of God."[444] He responds first by claiming the title "Son of Man," a reference to Daniel 7:13–14. Generally speaking, the Son of Man is an end-time figure who is given authority by God to rule his kingdom. In addition, Jesus alludes to Psalm 110:1 again when he says the Son of Man will be *seated at the right hand of God*. This is an image of regal and divine authority. According to Jewish tradition, only God sits in heaven.[445] Astoundingly, Jesus says to the Sanhedrin that "from now on" they'll see the Son of Man seated at God's right hand. In effect, Jesus is claiming that he will sit and rule with God after his impending death. What's more, God will do this for him as the ultimate act of vindication. The implications are staggering, which is why the Sanhedrin proceeds to charge Jesus with blasphemy. As Bock states, "This title 'Lord' is a more important title than Messiah, for it pictures Jesus's total authority and his ability and right to serve as an equal with God the Father."[446] Luke presents Jesus not only as the Messiah who saves God's people but also as the exalted Lord who reigns with God forever.

441. Luke 20:42–43.
442. Luke 20:41; cf. 20:44.
443. Bock, *Theology of Luke and Acts*, 180.
444. Luke 22:69.
445. Bock, *Theology of Luke and Acts*, 181.
446. Bock, *Theology of Luke and Acts*, 182.

JESUS'S WORK IN JERUSALEM (19:28–24:49, CONT.)

The Last Supper and Jesus's Arrest, Crucifixion, and Resurrection (22:1–24:49, cont.)

The Roman Trial (23:1–25)

The Crucifixion and Burial (23:26–56)

JESUS'S WORK IN JERUSALEM (19:28–24:49, CONT.)

The Last Supper, Jesus's Arrest, Crucifixion, and Resurrection (22:1–24:49, cont.)

The Roman Trial (23:1–25)

Next, the Jewish leaders rush Jesus over to Pontius Pilate, the Roman governor of Judea.[447] Shrewdly, they frame their charges against Jesus in political terms, knowing that the Romans kept a watchful eye on any potential Jewish rebellion. They tell Pilate that Jesus (1) was misleading their nation, (2) forbade them to pay taxes to Caesar, and (3) claimed to be "Christ, a king."[448] While in their Sanhedrin meeting they focused on theological charges (i.e., blasphemy), when talking to Pilate they make Jesus out to be a threat to Roman rule, something they had to know was disingenuous and completely unfounded.

Nevertheless, despite the travesty of justice that is rapidly unfolding, Jesus maintains his composure. Acknowledging that Jesus, whose home was in Galilee, belonged to Herod Antipas' jurisdiction,[449] Pilate sends him to Herod, who, Luke tells us, was glad to see Jesus, "for he had long desired to see him, because he had heard about him, and

447. Luke 23:1–5. Note how Luke gives a very succinct account of Jesus's Jewish trial (22:66–71; six verses) while covering his Roman trial in considerably greater detail (23:1–25; twenty-five verses). This is in keeping with his Gentile focus and his larger purpose of defending Christianity as innocent of all the charges leveled against it by its (Jewish) opponents following the crucifixion and resurrection (see the book of Acts and the following note).

448. Luke 23:2.

449. Luke's account here is distinctive, as he was keen to show that Jesus was examined by both Herod Antipas, ruler of Galilee, and Pontius Pilate, governor of Judea, and found innocent by both. This would be of special interest and importance for Theophilus, who most likely was a Roman government official (see "Preface: Luke's Purpose (1:1–4)" above). This, in turn, was part of Luke's larger purpose of providing a defense (*apologia*) of Christianity in a first-century Greco-Roman context.

he was hoping to see some sign done by him."[450] Herod questions Jesus at length, but Jesus says nothing. At the same time, the Jewish leaders are there, "vehemently accusing him"![451] One can just picture the scene: Herod presiding, Jesus in front of him saying nothing, and the Jewish authorities lobbying Herod intensely to take action against Jesus. In the end, Herod and his soldiers treat him with contempt, putting a robe on him to mock his royal claims.[452] This shows that unbelieving, sinful humanity has nothing but contempt for Jesus and the good news and salvation he came to bring. In fact, the sinful response is to ridicule Jesus's claims and to despise his apparent weakness.

I still remember when I, shortly before my conversion, mocked my own sister for her interest in Christianity. Then, in his great mercy, God got hold of me, and I experienced a radical conversion. I believe God allowed me to mock Jesus just shortly before my conversion to help me realize that I, too, am one of those sinners who would have mocked Jesus's claims if I had been alive during the proceedings against Jesus. As Pilate is about to find out, you can't take a neutral stance regarding Jesus. You must be either for or against him. I once, as a young Christian, asked a missionary to my native Austria what was the greatest obstacle to his missionary efforts. I'll never forget his one-word answer: "Apathy." I remember thinking, "What?" I thought he was going to say opposition from established religion, or spiritual warfare, or some other major obstacle, but apathy? Over the years, however, I've come to realize just how profound my missionary friend's answer really was.

Ironically, as Luke notes, while Pilate and Herod had previously been enemies, their common contempt for Jesus made them allies.[453] Nevertheless, Pilate realizes that despite the ferocity of the Jewish leaders' accusations, there were no objective grounds for indicting Jesus. So he calls the Jewish leaders and the people together to inform them of the outcome of his investigation: "After examining him before you, behold, I did not find this man guilty of any of your charges against him. Neither did Herod." He adds, "Look, nothing deserving death has been done by him. I will therefore punish and release him."[454] Nothing deserving death? Punish for doing *what*? Luke's reader realizes that Pilate is squirming to get out of a very uncomfortable situation. He also looks incredibly weak, acting as if he needs the Jewish leaders' permission to release Jesus. But he's the Roman governor! It is he who has the authority to release Jesus if he has determined that none of the charges against him is true; that's why the Jewish leaders brought Jesus to him in the first place! Truth is, they need him to pronounce the death sentence, as this was the prerogative of the Romans. Will he oblige, despite his own better judgment?

---

450. Luke 23:8; cf. Mark 6:14; 8:28.
451. Luke 23:10.
452. Luke 23:6–12.
453. Luke 23:12.
454. Luke 23:14–16.

Meanwhile, the crowd refuses to relent and ratchets up their demands. They even ask for the release of Barabbas, a murderer and rebel, in the place of Jesus.[455] The irony here is dreadfully thick. The crowd chooses to call for the release of a proven criminal while urging Pilate to convict an innocent man! What's more, as David Garland explains, "By choosing an insurrectionist over Jesus, the hypocrisy behind the leaders' charges against him is exposed."[456] The release of Barabbas simply reinforces the unmistakable impression that a terrible injustice is being carried out against Jesus. Nevertheless, as the Roman governor, Pilate is in a position to do what's right and release him. He repeats a third time, "What has this man done wrong?"[457] Clearly, the implied answer is "Nothing, nothing at all!" But instead of taking command of the situation, Pilate is pitifully swayed by the rabid voices of the crowd. In the end, he takes the politically expedient route of pacifying the Jewish leaders and sentencing Jesus to be crucified.[458]

The Crucifixion and Burial (23:26–56)

The hour of Jesus's crucifixion has arrived. Luke presents the events surrounding the crucifixion in five scenes:

1. The way to the cross (23:26–31)
2. The crucifixion (23:32–38)
3. The mockery (23:39–43)
4. Jesus's death (23:44–49)
5. Jesus's burial (23:50–56)

In each section, Luke is careful to highlight Jesus's faithfulness in the face of death. In addition, Luke presents a full range of responses to Jesus's death. As Darrell Bock points out, "Luke portrays Jesus's death as a public event that impressed a variety of people in a variety of ways."[459]

On the way to the cross, we see a large crowd of people who lament Jesus's fate. Simon from Cyrene is enlisted to help Jesus carry the cross. He is depicted as a model disciple—one who takes up his cross to follow Jesus.[460] Among the crowd of onlookers,

455. Luke 23:18–19. Even Barabbas's name is deeply ironic: "Bar-abbas," in Aramaic, means "son of the father."
456. Garland, *Luke*, 908. He adds, "Barabbas is truly guilty of the very crimes they have charged Jesus with committing—inciting the people. He has actually sparked an insurrection, and worse, he has committed murder. Jesus has rejected violence and poses no overt threat to Roman order."
457. Luke 23:22 CSB.
458. Luke 23:24–25.
459. Bock, *Luke 9:51–24:53*, 1860.
460. Even though in his case he literally takes up, not his, but Jesus's cross on his behalf! Luke 23:26; cf. Luke 9:23.

a group of women follow Jesus in mourning. Jesus responds to them with a prophetic warning about the destruction of Jerusalem.[461]

At the scene of Jesus's crucifixion, the reaction is drastically different, shifting from mourning to scoffing. The Jewish leaders ridicule Jesus: "He saved others; let him save himself, if he is the Christ of God, his Chosen One!"[462] The Roman soldiers join in the mockery. The climax of humiliation comes when one of the criminals crucified with Jesus echoes the taunts of the leaders.[463] The irony at the scene of the cross is again very thick. It's precisely because he's the Messiah that he must suffer and die to save his people from their sins.

Despite the cruelty and abuse, Jesus is undaunted in fulfilling God's plan. Luke highlights Jesus's faithfulness to the very end in several ways. First, Jesus prays for the forgiveness of his enemies.[464] Jesus's prayer underscores the purpose of his death—to atone for the sins of humanity. Second, he ministers to the repentant criminal crucified next to him. The criminal is convicted about his sin and recognizes that Jesus "has done nothing wrong."[465] Jesus assures him with the promise, "Today you will be with me in paradise."[466] The criminal's repentance and faith is a portrait of salvation. Third, Jesus's death is accompanied by several remarkable signs including darkness at midday and the curtain in the temple being torn in two.[467] These signs demonstrate that something far greater than a criminal's execution is taking place. In his final prayer, Jesus cries out, "Father, into your hands I commit my spirit!"[468] The Jewish leaders wanted to "lay hands on" Jesus,[469] but in the end Jesus commits his life into the Father's hands. Robert Karris comments, "Instead of trying to save himself, Jesus gave himself trustingly into the hands of his Father. . . . In this way, he proved himself to be the righteous one and son of God."[470]

After Jesus's final breath, Luke makes note of three specific responses to his death. Upon seeing what has happened, the centurion gives glory to God, exclaiming, "Certainly this man was innocent!"[471] Similar to the way it functions in Mark's Gospel, the

461. Luke 23:27–31; cf. Luke 13:34–35; 21:23; Hosea 10:8.
462. Luke 23:35.
463. Luke 23:36–39. Also, note the possible *inclusio* between Luke 4:23 ("Surely you will quote this proverb to me: 'Physician, heal yourself!'" [NIV]) and Luke 23:37 ("If you are the king of the Jews, save yourself" [NIV]).
464. Luke 23:34.
465. Luke 23:41.
466. Luke 23:43.
467. Luke 23:44–45.
468. Luke 23:46; cf. Psalm 31:5.
469. Luke 20:19.
470. Robert J. Karris, "Luke 23:47 and the Lucan View of Jesus's Death," *Journal of Biblical Literature* 105 (1986): 67, cited in Garland, *Luke*, 928.
471. Luke 23:47.

centurion's statement serves as the climax of a lengthy list of declarations of Jesus's innocence throughout the passion narrative.[472] The Greek word for "innocent" (*dikaios*) can also be translated as "righteous." Luke may be playing on both meanings here to emphasize that Jesus is both innocent of wrongdoing and righteous in his suffering. The same word is also used in the messianic prophecy of Isaiah 53.[473] There, Isaiah speaks of a suffering servant who is "the righteous one" and who will bear the sins of his people. The term is also picked up later in Acts, where it becomes a messianic title for Jesus: "The Righteous One."[474]

Next, Luke describes the reaction of the crowd that gathered to witness Jesus's death. They depart "beating their breasts," sensing the gravity of what has taken place.[475] In addition, Luke highlights "all his acquaintances" and "the women who had followed him from Galilee."[476] "Acquaintances" refers to a group of disciples larger than the Twelve (now minus Judas). Luke has mentioned some of the women previously during Jesus's ministry in Galilee.[477] They "stood at a distance" to separate themselves from the crowd and yet remain with Jesus until the very end.

Finally, Luke makes special note of Joseph of Arimathea.[478] While a member of the Sanhedrin, Joseph was not involved in the plot and decision to kill Jesus. He is depicted as a faithful disciple who honors Jesus with a proper burial. The women also honor Jesus by anointing his body with spices for burial. Each of the burial preparations is done in accordance with Jewish law before the Sabbath. The day of rest serves as a segue to the next scene.

472. Luke 23:4, 14–15, 22, 41.
473. Isaiah 53:11 LXX.
474. Acts 3:14–15; 7:52; 22:14. See Garland, *Luke*, 929.
475. Luke 23:48.
476. Luke 23:49.
477. Luke 8:1–3.
478. Luke 23:50–56.

JESUS'S WORK IN JERUSALEM (19:28–24:49, CONT.)
The Last Supper and Jesus's Arrest, Crucifixion, and Resurrection (22:1–24:49, cont.)
The Empty Tomb and Resurrection Appearances (24:1–53)
The Women at the Tomb (24:1–12)
The Two Disciples on the Road to Emmaus (24:13–35)
The Eleven Disciples in Jerusalem (24:36–49)

JESUS'S WORK IN JERUSALEM (19:28–24:49, CONT.)

The Last Supper, Jesus's Arrest, Crucifixion, and Resurrection (22:1–24:49, cont.)

The Empty Tomb and Resurrection Appearances (24:1–53)

Following the Messiah's crucifixion and burial, Jesus, the Righteous One, is vindicated by God through his resurrection. Luke records three separate resurrection appearances on "the first day of the week" (i.e., Sunday):[479] (1) to the women at the tomb (24:1–12); (2) to the two disciples on the road to Emmaus (24:13–35); and (3) to the eleven disciples in Jerusalem (24:36–49).[480]

The Women at the Tomb (24:1–12). The women are first to arrive at Jesus's tomb early that morning. They come to bring the spices they had prepared with no expectation that Jesus would be raised from the dead. They're "perplexed" to find the body of Jesus missing.[481] They're greeted by two angels, who announce, "He is not here, but has

479. Luke 24:1.

480. See Perry G. Phillips, "The Post-Resurrection Appearances of Christ (Luke 24)," in Beitzel, *Lexham Geographic Commentary*, 518–26.

481. Luke 24:4.

risen."[482] In the mind of the readers of Luke's Gospel, this triggers the memory of Jesus's words during his ministry that he would "rise on the third day."[483] The women "remembered his words" and relay the message to the apostles. Peter responds emphatically and goes to see the empty tomb for himself.

The Two Disciples on the Road to Emmaus (24:13–35). In the next scene, Jesus appears to two disciples on the road to Emmaus, a village about seven miles outside Jerusalem.[484] This episode represents Luke's unique contribution to the resurrection accounts in the Gospels; he places this appearance prominently in his resurrection narrative and presents it at great length. Like the women, the two disciples—one named (Cleopas), one unnamed—have no expectation of Jesus's resurrection as they're leaving Jerusalem for the nearby village of Emmaus.[485] Upon meeting Jesus on the road—with his identity hidden from them—they express their profound disappointment at his tragic death. As Mark Strauss explains, "Cleopas and his companion represent the discouragement and unbelief of Jesus's followers."[486] Jesus responds by rebuking them for their hardness of heart and points them back to the Scriptures: "And beginning with Moses and all the Prophets, he interpreted to them in all the Scriptures the things concerning himself."[487]

The two disciples invite Jesus to their home to share a meal with them. When they break bread together, "their eyes [are] opened, and they [recognize] him."[488] At this, they respond exuberantly, saying, "Did not our hearts burn within us while he talked to us on the road, while he opened to us the Scriptures?"[489] They proceed to find the apostles already announcing, "The Lord has risen indeed, and has appeared to Simon!"[490] This is yet another report of a resurrection appearance that clearly was totally unexpected

482. Luke 24:6.
483. Luke 24:7 CSB.
484. Bock (*Luke 9:51–24:53*, 1908) mentions that there is a textual variant, and the location of Emmaus is uncertain. He notes that, in any case, Emmaus is in the vicinity of Jerusalem, which is of special interest to Luke. Also, he notes the historical value of this account as it is hard to imagine that the story would have been fabricated and attached to such an obscure village (*Luke 9:51–24:53*, 1909).
485. Cleopas may be named because he is Luke's eyewitness source for this account; see Bauckham, *Jesus and the Eyewitnesses*, 47, who contends that Cleopas is the husband of "Mary the wife of Clopas" (a Semitic form of the Greek name Cleopas), who is mentioned as one of the women near the cross in John 19:25. The other disciple is most likely another male disciple (assumed by Bock, who speaks simply of "the two men"; see *Luke 9:51–24:53*, 1909), though it could have been Cleopas's wife (see the list of options in Bock, *Luke 9:51–24:53*, 1911, who says "suggestions abound").
486. Strauss, *Four Portraits, One Jesus*, 279.
487. Luke 24:27.
488. Luke 24:31.
489. Luke 24:32.
490. Luke 24:34.

and certainly not imagined or invented. Luke did some excellent research here, since he, as mentioned, is the only Gospel writer to feature this amazing story. Seeing the great variety and large number of resurrection appearances of Jesus can strengthen our faith considerably, as it's highly unlikely that all of them are fictional or mere figments of imagination. This is yet another example of why we can be glad that we have four Gospels rather than only one.

The Eleven Disciples in Jerusalem (24:36–49). In the final episode, Jesus appears to the Eleven. The disciples are initially startled and frightened by his appearance, but Jesus seeks to allay their fears by issuing the invitation, "See my hands and feet, that it is I myself."[491] Throughout the entire scene, Luke emphasizes the reality of Jesus's bodily resurrection. He is not a spirit or ghost; he even eats a piece of broiled fish in the presence of his followers! Jesus proceeds to remind them that everything has happened in accordance with his words. In fact, "everything written about [him] in the Law of Moses and the Prophets and the Psalms must be fulfilled."[492] This reiterates his message to the Emmaus disciples: it was "necessary"[493] for Jesus to suffer that the Scriptures might be fulfilled. As Darrell Bock explains, "Jesus makes it clear that he is the subject of these Scriptures and that when it comes to God's promise, he is at the center of those events."[494] As in the case of the Emmaus disciples, Jesus "opened their minds to understand the Scriptures."[495] Do you remember that Jesus began his public ministry by reading Scripture and announcing its fulfillment?[496] Here, at the end of his ministry, he explains how the Scriptures have all been fulfilled.

491. Luke 24:39.
492. Luke 24:44. The Law, the Prophets, and the Psalms (or Writings) represent the three major divisions of the Hebrew Bible.
493. The same word for "necessary" is used in Luke 24:26, 44. The events surrounding Jesus's death and resurrection were ordained by God to accomplish salvation.
494. Bock, *Luke 9:51–24:53*, 1935.
495. Luke 24:45.
496. Luke 4:16–21.

JESUS'S RESURRECTION APPEARANCES

The four Gospels, the book of Acts, and Paul's first letter to the Corinthians mention at least twelve resurrection appearances of Jesus to individuals or groups totaling well over five hundred people. These appearances took place over a period of several weeks, starting with the day on which Jesus rose from the dead. None of the Gospels includes all the appearances, but each of them features (or at least alludes to) at least one. What follows is a likely reconstruction of the sequence of appearances.

Recipients/ Location	Date/ Time	Matt.	Mark	Luke	John	Acts	1 Cor.
Number of appearances		2	1	5	5	2	4
First Sunday							
1. Empty tomb	Early morning	28:1–10	16:1–8	24:1–12	20:1–9		
2. Mary Magdalene/tomb	Early morning				20:11–18		
3. Peter/Jerusalem	Late morning?			24:34			15:5
4. Two disciples/ Emmaus road	Midday/ afternoon			24:13–32			
5. Ten disciples/ Upper Room	Evening			24:36–43	20:19–25		
Second Sunday (one week later)							
6. Eleven/ Upper Room	Evening				20:26–29		15:5
Subsequently (prior to Pentecost)							

Recipients/ Location	Date/ Time	Matt.	Mark	Luke	John	Acts	1 Cor.
7. Seven disciples/ Sea of Galilee	Daybreak				21:1–23		
8. Eleven/mountain in Galilee	Sometime later	28:16–20					
9. More than five hundred	Sometime later						15:6
10. James	Sometime later						15:7
11. Disciples/ Mount of Olives	Forty days later			24:44–49		1:3–8	
12. Saul/road to Damascus	Later					9:1–19	

Throughout the resurrection narrative, Luke highlights the process by which one comes to recognize the risen Lord.[497] An essential step in this process is understanding the Scriptures in light of Christ's fulfillment. Jesus summarizes the basic content of Scripture by way of three verbs: (1) Christ would "suffer," (2) he would "rise," and (3) repentance for the forgiveness of sins would be "proclaimed" or "preached" to all nations.[498] Darrell Bock states, "They key point of Luke 24:46–47 is that everything from suffering to universal proclamation has been predicted in the Scriptures."[499] Many of the details in this last scene anticipate themes that will be picked up in the book of Acts. The disciples are "witnesses" to the things Jesus did and taught. Jesus also promises to send "the promise of my Father," the Holy Spirit.[500] He directs his followers to stay in Jerusalem until the pouring out of the Spirit.

497. Garland, *Luke*, 935.

498. Regarding Jesus's suffering, Luke has invoked various psalms, such as Psalms 22, 31, 69, and 118. He has also referred to Isaiah 53. The resurrection is defended in Acts 2 from Psalms 16:10 and 110:1. The focus on preaching is Luke's version of the Great Commission (cf. Matthew 28:18–20) and constitutes the future mission of the church. See Bock, *Theology of Luke and Acts*, 130–34.

499. Bock, *Theology of Luke and Acts*, 133.

500. Luke 24:49.

EPILOGUE: THE ASCENSION (24:50–53)

EPILOGUE: THE ASCENSION (24:50–53)

The Gospel ends with a brief epilogue. In an unusual, distinctive scene, Jesus is shown to ascend to heaven from Bethany outside Jerusalem.[501] The disciples return to Jerusalem, praising God with boundless joy.[502] This ending prepares the reader for the opening scene of Acts and all that Jesus will continue to do through his apostles and the community of believers in the years following his ascension. While coverage of the book of Acts goes beyond the scope of the present volume, the fact remains that Acts is volume 2 of Luke (making Luke's the only Gospel with a sequel). The book of Acts starts out with the following preface: "In the first book, O Theophilus, I have dealt with all that Jesus began to do and teach, until the day when he was taken up, after he had given commands through the Holy Spirit to the apostles whom he had chosen. He presented himself alive to them after his suffering by many proofs, appearing to them during forty days and speaking about the kingdom of God."[503] We can reasonably infer that in Luke's second book, the book of Acts, he narrated what Jesus *continued* to do in and through his successor on earth, the Holy Spirit, and his apostles. In this way, Jesus didn't vanish from the scene but continued to be a major player (to put it mildly) in the emergence of the church.

What's more, in the following verses in the book of Acts, Luke tells us that the risen Jesus told his followers not to leave Jerusalem but to wait for the coming of the Holy Spirit, which he had promised and which would take place "not many days from now."[504] Again, they asked him the question all Jews were wondering about: "Lord, will

501. Luke 24:50–51. Note that the references to the ascension provide a literary bookend (*inclusio*) connecting Luke 9:51 with 24:50, encompassing Luke 9:51–53 under the rubric of preliminaries to Jesus's ascension.
502. Luke 24:52–53. Note that while Matthew and Mark end in Galilee, Luke ends in Jerusalem. This may be because Luke's sequel, the book of Acts, begins in Jerusalem, especially with the pouring out of the Spirit at Pentecost. It may also be because of Luke's special focus on Jerusalem as part of his geographical plan, which sees the gospel move from Galilee via the lengthy travel narrative to Jerusalem (Luke's Gospel) and subsequently from Jerusalem and Judea to Samaria and the empire's capital, Rome (cf. Acts 1:8). Compare also the temptation narratives in Matthew 4 and Luke 4, where Luke features the temptation that takes place in Jerusalem at the temple as the third and final one (compared to Matthew, who features it second), possible indicating Luke's emphasis on Jerusalem.
503. Acts 1:1–3.
504. Acts 1:5.

you at this time restore the kingdom to Israel?"[505] Jesus didn't directly answer the question but implied that this would have to wait until his return, which would happen at a time known only to the Father. In the meantime, his followers would "receive power when the Holy Spirit has come upon" them, and they would be his "witnesses in Jerusalem and in all Judea and Samaria, and to the end of the earth."[506]

At this, Jesus "was lifted up," and a cloud hid him from their sight.[507] In what is one of my favorite humorous moments recorded in Scripture, the disciples are still staring into the sky as two angels suddenly appear and address them, saying, "Men of Galilee, why do you stand looking into heaven? This Jesus, who was taken up from you into heaven, will come in the same way as you saw him go into heaven."[508] The disciples may have felt a little sheepish at that point, their heads spinning after all they had recently witnessed. What a roller coaster it had been! They had been punched in the stomach at Jesus's crucifixion and burial, but then sorrow had turned into hopeful expectation and even jubilant celebration when they had seen the resurrected Jesus. After this, there had been a brief time when Jesus had further instructed them about God's kingdom before he had left them in eager anticipation of the arrival of the Holy Spirit at Pentecost. In this way, the reach of Jesus's mission would continue, and he would personally direct the church's mission from his exalted state.

505. Acts 1:6.
506. Acts 1:8.
507. Acts 1:9.
508. Acts 1:11.

CHAPTER 5

The Good News according to JOHN

Jesus the God-Man and Revealer of God the Father

JUST THE FACTS

The good news of eternal life for all who believe in Jesus the Messiah and Son of God

Written by John the apostle, the son of Zebedee, one of the twelve apostles of Jesus

John was closest to Jesus during his earthly ministry and reveals his true divine identity

WHO WAS JOHN?

Like Matthew, John was a member of the twelve apostles.[1] John was one of the first followers of Jesus. What's more, John was a member of Jesus's inner circle of three apostles consisting of Peter, John's brother James, and John himself. As such, John was privileged to witness momentous events such as the raising of Jairus's twelve-year-old daughter, Jesus's glorious transfiguration, and Jesus's agonizing prayer in the garden of Gethsemane.

In his Gospel, John stakes a bold claim of eyewitness testimony that is second to none, including even the apostle Peter.[2] A Galilean fisherman, he may have been the youngest member of the twelve and the only apostle to live to a ripe old age without being martyred for his faith.[3] In his Gospel, John modestly calls himself "the disciple whom Jesus loved."[4] There is little doubt that John was one of the greatest theologians the world has ever known.[5]

HOW DOES JOHN TELL THE STORY OF JESUS?

Like Matthew, Mark, and Luke, John writes a Gospel—that is, a narrative centered on Jesus's life and earthly ministry culminating in his crucifixion, burial, resurrection,

1. See Andreas J. Köstenberger, L. Scott Kellum, and Charles L. Quarles, *The Cradle, the Cross, and the Crown: An Introduction to the New Testament* (Nashville: B&H, 2009), 351–54.
2. See esp. John 21:15–25.
3. John's brother James was martyred in the year 42 (see Acts 12:2).
4. See, e.g., John 21:20.
5. For a thorough discussion of the authorship of John's Gospel and why it matters, see Andreas J. Köstenberger, "FTC Workshop on the Gospel of John: Authorship, John's Prologue, and the Cana Cycle (John 2–4)," *Midwestern Journal of Theology* (Spring 2019): 2–11.

and commissioning of his followers. There is a nice symmetry to his Gospel, as John begins with a lengthy prologue and concludes with an extended epilogue.[6] In between these sections, John presents the life of Jesus in the form of a two-part drama: the Book of Signs and the Book of Exaltation.[7] The backbone of the Book of Signs, as its name suggests, consists of selected messianic signs performed by Jesus, most likely seven in number. The Book of Signs ends with a lament over the Jewish rejection of Jesus.[8]

The second half of the Gospel, the Book of Exaltation, then shows Jesus's final instruction of his inner circle, the twelve apostles. In this Upper Room or Farewell Discourse, which is unique to John's Gospel, Jesus talks to his followers about life after his departure: the implications of his death on the cross, the coming of the Holy Spirit after his ascension, and the inevitable persecution that will ensue.[9] The second half of the Gospel climaxes in the passion narrative, which exhibits a special focus on Jesus's sovereign control of events and provides a detailed account of his Roman trial before the governor, Pontius Pilate.[10] The account of Jesus's crucifixion, burial, and resurrection is followed by a narration of the risen Jesus's appearances to Mary Magdalene and three groups of disciples, as well as an account of Jesus's final words to Peter and to the author himself, the apostle John.[11]

WHAT ARE SOME OF JOHN'S DISTINCTIVE EMPHASES?

Writing a generation after the other three Gospels included in our Bibles, John, soaring like an eagle, penned a Gospel that is truly the high point of the fourfold Gospel according to Matthew, Mark, Luke, and John in our New Testament. While the Synoptic Gospels—Matthew, Mark, and Luke—resemble each other in many ways, John breaks new ground. This is even more remarkable as the three evangelists preceding him include a large amount of material in their respective accounts of Jesus's three-and-a-half-year ministry. John, it seems, is determined not merely to repeat what has already been covered in the other Gospels (though he does, of course, include indispensable material such as Jesus's crucifixion, burial, and resurrection). Instead, he is going out of his way to present fresh information. What's more, where he does overlap with Matthew, Mark, and/or Luke, he significantly deepens our understanding of the theological significance of events in the life of Jesus, a fact that has earned his work the epithet "the spiritual Gospel."[12]

6. John 1:1–18 and chap. 21, respectively.
7. Chaps. 2–12 and 13–20, respectively. John 1:19–51 provides the introduction to Jesus's ministry (see below).
8. John 12:36b–50.
9. Chaps. 13–17.
10. Chaps. 18–20.
11. Chap. 21.
12. Clement of Alexandria, cited in Eusebius, *Ecclesiastical History* 6.14.

John starts out his Gospel with a magnificent prologue that sets Jesus's coming into this world into an eternal, cosmic perspective. In a masterful, even stunning opening, John begins his prologue with the assertion, "In the beginning was the Word, and the Word was with God, and the Word was God."[13] In introducing his account of the life and ministry of Jesus in this way, John echoes the opening words of the entire Bible: "In the beginning God created the heavens and the earth."[14] This underscores the momentous significance of Jesus's coming. He was the Word who was in the beginning. Not only did he—prior to his coming into this world—exist *with* God, the eternal Creator; he himself *was* God! For any Jew reading this opening claim—that Jesus was to be placed alongside God the Creator—this assertion wouldn't only have been shocking; it would have been deeply offensive, as it flew in the face of the most distinctive belief of Judaism—that there was one, *and only one*, God, in contrast to the many gods of the surrounding nations.[15] But John, the author, himself a Jew, is unapologetic that while "no one has ever seen God," "the one and only Son, who is himself God and is in closest relationship with the Father"—Jesus!—"has made him known."[16] In this way, John's prologue sets up the following account of Jesus's life and ministry as a narration of how Jesus made God the Father known in both word and deed.

In comparison to the Synoptics, John's worldview is rather unique. John sees the world in polarities—that is, in sets of opposites: above and below, light and darkness, love and hate. John's favorite Old Testament theologian is doubtless the prophet Isaiah, from whom he derives his "sending Christology"—his presentation of Jesus as the Word sent by God to accomplish his mission on earth, and to return to his sender once the mission is accomplished.[17] He also borrows from Isaiah the depiction of Jesus as "lifted up"—that is, both physically lifted up in crucifixion and spiritually exalted by God in resurrection. Also, in a dual quotation from both major portions of Isaiah, John closes his Book of Signs to show that Israel's rejection of Jesus's messianic mission fulfilled Old Testament prophecy. You can see John's indebtedness to Isaiah on virtually every page of his Gospel. Another unique feature of John's Gospel is his realized eschatology—that is, his belief that we can experience Jesus's presence and an abundant life already in the here and now.

---

13. John 1:1.
14. Genesis 1:1 NIV.
15. See Deuteronomy 6:4: "Hear, O Israel: The Lord our God, the Lord is one." If you are interested in exploring this topic further, you may want to read chapter 1 in Andreas J. Köstenberger and Scott R. Swain, *Father, Son and Spirit: The Trinity and John's Gospel*, New Studies in Biblical Theology 24 (Downers Grove, IL: InterVarsity Press, 2008).
16. John 1:18 NIV.
17. Cf. Isaiah 55:10–11; see below.

WHAT ARE THE MAJOR CONTOURS OF JOHN'S ACCOUNT?

Prologue: The Word Became Flesh (1:1–18)

The Voice in the Wilderness and the Promise of Greater Things (1:19–51)
- Day 1: John's Witness regarding Himself (1:19–28)
- Day 2: John's Witness regarding Jesus (1:29–34)
- Days 3 and 4: Jesus's Call of His First Disciples (1:35–42)
- Day 5: Jesus's Call of Additional Disciples and Promise of "Greater Things" (1:43–51)

The Book of Signs: The Seven Signs of Jesus the Messiah (2:1–12:50)
- *The Cana Cycle (2:1–4:54)*
  - Day 7: The First Sign of Jesus: Turning Water into Wine (2:1–12)
  - The First Passover and Second Sign: Clearing the Jerusalem Temple (2:13–22)
  - Jerusalem: Jesus's Conversation with Nicodemus (2:23–3:21)
  - Judea: John's Continued Witness regarding Jesus (3:22–36)
  - Samaria: Jesus's Conversation with a Samaritan Woman (4:1–42)
  - Galilee: The Third Sign: Healing a Gentile Official's Son (4:43–54)
- *The Festival Cycle (5:1–10:42)*
  - The Fourth Sign: Healing an Invalid (5:1–17)
  - The Sabbath Controversy (5:18–47)
  - The Fifth Sign: Feeding the Five Thousand (6:1–15)
  - Jesus Walks on Water (6:16–21)
  - The Bread of Life Discourse (6:22–71)
  - Jesus at the Feast of Tabernacles (7:1–8:59)
  - The Sixth Sign: Healing a Man Born Blind (9:1–41)
  - The Good Shepherd Discourse (10:1–21)
  - Jesus at the Feast of Dedication (10:22–42)
- *The Climactic Sign and the Jewish Rejection of the Messiah (11:1–12:50)*
  - The Seventh Sign: The Raising of Lazarus (11:1–44)
  - The Sanhedrin's Plot against Jesus (11:45–57)
  - The Anointing of Jesus (12:1–11)
  - The Triumphal Entry (12:12–19)
  - The Dawning Era of the Gentiles (12:20–36a)
  - Conclusion to the Book of Signs: Jewish Unbelief toward Jesus the Messiah (12:36b–50)

WHAT ARE THE MAJOR CONTOURS OF JOHN'S ACCOUNT?

The Book of Exaltation (13:1–20:31)

The Last Supper and the Farewell Discourse (13:1–17:26)

The Last Supper and the Departure of the Betrayer (13:1–30)

The Farewell Discourse (13:31–16:33)

First and Second Teaching Cycles on Life after Jesus's Departure (13:31–14:31; 15:1–16:33)

Jesus's Final Prayer (17:1–26)

The Passion Narrative (18:1–20:31)

Jesus's Arrest and Jewish Trial before Annas, and Peter's Denials (18:1–27)

Jesus's Roman Trial before Pilate (18:28–19:16a)

Jesus's Crucifixion and Burial (19:16b–42)

The Empty Tomb and Jesus's Resurrection Appearances to Mary Magdalene and the Eleven (20:1–29)

Conclusion to the Book of Exaltation and Gospel Proper: John's Purpose for Writing (20:30–31)

Epilogue: Jesus's Final Appearance and Words (21:1–25)

Jesus's Third Resurrection Appearance and Final Words to Peter and the Beloved Disciple (21:1–23)

Conclusion to Entire Gospel (21:24–25)

PROLOGUE: THE WORD BECAME FLESH (1:1–18)

THE WORD

What is truly distinctive about John's presentation of Jesus is found at the very beginning. While Mark jumps right into the ministry of John the Baptist and the adult Jesus, and Matthew and Luke start with Jesus's infancy narrative and the virgin conception and birth, John begins in eternity past—with the Word's presence already at creation alongside God the Creator. Not merely is Jesus the "son of Abraham" and "son of David" as Matthew tells us, or even the "son of Adam" as Luke contends; Jesus's roots go back all the way to eternity past, when "in the beginning God created the heavens and the earth."[18] It is this Word of God, his self-expression and himself God, that became flesh in Jesus. In this striking assertion, John considerably deepens our understanding of who Jesus truly is.

As Lewis Carroll once wrote, "'Begin at the beginning,' the King said, very gravely, 'and go on till you come to the end: then stop.'"[19] John starts at the beginning—but not, as the Gospels before him did, the beginning of Jesus's human existence (his birth as a baby in a Bethlehem manger). Instead, he reaches all the way back into eternity and observes that in the very beginning Jesus—the Word—was already there! Thus, John peels back the layers of time and shows that Jesus's birth as a human child didn't mark the beginning of his existence; it merely constituted the momentous event when the preexistent Word took on human form:

In the beginning was the Word,
    and the Word was with God,
    and the Word was God.
    He was in the beginning with God. . . .
And the Word became flesh . . .[20]

---

18. Genesis 1:1 NIV.
19. Lewis Carroll, *Alice's Adventures in Wonderland* (New York: Macmillan, 1898), 182.
20. John 1:1–2, 14 (formatting here and below my own). For the grammatical issues involved in verse 1, especially in the translation "the Word was God," see Murray J. Harris, *John*, Exegetical Guide to the Greek New Testament (Nashville: B&H, 2015), 18–20.

Yet John doesn't present himself merely as an armchair theologian or objective, neutral historian. Rather, he identifies himself as a participant in the events he is about to narrate; in fact, he is a primary eyewitness:

> . . . and we have seen his glory,
> glory as of the only Son from the Father,
> full of grace and truth.[21]

"We" in the above statement most likely refers to the apostle John, the author of this Gospel, as well as the other members of the Twelve who accompanied Jesus throughout his earthly ministry, witnessed his messianic signs, and heard his extended discourses that revealed Jesus's true nature and unique relationship with God. As John continues in his prologue,

> For from his fullness we have all received,
> grace instead of grace. . . .
> No one has ever seen God;
> the only God, who is at the Father's side,
> he has made him known.[22]

Read through John's prologue reflectively and slowly, even reverently, and ponder John's words regarding Jesus "the Word." In verses 1–5, John speaks of the Word's activity in creation:

> All things were made through him,
> and without him nothing was made that was made.
> In him was life . . .[23]

Because everything was created in and through the Word, and because the Word has life in himself, the Word (Jesus) can give life (eternal life) to those who trust in him.[24] This will be John's message in the remainder of the Gospel. John's Gospel is an invitation for

21. John 1:14.
22. John 1:16, 18. The ESV translates "grace upon grace," though the Greek original for "upon" is *anti*, which is better translated "instead of." The idea here is that God had previously revealed himself in the law given through Moses; now he revealed himself in an even more perfect way, the person of Jesus Christ, in both word and deed.
23. John 1:3–4.
24. See John 1:12.

you, and all who read it, to believe in Jesus, the Word-become-flesh, the Messiah and Son of God![25]

Then, in verses 6–8, and again in verse 15, John (the evangelist) introduces another John, who will turn out to be a significant character in the story of Jesus—John the Baptist (to avoid confusion, the evangelist calls himself "the disciple whom Jesus loved" and reserves the name "John" exclusively for the Baptist). This John, as Jesus's forerunner, bore witness to Jesus as the first of a series of witnesses to Jesus throughout the Gospel. In this way, the evangelist assembles a veritable cloud of witnesses attesting to Jesus's true messianic identity that would put the world on trial for its rejection of Jesus. While later the Jewish high priest and the Roman governor were putting *Jesus* on trial, the evangelist pointedly observes that it was in fact *they* who were on trial for rejecting Jesus.[26] What a powerful way of turning the tables on those who put Jesus on the cross rather than worshiping him as Lord and God![27]

Next, in verses 9–14, John highlights the incarnation ("enfleshment") of the Word and extols the privilege of becoming a child of God through faith in Jesus. This portion of the prologue is at the very heart of John's message regarding what Jesus means for you and for me.[28] Take a closer look at the staircase-like structure of the prologue:

The Word's activity in creation (vv. 1–5)
  John's witness regarding Jesus (vv. 6–8)
    The Word's incarnation and the privilege of becoming God's children (vv. 9–14)
  John's witness regarding Jesus (v. 15)
The final word in the revelation of God the Father (vv. 16–18)

In the above diagram, you can see that verses 9–14 on the Word's incarnation and the privilege of becoming God's children epitomize the good news John has for his readers. Starting in verse 10, we read:

25. See John's purpose statement in 20:31: "These [messianic signs of Jesus] are written so that you may believe that Jesus is the Christ, the Son of God, and that by believing you may have life in his name."

26. Scholars refer to this as the "cosmic trial motif" in John's Gospel. See esp. Andrew T. Lincoln, *Truth on Trial: The Lawsuit Motif in the Fourth Gospel* (Peabody, MA: Hendrickson, 2000); and Andreas J. Köstenberger, *A Theology of John's Gospel and Letters: The Word, the Christ, the Son of God*, Biblical Theology of the New Testament (Grand Rapids: Zondervan, 2009), chapter 11, "The Cosmic Trial Motif."

27. As one of the Twelve, Thomas, does at the climax of the Gospel: see John 20:28.

28. See R. Alan Culpepper, "The Pivot of John's Prologue," *New Testament Studies* 27 (1980–81): 1–31. On "believing," see Harris, *John*, 31–32.

He was in the world,
    and the world was made through him,
    yet the world did not know him.
He came to his own,
    and his own people did not receive him.
But to all who did receive him,
    who believed in his name,
    he gave the right to become children of God.[29]

In these verses, John strikes an ominous note: the rejection of the Word by the world he had made. There is profound irony—even tragedy—in this: How could the world reject its Creator? How could people reject the very one who made them? This seems utterly preposterous and inconceivable. Yet this is exactly what happened, as the remaining narrative will show. At the climax of the escalating conflict between Jesus and the Jewish authorities, Jesus was put on a cross. He was buried, and on the third day rose from the dead—the gospel in a nutshell! The eternal Word in the flesh, Jesus the God-Man, died a real human death, so that everyone who believes in him can receive eternal life and become a child of God.

After returning briefly to the witness of John the Baptist in verse 15, the evangelist concludes his preamble to the story of Jesus with a reference to the grace and truth that came through Jesus, relating his coming to "the law . . . given through Moses."[30] The law, John observes, furnished evidence of God's gracious self-disclosure, for in it God revealed a glimpse of his righteous and holy character and laid down his expectations for how his people should live. And yet, in Jesus, God's self-revelation has reached new, unprecedented heights. For as we read in the book of Exodus, Moses, while serving as the vehicle of God's revelation at the giving of the Law, couldn't see God and live. By contrast, Jesus not only saw God but is continually present with him at his side; thus he could make him known in an infinitely greater and more definitive way than Moses ever could.[31]

This, then, is how the evangelist wants us to read the rest of his Gospel. Jesus is the eternal Word who had been active in creation and had now become flesh in the man named Jesus (which, coming from the Hebrew word *Yeshua*, means "salvation"). Note

29. John 1:11–12.
30. John 1:17.
31. Regarding the textual issues involved in verse 18 (as to whether John wrote "the only Son" or "the only God"), see Harris, *John*, 38. If the latter, verses 1 and 18 would form a literary *inclusio*, opening and concluding John's prologue with a reference to the deity of the Son. An *inclusio* is a literary device of beginning and ending a unit with the same or a very similar phrase or topic.

how now the evangelist completely skips over Jesus's human birth—narrated in both Matthew and Luke, though not in Mark—and starts immediately with the testimony of John the Baptist in verse 19. In this way, the fourth evangelist's account of the eternal Word becoming flesh in Jesus provides an important supplement to Matthew's and Luke's infancy narratives. This is exactly what one would expect in light of the fact that John most likely wrote a generation after the other Gospels had been written.

If you've read through the first three Gospels already and are now ready to embark on your reading of the fourth and final Gospel in the New Testament, you're well equipped for your journey. John won't duplicate much material from the other Gospels at all. There's inevitable overlap—especially in the passion narrative, which is indispensable to a Gospel—but for the most part John will add to your understanding of who Jesus is and what he said and did. You'll see that John, like a laser, focuses on Jesus's claim to deity, which is amply borne out by his messianic signs but which is rejected by the Jewish leadership. You'll also learn more about different kinds of faith—both temporary and abiding—through a series of representative characters.

THE VOICE IN THE WILDERNESS AND THE PROMISE OF GREATER THINGS (1:19–51)

Day 1: John the Baptist's Witness regarding Himself (1:19–28)

Day 2: John the Baptist's Witness regarding Jesus (1:29–34)

Days 3 and 4: Jesus's Call of His First Disciples (1:35–42)

Day 5: Jesus's Call of Additional Disciples and Promise of "Greater Things" (1:43–51)

THE VOICE IN THE WILDERNESS AND THE PROMISE OF GREATER THINGS (1:19–51)

Now that the fourth evangelist has set the stage with his carefully crafted prologue, he jumps right into the action, fast-forwarding to the days of John the Baptist in AD 29. We've already seen that the evangelist drew a connection between the Word's instrumentality in creation and Jesus's taking up residence among his people in the recent past (from the evangelist's vantage point). Now he takes this "new creation theology" a step farther, narrating the first week of Jesus's public activity in a way that mirrors the seven days of creation.[32] The following pattern emerges from the remainder of chapter 1, regularly punctuated by references to "the next day":[33]

Day 1: John the Baptist's witness regarding himself (1:19–28)
Day 2: John the Baptist's witness regarding Jesus (1:29–34)
Days 3 and 4: Jesus's call of his first disciples (1:35–39, 40–42)
Day 5: Jesus's call of additional disciples and promise of "greater things" (1:43–51)

Then chapter 2 begins with a reference to the wedding at Cana—the site of Jesus's first messianic sign—which took place "on the third day" (a possible allusion to Jesus's

32. On John's "new creation theology," see Köstenberger, *Theology of John's Gospel and Letters*, chapter 8.
33. John 1:29, 35, 43.

resurrection, which also took place "on the third day"). Thus, from 1:19 until 2:11, John narrates the first week of Jesus's ministry, even skipping over day 6, which may represent the Sabbath, the Jewish day of rest. Thus:

Day 6: No record of activity
Day 7: Jesus's turning of water into wine at the Cana wedding (2:1–11)

Day 1: John the Baptist's Witness regarding Himself (1:19–28)

Verses 19–28, then, narrate "the testimony of John" that the fourth evangelist anticipated in the prologue.[34] First, John bore witness regarding himself. Yet before he tells us who he is, he emphatically makes clear who he is not:

- *The Messiah*: while the word "Messiah" is surprisingly rare in the Old Testament, the message is clear that God would send his messenger and deliver his people one day.
- *Elijah*: some Jews expected Elijah—who had never died but was taken up to heaven—to return.[35]
- *The Prophet*: on the basis of Moses's prediction in the book of Deuteronomy that God would send a prophet like himself, many expected "the Prophet like Moses."[36]

As a ground-clearing exercise, John the Baptist makes clear from the very start that he is neither the Messiah nor Elijah nor the Prophet. Then who is he? Says John: "I am the voice of one crying out in the wilderness, 'Make straight the way of the Lord,' as the prophet Isaiah said."[37] Well, then, the people ask John: "If you're neither the Messiah, nor Elijah, nor the Prophet, why are you baptizing?"[38] Fair question. John's answer is this: he baptized with water in order to prepare the way for the coming Messiah, yet he is "not worthy to untie" even "the strap of [his] sandal."[39]

In this and the other Gospels, John serves as the epitome of humility, which all of us would do well to emulate. He is content to play second fiddle to Jesus and does so

34. See Benjamin A. Foreman, "Locating the Baptism of Jesus (John 1:19–2:1)," in *Lexham Geographic Commentary*, ed. Barry J. Beitzel (Bellingham, WA: Lexham, 2017), 65–73.
35. Note that Jesus does identify John with Elijah at one point during his ministry when asked about the Baptist (Matthew 11:14). This is not a real contradiction, however, as John is not literally Elijah who has returned, although he exhibits some similar characteristics in his outward appearance, style of clothing, and fiery demeanor.
36. See John 1:20–21; regarding the Prophet like Moses, see Deuteronomy 18:15. Notice that later in John's Gospel, people believe Jesus is "the Prophet who is to come into the world" (John 6:14).
37. John 1:23; cf. Isaiah 40:3. See the discussion of Mark 1:2–3 above.
38. John 1:25 (my own paraphrase).
39. John 1:26–27. The reader of John's Gospel already knows this from the prologue; see John 1:6–8, 15.

with distinction. Of how many of us could that be said? Everyone wants to be a leader, but who wants to be a follower? It's great to be the "*First* Baptist Church of [fill in the place]," but what about the "*Second* Baptist Church"? As Jesus would later teach, God will effect a reversal in which those who are first in this world will be last, and those who are last will be first. The Baptist serves as a perennial example of one who knew his vital supportive role and embraced it wholeheartedly.

Day 2: John the Baptist's Witness regarding Jesus (1:29–34)

"The next day" John calls Jesus "the Lamb of God, who takes away the sin of the world," and says the reason he was baptizing people was "that he might be revealed to Israel."[40] This shows that Jesus came first to the Jews, God's chosen Old Testament people, who were promised that a Messiah would come to lead and deliver them.[41] The Baptist humbly acknowledges that he could identify Jesus as Messiah only because the Holy Spirit descended from heaven like a dove and rested on Jesus.

Days 3 and 4: Jesus's Call of His First Disciples (1:35–39, 40–42)

Then, on "the next day," John points two of his own disciples to Jesus, "the Lamb of God"—a very humble thing to do—and they begin following Jesus.[42] One of them was Andrew, who is here identified as "Simon Peter's brother," even though Peter himself hasn't yet been mentioned in the Gospel. Apparently, John, writing a generation later than the other Gospels, expects his readers to know who Peter is already. The other disciple remains unnamed, but many believe it was none other than the apostle John, the author of the Gospel, himself.

Day 5: Jesus's Call of Additional Disciples and Promise of "Greater Things" (1:43–51)

In what follows, the evangelist highlights a pattern of pointing others to the Messiah:

---

40. John 1:29, 31.
41. In the remainder of his Gospel, John often refers to "the Jews" in a pejorative sense, so much so that some have alleged that John is anti-Semitic. However, most likely John (who himself was Jewish) refers to the Jewish leaders who, as representatives of the Jewish nation, rejected Jesus the Messiah. As Harris (*John*, 184) rightly points out, (1) both John (the author) and Jesus (the main character) are Jews; (2) the Gospel states that "salvation is from the Jews" (John 4:22); (3) Jesus is explicitly identified as "a Jew" (John 4:9, 20); (4) the Twelve were all Jewish; and (5) there are other positive (or at least neutral) Jewish characters in the Gospel, such as in the account of the raising of Lazarus (John 11:19, 31) and the burial of Jesus (John 19:38–42; i.e., Nicodemus and Joseph of Arimathea).
42. John 1:36–37.

- Andrew finds his brother Simon (Peter) and brings him to Jesus.[43]
    - "We have found the Messiah."
    - No response is recorded, but it is implied that Peter followed Jesus.
- Philip finds Nathanael and tells him to come to Jesus.[44]
    - "We have found him of whom Moses in the Law and also the prophets wrote."
    - "Rabbi, you are the Son of God! You are the King of Israel!"

Whom are you and I pointing to the Messiah?

When Nathaniel is amazed at Jesus's supernatural knowledge—Jesus tells him he saw him under the fig tree—Jesus in effect replies, "You ain't seen nothin' yet!" Alluding to Jacob, the patriarch, whom God later renamed "Israel," Jesus asserts that he—the Son of Man—will be the source of even more amazing revelation. Those who follow him "will see heaven opened"![45] What a teaser and cliff-hanger at that early stage in the Gospel! I guess we'll have to keep reading to find out what Jesus was talking about.[46]

RECAP

In the opening chapter to his Gospel, John has already covered a lot of ground. As we've seen, he has introduced Jesus in lofty terms as the Word who existed with God in eternity past and became flesh to dwell among his people and to reveal the Father. Just as the law was God's gracious gift to his people in the days of Moses, so Jesus, God's one and only Son, was full of grace and truth—only even more so. As the first of many witnesses to Jesus, John the Baptist arises as a "voice in the wilderness" that prepares the way for the coming of the Messiah. Not only does he bear witness to Jesus; he also points his followers to him, and they transfer their allegiance from John to Jesus. At this, Jesus calls his first followers, triggering a chain reaction: Andrew recruits his brother Simon, and Philip recruits Nathanael. While the latter initially is skeptical, Jesus wins him over by a display of supernatural insight. The chapter closes with Jesus providing a teaser, promising his disciples that they will witness amazing things if they stick with him.

---

43. John 1:40–42.
44. John 1:43–51.
45. See John 1:50–51.
46. Though, ultimately, see the book of Revelation, which John also wrote, most likely after his Gospel and letters. See Andreas J. Köstenberger, *Baker Handbook on the New Testament: General Epistles and Revelation*, ed. Benjamin Gladd (Grand Rapids: Baker, 2020).

THE BOOK OF SIGNS: THE SEVEN SIGNS OF JESUS THE MESSIAH (2:1–12:50)

The Cana Cycle (2:1–4:54)

Day 7: The First Sign of Jesus: Turning Water into Wine (2:1–11)

The First Passover and Second Sign: Clearing the Jerusalem Temple (2:13–22)

THE BOOK OF SIGNS: THE SEVEN SIGNS OF JESUS THE MESSIAH (2:1–12:50)

The Cana Cycle (2:1–4:54)

Day 7: The First Sign of Jesus: Turning Water into Wine (2:1–11)

We've already seen how John organized the inception of Jesus's ministry in the form of a week of activity ("The next day . . . ," "The next day . . . ," etc.). The week culminates "on the third day" with a wedding in a village called Cana, not far from Jesus's hometown of Nazareth, in Galilee, at which Jesus performs the first of his seven signs recorded in this Gospel.[47] Not only do we see the conclusion of Jesus's first week of ministry, therefore; we also witness the beginning of Jesus's signs that will span the remainder of the first half of John's Gospel—the Book of Signs.

What's more, John organizes this early stage of Jesus's ministry in the form of what scholars call the "Cana Cycle," showing Jesus's movement from Cana (the wedding at the beginning of chapter 2) to Jerusalem, Judea, Samaria, and back to Cana (healing an official's son at the end of chapter 4).[48] Thus, John shows how Jesus quite literally comes full circle, going on a circuit that leads him from Cana in the Galilean north, to Jerusalem

47. John 2:1; cf. 2:11: "This, the first of his signs, Jesus did at Cana in Galilee." On the seven signs, see Andreas J. Köstenberger, "The Seventh Johannine Sign: A Study in John's Christology," *Bulletin for Biblical Research* 5 (1995): 87–103. On the setting, see Emily J. Thomassen, "Jesus's Ministry at Cana in Galilee (John 2:1–11; 4:46–54; 21:2)," in Beitzel, *Lexham Geographic Commentary*, 74–83. For a discussion of John 2:1–11, see Köstenberger, "FTC Workshop on the Gospel of John."
48. See, e.g., Francis J. Moloney, "From Cana to Cana (John 2:1–4:54) and the Fourth Evangelist's Concept of Correct (and Incorrect) Faith," *Salesianum* 40 (1978): 817–43.

(where he clears the temple, celebrates the Passover, and engages in conversation with Nicodemus), to Judea and Samaria (where he converses with a woman at a historic well, again invoking memories of Jacob the patriarch), all the way back to Cana where the cycle started. As with Jesus's "creation week" of ministry, the Cana Cycle thus exhibits a nice pattern of organization and symmetry, which makes Jesus's early movements appear even more coherent and well-ordered, unfolding according to the divine plan.

First, then, we witness a wedding. Many believe that the family of the bride or groom may have been friends with Jesus's mother, who features prominently in the story. Interestingly, Jesus's mother remains unnamed—though many readers of the Gospel would no doubt have known that her name was Mary, just as they would have known about the apostle Peter, who, as mentioned, has been obliquely introduced into the narrative with the earlier reference to Andrew being "Peter's brother."[49] Just as John calls himself "the disciple Jesus loved" so that no one other than John the Baptist bears the name "John" in the Gospel, so here the evangelist simply calls Mary "Jesus's mother" so he can reserve the first name "Mary" for Mary Magdalene later in the Gospel. In this way, there'll be no confusion regarding multiple people with these common first names.

When the wedding hosts run out of wine—considered to be a major *faux pas* at festive occasions such as weddings in the ancient world (even though this could easily happen, as weddings often lasted for days if not an entire week)—Jesus's mother gently goads her son to help. Does she know that he can create new wine because he has performed miracles previously? When Mary approaches him and asks him to help the bride's or groom's family out of their predicament, Jesus's response is remarkably pointed: his hour, he tells his mother, has not yet come.[50] This statement represents a common feature in John's narrative—a misunderstanding of Jesus's identity and a lack of understanding of the purpose of his messianic mission, and in the present case specifically of his timing: he would not be revealed as the Messiah until a later time.

Unperturbed, Jesus's mother tells those helping at the wedding, "Do whatever he tells you."[51] At this, Jesus miraculously turns a large amount of water into wine, entirely behind the scenes (presumably so as not to steal the show). This makes clear that the purpose of Jesus's miracles—or "signs," as John prefers to call them—was not primarily to wow his audience but to reveal himself to his followers as the Messiah. When John tells us at the end of this account that by performing this sign Jesus "manifested his glory" to his disciples, and they "believed in him," he signals that Jesus's purpose for

49. See John 2:1, 3, 5, 12. Regarding Peter, see John 1:40 and the discussion above.

50. John 2:4.

51. John 2:5. Note the unmistakable echo of Pharaoh's words to Joseph in Egypt at the inception of the famine there: "Go to Joseph and do whatever he tells you" (Genesis 41:55 CSB).

performing his sign had been fulfilled: his followers had come to see a glimpse of his messianic identity and placed their faith in him.[52] Plus, he had helped the family save face and done a very nice thing for the young couple!

The First Passover and Second Sign: Clearing the Jerusalem Temple (2:12–23)

After spending a few days in Capernaum, a nearby town, with his mother, brothers, and disciples, Jesus travels to Jerusalem for the Passover.[53] The Passover, of course, commemorated the occasion just prior to Israel's exodus from Egypt when the death angel "passed over" those who had smeared blood on their doorposts as a sign of their trust in God.[54] Ever since, the Israelites celebrated God's miraculous deliverance from their enemies with a festive meal—the Passover—and a subsequent week of festivities, the Feast of Unleavened Bread.[55] John records Jesus attending three such Passovers during his earthly ministry—the first one here, a second one in Galilee midway through his ministry, and a third and final Passover at which he would be crucified as "the Lamb of God"—the perfect Passover lamb who "takes away the sin of the world."[56]

At this, his first Jerusalem Passover during his public ministry, Jesus goes straight to the temple and finds it to be a place of shameful, irreverent commercialism. In passionate, consuming zeal for God's honor and glory, and in righteous anger and indignation at the scene he witnesses—money changers, dove sellers, and a variety of sacrificial animals—Jesus clears the temple area to purify his "Father's house" for worship, the temple's God-intended purpose. Now it is the Jewish authorities' turn to be indignant, pressing Jesus to present a sign of his authority to act in this way. Ironically, however, Jesus had just performed the sign they were asking for—the temple clearing—but they had entirely missed it!

In true prophetic style, Jesus's action of confronting those merchants who had made worship in God's house a matter of crass profiteering symbolized God's judgment on the temple. It would soon be destroyed—in fact, it was destroyed about forty years later in the year 70, as John most likely knew when writing the Gospel a decade or two

52. John 2:11.

53. For a slightly more thorough discussion of John 2:13–22 than the one provided below, with some helpful additional details, see Köstenberger, "FTC Workshop on the Gospel of John," 26–28.

54. You can read the story in Exodus 12.

55. See Exodus 13:1–16; Leviticus 23:5–8; Deuteronomy 16:1–8; Mark Strauss, "Passover and the Feast of Unleavened Bread," in *Luke*, in *Zondervan Illustrated Bible Backgrounds Commentary*, vol. 1, *Matthew, Mark, Luke*, ed. Clinton E. Arnold (Grand Rapids: Zondervan, 2002), 350.

56. John 1:29. See John 2:13, 23 (first Passover in Jerusalem); 6:4 (second Passover in Galilee); 11:55; 12:1, 12, 20; 13:1; 18:28; 19:14 (third Passover in Galilee, including the Last Supper). In addition, there may have been another Passover not recorded in John only hinted at in the Synoptic Gospels (Matthew 12:1: "At that time"; Mark 2:23; Luke 6:1?).

later—and Jesus's broken and raised body would take the temple's place as the proper realm of worship. "Destroy this temple," Jesus dared his detractors, "and in three days I will raise it up."[57] In fact, they would try to destroy Jesus's body, and apparently succeed, but three days later he would rise. Another prophecy fulfilled! In this way, the temple clearing furnished a second sign—this time in Jerusalem—of Jesus's messianic authority, though the Jewish authorities tragically failed to understand the true meaning of Jesus's words and were unable to perceive the significance of his actions.[58]

THE NEW TEMPLE

A study of the "temple" theme in Scripture is highly instructive.[59] In the original creation, Adam and Eve lived continually in God's presence in the garden of Eden. There was no need for a special building where God would manifest his presence, much less a need for sacrifices, as the fall had not yet occurred, and Adam and Eve enjoyed close and direct fellowship with their Creator.

Then, at the fall, this fellowship was broken. Adam and Eve rebelled against God and as a result were expelled from God's immediate presence in the garden.[60] Later, God manifested his presence among his people Israel through temporary structures such as the tabernacle (built by Moses) and then the temple (built by Solomon). The "glory of the Lord" was said to fill these sanctuaries where God was worshiped.[61]

Still later, Israel was taken into exile, and the temple was destroyed. People languished far away from their homeland and central sanctuary. Following the exile, the temple was rebuilt and rededicated by those who returned (though many did not). In Jesus's day, his disciples marveled

57. John 2:19.
58. For references to Jesus's Jerusalem signs, see John 2:23 and 3:2.
59. See Peter W. L. Walker, *Jesus and the Holy City: New Testament Perspectives on Jerusalem* (Grand Rapids: Eerdmans, 1996). On the temple in John's Gospel, see Andreas J. Köstenberger, "The Destruction of the Second Temple and the Composition of the Fourth Gospel," in *Challenging Perspectives on the Gospel of John*, Wissenschaftliche Untersuchungen zum Neuen Testament 2/219 ed. John Lierman (Tübingen: Mohr Siebeck, 2006), 69–108.
60. Genesis 3:23–24.
61. See, e.g., Exodus 40:34; 1 Kings 8:11; 2 Chronicles 5:14; 7:1; Ezekiel 43:5.

at its beauty, though he predicted its destruction.[62] Jesus's prophecy was fulfilled when the Romans under Titus destroyed the temple in AD 70.[63]

The apostle John tells us that Jesus manifested God's presence in our midst and became the "new temple." His body would be "destroyed" (the cross) and "raised up" (the resurrection) on the third day.[64] No longer would people worship on Mount Gerizim or in Jerusalem (or any other location), but worship would be offered "in spirit and truth."[65] And the object of worship would be the crucified and risen Lord Jesus himself!

Extending the New Testament temple motif yet further, Peter tells us that the church is now a "spiritual temple" with believers being "living stones."[66] Then, we see in the book of Revelation that in heaven there is "no temple" anymore because God himself is there![67] This shows that our relationship with God has been fully restored, and we'll be able to live in his presence as was his plan from the very beginning. Praise the Lord!

62. Matthew 24:1–2; Mark 13:1–2; Luke 21:5–6.
63. This ended what is commonly referred to as the "Second Temple period," which extended from the rebuilding of the temple following the exile until its destruction in AD 70.
64. John 2:18–21.
65. John 4:19–24.
66. 1 Peter 2:5.
67. Revelation 21:22.

THE BOOK OF SIGNS: THE SEVEN SIGNS OF JESUS THE MESSIAH (2:1–12:50, CONT.)

The Cana Cycle (2:1–4:54, cont.)

Jerusalem: Jesus's Conversation with Nicodemus (2:23–3:21)

Judea: John's Continued Witness regarding Jesus (3:22–36)

THE BOOK OF SIGNS: THE SEVEN SIGNS OF JESUS THE MESSIAH (2:1–12:50, CONT.)

The Cana Cycle (2:1–4:54, cont.)

Jerusalem: Jesus's Conversation with Nicodemus (2:23–3:21)

Still in Jerusalem, Jesus receives a nightly visitor, a Pharisee named Nicodemus who was "a ruler of the Jews"—that is, a member of the powerful assembly called the Sanhedrin. This "man of the Pharisees," John makes clear, was one of the "men" regarding whom Jesus needed no witness—he knew that people couldn't be trusted because of their sin nature. As you read the narrative about Nicodemus, therefore, you should start reading in chapter 2, verse 23, as 2:23–25 serves as an introduction to the actual narrative that spans 3:1–15.[68] This, in turn, is followed by the evangelist's own commentary in 3:16–21—including the famous verse John 3:16—after which the narrative moves from Jerusalem, the Jewish capital, to the countryside of Judea, as Jesus embarks on the return journey to Galilee via Samaria.[69]

In a nutshell, Jesus tells Nicodemus that he lacks one very important thing—spiritual rebirth: "You must be born again."[70] Nicodemus should have realized from reading Scriptures such as the prophet Ezekiel that Israel must be restored and revitalized, which entailed a real spiritual awakening. As the "teacher of Israel," he should have understood

68. See Köstenberger, "FTC Workshop on the Gospel of John," 29–37, esp. 29–30.
69. See the reference to the "Judean countryside" in John 3:22. For an interesting discussion of the Nicodemus narrative, see Peter Cotterell and Max Turner, *Linguistics and Biblical Interpretation* (Downers Grove, IL: InterVarsity Press, 1989), 275–78.
70. John 3:7; cf. 3:3, 5.

this but tragically had missed the vital spiritual reality conveyed by these prophecies. This is what happens when one gets bogged down in the minutiae of the law and fails to pay attention to the overarching prophetic thrust of the Scriptures! In this, Nicodemus serves as an abiding example of a nominal Christian, even in a position of leadership. Yes, one can have impressive religious credentials and yet not be part of Christ's kingdom! This is the sobering truth with which Jesus confronts Nicodemus, and all of us today.

What is God's will? How can we please God? In the end, we must realize that before we can do anything for *him*, we must first allow him to do something for *us*—save us from our sins, help us trust in Christ, and give us new life in the Spirit. In this way, John depicts Nicodemus as a representative of official Judaism that scrupulously observed the law but lacked true spiritual life and vitality, so much so that when the long-awaited Messiah came to the Holy City, those who were supposed to recognize him and welcome him with open arms had no use for him and missed out on benefiting from his coming altogether. What's more, they found him to be an inconvenient nuisance who kept them from engaging in business as usual, threatened their powerful positions and livelihood, and rivaled their sway over the common people.

Nicodemus doesn't understand the mysterious operation of the Spirit, though Jesus tries to explain it to him by using the analogy of the wind.[71] Neither does Nicodemus understand Jesus's statement that "as Moses lifted up the serpent in the wilderness, so must the Son of Man be lifted up."[72] Jesus here refers to an incident during the Israelites' exodus in the wilderness when people were dying of snakebites and God told Moses to make a bronze serpent and raise it in plain view of the people. Everyone who looked at the raised-up serpent in faith would live.[73] Jesus explains that it would be the same with him: God would raise him, the Son of Man, up on the cross, and everyone who looked at him in faith, trusting him for salvation from sin, would live—and receive eternal life. What a beautiful picture!

At this point, the narrative transitions from the actual story of Jesus and Nicodemus to the evangelist's commentary: "For God so loved the world. . . ."[74] John's point here is that, at the cross, God's great love for sinful humanity was revealed, at great sacrifice to himself: "he gave his only Son."[75] This recalls Abraham's giving of his son Isaac at a critical juncture in his journey of faith.[76] But now, John explains, God himself gave his

71. John 3:8.
72. John 3:14.
73. Numbers 21:4–9.
74. John 3:16. For a thorough exposition, see Murray J. Harris, *John 3:16: What's It All About?* (Eugene, OR: Cascade, 2015).
75. John 3:16.
76. See Genesis 22.

only Son for the life of the entire world—not merely the Jewish people.[77] God gave his only Son "that whoever believes in him should not perish but have eternal life"![78] For this reason, John is rightly considered the universal Gospel, the Gospel that presents good news for all those who are willing to put their trust in Jesus the Messiah. In the ultimate analysis, the evangelist contends, God judges no one; people bring judgment on themselves if they persist in sin.[79]

Judea: John's Continued Witness regarding Jesus (3:22–36)

OK, time to move on. Jesus and the disciples travel to the Judean countryside where they perform baptisms, similar to John the Baptist. As at previous occasions, the evangelist's parenthetical remark, "For John had not yet been put in prison,"[80] seems to indicate that he expects his readers already to be familiar with the basic gospel story, whether from previous written accounts or oral reports. And once again, John the Baptist clarifies his role in relation to Jesus. This time he uses the illustration of the friend of a bridegroom. Just as that friend is content to assist the bridegroom on his special day, so the Baptist is happy to point people to Jesus rather than himself: "He must increase, but I must decrease."[81] With this kind of attitude, as mentioned, John can serve as an example for all of us: it's not about us; it's all about Jesus! The rest of the chapter contains additional commentary by the Baptist, pointing people to Jesus.[82]

77. See Andreas J. Köstenberger, "Lifting Up the Son of Man and God's Love for the World: John 3:16 in Its Historical, Literary, and Theological Contexts," in *Understanding the Times: New Testament Studies in the 21st Century; Essays in Honor of D. A. Carson on the Occasion of His 65th Birthday*, eds. Andreas J. Köstenberger and Robert W. Yarbrough (Wheaton, IL: Crossway, 2011), 141–59.
78. John 3:16.
79. John 3:19–21.
80. John 3:24.
81. John 3:30.
82. John 3:31–36.

THE BOOK OF SIGNS: THE SEVEN SIGNS OF JESUS THE MESSIAH (2:1–12:50, CONT.)

The Cana Cycle (2:1–4:54, cont.)

Samaria: Jesus's Conversation with a Samaritan Woman (4:1–42)

Galilee: The Third Sign: Healing a Gentile Official's Son (4:43–54)

THE BOOK OF SIGNS: THE SEVEN SIGNS OF JESUS THE MESSIAH (2:1–12:50, CONT.)

The Cana Cycle (2:1–4:54, cont.)

Samaria: Jesus's Conversation with a Samaritan Woman (4:1–42)

On his way back from Judea to Galilee, the evangelist tells us, Jesus "had to pass through Samaria."[83] In one sense, this needs elaboration. There was a shorter way, but John is here speaking of God's sovereign will. God wanted Jesus to go through Samaria because he had a special mission for him there. The place is historic—Jacob's well (though note that this well is not mentioned in the Old Testament).[84] As Jesus sits down by the well, thirsty and tired (he was, after all, not only God in the flesh but also fully human), a Samaritan woman comes to the well at noon—when the sun would have been at its peak—to draw water. What ensues is a remarkable conversation in which Jesus engages the unnamed woman with her sin, her spiritual thirst, and her need for a Savior.

The evangelist juxtaposes this story with the Nicodemus narrative in the previous chapter as a study of contrasts. Nicodemus is a man—a Jew, a member of the Sanhedrin (the highest Jewish council), the "teacher of Israel." The woman—who, unlike the highly prominent Nicodemus, remains unnamed—is a Samaritan, part of a people with whom the Jewish people did not associate because they considered them racially and

83. John 4:4. For a discussion of Jesus's conversation with the Samaritan woman in John 4, see Köstenberger, "FTC Workshop on the Gospel of John," 37–39.

84. John 4:5–6. See Perry G. Phillips, "At the Well of Sychar (John 4:1–42)," in Beitzel, *Lexham Geographic Commentary*, 92–99.

ritually unclean, a mixed race with heretical views, such as that people ought to worship God on Mount Gerizim in Samaria rather than in the temple in Jerusalem. Nicodemus and the Samaritan woman couldn't be more different! Consider the following:

- Nicodemus is a man; she is a woman.
- Nicodemus is a Jew; the woman is a Samaritan, a hated hybrid race.
- Nicodemus is the "teacher of Israel"; the Samaritan woman remains unnamed.
- He is a member of the Jewish highest court, the Sanhedrin; she is a nobody.
- He knows the Scriptures; she is mired in folklore and tradition.
- He is the epitome of morality; she is engaged in a series of immoral relationships.
- He comes by night; she comes at noon.[85]

The list goes on and on. And yet what they both have in common is their need for a Savior. But while Nicodemus proves intransigent in the course of his conversation with Jesus, the Samaritan woman is willing to be engaged by Jesus and grows increasingly animated.[86] She first recognizes Jesus as a Jew, then calls him a prophet, and finally asks hopefully, "Can this be the Christ?"[87] What a progression—Jew, prophet, Messiah! In the end, the woman turns into an evangelist herself, bringing her entire town to Jesus, saying in effect, "But don't take my word for it!"[88] In this way, John shows that God is no respecter of persons. It really is true that God so loved the world that whoever believes in him can have eternal life—even an immoral Samaritan woman from a mixed, "impure" race despised by the Jewish people! That's grace.

You may be reading this and thinking, "God can never forgive me." You may be thinking, "I can't get over some of the terrible things I've done. I can't come to Jesus!" Not true. Look at the Samaritan woman! She had a very checkered past, and present—and yet Jesus accepted her and loved her as a human being while confronting her about her sin. And she responded, gladly, even excitedly, becoming a representative figure of those who are steeped in immorality and yet have a heart that longs for meaning in life, for significance in relationships, and who ultimately want to be loved and accepted. Jesus loves you and will accept you—but he will confront you with your sin. And if you

85. This list was adapted from a workshop on John's Gospel that I gave at Midwestern Seminary. See Köstenberger, "FTC Workshop on the Gospel of John," 38. You may find the entire article worth reading as a thorough survey of the first four chapters of John's Gospel.
86. See Murray, *John*, 96, who sketches the following stages: (1) a certain sauciness (v. 9); (2) a tempered respect (v. 11); (3) a gentle humoring of Jesus (v. 15); (4) a developing recognition of Jesus's identity (v. 19); and (5) embryonic belief (v. 29).
87. See John 4:9, 19, 29.
88. John 4:28–30, 39–42.

believe in him and give your life to him, he will change you. To paraphrase Tim Keller, "God loves you just the way you are. But he doesn't want you to stay that way."[89]

Galilee: The Third Sign: Healing a Gentile Official's Son (4:43–54)

After staying in Samaria for two days, Jesus returns to Galilee and arrives back in Cana, where he started his journey.[90] What brings Jesus to this inconspicuous village this time is not a wedding but a message from an official from the nearby town of Capernaum. That official sent word to Jesus that his son had fallen ill, and asked him to come and heal his son. Strikingly, Jesus doesn't bother coming but heals the boy long-distance, simply by speaking the word! This is one of only a small number of long-distance healings recorded in any of the Gospels. In this way, the evangelist teaches us a lesson about prayer and faith. We may expect God to answer our requests by acting in a certain way, but God may choose to answer our prayers differently than we might imagine. After all, as the Old Testament prophet Isaiah wrote, God's ways are infinitely higher than ours![91] So we can simply share our requests with God and then wait expectantly to see what God will do. John closes out the Cana Cycle by writing that "this was now the second sign that Jesus did" in Cana of Galilee, reminding the reader of Jesus's first Cana sign when he turned water into wine at the wedding.[92] If the temple clearing in Jerusalem constituted a sign as well, this means that Jesus has now manifested his messianic identity both in Galilee and in Judea—and, for good measure, in Samaria as well.[93]

RECAP

Chapters 2–4 depict the early goings of Jesus's ministry from Cana, a small Galilean village, back to Cana. The initial episode at the Cana wedding marks at the same time day 7 in the first week of Jesus's ministry, which the fourth evangelist depicted in the second half of chapter 1. The turning of water into wine at the Cana wedding is the first of seven signs of Jesus showcased in the first half of John's Gospel, the so-called Book

89. The verbatim quote is this: "God sees us as we are, loves us as we are, and accepts us as we are. But by His grace, He does not leave us as we are." Timothy Keller (@timkellernyc), Twitter, May 16, 2014, https://twitter.com/timkellernyc/status/467333916303839232.
90. See the discussion of the Cana Cycle in the introduction at 2:1 above.
91. Isaiah 55:8–9.
92. John 4:54; cf. 2:11.
93. Albeit not by way of a sign. Notice that by going from Jerusalem to Judea, and from there to Samaria and to a Gentile in Galilee, Jesus anticipates the movement of the early Christian mission; see Acts 1:8. This may be coincidental, but more likely the fourth evangelist, writing toward the end of the first century AD, sought to show that the early Christian mission was grounded in the mission of none other than Jesus himself.

of Signs. The purpose of these messianic displays of Jesus is to reveal himself to Israel as its Messiah. Following the first sign at the Cana wedding, we see Jesus clear the temple in Jerusalem in a prophetic display of zeal for God's house. This sign, performed in Jerusalem, is different from the first in that it is not miraculous in a narrow sense, but it still serves as a prophetic sign of the upcoming "destruction" of Jesus's body, the new temple, followed by his miraculous resurrection.

Chapter 3 opens with Jesus's conversation with Nicodemus, the teacher of Israel and Sanhedrin member. As a representative of official Judaism, Nicodemus displays ignorance of his need for a spiritual rebirth. Chapter 4 features Jesus's conversation with an unnamed Samaritan woman. While the diametrical opposite of Nicodemus, the woman progresses in her understanding of Jesus to the point of recognizing him as Messiah and goes on to bring her fellow Samaritans. In this way, Jesus is shown to engage in a mission starting in Jerusalem and moving on to Judea and Samaria. At the close of the Cana Cycle, he heals a royal official's son (almost certainly a Gentile). By his arrangement of Jesus's early ministry in the form of a week of activities (mirroring creation week) followed by a sketch of Jesus's mission from Jerusalem to Judea, Samaria, and the Gentile world, John has organized his material in a way that is both memorable and easy to follow.

THE BOOK OF SIGNS: THE SEVEN SIGNS OF JESUS THE MESSIAH (2:1–12:50, CONT.)

The Festival Cycle (5:1–10:42)

The Fourth Sign: Healing an Invalid (5:1–17)

The Sabbath Controversy (5:18–47)

THE BOOK OF SIGNS: THE SEVEN SIGNS OF JESUS THE MESSIAH (2:1–12:50, CONT.)

The Festival Cycle (5:1–10:42)

The next, larger cycle of Jesus's activities is often called the Festival Cycle, spanning chapters 5–10. During this critical phase of his ministry, Jesus encounters increasing opposition from the Jewish authorities as he attends various Jewish festivals—an unnamed feast in Jerusalem (chap. 5); Passover in Galilee (chap. 6); Tabernacles, also called the Feast of Booths (chaps. 7–8, plus the aftermath in 9:1–10:21); and the Feast of Dedication, also called Hanukkah (10:22–39). As in the Cana Cycle, Jesus is shown to perform three messianic signs: the healing of a lame man (chap. 5), the feeding of the five thousand (chap. 6), and the healing of a man born blind (chap. 9). In this manner, the evangelist continues to demonstrate that Jesus manifested his messianic identity to the Jewish people in tangible and ever more powerful ways.

By now you've probably noticed that while the other Gospels include more events and move from one scene to the next more quickly, John tends to linger much longer in one place and is considerably more selective. He includes fewer events but covers them in greater detail. In this way, he allows the reader to ponder the meaning of a given event or conversation and to reflect on its significance in relation to Jesus's messianic identity and mission.

Another literary device John uses with considerable skill and artistry is that of representative figures.[94] We've already seen this in John's characterization of Nicodemus and the Samaritan woman, a veritable study in contrasts. Another example of contrasting,

94. See Raymond F. Collins, "Representative Figures," in *These Things Have Been Written: Studies on the Fourth Gospel* (Grand Rapids: Eerdmans, 1991), 1–45.

representative figures is furnished by the characters of the lame man in chapter 5 and the blind man in chapter 9.[95] While both are healed by Jesus, and both healings take place on a Sabbath, the two healed men respond in markedly different ways. When confronted by the Jewish leaders, the lame man blames Jesus for an infraction of the law and reports him to the authorities, appearing utterly intransigent to Jesus's messianic identity.[96] The blind man, on the other hand, defends Jesus—even though the Pharisees hurl repeated insults at him—and in the end even worships Jesus.[97]

The Fourth Sign: Healing an Invalid (5:1–17)

In the case of the lame man, his healing—if you're keeping track, Jesus's fourth messianic sign in this Gospel—triggers a significant wave of opposition and persecution.[98] The fact that Jesus healed the man on a Sabbath made him a breaker of God's law in the eyes of the authorities who took the commandment to keep the Sabbath day holy with utmost seriousness and observed it obsequiously and assiduously. Yet while their zeal for God's word was commendable, they failed to realize that as God's Son, who was himself divine, Jesus had authority over the Sabbath rather than the Sabbath having authority over him. Not that Jesus brazenly disregarded or arbitrarily set aside scriptural Sabbath regulations. Rather, he interpreted the Sabbath in light of God's underlying purpose. What's more, he himself fulfilled the Sabbath by giving people abiding rest.[99]

In fact, Jesus used the occasion to affirm his equality with God the Father ("My Father is working until now, and I am working"),[100] which made the Jewish leaders even more furious, because "not only was he breaking the Sabbath [at least in their eyes], but he was even calling God his own Father, making himself equal with God."[101] In this way, the evangelist keeps his narrative's single-minded focus on what he believed was the central issue in the entire story of Jesus: his implicit and explicit claim to be none other than God in the flesh. As a matter of fact, as we'll see below, the Festival Cycle will end exactly as it began, with Jesus claiming equality with God the Father—"The Father and I are one"—and the Jews picking up stones to kill him because of perceived blasphemy.[102]

---

95. See Dorothy A. Lee, *The Symbolic Narratives of the Fourth Gospel: The Interplay of Form and Meaning*, Journal for the Study of the New Testament Supplement Series 95 (Sheffield: JSOT Press, 1994), 105–7; and R. Alan Culpepper, *Anatomy of the Fourth Gospel: A Study in Literary Design* (Philadelphia: Fortress, 1983), 139.
96. John 5:10–17.
97. John 9:13–38.
98. On the setting, see Gordon Franz, "Jesus at the Pool of Bethesda (John 5:1–9)," in Beitzel, *Lexham Geographic Commentary*, 125–33.
99. See Matthew 11:28–29 and Hebrews 3–4.
100. John 5:17.
101. John 5:18.
102. John 10:30–33.

The Sabbath Controversy (5:18–47)

The remainder of the chapter is given to a close narration of the controversy surrounding the Sabbath between Jesus and the authorities. In the process, Jesus not only claims authority over the Sabbath but also affirms that as the Son of Man he has authority to execute judgment on the last day.[103] In addition, he calls several witnesses to the stand who attest to the truthfulness of his claims, including John the Baptist (5:33–35), the works Jesus is performing (including the signs; 5:36), God the Father (5:37–38), and Moses and the (Old Testament) Scriptures (5:39–47).[104] The chapter ends with Jesus's parting challenge that is ringing in the reader's ears: "If you do not believe his writings, how will you believe my words?"[105]

Today, some are saying we should "ditch the Old Testament."[106] It only gets in the way in evangelism. After all, as the book of Hebrews tells us, the old covenant is obsolete; the New Testament is all we need. Jesus's words here don't seem to support this argument. Rather, he points to the continuity between Moses's words and his own words. Both are revelation from God and should be taken seriously (in fact, they are authoritative). The element of truth in the abovementioned argument is that there is certainly a progression: as Matthew, in particular, makes clear, Jesus interpreted the Old Testament at a deeper level in light of God's underlying purposes. What's more, he fulfilled the Old Testament in many absolutely critical ways. But that hardly means that we should dispense with the Old Testament and cut it out from our Bibles! I believe Jesus would be aghast at such a notion. In fact, in the present passage he seems to indicate that the Old Testament is important preparation for the New. In fact, Moses wrote about him! "For if you believed Moses, you would believe me; for he wrote of me."[107]

---

103. John 5:19–29.
104. John 5:30–47. Later, John will add the witness of the Holy Spirit and the disciples (15:26–27), as well as his own witness (21:24–25).
105. John 5:47.
106. E.g., Andy Stanley, *Irresistible: Reclaim the New That Jesus Unleashed for the World* (Grand Rapids: Zondervan, 2018). See my "Editorial," *Journal of the Evangelical Theological Society* 62 (2019): 1–3. See also the excellent critiques by Owen Strachan, "We Have No Divided God: A Review of 'Irresistible' by Andy Stanley," Center for Public Theology at Midwestern Seminary, October 15, 2018, https://cpt.mbts.edu/2018/10/15/we-have-no-divided-god-a-review-of-irresistible-by-andy-stanley, and Michael Kruger, "Why We Can't Unhitch from the Old Testament," The Gospel Coalition, October 22, 2018, https://www.thegospelcoalition.org/reviews/irresistible-andy-stanley.
107. John 5:46.

THE BOOK OF SIGNS: THE SEVEN SIGNS OF JESUS THE MESSIAH (2:1–12:50, CONT.)

The Festival Cycle (5:1–10:42, cont.)

The Fifth Sign: Feeding the Five Thousand (6:1–15)

Jesus Walks on Water (6:16–21)

The Bread of Life Discourse (6:22–71)

THE BOOK OF SIGNS: THE SEVEN SIGNS OF JESUS THE MESSIAH (2:1–12:50, CONT.)

The Festival Cycle (5:1–10:42, cont.)

The Fifth Sign: Feeding the Five Thousand (6:1–15)

The beginning of chapter 6 finds Jesus suddenly in Galilee (chapter 5 has taken place in Jerusalem). As a result, some scholars have posited ingenious rearrangement theories, arguing that somehow the order got jumbled up, and the Gospel originally had chapter 6 ahead of chapter 5. Of course, all of this is unnecessary (not to mention that no available manuscripts display a different order than the one we have in our Bibles today), because even though John doesn't explicitly narrate Jesus's movement from Jerusalem to Galilee, he certainly implies it, as he does in many other places in his Gospel.[108]

As mentioned, this is now the second Passover Jesus observes in this Gospel, and this time Jesus, for some unknown reason (it was usually expected that Jews travel to Jerusalem for the major "pilgrim feasts"), stays in Galilee. In an event recorded in all four Gospels, Jesus there miraculously feeds five thousand men, plus women and children. In the Johannine narrative, this constitutes Jesus's fifth messianic sign. Philip and Andrew (Peter's brother) emerge as characters here in the buildup to the miracle. Jesus is shown to take the initiative by asking Philip, "Where are we to buy bread, so that

108. Perhaps most famously in John 14:31.

these people may eat?" (as the fourth evangelist tells us, "he said this to test him, for he himself knew what he would do").[109]

It's interesting that Jesus here involves his followers in the miracle at all, as he could have simply performed it by himself. This shows that Jesus's working of messianic signs was part of his larger purpose of training the Twelve and letting them in on what went on behind the scenes, as it were, in engaging in his messianic ministry. Philip assesses the situation realistically: "Two hundred denarii worth of bread would not be enough for each of them to get a little."[110] A denarius was a day's wage, so if a person in Jesus's day would have made the equivalent of, say, $15,000 a year, Philip was suggesting that even $10,000 would not have been enough to buy bread for everyone! (Remember, people didn't work on the Sabbath and so didn't earn any money then either.) That showed that Jesus's idea of feeding all these people was completely beyond the realm of possibility, humanly speaking.

At this, a second disciple, Andrew, provides a glimmer of hope (though it seems like a long shot): "There is a boy here who has five barley loaves and two fish, but what are they for so many?"[111] One wonders why Andrew even mentioned this; it's almost laughable to think that Jesus could feed all these people with five loaves of bread and two fish! Or is it? Jesus, again involving the disciples in the process, tells them to have people sit down. Then he takes the loaves, gives thanks, and has the disciples distribute them and also the fish. And miraculously there's enough to feed them all! He even has the disciples gather twelve basketsful of leftovers. When people see Jesus's sign, they exclaim that Jesus is the Prophet like Moses (who John the Baptist denied being) and want to compel him to be their king.[112] But Jesus withdraws to a mountain by himself.

What we see here is that Jesus can use our humble resources—a few loaves of bread, a couple fish—if we only give them to him, to accomplish something truly miraculous. He has the power to multiply our resources exponentially. This is a powerful incentive, not only to sacrificial giving to God's work, but even more importantly to give ourselves to him so he can use us. The disciples (hopefully) learned a powerful ministry lesson that day: if they let God work through them, he will accomplish powerful things through their limited means. God doesn't need us, but he wants to use us. And our humble resources don't limit what God can do through them at all if we let him get to work and use them the way he sees fit. He has the vision, and the power, and the will, to do great things. And he is willing to use humble human means to do them.

109. John 6:5–6.
110. John 6:7.
111. John 6:9.
112. John 6:14–15.

Jesus Walks on Water (6:16–21)

Meanwhile, his disciples embark on a boat on their own to cross the sea of Galilee to Capernaum. Even though several of them are fishermen (and thus should be used to the stormy weather), they get scared when a gust comes up and the sea gets very rough. At this, Jesus walks toward them on the surface of the large lake (I'm sure it's an exceedingly surreal-looking scene), and now they get really scared and think Jesus is a ghost! When they recognize him and take him into the boat, a second miracle occurs—the boat immediately reaches the shore! Again, Jesus displays an attribute of deity—walking on the water—and identifies himself as "I am," the name with which God identified himself to Moses in the burning bush and the name Isaiah repeatedly uses with reference to YHWH.[113]

In an earlier chapter we introduced you to the literary device of a "Markan sandwich," the technique of framing a given event by interposing a second event right in the middle of it. Apparently, John knew the technique as well because he uses it here, sandwiching the walking on the water between the narrative of Jesus feeding the crowd on the one hand and the crowd reconnecting with Jesus to follow up with him about the previous event on the other hand.

A JOHANNINE SANDWICH

6:1–15 Feeding the five thousand
  6:16–21 Walking on water
6:22–59 Follow-up on the feeding (the Bread of Life Discourse)

In the present case, Jesus, who "knew all people,"[114] immediately discerns their true motives. It's not that they're drawn to the Messiah because of the sign he has recently performed; they simply want the thrill of having their stomachs filled without having to work for it (and many of us can relate: who wouldn't love to win the lottery so they didn't have to work ever again?).

113. John 6:20; cf. Exodus 3:14; Isaiah 40–66. Many consider the walking on the water a sign but note that the event is not actually identified as such in John's Gospel. What's more, signs in this Gospel are typically public in nature, aiming to elicit faith in the unbelieving crowd, while the walking on the water was private, seen only by Jesus's disciples. More likely, therefore, the walking on the water is a theophany, a manifestation of God. On Jesus's "I am" sayings in John's Gospel, see Andreas J. Köstenberger, "7.3 'I Am' Sayings," in *Handbook of Jewish Roots of the Christian Faith*, eds. Craig A. Evans and David Mishkin (Peabody, MA: Hendrickson, 2019).

114. John 2:24.

In our own lives, too, we often approach God not for who he is in himself but because we want him to do something for us. That's like one of our children coming to us with a request. Not that we don't delight in our children and want to give them what they would like to have (if it's good for them), but if all they ever do is come to us with their requests, we'll be grieved because we cherish our relationship with them even more than giving them what they want. It's like the bumper sticker I once saw: "My children think I'm an ATM." I'm sure God often feels that way. In fact, I'm confident Jesus often felt that way in his dealings with people. He was very gracious, but no doubt he was still grieved that so few cared to take a personal interest in him. What Jesus desires more than anything is to enter into a personal relationship with us.

The Bread of Life Discourse (6:22–71)

This desire for relationship is borne out in what follows as soon as Jesus and the disciples land on the other side of the lake. People track Jesus down in an instant, but he says to them, "Truly, truly, I say to you, you are seeking me, not because you saw signs, but because you ate your fill of the loaves. Do not work for food that perishes but for the food that endures to eternal life." People reply, "What must we do, to be doing the works of God?" Jesus's response is profound: "This is the work of God, that you believe in him whom he has sent."[115] In other words, you don't need to do anything except believe! The only "work" you have to do is believing in Jesus! And even that is really the work of God, as no one can come to Jesus unless the Father draws him. The apostle Paul's references to "works of the law" are the subject of much scholarly discussion, but here we have an equally profound word from Jesus that makes clear that people are saved by grace alone through faith alone.

Sadly, people fail to understand. In the ensuing interchange, they again ask Jesus for a sign, tragically revealing that they've failed to perceive the sign he has just performed when feeding the multitudes. Will Jesus provide yet another sign? No. Instead, he proceeds to explain the significance—or shall we say "sign-ificance"—of the sign he has just performed.[116] The crowd wants Jesus to duplicate Moses's feeding miracle of providing the Israelites in the wilderness during the exodus from Egypt with the mysterious manna, the "bread from heaven." They even have the *chutzpah* to pit Jesus against Moses: "Moses fed us with manna from heaven. What are you going to do to top this?"[117] What they conveniently ignore, however, is that in the original instance when Moses gave people the manna, they complained! The more

115. John 6:26–29.
116. John 6:30. For a similar dynamic, see John 2:18 and the discussion above.
117. My paraphrase. See John 6:30–31.

things change, the more they stay the same. In response, Jesus graciously explains that, in truth, he himself, in his very own person, is the God-sent bread from heaven that gives life, and this not merely to the Jews, but to the entire world![118] This is truly a breathtaking claim, putting Jesus way above Moses to an elevated status occupied otherwise only by God the Father, the one who "sent" Jesus into the world and "gave" him as a sin offering for the world.

Just like their ancestors, as mentioned, the Jews grumble at Jesus's words and take offense at his language that people must eat his flesh and drink his blood. (The scene now takes place in the synagogue at Capernaum, having shifted almost imperceptibly from an outdoor to an indoor venue.) We don't have time for a blow-by-blow commentary here; please make sure to read the account in John 6:25–69. As it turns out, this occasion became a watershed moment in Jesus's ministry, because many of his disciples (Jesus's close followers) stopped following him at this point, so offended were they at his teaching. Only the Twelve remain, the positive example and representative figure being Peter, who, at Jesus's challenge, responds, "Lord, to whom shall we go? You have the words of eternal life."[119] Judas, on the other hand, another member of the Twelve, will betray Jesus not long after this scene.[120] Remarkably, the fourth evangelist unveils the identity of the betrayer early in the narrative, so his readers can track Judas's movements and actions in light of this fact (even though his fellow disciples appear to have been in the dark about Judas's devious designs until the very end).

RECAP

Following the Cana Cycle, John has showcased Jesus's appearance at various Jewish festivals in the first half of the Festival Cycle. In chapters 5 and 6, we've seen how John first records a "sign" followed by a lengthy discourse or series of interchanges based on the initial sign. This helps the reader process the significance of the sign and ponder how it points to Jesus's messianic identity. In chapter 5, Jesus heals a lame man in Jerusalem—on the Sabbath (the fourth sign overall and the first in the Festival Cycle). This healing provided the occasion for the Sabbath controversy narrated in the remainder of the chapter. In the ensuing dialogue, Jesus adduces a series of witnesses attesting to his identity as the Son sent from God the Father. Just as God the Creator has authority over the Sabbath, so does Jesus the Son.

118. John 6:33.
119. John 6:68.
120. In the Gospel, that is; in real time, another year will pass until the next Passover, which Jesus spends in Jerusalem and at which occasion he will be crucified after Judas betrays him to the high priest.

Then, in chapter 6, we find Jesus in Galilee at the Passover, feeding the multitudes (the fifth sign overall and the second sign in the Festival Cycle). This feeding, which is featured in all four Gospels, leads many to wonder whether Jesus is the Prophet like Moses whom they expected to appear. Jesus, however, eludes their grasp and provides his closest followers with a private manifestation of his deity by walking on the water. What follows is the so-called Bread of Life Discourse in the remainder of chapter 6. Here Jesus reveals himself as the end-time "manna," the "bread from heaven" God gave to the Israelites in the wilderness during the exodus. Now, Jesus claims, he himself has come down from heaven so that people may "eat his flesh" and "drink his blood" and thus have eternal life. Jesus's words prove too tough to stomach even for many of his disciples.

THE BOOK OF SIGNS: THE SEVEN SIGNS OF JESUS THE MESSIAH (2:1–12:50, CONT.)

The Festival Cycle (5:1–10:42, cont.)

Jesus at the Feast of Tabernacles (7:1–8:59)

Opposition to Jesus is not limited to his disciples, however. Rejection and misunderstanding meet him at every turn, even in his own family. We've already seen how earlier, at the Cana wedding, Jesus's own mother didn't understand his messianic timing.[121] His brothers were mentioned right after that occasion, but nothing was said about their stance toward Jesus's messianic mission then. Now we see them urging Jesus to come out into the open so that he can show himself to the world, because, as the evangelist tells us, "not even his brothers believed in him."[122] As one might expect, just as Jesus had earlier refused his mother, he now reiterates to his brothers that his time has not yet come.[123] Humanly speaking, this surely must have been a very discouraging time in Jesus's ministry. Most of his disciples stopped following him, and even his own brothers didn't believe in him. Have you ever experienced discouragement in your ministry? If so, know you're not alone. In such situations, we need to focus on what we can control and remain faithful. Also, we need to focus on what we still have. Jesus still had the Twelve! While unbelief in others can be disheartening, there will be those who respond positively, and we should pour our lives into them as Jesus did with the Twelve.

---

121. John 2:4.
122. John 7:5.
123. John 7:6. Note that nothing is said about Jesus's sisters (cf. Matthew 13:56); one presumes that they didn't believe in Jesus either at this point.

This being part of the Festival Cycle, it's now the Feast of Booths or Tabernacles, at which time the Jewish people celebrated their dwelling in tents during the exodus in the wilderness. In keeping with Jesus's reluctance to reveal himself openly as the Messiah before his time has come, we witness no sign in chapters 7–8 but instead are treated to a smorgasbord of messianic expectations that swirl around Jesus's appearance at the feast, as well as Jesus's claim that, in fulfillment of Tabernacles' symbolism, he is "the light of the world."[124] I've already mentioned the evangelist's skillful use of the literary device of representative characters. In chapter 7, he uses various anonymous people in the crowd to represent a variety of messianic expectations. Don't be confused—some of these are contradictory! All of this is to show that people had different expectations as to who the Messiah would be and what kind of figure he would turn out to be; there was little uniformity in this regard. This explains why in many cases Jesus didn't meet people's expectations and thus encountered resistance from many quarters.

Remember: just because the Old Testament tells us about a descendant of David who would come and reign on his throne, as well as about a suffering servant who would give his life for people's transgressions, doesn't mean people always understood what that meant or were able to put all the pieces of the puzzle together in the right way. As a matter of fact, Peter writes that "the prophets [themselves] who prophesied . . . searched and inquired carefully, inquiring what person or time the Spirit of Christ in them was indicating when he predicted the sufferings of Christ and the subsequent glories."[125] So there was considerable uncertainty, and much confusion, surrounding the exact person, time, and circumstances of the Messiah's coming. Would he come to suffer and die or to rule and reign? (Most thought the latter.) Would he come just for Israel or for Gentiles as well? (Most thought just for Israel.)[126] Where would the Messiah come from—would he be of mysterious origin or would he be born in Bethlehem in keeping with biblical prophecy? (Many, though not all, believed the latter.) This is the kind of matrix against which people

124. John 8:12; repeated in 9:5. Note that chapters 7–8 are a unity; 7:53–8:11, which contains the story of the adulterous woman and the Pharisees, has been inserted at a later point after 7:52 but is almost certainly not original with John. Not only does the story interrupt the flow of the narrative; it is not found in the best and earliest manuscripts. The story may be historical, but it is not properly part of John's Gospel, so we will not further discuss it below. See the discussions in Harris, *John*, 166; Bruce M. Metzger, *A Textual Commentary on the Greek New Testament*, 2nd ed. (Stuttgart: Deutsche Bibelgesellschaft; New York: United Bible Societies, 1994), 187–89.

125. 1 Peter 1:10–11.

126. Including, one presumes, Nicodemus. This is why the evangelist's commentary that God so loved "the world"—including Gentiles—would have been truly shocking to most first-century Jews (see discussion at chapter 3 above and at 12:20 below).

compared anyone who appeared claiming to be the Messiah—and there were several false messianic claimants in the first century—to see whether they fit the bill, as it were.[127]

In the present instance, the evangelist skillfully uses the Feast of Tabernacles to sketch the spectrum of popular opinion regarding Jesus. In short, people were divided. Some said, "He is a good man," while others countered, "He is leading the people astray."[128] Yet others were wondering if the authorities had concluded that Jesus really was the Messiah because they allowed him to teach openly in public at the feast.[129] Regarding the Messiah's origin, some opined that "when the Christ appears, no one will know where he comes from."[130] Yet Jesus's origins, it was thought, were known—he was Joseph and Mary's son and hailed from Nazareth in Galilee. The reader of John's Gospel, of course, knows better—Jesus was the preexistent Word become flesh![131]

Others were not so skeptical, pointing to Jesus's signs. They asked, "When the Christ appears, will he do more signs than this man has done?"[132] The implied answer seems to be no. Because of his many signs, Jesus fit the bill. Maybe he was the Messiah after all?

As a structuring device, the evangelist divides his account of Jesus's appearance at the Feast of Tabernacles as follows. Starting in verse 14, Jesus teaches at "about the middle of the feast." Then, in verse 37, Jesus teaches again "on the last day of the feast." At the former occasion, Jesus revisited the Sabbath healing of the lame man in chapter 5, pointing out that even the Jewish rabbis conceded that baby boys may be circumcised on the Sabbath, so why not heal a man on the Sabbath?[133] At the latter occasion, at Tabernacles, a feast known for its water-pouring ceremonies, Jesus invited spiritually thirsty people to come to him, the one through whom the Holy Spirit would be given not many days later.[134]

---

127. Jesus himself warned against false Christs or prophets in his Olivet Discourse (Matthew 24:5, 11, 23–24). In the book of Acts, the famous Jewish rabbi Gamaliel refers to imposters such as Theudas or Judas the Galilean (Acts 5:35–37). The first-century Jewish historian Josephus, likewise, mentions several messianic pretenders. See Paul W. Barnett, "The Jewish Signs Prophets—A.D. 40–70: Their Intentions and Origin," *New Testament Studies* 27 (1981): 679–97.
128. John 7:12.
129. John 7:26.
130. John 7:27.
131. John 1:1, 14.
132. John 7:31.
133. John 7:22–23.
134. John 7:37–39. See Cyndi Parker, "The People's Thirst at the Feast of Tabernacles (John 7:37–39)," in Beitzel, *Lexham Geographic Commentary*, 356–64.

JESUS AT THE FEAST OF TABERNACLES

7:1–13	Preamble: Jesus and his brothers and his private journey to the feast
7:14–36	Middle of the feast: Jesus commences his teaching
7:37–52	Last day of the feast: Jesus continues his teaching, Pharisaic opposition
8:12–59	Jesus continues his teaching, escalating controversy

At this, multiple opinions regarding Jesus surface again. Some affirmed, "This really is the Prophet." Others even opined, "This is the Christ." Yet others objected that the Messiah was to be born in Bethlehem, yet Jesus came from Galilee![135] While not mentioned in this Gospel, the informed reader will immediately recognize that people here are victims of misunderstanding: while having grown up in Nazareth and having taken up residence in Capernaum (both of which were in Galilee), Jesus had in fact been born in Bethlehem, as the Gospels of Matthew and Luke make clear, in keeping with messianic prophecy in the Old Testament book of Micah.[136]

These kinds of conversations are sandwiched between the reference to the Jewish authorities sending officers to arrest Jesus in verse 32 and the return of these officers to the chief priests and Pharisees in verse 45—without Jesus! It appears even the officers had fallen under the spell of Jesus's teaching. What's more, even among the Sanhedrin—the Jewish ruling council—were those, like Nicodemus (who had come to Jesus earlier), who defended him and urged that he be treated fairly.[137] Things seem to be turning out in Jesus's favor—or do they?[138]

135. John 7:40–43.
136. Matthew 2:1–6; cf. Micah 5:2; Luke 2:4–6.
137. John 7:50–51; cf. 3:1.
138. Note that we move straight from 7:52 to 8:12; see discussion of the pericope of the adulterous woman (which is likely not original with the fourth evangelist) in note 124 above.

VARYING OPINIONS REGARDING JESUS VOICED BY REPRESENTATIVE CHARACTERS

Passage in John	*Opinion regarding Jesus*
7:12	"He is a good man."
7:12	"He is leading the people astray."
7:27	The Messiah will be of mysterious origin.
7:31	Will the Messiah perform more signs than Jesus?
7:41	"This really is the Prophet."
7:41	"This is the Christ."
7:41	The Messiah was to be born in Bethlehem, yet Jesus came from Galilee.

Continuing his teaching at the feast, Jesus now boldly states, "I am the light of the world."[139] Readers of John's Gospel have already been introduced to Jesus "the light" in the prologue.[140] Now we see Jesus himself affirm being "the light" at a festival known for its torch-lighting ceremonies. The Pharisees promptly challenge him, objecting that a person's witness regarding himself cannot be accepted without additional witnesses.[141] Jesus retorts that his testimony is true, but it doesn't stand alone; God the Father attests to Jesus's messianic identity and divine commission as well.

This moves discussion to Jesus's relationship with the Father, which, as the readers of the Gospel already know, is unique and entails Jesus's equality with God.[142] From chapter 5 to chapter 8 to, as we'll see, chapter 10, therefore, the Festival Cycle is pervaded by Jesus's repeated and explicit claims of deity and of equality with God.[143] This sets him on

139. John 8:12.
140. John 1:4–9.
141. Cf. Deuteronomy 19:15.
142. John 1:1–2, 18.
143. See especially John 5:18 and 10:33.

an inevitable collision course with the Jewish authorities who tenaciously defend monotheism, the belief in one and only one God.[144] In this way, the fourth evangelist makes his entire Gospel a referendum on Jesus's deity; all other issues pale by comparison.

The Jewish authorities believe he is a mere man whose origin and family background they know. In fact, Jesus came from heaven as the God-sent Messiah to accomplish his mission (attested by his messianic signs). Upon completing his mission, he will return to his divine glory by way of the cross, where he will be "lifted up" both physically and spiritually—crucified by humans but exalted by God. In John 3:14, Jesus presented his own "lifting up" in analogy with the bronze serpent Moses had "lifted up" in the wilderness. In John 8:28, we find the second such reference: "When you have lifted up the Son of Man, then you will know that I am he." This shows that Jesus's crucifixion is inescapable and part of God's sovereign plan, and that Jesus is consciously and deliberately moving toward the cross. While the Jewish and Roman authorities are dead set on destroying him, and Satan will use Judas as a human instrument of betrayal, God will use human evil to accomplish his good and sovereign divine purposes. He won't allow crucifixion to be the last word but will override and overrule it by raising Jesus from the dead. As Jesus had said previously, "Destroy this temple [i.e., his body], and in three days I will raise it up."[145]

The remainder of the chapter finds a truly astonishing dynamic at work: the same "Jews who had believed" Jesus,[146] when challenged to continue in Jesus's word so as to prove that they're really Jesus's disciples, turn out at closer scrutiny to be slaves to sin and children of the devil! In this way, Jesus confronts the Jewish people's presumption that just because they were Jews ethnically, this meant they were also God's children spiritually. This is borne out by numerous passages in the other Gospels in which Jews customarily refer to Gentiles as "sinners," implying that they themselves were not! Yet, while they were God's chosen people and God had indeed entered into covenant with Abraham, they were still sinners and in need of God's grace. Merely affirming, as they did, "Abraham is our father," was inadequate, because, as Jesus pointed out, "If you were Abraham's children, you would be doing the works Abraham did."[147] In other words,

144. Note that John himself, who is Jewish, affirms both monotheism and Jesus's deity, contending that there is indeed one God, but that this God exists in two related yet distinct persons—Jesus the Son and God the Father. John also mentions later in the Gospel that both Jesus and the Father will send the Spirit, who thus is the third person in the one Godhead. Later, the church would use John's Gospel to develop the doctrine of the Trinity—God existing eternally as Three-in-One, one God in three persons, Father, Son, and Spirit. See Köstenberger and Swain, *Father, Son and Spirit*, especially chapter 1 on John's Gospel and Jewish monotheism.

145. John 2:19. The third "lifted-up saying" in John's Gospel is found in 12:32, on which see the discussion below.

146. John 8:31.

147. John 8:39.

"show me"[148]—prove to me your faith by your works. James and Paul would later address this same issue, as did the Jerusalem Council in the early days of the church.[149]

The debate between Jesus and the Jewish leaders gets increasingly heated. They accuse him of demon possession, while he points out that their true father is not Abraham but the devil![150] The interchange culminates in Jesus's claim, "Before Abraham was, I am"—affirming that Jesus existed prior to Abraham—at which the Jews once again pick up stones to throw at Jesus because of perceived blasphemy.[151] This is an incredibly climactic moment at this point in John's Gospel, because it continues the string of references to Jesus's claim to deity that proves deeply offensive to his monotheistic Jewish contemporaries (though not the Twelve!). In fact, the entire Festival Cycle is enveloped by bookends where Jesus affirms his deity and his Jewish opponents attempt to stone him on account of blasphemy.[152] In the end, it's the charge of blasphemy that is leveled against Jesus before Pilate.[153]

The Sixth Sign: Healing a Man Born Blind (9:1–41)

With the merest of transitions ("As he passed by"), John continues the narrative by recounting Jesus's healing of a man born blind, another astonishing messianic sign performed by Jesus that attests to his messianic identity.[154] At the outset, Jesus is addressing some false preconceived notions about the nature of suffering—namely, that suffering is always a result of a person's sin, or at least that of his parents. In the present case, at least—the predicament of the man having been born blind—Jesus notes that the man's blindness was to serve to reveal the glory of God in Jesus, who, as mentioned, is "the light of the world."[155]

The story is told in a highly entertaining fashion and spans the entire chapter. First, John records the actual healing (9:1–12). Then, he features the Pharisees' initial interrogation of the formerly blind man (9:13–17). After this, he narrates the Pharisees' interrogation of the man's parents (9:18–23). This is followed by a second round of questioning of the healed man by the Pharisees (9:24–34). Finally, John uses the event as a

148. Can't resist—I'm writing this in the "Show Me" state!
149. See esp. James 2:14–26; Galatians; Acts 15.
150. John 8:44, 48, 52.
151. John 8:58–59.
152. John 5:17; 10:30–33.
153. John 19:7.
154. On the setting, see Elaine A. Phillips, "Healing by Living Water at the Pool of Siloam (John 9:1–41)," in Beitzel, *Lexham Geographic Commentary*, 365–73.
155. John 9:5; cf. 8:12. Note also the affinity between 2:11 (the first, "head" sign) and 9:5 (the sixth sign). In both cases, Jesus's disciples see Jesus's glory and believe on account of his messianic sign.

sort of real-life parable illustrating the spiritual blindness of the Pharisees (9:35–41).[156] It's as if the evangelist is saying: Jesus can open the eyes of those who are physically blind, but he can't help those who claim to see while being spiritually blind!

THE STORY OF THE HEALING OF THE MAN BORN BLIND

9:1–12	Healing of the blind man
9:13–17	Pharisees' initial interrogation of the man
9:18–23	Interrogation of the man's parents
9:24–34	Second round of questioning of the man
9:35–41	On the Pharisees' spiritual blindness

As mentioned above, the healed blind man provides a striking contrast with the healed lame man at the beginning of the Festival Cycle in chapter 5. While the lame man blames Jesus and reports him to the authorities, the healed blind man defends Jesus and ultimately worships him. This again illustrates the importance of responding to Jesus in faith, discerning the way in which his messianic signs reveal his identity—Jesus is the Messiah, the Son of God! In this way, once again, this sign, carefully selected by the evangelist, becomes the vehicle of the evangelist's message that undergirds his entire Gospel. His burning desire is that people believe in Jesus and as a result have eternal life in him.[157] Do you believe yet? Are you reading John's Gospel as good news? Have you come to know Jesus for who he really is? Who do you say that he is?

156. Note that, in stark contrast to the other Gospels, John doesn't feature a single parable. It's as if John were saying Jesus's life contains more than enough real-life encounters and events that are pregnant with meaning; who needs parables—made-up stories—when deeper spiritual meaning can be readily gleaned from actual historical events such as Jesus's healing of a blind man (which revealed the Pharisees' spiritual blindness)?

157. John 20:30–31.

THE BOOK OF SIGNS: THE SEVEN SIGNS OF JESUS THE MESSIAH (2:1–12:50, CONT.)

The Festival Cycle (5:1–10:42, cont.)

The Good Shepherd Discourse (10:1–21)

Jesus at the Feast of Dedication (10:22–42)

THE BOOK OF SIGNS: THE SEVEN SIGNS OF JESUS THE MESSIAH (2:1–12:50, CONT.)

The Festival Cycle (5:1–10:42, cont.)

The Good Shepherd Discourse (10:1–21)

With no transition whatsoever, chapter 10 picks up seamlessly where chapter 9 left off, starting with an authoritative pronouncement of Jesus regarding legitimate and illegitimate shepherds of God's sheep.[158] The so-called Good Shepherd Discourse by Jesus contained in this chapter is one of two sustained symbolic discourses in this Gospel,[159] the other being the discourse on the vine and the branches in chapter 15. Both highlight corporate metaphors for God's people: God's flock (chapter 10) and God's vineyard (chapter 15). Both metaphors are used for Israel in the Old Testament but are now applied by Jesus to his new messianic community made up of all believers in him, both Jewish and Gentile.

The Good Shepherd Discourse contains two of the seven "I am" sayings of Jesus in this Gospel: "I am the door (or gate)" and "I am the good shepherd."[160] How can Jesus

158. Note that chapter divisions were not added to our Bibles until 1205 by professor Stephen Langton, and verse numbers were added even later, in 1551, by the printer Robert Stephanus.

159. The ESV renders the Greek word *paroimia* in John 10:6 as "figure of speech," but "illustration" may be a better translation. In the other instance of the same word, in John 16:25, the expression is used to refer to Jesus's illustration of a woman having a baby as an analogy for the grief his followers would experience when he would be crucified to be followed by their joy when they would see him again after his resurrection.

160. John 10:11. See Köstenberger, "'I Am' Sayings." See also Vernon H. Alexander, "The 'Good Shepherd' and Other Metaphors of Pastoralism (Matt 18:10–14; 25:31–46; Luke 15:1–7; John 10:1–15; Acts 8:26–35)," in Beitzel, *Lexham Geographic Commentary*, 374–84.

be both the gate to the sheep and their shepherd? This shows the fluidity that one often finds in these kinds of symbolic discourses. The fact is, Jesus is both: he is the only legitimate way of access to God's flock—he is "the way";[161] and he is also the divinely appointed shepherd of God's flock, in contrast to Israel's faithless shepherds who, as Ezekiel lamented in his day, used their sacred office only to enrich themselves at the sheep's expense.

All of this makes clear that Jesus is still talking about the very same Pharisees who had opposed his healing of the blind man in the previous chapter. The connection with the preceding chapter is underscored by the renewed charge of demon possession hurled toward Jesus, and people's response: "These are not the words of one who is oppressed by a demon. Can a demon open the eyes of the blind?"[162] Again, we see John's skillful use of representative characters. It's as if he is exploring C. S. Lewis' threefold set of options as to Jesus's identity: Is he a lunatic? Hardly. Lunatics don't usually go around performing amazing miracles that show mastery over the spirit world and that benefit other people!

Actually, that's an interesting aspect of people's response to Jesus. It seems they couldn't deny that he had something supernatural about him and that he commanded the spirit world. They saw how he in many ways transcended the mundane scene of your average Jewish rabbi. It would have been easy just to label him as a Galilean miracle worker, but that hardly did justice to who he was in his totality. He was that, but he was so much more. It is this multifaceted nature of Jesus's mission and identity that his contemporaries, and scholars to this day, have found so difficult to grasp. How do you bring the different roles and identities combined in Jesus all under one hat? That's what we see both the crowds and the Jewish leaders grappling with. Could it be that Jesus was the Messiah, the Son of God?

Jesus at the Feast of Dedication (10:22–42)

With this, the scene transitions to yet another feast, the last one mentioned in the Festival Cycle that is slowly but surely drawing to a close—namely, the Feast of Dedication. This festival is not mentioned in the Old Testament because it was instituted only in the intertestamental or Second Temple period, during the time of a Jewish revolutionary movement led by the Maccabees in the second century BC.[163] At that time, the Seleucid (Greek) ruler Antiochus Epiphanes IV, a prototype of the Antichrist, erected a

161. John 14:6.
162. John 10:21.
163. On Jewish Second Temple history and literature, see Köstenberger, Kellum, and Quarles, *The Cradle, the Cross, and the Crown*, chapter 2.

statue of Zeus in the Jerusalem temple and—horror of horrors—sacrificed a pig at the altar.[164] A Jewish revolt predictably ensued, and miraculously Antiochus was defeated by a local militia and the temple rededicated in 164 BC, giving birth to the annual Feast of Dedication (celebrated in mid-December).[165]

While the locale is different—Jesus is now moving about in the temple area, in a place called Solomon's Colonnade—the topic is much the same as earlier in the chapter: Jesus's rightful authority over God's "flock" or "sheep" and his role as the "good shepherd." In a passage often mentioned in conjunction with the biblical teaching of "eternal security"—that is, the fact that once a person is saved, they cannot lose their salvation (though they may suffer loss of rewards)—Jesus insists that no one can snatch his sheep (i.e., believers) out of his hand because God the Father, who has given those sheep to Jesus, is greater than all. In other words, God is greater than all our sin, greater than the worst sin any of us can ever commit! That's why our salvation ultimately depends on God's ability to save, and preserve us once saved, not on our own ability to stay saved—a deeply reassuring realization, as all of us are weak and susceptible to temptation. Jesus proceeds to depict God the Father and himself—God the Son—as working in tandem throughout Jesus's messianic mission, boldly asserting, "I and the Father are one."[166]

For the third time in the Festival Cycle, the Jews are picking up stones to throw at Jesus because of alleged blasphemy.[167] At this, Jesus engages them in a rather technical rabbinic debate about whether it is ever appropriate to call someone other than God "Son of God." The implied answer is yes—but the Jews aren't convinced. For now, Jesus continues to elude their grasp, however, and returns to the place where John the Baptist had started his baptizing ministry.[168] This is now the last time the evangelist refers to John the Baptist in what scholars identify as a literary *inclusio*.[169] This portion of the

164. See Jesus's reference in the so-called Olivet Discourse to the "abomination of desolation spoken of by the prophet Daniel" (Matthew 24:15; Mark 13:14; cf. Daniel 9:27). On Jesus's teaching on the end times, see Andreas J. Köstenberger, Alexander E. Stewart, and Apollo Makara, *Jesus and the Future: Understanding What Jesus Taught about the End Times* (Bellingham, WA: Lexham, 2017).

165. Cf. John 10:22: "It was winter."

166. John 10:30. Note that the word "one" is *neuter* rather than masculine in the Greek, which means that Jesus is affirming that he and the Father are one *entity*, not that they're one *person*. In fact, they are *two* distinct persons, yet united in their mission to save and to preserve all genuine believers.

167. John 10:31–33; cf. 5:18; 8:59.

168. See Mark W. G. Stibbe, "The Elusive Christ: A New Reading of the Fourth Gospel," *Journal for the Study of the New Testament* 44 (1991): 19–38.

169. That is, the Book of Signs starts and ends with a reference to John the Baptist in 1:19 and 10:40–41. Another such *inclusio* is the reference to Jesus's first and second sign in Cana of Galilee in 2:11 and 4:54. In both cases, the repeated reference serves as a sort of bookend indicating the beginning and end of a literary unit in John's Gospel, whether the Book of Signs or the Cana Cycle.

Gospel thus ends the same way it began: with Jesus's forerunner, John the Baptist.[170] As the evangelist points out, unlike Jesus, John performed no sign, yet everything he said regarding Jesus was true. He was the foundational witness to Jesus the Messiah.[171]

RECAP

We've already summed up the first couple chapters in the Festival Cycle (chaps. 5 and 6) above. In the remainder of this portion of John's Gospel, we see Jesus attend the Feast of Tabernacles in Jerusalem. Throughout this extended eight-day festival, Jesus is manifested as the "light of the world." In many ways, Jesus represents the very essence of each feast in the Jewish festal calendar. At the same time, chapters 7 and 8 feature no further messianic signs of Jesus. The next and final sign in the Festival Cycle, the healing of the man born blind, is found in chapter 9 (the sixth sign overall and the third sign in the Festival Cycle). Jesus's identity as the "light of the world" ties chapters 8 and 9 together.

At this occasion, Jesus opens the eyes of the blind—and of a man *born* blind at that!—in vintage messianic fashion. What more can Jesus do? How about raise the dead? As it turns out, that's exactly what he'll do for an encore, as the final, seventh sign in John's Gospel (chap. 11; see below). For now, John presents Jesus as the caring and compassionate messianic shepherd who protects his flock and sustains an intimate relationship with his spiritual sheep. The Festival Cycle ends with a reference to Jesus's appearance at the Feast of Dedication and reference to John the Baptist who had performed no signs, yet whose witness regarding Jesus was found to be true.

170. See John 1:19.
171. John 10:41.

THE BOOK OF SIGNS: THE SEVEN SIGNS OF JESUS THE MESSIAH (2:1–12:50, CONT.)

The Climactic Sign and the Jewish Rejection of the Messiah (11:1–12:50)

The Seventh Sign: Raising Lazarus (11:1–44)

The Sanhedrin's Plot against Jesus (11:45–57)

THE BOOK OF SIGNS: THE SEVEN SIGNS OF JESUS THE MESSIAH (2:1–12:50, CONT.)

The Climactic Sign and the Jewish Rejection of the Messiah (11:1–12:50)

Following the Cana Cycle (chaps. 2–4) and the Festival Cycle (chaps. 5–10), each of which features three of Jesus's messianic signs, a bridge section spanning chapters 11–12 narrates the seventh, climactic sign—the raising of Lazarus—and closes the book (the Book of Signs) on the Jewish rejection of Jesus the Messiah, in keeping with biblical prophecy. (John quotes two passages from the prophet Isaiah; see discussion at 12:38–40 below.) While two chapters remain, Jesus's public ministry has all but come to a close with the third and final attempt to stone him at the conclusion of the Festival Cycle at the end of chapter 10. All that's left for Jesus to do is perform his final sign.

THE SEVEN SIGNS OF JESUS IN THE BOOK OF SIGNS (JOHN 2–12)

Cana Cycle (John 2–4)

2:1–11	#1: Turning water into wine at the wedding at Cana	Galilee
2:13–22	#2: Clearing the temple as a sign of God's judgment	Jerusalem
4:46–54	#3: Healing the official's son	Galilee

THE SEVEN SIGNS OF JESUS IN THE BOOK OF SIGNS (JOHN 2–12)		
	Festival Cycle (John 5–10)	
5:1–15	#4: Healing the invalid	Jerusalem
6:1–15	#5: Feeding the multitude	Galilee
9:1–41	#6: Opening the eyes of the blind man	Jerusalem
	Conclusion of Book of Signs (John 11–12)	
11:1–44	#7: Raising Lazarus from the dead	Outside Jerusalem

The Seventh Sign: Raising Lazarus (11:1–44)

The story of the raising of Lazarus is well known. Lazarus was the brother of Mary and Martha, a pair of sisters also featured in Luke's Gospel where Jesus defends Mary against Martha's complaint that she should help her host Jesus while she chose instead to sit at Jesus's feet to learn from him.[172] John expects his readers to be already familiar with Mary, as he mentions at the beginning of chapter 11 that it was Mary who anointed Jesus's feet with perfume and wiped his feet with her hair—even though he doesn't recount this story until the next chapter in his Gospel![173] As at the healing of the blind man, Jesus notes at the outset that Lazarus's illness occurred so that the glory of God could be manifested in and through Jesus.[174]

There is a dramatic delay in that Jesus, when hearing of Lazarus's illness, "stayed two days longer in the place where he was."[175] In the interim, it turns out, Lazarus has died. When Jesus arrives on the scene, Lazarus has already been in the tomb for four days.

172. Luke 10:38–42. Sitting at someone's feet was the characteristic posture of a disciple. On the fourth evangelist's portrayal of Jesus as a rabbi and of his relationship with his followers in terms of first-century Jewish rabbi-disciple relationships, see Andreas J. Köstenberger, "Jesus as Rabbi in the Fourth Gospel," *Bulletin for Biblical Research* 8 (1998): 97–128.
173. John 11:2; cf. 12:1–8.
174. John 11:4; cf. 9:5.
175. John 11:6.

Jesus is initially met by Lazarus's (older) sister Martha and assures her that her brother will rise again. Again, utilizing the literary device of representative figures, the evangelist quotes Martha as saying that, yes, she knows Lazarus will rise again "in the resurrection on the last day."[176] Martha's statement promptly triggers another "I am" saying of Jesus: "I am the resurrection and the life."[177] In context, Jesus makes clear that, as the resurrection and the life, he has the power to raise Lazarus not only on the last day but right then! When he challenges Martha and asks if she believes this, she responds, "Yes, Lord; I believe that you are the Christ, the Son of God, who is coming into the world."[178] In this (albeit slightly elusive) confession, Martha anticipates almost verbatim John's purpose statement at the end of this Gospel. This shows the remarkable place John assigns to women in his account.

Next, Jesus meets up with Lazarus's younger sister Mary, who, heartbroken yet full of confident faith in Jesus, simply tells him, "Lord, if you had been here, my brother would not have died."[179] Notice that Mary, like Martha, had enough faith to believe Jesus could have kept Lazarus from dying but perhaps not quite enough faith to believe that now that her brother had died, Jesus could raise him from the dead—at least not right now. When Jesus sees Mary and others weep, he, too, bursts into tears.[180] How touching! As at previous occasions, John helps his readers connect the present event with the preceding sign when he quotes some Jews as saying, "Could not he who opened the eyes of the blind man also have kept this man from dying?"[181] Like Mary, these Jews fall short of believing that now that Lazarus has died, Jesus can do anything about this tragedy, much less raise him from the dead.

The remainder of the narrative is told rather tersely with great economy of words. Jesus arrives at the tomb, issuing the directive, "Take away the stone," and—Martha's protestations notwithstanding that Lazarus would exude an odor of death as he has already been in the tomb for four days—they take away the stone.[182] Jesus utters a short prayer and commands with a loud voice, "Lazarus, come out!"[183] At this, the dead man walks out of the tomb, still bound with linen strips and a face cloth! Jesus says simply,

176. John 11:24.

177. John 11:25.

178. John 11:27; cf. 20:30–31.

179. John 11:32.

180. John 11:35, the shortest verse in the Bible, at least in English: "Jesus wept." There is good reason to believe that the aorist tense-form in the Greek original is to be taken ingressively—that is, as focusing on the beginning of Jesus's action: he "burst into tears," being suddenly overwhelmed by the evil of death and sin in this fallen world.

181. John 11:37; cf. 12:17 below.

182. John 11:39–41.

183. John 11:43.

"Unbind him, and let him go,"[184] at which the scene shifts abruptly from Lazarus's tomb to a meeting of the Sanhedrin. This is one of several junctures in John's Gospel that has all the makings of a stage play.

As mentioned, the raising of Lazarus is Jesus's climactic, seventh messianic sign in John's Book of Signs, which makes up the first half of his Gospel. In this first half, the fourth evangelist depicts Jesus's mission to the Jews as their God-sent Messiah. Tragically, they will reject him, despite the abundant proof he furnished for being the Messiah in keeping with the messianic expectations voiced by the Old Testament prophets, especially Isaiah.[185] As a raising from the dead, the raising of Lazarus, even more than the other signs, points to Jesus's own resurrection, proving that he is indeed "the resurrection and the life" in his very being.[186] If people don't believe in Jesus when he raises people from the dead, how will they believe in the resurrected Jesus?[187]

The Sanhedrin's Plot against Jesus (11:45–57)

In their meeting, the chief priests and Pharisees are exasperated. What can they do? Jesus's popularity is meteorically on the rise. Then Caiaphas the high priest speaks up, arguing that "it is better for you that one man should die for the people, not that the whole nation should perish."[188] The evangelist astutely observes that Caiaphas, speaking better than he knew, here unwittingly prophesied that Jesus would die on the cross for people's sins—what's more, not only for Jews but also for Gentiles. The chapter ends on the ominous note that the third Passover recorded in John's Gospel is at hand and orders are out for Jesus's arrest. Will he even come to the feast? Once again, John proves to be a master storyteller who keeps his readers on the edge of their seats.

184. John 11:44.
185. See further John 12:38–41 below.
186. Cf. John 11:25; cf. 1:4–9; 14:6.
187. This is essentially the point Jesus makes in the parable of the rich man and Lazarus in Luke 16:19–31.
188. John 11:50.

THE BOOK OF SIGNS: THE SEVEN SIGNS OF JESUS THE MESSIAH (2:1–12:50, CONT.)
The Climactic Sign and the Jewish Rejection of the Messiah (11:1–12:50)
The Anointing at Bethany (12:1–11)
The Triumphal Entry (12:12–19)
The Dawning Era of the Gentiles (12:20–36a)
Conclusion of the Book of Signs: Jewish Unbelief toward Jesus the Messiah (12:36b–50)

THE BOOK OF SIGNS: THE SEVEN SIGNS OF JESUS THE MESSIAH (2:1–12:50, CONT.)

The Climactic Sign and the Jewish Rejection of the Messiah (11:1–12:50, cont.)

The Anointing at Bethany (12:1–11)

The chapter opens with a remarkable scene: a dinner given in Lazarus's honor, the very one whom Jesus had raised from the dead. As anticipated in the previous chapter, Mary anoints Jesus's feet with precious, expensive perfume, intuitively sensing that Jesus's crucifixion and burial are imminent.[189] While the other Gospels don't reveal the identity of the one who objected to this "extravagant waste," the fourth evangelist notes that the anointing served as an occasion for the antagonism of Judas to be revealed, as pious posturing masked the fact that he was a thief. Notice how a single verse is devoted to Mary's act of devotion, while five verses are given to Judas's objection and Jesus's response.[190] The mention that "the house was filled with the

189. Cf. John 11:1–2 and discussion above.

190. John 12:3 on Mary, and John 12:4–8 on Judas. Regarding Mary's actions, Harris (*John*, 224) notes several irregularities: (1) she anointed Jesus's feet; (2) she did so during a meal; (3) she wiped Jesus's feet with her hair rather than a towel; (4) she let down her hair in public; (5) she wiped off the oil.

fragrance of the perfume" is a nice touch, reminding the reader that the author is an eyewitness.[191]

The Sanhedrin's desperation is underscored further by the fact that now they resolved to kill not only Jesus but Lazarus as well, because his very presence constituted incontrovertible evidence that Jesus had the power to raise the dead. It's hard to argue with a dead man come to life (though some diehard skeptics will simply not believe no matter what evidence they're presented with)![192] Needless to say, John here provides us with both a positive example of devotion to Jesus (Mary) and a negative example of antagonism toward Jesus (Judas). This shows how Jesus was a polarizing figure who forced people to make a decision regarding who he was and how we should relate to him. We must either pledge allegiance to Jesus in loyalty and faith or reject him and suffer the consequences. There's simply no middle ground—as Pilate, the Roman governor, would soon find out.

The Triumphal Entry (12:12–19)

The final week of Jesus has now begun. It's Palm Sunday, and Jesus enters Jerusalem in what is known as the "triumphal entry." Throngs of people welcome him into the city, waving palm branches from nearby Jericho, the "City of Palms," a nationalistic symbol found on coins celebrating Jewish national pride in the face of foreign oppression and occupation. By riding into the city on a lowly donkey, Jesus not only emulates King Solomon's mode of entry into the city; he also evokes the memory of the coming lowly king envisioned in the Old Testament prophet Zechariah's prophecy: "behold, your king is coming, sitting on a donkey's colt!"[193] Again, the evangelist connects this event to what had happened previously, in the present case the raising of Lazarus.[194]

The triumphal entry is covered in all four Gospels. As mentioned, it's deeply tragic and ironic that people here acclaim Jesus on the basis of a shallow notion of who the Messiah was going to be. Later the same week, they will shout, "Crucify! Crucify!" This shows that Jesus was right when he chose not to entrust himself to anyone.[195] Public adulation is extremely fickle, and you may find yourself "the flavor of the day" for a season before people move on to someone more "exciting" than you. What others think about you is simply no reliable grounds on which to base your self-worth. Jesus was se-

191. John 12:3.
192. See Jesus's parable of the rich man and Lazarus in Luke 16:19–31, especially the punch line in verse 31: "If they do not hear Moses and the Prophets, neither will they be convinced if someone should rise from the dead."
193. John 12:15; cf. Zechariah 9:9; 1 Kings 1:33, 38, 44.
194. John 12:17–18.
195. John 2:23–25.

cure in himself and in his relationship with God the Father, which enabled him to deal with seismic shifts in popular opinion. You and I, likewise, should ground our identity in being loved and accepted by God in Christ, which is true no matter what others are saying about us.

The Dawning Era of the Gentiles (12:20–36a)

Jesus's popularity is further underscored by the fact that some Greeks (i.e., Gentiles) ask to see him. This, stunningly, triggers Jesus's pronouncement, "The hour has come for the Son of Man to be glorified."[196] As we've seen, starting in chapter 2, Jesus has repeatedly affirmed, both to his mother and to his brothers, that his "time"—that is, the time at which he would publicly reveal his messianic identity—has not yet come.[197] But now, it appears, it is approaching Gentiles who signal to Jesus that his "time"—that is, his saving cross-death—is near. In an agricultural metaphor, Jesus likens himself to a grain of wheat that must fall into the ground and die in order to bring much fruit—apparently, including many Gentiles—and speaks of losing his life. This shows that throughout his life Jesus was focused on the work of redemption that he was about to accomplish.

When a heavenly voice promises to glorify God's name, Jesus utters his third "lifted up" saying in this Gospel, averring, "And I, when I am lifted up from the earth, will draw all people to myself."[198] Doubtless by "all people" Jesus means "both Jews and Gentiles." And yet the evangelist doesn't say whether the Gentiles who had asked to see Jesus got their wish. One surmises they did not, as Jesus had not yet been "lifted up" on the cross for the salvation of all who would believe in him regardless of ethnic background.[199] At the end of the Book of Signs, this gives a heads up to the reader that Jesus would surmount his rejection by the Jewish leaders and that his death would open the door to salvation to all, Jews and non-Jews alike. People might reject him, but God would accept his sacrifice on our behalf! And that's in the end all that matters. As Paul would write later, "If God is for us, who can be against us?"[200]

Conclusion of the Book of Signs: Jewish Unbelief toward Jesus the Messiah (12:36b–50)

At this, Jesus hides himself, most likely conveying God's judgment and hiddenness for those who are about to reject him as Messiah and God-sent king. John draws

196. John 12:23.
197. Cf. John 2:4; 7:6; cf. 7:30.
198. John 12:32.
199. Or gender or social status; see Paul's words in 1 Corinthians 12:13; Galatians 3:28.
200. Romans 8:31.

the somber spiritual conclusion: "Though he [Jesus] had done so many signs before them, they still did not believe in him."[201] Even this unbelief however, John points out, fulfilled biblical prophecy. As in Isaiah's day, God's message through Jesus has largely fallen on deaf ears among the Jewish people. As Isaiah lamented, "Lord, who has believed what he heard from us, and to whom has the arm of the Lord been revealed?"[202] "Arm of the Lord" refers to God's power, which had been on ample display in Jesus's powerful works (his seven messianic signs). Tellingly, this first of two Isaianic passages John quotes, Isaiah 53:1, is part of the Song of the Suffering Servant that is fulfilled in Jesus.

The second passage, Isaiah 6:10, is one of the most frequently cited passages in the entire New Testament, being found in all four Gospels as well as in the book of Acts and Romans. In it Isaiah proclaims,

> He has blinded their eyes
> 	and hardened their heart,
> lest they see with their eyes,
> 	and understand with their heart, and turn,
> 	and I would heal them.

Remarkably, this passage immediately follows Isaiah's throne-room vision of the holy God. At his realization of being a "man of unclean lips," God cleanses the prophet, who says, "Here I am! Send me," and commissions him to his prophetic ministry.[203] The fourth evangelist introduces this second passage from Isaiah, which speaks of the people's hardening toward God's message and work among them by commenting, "Therefore they could not believe."[204]

Notice he doesn't say "*did* not" but "*could* not," which raises all kinds of complex theological questions regarding the relationship between God's sovereignty and human responsibility. If they couldn't believe, then how can God still hold them responsible? Well, they couldn't, but God still can; both are true. How can this be? On one level, it's a paradox. On a higher plane of spiritual reality, however, God is sovereign (the final authority), which includes being sovereign even over human sin. In a sense, it can even be said that God was responsible for people's hardening their hearts toward Jesus. Yet at the same time it's still true that they shouldn't have done so and are responsible for the

201. John 12:37.
202. John 12:38–40; cf. Isaiah 53:1 and 6:10 (see discussion below).
203. Isaiah 6:1–9.
204. John 12:39.

fact they did. Make sense? If not, I'm sorry! It's one of the deep mysteries of the faith that defies simple explanation.[205]

The Book of Signs closes on an almost surreal note. The entire cast, it appears, has left the stage. Only Jesus "the light" remains, engaging in dramatic monologue:

> Whoever believes in me, believes not in me but in him who sent me. And whoever sees me sees him who sent me. I have come into the world as light, so that whoever believes in me may not remain in darkness. If anyone hears my words and does not keep them, I do not judge him; for I did not come to judge the world but to save the world. The one who rejects me and does not receive my words has a judge; the word that I have spoken on my own authority, but the Father who sent mee has himself given me a commandment—what to say and what to speak. And I know that his commandment is eternal life. What I say, therefore, I say as the Father has told me.[206]

With that, the curtain closes. Act I of the Johannine drama has come to an end. After a brief intermission, Act II will begin.

205. My mentor D. A. Carson has written his doctoral dissertation on the subject, in which he advocates a view called "compatibilism" (both are true: God is sovereign and we're responsible for our actions). See *Divine Sovereignty and Human Responsibility: Biblical Perspectives in Tension* (Atlanta: John Knox, 1981).

206. John 12:44–50.

THE BOOK OF EXALTATION (13:1–20:31)
The Last Supper and the Farewell Discourse (13:1–17:26)
The Last Supper and the Departure of the Betrayer (13:1–30)
The Farewell Discourse (13:31–16:33) First and Second Teaching Cycles on Life after Jesus's Departure (13:31–14:31; *15:1–16:33)*
Jesus's Final Prayer (17:1–26)

THE BOOK OF EXALTATION (13:1–20:31)

The Book of Signs (chaps. 1–12) is now followed by Act II in John's two-part drama, The Book of Exaltation. The Book of Signs narrated Jesus's performance of seven messianic signs to demonstrate to the Jewish people that is the expected Messiah. However, their rejection of Jesus is signaled at the end of the Book of Signs, so the Book of Exaltation starts out with Jesus's gathering of a believing remnant, the Twelve. In the Farewell or Upper Room Discourse, Jesus celebrates the Last Supper with his new messianic community. After Judas's departure, Jesus instructs the Eleven about his imminent departure and the coming of the indwelling Holy Spirit. The Passion Narrative ensues, including Jesus's arrest, trials, crucifixion, resurrection appearances, and final commissioning.

The Last Supper and the Farewell Discourse (13:1–17:26)

The Last Supper and the Departure of the Betrayer (13:1–30)

Moving from the end of chapter 12 to the beginning of chapter 13, it's as if you're starting to read a new book, complete with a new introduction. In the preamble, we're told that "when Jesus knew that his hour had come to depart out of this world to the Father, having loved his own who were in the world, he loved them to the end. . . . Jesus, knowing that the Father had given all things into his hands, and that he had come from God and was going back to God, rose from supper."[207] While the focus in the first half of John's Gospel was on Jesus's public performance of striking messianic signs, the focus now shifts to Jesus's private instruction of his new messianic community, the Twelve. This community is cleansed, first literally (the footwashing) and then figuratively (by the removal of Judas the betrayer).

Jesus himself, it appears, is no longer engaged in acrimonious debate with his opponents. Rather, he anticipates that he will shortly die on the cross and subsequently return to his heavenly glory. The main need now is to provide final instruction to his followers. In typical rabbinic fashion, Jesus engages in a didactic action, washing his disciples' feet in order to demonstrate their need to serve one another humbly in love. It's almost as if, for the fourth evangelist, the footwashing serves as an anticipatory commentary on the meaning of the cross before he recounts the ensuing events surrounding Jesus's crucifixion in the passion narrative.[208] The lesson of the footwashing, then, is this: "If I then, your Lord and Teacher, have washed your feet, you also ought to wash one another's feet. For I have given you an example."[209]

In that day, people would walk, sometimes for miles, in sandals on dusty roads; when they arrived at their host's house for dinner, a household servant would greet them at the door and wash their feet, so when they reclined to eat beside one other, resting on one elbow, the person beside them didn't have to smell their dirty, stinky, unsanitary feet! Problem was, at Jesus's last supper with his apostles, they rented an upper room, but apparently the household servant was not included! So who would rise to the task? No one did—except for Jesus. The disciples, for their part, were aghast—how could their Master condescend to the lowly stature of a slave? The evangelist tells us that the reason why Jesus engaged in the footwashing was because of love: "Having loved his own who were in the world, he loved them to the end."[210]

The touching footwashing scene gives way to Jesus's gentle but pointed exposure of Judas, the betrayer. The reader has been told a while back that in due course Judas, one of the Twelve, would betray Jesus.[211] It appears, however, that at the time the other apostles were completely unaware of who it was who would commit such an egregious act of treachery. We've seen how, at the recent anointing of Jesus by Mary of Bethany, Judas's antagonism reared its ugly head, but nonetheless Judas's Janus-faced nature was

207. John 13:1, 3.

208. I develop this idea in *Theology of John's Gospel and Letters*, chapter 13, "The Johannine Love Ethic."

209. John 13:14–15.

210. John 13:1. "Loved them to the end" ("to the end" is *eis telos* in Greek) was true both *literally* in that Jesus loved his disciples all the way to the cross, the ultimate expression of his love (John 3:16), and *figuratively* in that Jesus's love was perfect and complete.

211. John 6:70–71.

largely lost on the disciples.[212] During the Last Supper in the upper room, we see the "beloved disciple" (the author of the Gospel) and Peter engage in an exchange regarding the identity of the betrayer, and Jesus indicate that it was Judas, apparently seated at Jesus's right, the place of honor, who would point him out to the authorities.[213]

It's gripping to realize that this very Judas was among those whose feet Jesus had just finished washing! Jesus loved Judas, even though he knew he would shortly betray him, a tangible and moving expression of Jesus's maxim that his followers should love even their enemies.[214] The scene ends with Judas stepping out of the room into the night, ominously foreshadowing the hour when darkness would reign and Judas would betray Jesus with a kiss in the garden of Gethsemane.[215] Put yourself in the upper room, and in the shoes of the disciples: How would you have felt? There was probably quite a bit of tension in the air and a measure of uncertainty. People didn't know what would happen and how it would affect them. They had staked their lives on following Jesus, and now it looked like the gamble had not paid off. What would Jesus say next?

The Farewell Discourse (13:31–16:33)

Now that his inner circle of followers had been cleansed—not merely physically by the footwashing but also spiritually by the removal of the betrayer—Jesus begins to instruct his followers. He first enunciates "a new commandment" he gives to them: "that you love one another: just as I have loved you, you also are to love one another."[216] This is how people will know that they are Jesus's disciples—by their love for one another. At this, Peter pledges undying loyalty, but Jesus predicts that even Peter, the apostles' unquestioned leader and spokesman, would shortly deny him three times.[217] It's interesting that Jesus speaks first and foremost of love and loyalty. In the face of Judas's defection and the prospect of Peter's denials, Jesus unconditionally loves his followers all the way to the cross and talks to them about selfless love. He definitely walked his talk and would amply earn the right to talk about the "glory of love."[218]

212. John 12:4–8.
213. John 13:21–27.
214. Matthew 5:44.
215. John 13:30; cf. Luke 22:47–48, 53.
216. John 13:34.
217. Jesus's prophecy came true: see John 18:17, 25–27.
218. Excuse the allusion to an old Peter Cetera song (1986) by the same title! Obviously, Jesus talks about a totally different kind of love than the lyrics of this song.

The First and Second Teaching Cycles on Life after Jesus's Departure (13:31–14:31; 15:1–16:33). The next three chapters contain what is commonly referred to as the Upper Room or Farewell Discourse.[219] The first teaching cycle of Jesus spans from 13:31 to 14:31, and the second extends from 15:1 to 16:33. In this material, unique to John, Jesus engages in a sort of Q and A with his followers who are deeply perturbed and perplexed at the prospect of his imminent departure and the loss they would suffer because of the removal of their beloved teacher. The following disciples take turns asking questions or making a request:

- Thomas (14:5): "How can we know the way?"
- Philip (14:8): "Lord, show us the Father, and it is enough for us."
- Judas (not Iscariot; 14:22): "Lord, how is it that you will manifest yourself to us, and not to the world?"

It's very important that you read this portion with a healthy dose of historical imagination. Put yourself in the disciples' shoes: How would you have felt if you had been in their place? They had put their lives, family ties, and possessions on the line for Jesus; now, it seemed, all their investments were going to be reduced to zero in a matter of days (think Great Depression or stock-market crash). Had they made the wrong decision? And what would life be like without Jesus? It is these kinds of questions that Jesus addresses in the last few hours before his betrayal, arrest, Jewish and Roman trials, and crucifixion.

Jesus's main burden here seems to be to convince his disciples that, contrary to their own expectations, it would in fact turn out to their advantage for him to go away, because once he was exalted with God, the Father and he would send the Spirit. What's more, Jesus had been *with* them—the Holy Spirit would be *in* them.[220] Using the illustration of branches' close connection to the vine, Jesus explains the way in which they would be able to remain connected with him and the Father through the Spirit.[221] These are truths familiar to us, but they were all news to the disciples!

Jesus also prepares his followers for upcoming persecution and reassures them that the Spirit would bear witness alongside them.[222] Not only does Jesus instruct the dis-

219. Some start the Farewell Discourse at 13:31 and end it at 16:33 (e.g., Aelred Lacomara, "Deuteronomy and the Farewell Discourse [Jn 13:31–16:33]," *Catholic Biblical Quarterly* 36 [1974]: 65–84). Others include chapter 17, Jesus's final prayer, as well.

220. John 14:18.

221. John 15:1–11. See Carl J. Laney, "The Vine, the Branches, and What It Means to Abide (John 15:1–11)," in Beitzel, *Lexham Geographic Commentary*, 431–41.

222. John 15:18–16:4, esp. 15:26–27.

ciples about the work of the coming Holy Spirit; he also equips them for the "little while" during which they would no longer see him—the interim between his burial and resurrection—and the time following the resurrection when they would see him again before he would be exalted with God (the ascension and exaltation). Their emotional roller-coaster ride would be comparable to that of a woman giving birth.[223]

Jesus's Final Prayer (17:1–26)

After this, Jesus prays to the Father—for himself, his followers, and even later generations of believers:

- for himself (17:1–5)
- for his followers (17:6–19)
- for later believers (17:20–26)

Essentially, this is the report of the Word who had come into the world, accomplished his mission, and was about to return to his sender: "Mission accomplished!" In this, as in so many other ways, John seems strongly dependent on the theology of the Old Testament prophet Isaiah, who had memorably written,

> For as the rain and the snow come down from heaven
>   and do not return there but water the earth,
> making it bring forth and sprout,
>   giving seed to the sower and bread to the eater,
> so shall my word be that goes out from my mouth;
>   it shall not return to me empty,
> but it shall accomplish that which I purpose,
>   and shall succeed in the thing for which I sent it.[224]

Doesn't this sound very similar to John's portrayal of Jesus's mission? Jesus, the Word, was sent by God to earth and didn't return to him empty; he accomplished all that God intended and succeeded in the thing for which God sent him. Thus, he would cry on the cross, "It is finished!"[225] This mission, in turn, was bound up with those whom the Father had given Jesus out of the world—his disciples—who would serve as his representatives in this world and pass on the good news of salvation in him to subsequent generations.

223. John 16:16–24.
224. Isaiah 55:10–11.
225. John 19:30.

Here Jesus's three-pronged vision comes into sharp focus: (1) setting apart believers from the world, (2) helping them grow in the truth, and (3) sending them back into the world to proclaim the saving message of Christ: "They are not of the world, just as I am not of the world. Sanctify them in the truth; your word is truth. As you sent me into the world, so I have sent them into the world."[226] Three chapters—and three days—later, this vision would become a reality.[227]

RECAP

Following the Book of Signs in chapters 1–12, we've moved into the Book of Exaltation starting in chapter 13. The stage was set by Jesus's washing of his disciples' feet in the upper room just prior to the Last Supper. Following this moving scene at which Jesus revealed the full extent of his love for his own and took on the menial stance of a slave, Judas the betrayer slips into the night. This triggers the Farewell Discourse, which starts at 13:31 and continues until the end of chapter 16. The discourse proceeds in two parts, 13:31–14:31 and chapters 15–16. The break is marked by the disciples' departure from the upper room in 14:31 and the discourse on the vine and the branches, which starts at the beginning of chapter 15.

At the same time, several themes are shared in both portions of the Farewell Discourse, most notably Jesus's announcement of the coming of "another Helping Presence"—that is, the Holy Spirit.[228] While Jesus had been (physically) *with* his followers, the Spirit would be (spiritually) *in* them. In this way, Jesus assures his disciples, it will actually be to their advantage if he goes away and returns to the Father. While this proved to be a tough sell, and the disciples had many questions, John shows that Jesus will direct the mission of his followers from his exalted position at the Father once he has been "lifted up" at the cross (hence the Book of Exaltation).

226. John 17:16–18.
227. John 20:21.
228. "Another helping Presence" is the likely meaning of the Greek word translated in the ESV as "another Helper" in 14:16 or simply "Helper" in 15:26 and 16:7. Just as Jesus was physically present with his disciples, the Spirit would manifest Jesus's spiritual presence after his departure.

THE BOOK OF EXALTATION (13:1–20:31, CONT.)

The Passion Narrative (18:1–20:31)

Jesus's Arrest and Jewish Trial before Annas, and Peter's Denials (18:1–27)

Jesus's Roman Trial before Pilate (18:28–19:16a)

THE BOOK OF EXALTATION (13:1–20:31, CONT.)

The Passion Narrative (18:1–20:31)

Jesus's Arrest and Jewish Trial before Annas, and Peter's Denials (18:1–27)

The passion narrative—the account of Jesus's arrest, trials, crucifixion, burial, and resurrection—in John's Gospel in many ways resembles the accounts in the other three Gospels. This is to be expected, as Jesus's entire earthly ministry culminates in his saving mission at the cross, and all the Gospels are firmly grounded in actual history. Christianity is a historical religion![229] And yet there are ways in which John emphasizes particular aspects of Jesus's passion, in many cases filling in certain gaps left by the other Gospels.

First, John, more than the other Gospels, stresses Jesus's sovereignty throughout the proceedings against him. We've seen this already in the preamble to the Book of Exaltation, where John stressed that Jesus knew where he had come from and where he was going.[230] The arrest and crucifixion didn't take Jesus by surprise! He wasn't ambushed by Judas's betrayal, as the evangelist has gone to great lengths to demonstrate. Neither was Jesus a messianic pretender who miscalculated the extent of opposition to him and was swept away by a wave of popularity that suddenly turned into rejection. Contrary to Albert Schweitzer's thesis in *The Quest of the Historical Jesus* mentioned in the introduction, Jesus was not a deluded apocalyptic end-time prophet who indulged in visions of grandeur but ended up tragically betrayed by one of his confidants, forsaken by the

229. See 1 Corinthians 15:12–19.
230. See John 13:1–3.

leaders of his nation, and cast aside.[231] To stress this, the evangelist emphasizes Jesus being in control of his surroundings at every turn. At his arrest, it is Jesus who asks the soldiers, "Who are you looking for?"[232] When they tell him, "Jesus of Nazareth," he fearlessly replies, "I am [he]."[233] At which they draw back and fall to the ground, as in response to a theophany, a manifestation of God himself, whose name he had just invoked. Then Jesus tells those who are about to arrest him to let his disciples go, and when Peter draws a sword to defend him, he tells Peter to put his sword away. He must "drink the cup that the Father has given" him.[234] One marvels at such courage, composure, and sovereign handling of a very trying situation.

Second, John focuses less on the suffering of Jesus and more on the glory of the cross. While no one can deny that Jesus suffered excruciating pain for us when he endured countless humiliations and the most inhumane form of execution—what kinds of people are we to subject fellow human beings to this vile form of punishment?—John presents the cross as nothing but a station on Jesus's return to the Father and to the glory he had before the world began.[235] A representative statement is as follows: "I came from the Father and have come into the world, and now I am leaving the world and going to the Father."[236] Or consider Jesus's prayer: "But now I am coming to you. . . . Father, I desire that they also . . . may be with me where I am, to see my glory that you have given me because you loved me before the foundation of the world."[237] Then, when hanging on the cross, Jesus's last word in this Gospel is *tetelestai*, "It is finished."[238] Mission accomplished! It's a cry of triumph, not defeat. Jesus has completed his redemptive mission. After dying a real death, his body will be buried, and then, three days later, he will rise and never die again. In this way, as Peter puts it in his first letter, Jesus "suffered once for sins, the righteous for the unrighteous, that he might bring us to God."[239]

Third, John all but presupposes Jesus's Jewish trial before Caiaphas the high priest and supplements the accounts in the other Gospels in two ways: he records an informal hearing before Annas, the high-priestly patriarch and father-in-law of Caiaphas; and he recounts Jesus's interrogation by Pontius Pilate, the Roman governor, in considerably

231. On Schweitzer's views, see further the discussion in the introduction. For a brief sketch, see Andreas Köstenberger, "Albert Schweitzer," Biblical Foundations, September 21, 2015, https://www.biblicalfoundations.org/albert-schweitzer.
232. John 18:4, my paraphrase. ESV: "Whom do you seek?"
233. John 18:5.
234. John 18:11.
235. See Köstenberger, *Theology of John's Gospel and Letters*, chapter 14, "John's Theology of the Cross."
236. John 16:28.
237. John 17:13, 24.
238. John 19:30.
239. 1 Peter 3:18.

more detail than do the other Gospels.[240] By way of overview, John's account is structured like this:

- Jesus's arrest (18:1–11)
- Jesus's hearing before Annas (18:12–14, 19–24; sandwiched in between is Peter's first denial: 18:15–18)
- Jesus sent by Annas to Caiaphas (18:24)
- Jesus sent by Caiaphas to Pilate (18:28; sandwiched in between are Peter's second and third denials: 18:25–27; note that the fourth evangelist doesn't narrate the Jewish trial before Caiaphas at all)
- Jesus's interrogation before Pilate (18:28–19:16)

Note how the fourth evangelist devotes nine verses to the informal hearing before Annas, skips over the formal Jewish trial before Caiaphas and the Sanhedrin, and devotes twenty-nine verses to Jesus's Roman trial before Pilate.

Jesus's Roman Trial before Pilate (18:28–19:16a)

The trial before Pilate, for its part, is structured in the form of "an oscillating pattern of outdoor and indoor scenes":

- outside (18:29–32)
- inside (18:33–38a)
- outside (18:38b–40)
- inside (19:1–3)
- outside (19:4–7)
- inside (19:8–11)
- outside (19:12–15)[241]

In this way, John graphically depicts the dramatic back-and-forth between Pilate and the Jewish leaders who accused Jesus before the Roman governor. Notice also that the Jewish leaders initially try to sway Pilate by bringing against Jesus a vague, general criminal charge—he is an evildoer (which is hardly the case!).[242] They also seem to have hinted at a political charge, knowing that Rome was very sensitive to any threats to

240. For a close reading, see Andreas J. Köstenberger, "'What Is Truth?' Pilate's Question in Its Johannine and Larger Biblical Context," in *Whatever Happened to Truth?*, ed. Andreas J. Köstenberger (Wheaton, IL: Crossway, 2005), 19–51.
241. Köstenberger, Kellum, and Quarles, *The Cradle, the Cross, and the Crown*, 371.
242. John 18:30.

Roman rule. Therefore, the next round of interrogation before Pilate revolves around the question of whether Jesus is "king of the Jews." In response, Jesus pointedly tells the Roman governor that his kingdom "is not from the world."[243] In other words, Pilate has nothing to worry about; Jesus is no threat to Roman imperial power in Palestine.

When neither the general nor the political charge seems to sway Pilate, the Jewish leaders move to the (for them) heart of the matter: "We have a law, and according to that law he ought to die because he has made himself the Son of God."[244] In this way, too, the evangelist sharpens the focus of the other Gospels: at the core, what got Jesus on the cross was a theological charge, that is, alleged blasphemy—his claim to be God.[245] The entire Gospel narrative has been building up to this moment. Repeatedly, the Jews have picked up stones to throw at Jesus because of perceived blasphemy. Now they press their case before the Roman governor, and at last Pilate succumbs to the political pressure and—against his better judgment—condemns Jesus to die.

243. John 18:36.

244. John 19:7.

245. Though this is nicely corroborated by the accounts of the Jewish trial in the other Gospels: see esp. Mark 14:60–64.

THE BOOK OF EXALTATION (13:1–20:31, CONT.)

The Passion Narrative (18:1–20:31, cont.)

Jesus's Crucifixion and Burial (19:16b–42)

The Empty Tomb and Jesus's Resurrection Appearances to Mary Magdalene and the Eleven (20:1–29)

Conclusion to the Book of Exaltation and Gospel Proper: John's Purpose for Writing (20:30–31)

THE BOOK OF EXALTATION (13:1–20:31, CONT.)

The Passion Narrative (18:1–20:31, cont.)

Jesus's Crucifixion and Burial (19:16b–42)

The crucifixion itself is narrated in terse and somber tones: "So they took Jesus, and he went out, bearing his own cross. . . . There they crucified him."[246] After entrusting the care of his mother to the "beloved disciple" (none other than the fourth evangelist, the apostle John), Jesus says, "It is finished," bows his head, and dies.[247] Beyond this, the evangelist records several ways in which minor details surrounding the crucifixion fulfill biblical prophecy, again underscoring the fact that this was God's plan all long.[248]

An equally respectful and somber account of the burial rounds out John's passion narrative and concludes chapter 19. Two "secret disciples" of Jesus from among the Sanhedrin, Joseph of Arimathea and Nicodemus (mentioned only in John's Gospel), ask Pilate for Jesus's body and, with Pilate's permission, take Jesus's body down from the cross and hastily prepare it for burial, as the Jewish Sabbath, on which no work must be done, is about to begin.[249]

---

246. John 19:16–18.
247. John 19:25–30. For a listing of Jesus's seven sayings on the cross, see Harris, *John*, 318; more fully, Murray J. Harris, *The Seven Sayings of Jesus on the Cross: Their Circumstances and Meaning* (Eugene, OR: Cascade, 2016).
248. See John 19:24, 28, 36, 37. For details, see Andreas J. Köstenberger, "John," in *Commentary on the New Testament Use of the Old Testament*, eds. G. K. Beale and D. A. Carson (Grand Rapids: Baker, 2007), 500–506.
249. John 19:38–42.

The Empty Tomb and Jesus's Resurrection Appearances to Mary Magdalene and the Eleven (20:1–29)

At this, we've arrived on the "first day of the week." Mary Magdalene goes to Jesus's tomb early, no doubt to complete the work that had remained unfinished because of the inbreaking Sabbath, yet finds that the stone has been rolled away from the tomb. She tells John and Peter, who promptly rush to the tomb and find it empty, just as Mary had said. In another piece of eyewitness recollection, they find the linen cloths with which Jesus's body had been wrapped lying there, and Jesus's face cloth neatly folded up by itself. Even this apparently was not enough for them to understand that Jesus had risen from the dead.

Then Mary is back outside the tomb, crying. She sees two angels and then turns around and sees Jesus himself but fails to recognize him at first. Thinking he is the gardener, she asks him where he has taken Jesus's body. This proves that neither the disciples nor the women were looking for a *risen* Jesus; for them, the cross and burial of Jesus were the end of his earthly existence. At this, Jesus calls Mary by name: "Mary!" She recognizes him at once, exclaiming in Aramaic, "'Rabboni!' (which means Teacher)."[250] In this way, just as she was the first witness of the empty tomb, so now Mary becomes the first witness of the resurrection: "I have seen the Lord"![251]

After this, the risen Jesus appears to the disciples at three separate occasions:

1. On the evening of that first Sunday, to ten of the apostles (without Judas and Thomas; 20:19–23)

2. Eight days later, to the eleven apostles (including Thomas; 20:26–29)

3. Sometime later, to seven disciples who went fishing by the Sea of Tiberias (the Sea of Galilee; 21:1–14)

At the first occasion, Jesus commissions the disciples in the power of the Spirit: "As the Father has sent me, even so I am sending you. . . . Receive the Holy Spirit."[252] This is a pivotal point in the narrative, as thus far it has always been Jesus who was sent by the Father; now Jesus, the Sent One, has become the sender of his new messianic community. This verse, then, is the center of John's Trinitarian mission theology: the Father sent Jesus; now Jesus sends his disciples in the power of the Spirit. Some have called this

250. John 20:16.
251. John 20:18; cf. 20:2.
252. John 20:21–22.

account the "Johannine Pentecost." However, more likely this is an earlier occasion, later followed by the Pentecost recorded in the book of Acts when the Spirit was actually and historically sent jointly by the Father and the Son.

At the second occasion, Thomas (who for some reason was missing the first time Jesus appeared to his disciples; I'm sure he was kicking himself for not being there!) is now present with the rest of the Twelve (minus Judas, of course). When the other disciples told him about Jesus's first appearance among them, Thomas had been skeptical: "Unless I see in his hands the mark of the nails, and place my finger into the mark of the nails, and place my hand into his side, I will never believe."[253] Strong words! How will Jesus respond? Displaying divine knowledge, Jesus (who wasn't physically present when Thomas had expressed his doubts to his fellow disciples) simply tells him to put his finger in his wounds and look at his nail-scarred hands. At this, "doubting Thomas" turns into "believing Thomas."

Apparently without taking Jesus up on his offer, he throws his skepticism overboard and exclaims in worship: "My Lord and my God!"[254] Just as the fourth evangelist had affirmed Jesus's deity at the very outset of his Gospel ("The Word was with God, and the Word was God . . . And the Word became flesh. . . . No one has ever seen God; the only God, who is at the Father's side, he has made him known"[255]), he concludes his Gospel with an unequivocal affirmation of Jesus's deity. What's more, now it is one of the Twelve, a character in the narrative, who has arrived at the same conclusion (despite considerable skepticism) that Jesus is Lord and God (even *his* Lord and *his* God!). One might even say that, in a sense, what is the Roman centurion's confession of Jesus as the "Son of God" in the Synoptics is Thomas's confession of Jesus as his "Lord and God" in John.[256]

Jesus's response to Thomas's expression of worship seamlessly transitions from Thomas, a historical character, to the readers who never had the opportunity to see Jesus in the flesh: "Have you believed because you have seen me? Blessed are those who have not seen and yet have believed."[257] In this way, Thomas serves as an example of someone who has believed in Jesus because he saw him. Jesus's challenge, however, extends beyond Thomas to those who haven't seen him and yet have believed. In fact, he calls them "blessed"! Thomas's confession of Jesus as his Lord and God therefore provides an incredibly fitting climax to the Gospel's presentation of Jesus as Messiah and Son of God and even implicitly includes the readers in the orbit of John's message and purpose.

253. John 20:25.
254. John 20:28.
255. John 1:1, 14, 18.
256. Cf. esp. Mark 15:39.
257. John 20:29.

Conclusion to the Book of Exaltation and the Gospel Proper: John's Purpose for Writing (20:30–31)

With this, we've come to the end of the Book of Exaltation and the Gospel proper (though an epilogue is still to follow). Wrapping up the Gospel, the evangelist acknowledges that "Jesus did many other signs in the presence of the disciples, which are not written in this book."[258] This is certainly a proper disclaimer, especially when one thinks of all the material included in the Synoptic Gospels that John chose not to include: the Sermon on the Mount (including the Lord's Prayer), the transfiguration, the Olivet Discourse, Jesus's numerous kingdom parables, demon exorcisms—the list goes on and on. Clearly, John has been extremely selective in what he chose to include in his Gospel.

He continues, "but these [signs] are written so that you may believe that Jesus is the Christ, the Son of God, and that by believing you may have life in his name."[259] The first thing one notices is the highly unusual direct personal address: "that *you* may believe." It is virtually unprecedented for a Gospel writer to address his audience directly, but this is what John does here! He is not writing an impersonal treatise; he is writing for the purpose of leading his readers to Christ, whether directly (evangelism) or, perhaps more likely, indirectly (supplying believers with an evangelistic tool to use with unbelievers). One surmises that the other Gospel writers pursued a similar purpose.

In his concluding purpose statement, the fourth evangelist conveniently touches on virtually all of his key emphases throughout the Gospel. Pride of place goes to Jesus's messianic signs. As we've seen, John records seven particularly striking signs, including the raising of Lazarus as the seventh climactic sign, which remarkably has not been featured in the first three Gospels. Also, John is writing to encourage his readers to believe that Jesus is the Christ, the Son of God. In this, he is very much in line with the other Gospels. Throughout the Gospel, he has used representative characters to lead his readers to this intended conclusion. Finally, those who believe in Christ will have eternal life (John's substitute for the other Gospels' emphasis on God's kingdom).

---

258. John 20:30.
259. John 20:31.

THE CHRIST, THE SON OF GOD

John is the only evangelist who provides us with a clear purpose statement: "Now Jesus did many other signs in the presence of the disciples, which are not written in this book; but these are written so that you may believe that *Jesus is the Christ, the Son of God*, and that by believing you may have life in his name."[260] In seeking to demonstrate that Jesus is the Messiah, the Son of God, John concurs wholeheartedly with the other Gospel writers. All four insist that Jesus was the Messiah who fulfilled an entire matrix of biblical prophecy and was sent by God to save his people from their sins.

Yet John demonstrates Jesus's messianic identity in a creative way that doesn't merely repeat the message of the other Gospels but deepens it significantly. While the earlier Gospels narrate many miracles that Jesus performed during his earthly ministry, John selects seven such striking manifestations and calls them "signs"—signposts to Jesus's true nature and identity. In this way, he seeks to show that the purpose of Jesus's works was not to wow people with amazing feats in and of themselves but to point people to who he was in the core of his being and to elicit faith in him. After all, people could see the *miracle* and still miss its *significance*!

This was John's grave concern, that people might hear (or read) the story of Jesus and miss what mattered most—the true identity of Jesus. For this reason, he streamlined his presentation of what Jesus did and, like channeling a sprawling river, made all Jesus's activities tributaries to his personal identity. It's all about *Jesus*, John is saying. *He* is the one who came to earth to reveal God to us and to die for our sins on the cross. It's that simple, and yet that profound. With a single-minded, laser-like focus, John crystallizes all our reading of the Gospels into one solitary, penetrating question: *Who do you say that Jesus is?*

In the end, it doesn't matter what others are saying about him. The question is, who do *you* say that he is? Because one day you'll stand before

260. John 20:30–31, emphasis added.

God and he'll ask you, "What have you done with Jesus? I sent my Son to die for you. Did you believe? And if not, why not?" What's your answer going to be? I hope that this simple volume has helped you make progress in grasping the true essence of Jesus—not merely what he *did* but even more importantly who he *was*. May God give you grace as you contemplate the all-important question: *Who was Jesus? And how does he want me to live my short life here on earth?*

EPILOGUE: JESUS'S FINAL APPEARANCE AND WORDS (21:1–25)

Jesus's Third Resurrection Appearance and Final Words to Peter and the Beloved Disciple (21:1–23)

Conclusion to Entire Gospel (21:24–25)

EPILOGUE: JESUS'S FINAL APPEARANCE AND WORDS (21:1–25)

Two resurrection appearances to his disciples have already been recorded, in addition to Jesus's encounter with Mary Magdalene. The Gospel closes with a third appearance and Jesus's final instructions to Peter and John, the "beloved disciple" and author of the Gospel.

Jesus's Third Resurrection Appearance and Final Words to Peter and the Beloved Disciple (21:1–23)

At his third resurrection appearance, Jesus helps his followers catch a huge haul of 153 fish. In addition, he prepares breakfast for these men. After the meal, Jesus spends some one-on-one (or one-on-two) time with Peter and the "beloved disciple." In the course of the conversation, he predicts Peter's martyrdom. When Peter inquires as to the fate of the "other disciple," Jesus essentially tells him to mind his own business; he must follow Jesus!

This final interchange highlights the fact that while all of Jesus's followers must bear witness to him, there will be different individual callings within this general responsibility. Some, such as Peter, will be called on to give their very lives in martyrdom as an outflow of that witness. Others, such as John (the beloved disciple), will be called on to bear witness through writing or proclamation. In John's case, he had the unique privilege of writing the fourth and final Gospel included in the New Testament.

Conclusion to Entire Gospel (21:24–25)

The Gospel closes with an acknowledgment that John of necessity had to be highly selective in what he recorded, as the entire world could not contain the books that would need to be written if everything Jesus had said and done were recorded. This in fact is a fitting ending not just to John's Gospel but to the entire fourfold Gospel witness according to Matthew, Mark, Luke, and John in our New Testament. We aren't given an exhaustive account but only a selection of Jesus's words and deeds, and yet what we do have is more than enough to make an informed decision about who Jesus truly was and what was the significance of his coming.

EPILOGUE

I'll close by telling you a bit more about my personal story. The turning point came when I met an opera student, who shared her Christian faith with me on a train from my hometown of Vienna, Austria to Venice. When I heard God's Word for the first time with an open heart and mind that day, I didn't immediately drop everything and follow Jesus. That initial encounter with Jesus was just the beginning of what would turn out to be a life-changing relationship that continues to this very day. I first had to come to terms with my inner corruption and brokenness and my unconditional need for someone who could reconcile me to my Creator and mediate genuine removal of my guilt before God for all the wrong things I had done and for the self-centered, critical, unloving person that I was.

It took six months, two times of reading through the Bible cover to cover, and most importantly the convicting work of the Holy Spirit, to bring me to my knees—to bring me the point where I was willing and able to confess that I was a rebel, a transgressor of God's law, a sinner who continually missed the mark and who robbed God of the glory that was rightfully his. As Paul wrote in the book of Romans, "All have sinned and fall short of the glory of God"[1]—and that "all" most certainly included me. It's not just that I fell short of my divinely created potential, sad and tragic as that was; I fell "short of the glory of God"—that is, didn't bring God the glory he so richly deserved.

When I prayed to receive Christ—or rather, prayed to ask *him* to receive *me,* and to thank him that he had done so already—angels may have rejoiced in heaven but nothing happened immediately that very moment, at least nothing tangible or visible. Spiritually, I believe, however, everything changed: I received the Holy Spirit—God's continual, life-changing presence—into my heart, and my desire changed from pleasing myself to loving God and following Christ. There was a purity of desire I had never known before.

Over the next few months, I witnessed to all my family and friends about the life-changing experience I'd had with Christ. And I was resolved to strive for purity and

1. Romans 3:23.

integrity in all my relationships with others, both male and female. I confessed my sins to others. One Sunday during church, several weeks after my conversion, I almost physically felt that a load of guilt had been taken off my shoulders and wept uncontrollably out of relief and joy.

Also, by becoming a Christ-follower, I had become part of a new family, the family of God, that became increasingly precious to me—my fathers and mothers, and brothers and sisters, in Christ. In a very real sense, they replaced my natural family who didn't (yet) know Christ the way I'd come to know him. I craved spiritual fellowship with my new brothers and sisters and met with them for worship, Bible study, and prayer. We shared meals together and laughed and cried together. Everything changed, and I've never been the same—ask those who knew me before I became a Christian! As Paul wrote, "I have been crucified with Christ. It is no longer I who live, but Christ who lives in me. And the life I now live in the flesh I live by faith in the Son of God, who loved me and gave himself for me."[2]

I've written this book to introduce you to the person I love the most in this world and the next, the person I'm infinitely grateful to for saving me from my sins and for eternity with God in heaven. It's my desire that you get to know him the way I've come to know him. As Jesus said, "You are my friends if you do what I command you."[3] As you walk with him and talk with him, and as you obey his Word, you'll increasingly come to know him as your best friend, as one who offers you a supernatural and yet very real friendship that far exceeds any depth of relationship the world has to offer.

As one of my theological heroes, the twentieth-century German scholar Adolf Schlatter (1852–1938), asked his contemporaries: "Do we know Jesus?"[4] Let me ask you, then: Do *you* know Jesus? If you don't, why don't you make an effort to get to know him? You won't regret it. And if you do know him already, why don't you make knowing Jesus your first priority? There's so much more he can do in and through you if you yield your life unreservedly to him. As Jesus said, "For what will it profit a man if he gains the whole world yet forfeits his soul? Or what shall a man give in return for his soul?"[5] I'll close with the lyrics of a song that expresses the desire of my heart for you:

---

2. Galatians 2:20.
3. John 15:14.
4. Adolf Schlatter, *Do We Know Jesus? Daily Insight for the Mind and Soul*, trans. Andreas J. Köstenberger and Robert W. Yarbrough (Grand Rapids: Kregel, 2005). Schlatter was a prolific, though often underestimated, scholar. This devotional was Schlatter's last work, written at age eighty-five shortly before he died.
5. Matthew 16:26; cf. Mark 8:36–37; Luke 9:25.

O soul, are you weary and troubled?
No light in the darkness you see?
There's light for a look at the Savior,
And life more abundant and free.

Turn your eyes upon Jesus,
Look full in His wonderful face,
And the things of earth will grow strangely dim,
In the light of His glory and grace.

Through death into life everlasting
He passed, and we follow Him there;
O'er us sin no more hath dominion
For more than conqu'rors we are!

Turn your eyes upon Jesus,
Look full in His wonderful face,
And the things of earth will grow strangely dim,
In the light of His glory and grace.

His Word shall not fail you, He promised;
Believe Him and all will be well;
Then go to a world that is dying,
His perfect salvation to tell!

Turn your eyes upon Jesus,
Look full in His wonderful face,
And the things of earth will grow strangely dim,
In the light of His glory and grace.[6]

6. "Turn Your Eyes upon Jesus," lyrics by Helen Howarth Lemmel (1863–1961; lyrics are in the public domain). The underlying New Testament passage is Hebrews 12:1–2 (emphasis added): "Therefore, since we are surrounded by so great a cloud of witnesses, let us also lay aside every weight, and sin which clings so closely, and let us run with endurance the race that is set before us, *looking to Jesus*, the founder and perfecter of our faith, who for the joy that was set before him endured the cross, despising the shame, and is seated at the right hand of the throne of God."

SUGGESTED RESOURCES

Note: All of these resources have been written or cowritten by Dr. Andreas Köstenberger. For a full list of Dr. Köstenberger's publications and for additional resources, see www.biblicalfoundations.org.

Studying the Life of Jesus (The Gospels)

The First Days of Jesus: The Story of the Incarnation
Jesus and the Future: Understanding What He Taught about the End Times
The Final Days of Jesus: The Most Important Week of the Most Important Person Who Ever Lived

Growing in and Defending the Faith (Apologetics)

Truth Matters: Confident Faith in a Confusing World (introductory)
Truth in a Culture of Doubt: Engaging Skeptical Challenges to the Bible (more in depth)
The Heresy of Orthodoxy: How Contemporary Culture's Fascination with Diversity Has Reshaped Our Understanding of Early Christianity (more in depth)

Studying the New Testament (New Testament Introduction)

The Lion and the Lamb: New Testament Essentials from "The Cradle, the Cross, and the Crown" (introductory)
The Cradle, the Cross, and the Crown: An Introduction to the New Testament, 2nd edition (more in depth)
Handbook on Hebrews through Revelation (intermediate)

Studying the Bible (Hermeneutics)

For the Love of God's Word: An Introduction to Biblical Interpretation (introductory)
Inductive Bible Study: Observation, Interpretation, and Application through the Lenses of History, Literature, and Theology (introductory)
Invitation to Biblical Interpretation: Exploring the Hermeneutical Triad of History, Literature, and Theology (more in depth)

THIRTY-DAY GOSPELS READING PLAN

DAY	PASSAGE	CONTENT
1	Matthew 1–4	Introduction, Work in Galilee (1)
2	Matthew 5–7	Sermon on the Mount
3	Matthew 8–9	Work in Galilee (2)
4	Matthew 10:1–13:53	Work in Galilee (3), Stories about God's Kingdom
5	Matthew 13:54–18:35	Work Farther North, Stories about God's Kingdom
6	Matthew 19–23	Work in Judea and Jerusalem
7	Matthew 24–25	Teaching on End Times, Stories about God's Kingdom
8	Matthew 26–28	Death, Burial, Resurrection, Great Commission
9	Mark 1:1–3:12	Initial Ministry in Galilee
10	Mark 3:13–6:6a	Later Ministry in Galilee
11	Mark 6:6b–8:26	Ministry beyond Galilee
12	Mark 8:27–10:52	Journey to Jerusalem
13	Mark 11–13	Ministry in Jerusalem
14	Mark 14–16	Passion Narrative

DAY	PASSAGE	CONTENT
15	Luke 1–4:13	Preface, Birth, and Preparation for Ministry
16	Luke 4:14–7:50	Ministry in Galilee (1)
17	Luke 8:1–9:50	Ministry in Galilee (2 and 3)
18	Luke 9:51–12:59	Journey to Jerusalem (1)
19	Luke 13–15	Journey to Jerusalem (2)
20	Luke 16:1–19:27	Journey to Jerusalem (3)
21	Luke 19:28–22:38	Final Ministry in Jerusalem
22	Luke 22:39–24:53	Crucifixion, Resurrection, and Ascension
23	John 1	Prologue and Early Ministry
24	John 2–4	Cana Cycle
25	John 5–7	Festival Cycle (1)
26	John 8–10	Festival Cycle (2)
27	John 11–12	Bridge Section (Raising of Lazarus)
28	John 13–17	Farewell Discourse
29	John 18–19	Passion Narrative (1)
30	John 20–21	Passion Narrative (2) and Epilogue

SCRIPTURE INDEX

Luke

SUBJECT INDEX

NAME INDEX